# ONE WEEK LOAN

# Modern Theories
## of Drama

A Selection of Writings on Drama
and Theatre 1850–1990

Edited and annotated

by **George W. Brandt**

CLARENDON PRESS · OXFORD

1998

Oxford University Press, Great Clarendon Street, Oxford OX2 6DP

Oxford New York

Athens Auckland Bangkok Bombay
Calcutta Cape Town Dar es Salaam Delhi
Florence Hong Kong Istanbul Karachi
Kuala Lumpur Madras Madrid Melbourne
Mexico City Nairobi Paris Singapore
Taipei Tokyo Toronto Warsaw

and associated companies in
Berlin Ibadan

Oxford is a registered trade mark of Oxford University Press

Published in the United States
by Oxford University Press Inc., New York

British Library Cataloguing in Publication Data
Data available

Library of Congress Cataloging in Publication Data
Modern theories of drama : a selection of writings on drama and
theatre from the middle of the nineteenth to the latter part of the
twentieth century / edited and annotated by George W. Brandt.
Includes bibliographical references and index.
1. Drama.   2. Theater.   3. Drama—History and criticism.
I. Brandt, George W.
PN1655.M59 1998   809.2—dc21   97–27188
ISBN 0–19–871140–9
ISBN 0–19–871139–5 (pbk.)

1 3 5 7 9 10 8 6 4 2

Typeset by Alliance Phototypesetters, Pondicherry
Printed in Great Britain
on acid-free paper by
Biddles Ltd,
Guildford and King's Lynn

# Contents

*Acknowledgements*                                                              ix

*Introduction*                                                                  xiii


## PART I   **General Theory**

The Work of Art of the Future (1849)   Richard Wagner                            3

The Thirty-Six Dramatic Situations (1895)   Georges Polti                       12

The Law of the Drama (1894)   Ferdinand Brunetière                              19

The Comic in Situations (1900)   Henri Bergson                                  25

Melodrama (1966)   Eric Bentley                                                 35

For a Theatre of Situations (1947)   Jean-Paul Sartre                           42

Theatre Problems (1954–5)   Friedrich Dürrenmatt                                45

Theatre without a Conscience (1990)   Howard Barker                            55

Are There Universals of Performance in Myth, Ritual,
     and Drama? (1989)   Victor Turner                                          62


## PART II   **Varieties of Realism**

The Relationship of Dramatic Art to its Age and Allied Matters:
     The Preface to *Mary Magdalene* (1844)   Friedrich Hebbel                  71

Naturalism (1881)   Émile Zola                                                  80

Author's Preface to *Miss Julie* (1888)   August Strindberg                    89

Against the Well-Made Play (1911)   George Bernard Shaw                         99

*Death of a Salesman:* A Modern Tragedy? (1958)   Arthur Miller               106

## PART III. **Anti-Naturalism**

The Tragical in Daily Life (1894)   Maurice Maeterlinck                                     115

The Theatre (1899)   William Butler Yeats                                                   122

Certain Noble Plays of Japan (1917)   William Butler Yeats                                  126

On the Theatre: *The Fairground Booth* (1913)
Vsevolod Emilievich Meyerhold                                                               132

On the Art of the Theatre: The First Dialogue (1905)
Edward Gordon Craig                                                                         138

Organic Unity (1921)   Adolphe Appia                                                        145

Memoranda on Masks (1932)   Eugene O'Neill                                                  153

A Dramatist's Notebook (1933)   Eugene O'Neill                                              156

Author's Note to *A Dream Play* (1901)   August Strindberg                                  158

On the Futility of the 'Theatrical' in the Theatre (1896)   Alfred Jarry                    160

Preface and Prologue to *The Breasts of Tiresias* (1903)
Guillaume Apollinaire                                                                       165

Preface to *The Immortals* (1920)   Yvan Goll                                               171

Preface to *Methusalem, the Eternal Bourgeois* (1922)   Yvan Goll                           174

The Futurist Synthetic Theatre (1915)   Filippo Tommaso Marinetti                           176

On a New Type of Play (1920)   Stanisław Ignacy Witkiewicz                                  182

The Theatre of Cruelty: First Manifesto (1932)   Antonin Artaud                             188

An End to Masterpieces (1933)   Antonin Artaud                                              195

The Theatre's New Testament (1964)   Jerzy Grotowski                                        200

The Holy Theatre: Happenings (1968)   Peter Brook                                           205

The London Controversy: Tynan *v.* Ionesco (1958)                                           208

## PART IV. **Political Theatre**

Letter to a Creative Collaborator (1922)   Ernst Toller                                     217

The Programme of the Proletarian Theatre (1920)   Erwin Piscator                            220

The Modern Theatre is the Epic Theatre: Notes to the Opera
*Rise and Fall of the Town of Mahagonny* (1930)   Bertolt Brecht                            224

A Short Organum for the Theatre (1948)   Bertolt Brecht                                     232

The Material and the Models: Notes Towards a Definition
of Documentary Theatre (1968)   Peter Weiss                       247

Poetics of the Oppressed (1974)   Augusto Boal                    254

Political Dynamics: The Feminisms (1986)   Michelene Wandor       261

## PART V.   **Semiotics**

Dynamics of the Sign in the Theatre (1940)   Jindřich Honzl       269

Semiotics of Theatrical Performance (1977)   Umberto Eco          279

Psychic Polyphony (1986)   Marvin Carlson                         288

The Signs of Stage and Screen (1987)   Martin Esslin              299

Avant-Garde Theatre and Semiology: A Few Practices and
the Theory Behind Them (1982)   Patrice Pavis                     307

*Select Bibliography*                                             317

*Index*                                                          329

# Acknowledgements

I am deeply grateful to former colleagues in the Department of Drama of the University of Bristol, notably Professor Emeritus Edward Braun and Professor Martin White, the current Head of Department, for the support they have given me in my work of compiling this volume of modern theories of drama. Professor Braun's advice in particular has been invaluable from the very inception of the project. The bibliographical and other help I have had from Linda Fitzsimmons and Ted Freeman has been most useful. I am also happy to acknowledge the tireless assistance I have received from the staff of the Main Library of the University of Bristol as well as that of the British Library.

My warmest thanks go to Oxford University Press in the persons of Andrew Lockett, Jason Freeman, and Sophie Goldsworthy for their constant guidance in the preparation of this volume.

I am happy to acknowledge the generous financial assistance I have had from the Humanities Research Board of the British Academy, through the good offices of Mrs R. Sutton, Miss Elizabeth Ollard and Mrs Beryl Leaver, for the Small Personal Research Grant which enabled me to consult the British Library very much more extensively than would otherwise have been the case. I also owe a debt of gratitude to the University of Bristol which appointed me as a Senior Research Fellow for two years, thereby giving me additional assistance and enabling me to make full use of the University's facilities even though I had retired several years earlier.

Last but not least I wish to thank my wife, Toni Brandt, most sincerely for her patience, tolerance, and unfailing support during—and not only during —my work on the book.

The author would like to thank the relevant publishers for permission to reproduce the following texts. Every effort has been made to clear the necessary permissions. Any omissions will be rectified in future editions.

Georges Polti, *The Thirty-Six Dramatic Situations*, trans. Lucille Ray (Cincinatti: Writer's Digest, 1931), first published in Mercure de France, 1895. Ferdinand Brunetière, 'The Law of the Drama', trans. Philip M. Hayden (New York: Dramatic Museum of Columbia University, 1914); reprinted in Barrett

H. Clark, *European Theories of Drama* (New York: Crown Publishers, 1918). Henri Bergson, *Laughter* (first published 1900), trans. C. Brereton and F. Rothwell (London: Macmillan, 1911). Eric Bentley, *Melodrama*, from *The Life of the Drama* (London: Methuen, 1966). Jean-Paul Sartre, *For a Theatre of Situations*, trans. Richard McLeary; reprinted from Michel Contat and Michel Rybalka (eds.), *The Writings of Jean-Paul Sartre*, Vol. 2 (Evanston, Ill.: Northwestern University Press, 1972); English translation copyright © by Random House Inc; originally published by Editions Gallimard. Friedrich Dürrenmatt, *Theatre Problems*, trans. H. M. Waidson (London: Jonathan Cape, 1976). Howard Barker, *Theatre Without a Conscience* (1990), from *Arguments for a Theatre* (Manchester University Press, 1993). Victor Turner, 'Are There Universals of Performance?'; reprinted from *By Means of Performance* (Richard Schechner and Willa Appel, eds.; Cambridge University Press, 1990), by permission of the Wenner-Gren Foundation for Anthropological Research, New York. August Strindberg, Author's Preface to *Miss Julie* (1889), trans. Michael Meyer, from *August Strindberg, The Plays*, Vol. 1 (London: Secker & Warburg, 1964). Reproduced by courtesy of Reed Books and David Higham Associates Ltd. George Bernard Shaw, Preface to *Three Plays by Brieux* (London: A. C. Fifield, 1911). Arthur Miller, excerpt from the *Introduction to the Collected Works*, Vol. 1 (London: Cresset Press, 1958). Extracts from William Butler Yeats, *The Theatre* (1899) and *Certain Noble Plays of Japan* (1916), both from *Essays and Introductions* (London: Macmillan, 1969); reproduced courtesy of A. P. Watt Ltd on behalf of Michael Yeats. Vsevolod Emilievich Meyerhold, *The Fairground Booth* (1913), from Edward Braun (trans. and ed.), *Meyerhold on Theatre* (London: Methuen, rev. edn. 1991); copyright © 1969, 1991 by Edward Braun. Edward Gordon Craig, '1st and 2nd Dialogue', from *The Art of the Theatre* (London: Heinemann, 1911); copyright © Edward Gordon Craig, 1911. Adolphe Appia, 'Organic Unity' from *Adolphe Appia's 'The Work of Living Art'*, trans. H. D. Albright (University of Miami Press, 1960). Eugene O'Neill, *Memoranda on Masks* (1932) and *A Dramatist's Notebook* (1933) in *The American Spectator*, Nov. 1932 and Jan. 1933, repr. in Toby Cole (ed.), *Playwrights on Playwriting* (Dramabooks, New York: Hill and Wang, 1961). August Strindberg, Author's Note to *A Dream Play* (1901), trans. Michael Meyer, from *August Strindberg, The Plays*, Vol. 2 (London: Secker & Warburg, 1975). Reproduced by courtesy of Reed Books and David Higham Associates Ltd. Alfred Jarry, *On the Futility of the Theatrical in the Theatre* (Mercure de France, Sept. 1896), trans. Barbara Wright in *Ubu Roi* (London: Gaberbocchus Press, 1951). Preface and Prologue from 'The Breasts of Tiresias' by Guillaume Apollinaire; English translation © 1961 by Louis Simpson, from Michael Benedikt and George E. Wellwarth (eds.) *Modern French Plays: an Anthology from Jarry to Ionesco* (London: Faber & Faber, 1964); used by permission of Georges Borchardt, Inc. on behalf of the translator. Ivan Goll, Preface to *The Immortals* (1920), from I. G., *Dichtungen* © Argon Verlag GmbH, Berlin. Yvan Goll, Preface to *Methusalem: The Eternal Bourgeois* (1922) (Berlin: Walter de Gruyter, 1966).

Stanisław Ignacy Witkiewicz, *On a New Type of Play* (1920), from *The Mother and Other Unsavoury Plays*, trans. Daniel Gerould and C. S. Durer (New York: Applause Books, 1966). Jerzy Grotowski, *The Theatre's New Testament* (1964), trans. Jörgen Andersen and Judy Barba, in Jerzy Grotowski, *Towards a Poor Theatre* (London: Methuen, 1969); copyright © 1968 by Jerzy Grotowski and Odin Teatrets Forlag. Peter Brook, *Happenings* from *The Empty Space* (Harmondsworth: Pelican Books, 1972). Reproduced by permission of Harper-Collins Publishers Ltd. 'The London Controversy': Kenneth Tynan v. Eugene Ionesco, from Eugene Ionesco, *Notes and Counter Notes*, trans. Donald Watson (London: Calder, 1964); reproduced courtesy of Calder Publications Ltd. Erwin Piscator, *The Proletarian Theatre*, in *The Political Theatre*, trans. Hugh Rorrison (London: Methuen, 1980); reproduced by courtesy of Reed Books and Avon Books; copyright © by Rowohlt Verlag Publishing Co., Reinbek bei Hamburg. 1963. Excerpts from 'The Modern Theatre is the Epic Theatre', and excerpts from 'A Short Organum for the Theatre' from *Brecht on Theatre: The Development of an Aesthetic* by Bertolt Brecht, edited and translated by John Willett (London: Methuen, 1964); copyright © 1957, 1963, and 1964 by Suhrkamp Verlag, Frankfurt am Main; this translation and notes © 1964 by John Willett. Translation copyright © 1964 and translation copyrights renewed © 1992 by John Willett. Reprinted by permission of Reed Books and by permission of Hill and Wang, a division of Farrar, Straus and Giroux, Inc. Peter Weiss, 'The Material and the Models: Notes Towards a Definition of Documentary Theatre', trans. Heinz Bernard in *Theatre Quarterly*, 1/1 (Cambridge University Press). Augusto Boal, *Poetics of the Oppressed* (1974), from Augusto Boal, *Theatre of the Oppressed*, trans. Charles A. and Maria Odilia Leal McBride (New York: Urizen Books, 1979). Michelene Wandor, 'Political Dynamics: Feminisms', from *Carry On, Understudies: Theatre and Sexual Politics* (London: Routledge and Kegan Paul, 1986). Jindřich Honzl, *Dynamics of the Sign in the Theatre* (1940), from Ladislav Matejka and I. R. Titunik (eds. and trans.), *Semiotics of Art* (Cambridge, Mass.: the MIT Press, 1976); copyright © 1976 by The Massachusetts Institute of Technology. Umberto Eco, *Semiotics of Theatrical Performance* in *The Limits of Interpretation* (Bloomington: Indiana University Press, 1994); reproduced by courtesy of Indiana University Press. Marvin Carlson, *Psychic Polyphony* in *Theatre Semiotics* (Bloomington: Indiana University Press, 1990); reproduced by courtesy of Indiana University Press. Martin Esslin, 'The Signs of Stage and Screen', from *The Field of Drama* (London: Methuen, 1987); reproduced by permission of Reed Books (Methuen) and Curtis Brown Ltd, London on behalf of Martin Esslin; copyright © 1987 Martin Esslin. Patrice Pavis, 'Avant-Garde Theatre and Semiology', from *Languages of the Stage*, trans. Jill Daugherty (New York: Performing Arts Journal Publications, 1982). Excerpts from 'The Theatre of Cruelty: The First Manifesto' (1932) © Gallimard 1974, and excerpts from 'An End to Masterpieces' (1933) © Gallimard 1966, from *Antonin Artaud: Selected*

*Writings* by Antonin Artaud, translated by Helen Weaver. Translation copyright © 1976 by Farrar, Straus and Giroux, Inc. Reprinted by permisssion of Farrar, Straus and Giroux, Inc. 'The Futurist Synthetic Theatre' from *Marinetti: Selected Writings* by F. T. Marinetti, edited by R. W. Flint, translated by R. W. Flint and Arthur A. Coppotelli. Copyright © 1972 by Farrrar, Straus and Giroux, Inc. Reprinted by permission of Farrar, Straus and Giroux, Inc.

# Introduction

In his *Poetics*, the fountainhead of Western speculation about drama, Aristotle presented tragedy as an intrinsic part of *literary* theory. He admitted that as a performance art it did have its non-literary aspects—spectacle and music; but these he considered secondary attractions, not to be ranked in critical importance with the text. He even suggested that a good drama might be spoilt by shortcomings in performance. This view has had a lasting effect on the Western view of drama. When literary theorizing was revived in the Renaissance along the lines laid down by the ancients, principally Aristotle and Horace, the primacy in drama of the text was taken for granted. For example, François Hédelin d'Aubignac had little to say about settings and machines (which in fact were a significant part of performance in the French theatre of his day) in his influential statement of the principles of neoclassical doctrine, *La Pratique du théâtre* (The Practical Art of the Theatre, 1657). The presentational elements of theatre he saw as mere adjuncts to the true business of the stage which was the delivery of the author's words.

The primacy of the text has continued to be the underlying assumption of much Western dramatic theory until quite recent times. But at least from Denis Diderot's *Discours sur la poésie dramatique* (On Dramatic Poetry, 1758) onwards the importance of visual signifiers in the theatre has been recognized. These came to be seen as necessary elements in a nascent bourgeois drama that aimed to be closer to its middle-class spectators than a courtly drama, situated in a non-specific and idealized sphere, could ever be. One important aspect of the evolution of dramatic theory over the last century or so has been the gradual but relentless downgrading of the dramatic text as the theoretical cornerstone of the whole theatrical edifice; more and more heed has been paid to other elements of performance, including and indeed particularly the art of acting.

Some of the kaleidoscopic succession of theories of the drama over the last 150 years have articulated problems at least embryonically present in the idea of theatre from the beginning. There is a fundamental distinction between drama and other forms of literature. The latter, no matter whether enjoyed individually or collectively, appeal wholly to the imagination. They address the inner man (and woman). But the contradiction embedded in the idea of a performance text is the ambiguous and shifting relationship between reality and enactment. On the one hand there is the physical presence of the actor in a three-dimensional space which he shares with the spectators during a time span which is also experienced jointly: this is a palpable piece of reality. On the other hand, the dramatic enactment—be it quasi-religious ritual, illusionistic make-believe or open acknowledgement of theatre *qua* theatre—invites the audience to contribute its imagination to this shared experience. In other words, reality interlocks with fiction in something like Coleridge's 'willing suspension of disbelief'—perhaps more than that: a moment of magic. The relative weight of these contradictory ingredients has shifted again and again in the theoretical debates of the last century and a half. A commitment to external reality on the one hand and an assertion of the self-sufficiency of art on the other have fought for dominance in a constant reinterpretation of the theatrical phenomenon. Which is the 'truer' kind of theatre?

An argument of venerable antiquity that recurs in various guises, loosely linked with the question of 'reality', is that of the *usefulness* of drama. Does it, can it, indeed should it provide the audience with guidance—be it in the religious, the moral, or the political sphere? Should it give moral uplift to the individual spectator, should it help to improve society as a whole? Conversely, is an aesthetic response not sufficient unto itself? Does such a response not *preclude* any moral considerations if it is to have its full effect? The question of which of the two functions that Horace demanded of drama—instruction and delight—should prevail crops up again and again, in ever new formulations.

Obviously, these tides of intellectual fashion have been stirred by the accelerating tempo of change which has characterized every aspect of life during the nineteenth and the twentieth centuries. New literary, philosophical, and political systems have sprung up in response to a dizzy flux of events: new industries have been created, new classes have come into being, the political map of the world has kept altering with the rapid expansion of empires followed by their collapse, new nations have emerged on the political stage. Wars have shattered the world, ideologies have been locked in conflict. It would have been astonishing if the theatre had failed to reflect this turmoil—although as an artistic practice dependent on audiences, i.e. on groups of people with shared tastes and interests, it tends to lag culturally behind other, more individually consumable, literary arts. New conditions of performance: playhouses designed for ever larger mass spectacles or conversely reduced to elitist intimacy; new stage technologies employing sophisticated mechanics, electrics, and electronics; the influence of different movements in the visual arts creating new ways of seeing; performances moving out of the theatre altogether into churches, onto open-air sites, into workshops or streets, either for aesthetic or for political reasons: these and the changing composition of the audience itself have all been reflected in dramatic, and latterly performance, theories. But such a reflection is not necessarily direct. While there *is* a link between theory and practice it may well be oblique, with a time lag between cause and effect. The earliest example of such a gap can be seen in the Greek theatre's period of greatest glory in the fifth century BC being followed by the *Poetics* rather later, in the latter part of the fourth century. Now practice, now theory comes first. Nor is there any direct correlation between theory and practice in terms of quality. Throughout the history of the theatre, there has not been an invariable coincidence in time or place between dramatic and theoretical productivity. Elizabethan and Jacobean drama in England as well as Golden Age drama in Spain were much poorer in the output of dramatic theorizing than was seventeenth-century France. But neither England nor Spain were necessarily any the worse off, as far as playwriting was concerned, because of that deficiency. In the period examined in this book, there has at certain times and in certain places been a similar mismatch between the quality of the drama produced and the theories woven around it. What is true of the overall picture may also apply to individual authors. Innovative writers often fail to provide an explicit theoretical framework for their plays. Ibsen, in giving his views on drama, did not go much beyond *obiter dicta*. Chekhov's opinions about his own drama can only be gathered in snippets. Beckett was as tight-lipped in terms of theory as his Lucky was loquacious in spouting *his* philosophy. The empirical tradition of English-speaking playwrights and thinkers has in general made them less theoretically articulate than their philosophically schooled French confrères; which is not to say that English-language drama has been consistently less rich and interesting than that of France. There are times when the output of theory outweighs the production of the material to be theorized about; the second half of the twentieth century may well in retrospect be seen as such a time. Nor do all plays attract the same degree of theoretical attention. Popular forms of drama have rarely been deemed worthy of scholarly attention until fairly recent times. To sum up: the history of dramatic theory is not the same thing as the history of drama, let alone the history of the theatre. The link is a loose one, and it is governed by diverse historical factors, such as the role played by the intelligentsia in different societies.

Dramatic theories come in various guises. They may overlap in any given case but, notionally at least, they tend to serve different purposes.

They may be *prescriptive*. This was certainly true of the neoclassical doctrine which, first elaborated in Italy in the sixteenth century, was to dominate French drama, and hence that of much of the rest of Europe, for some two centuries after the foundation of the French Academy in 1635. Such an authoritarian attitude might seem dead as the dodo nowadays, wholly irrelevant to modern concerns. In its unadulterated form it is of course a thing of the past. But the conveniently dated death of French neoclassicism in 1830—the so-called 'battle of *Hernani*', Victor Hugo's trail-blazing drama fought over by the young generation of romantics—was more apparent than real. It is true that nearly a century ago, Professor Saintsbury could write dismissively: 'It is part of the Neo-Classic error itself to assume some definite goal of critical perfection towards which all things tend, and which, when you have attained it, permits you to take no further trouble except of imitation and repetition.'[1] And yet, fragments of classical doctrine survive. A matter of constant theoretical/ critical concern is the question of the viability of tragedy in modern times. Eugene O'Neill is an outstanding example of a playwright much preoccupied with this problem. Some writers have declared tragedy to be impossible in a world secular in its beliefs and democratic in its aspirations. But others, such as Arthur Miller[2], have reformulated the neo-Aristotelian definition of tragedy, tinged as it was with Renaissance concepts of high social status, and have argued the continuing justification of tragedy in the Century of the Common Man. Indeed, the whole idea of *genre* derived from antiquity—drama falling into distinct and mutually exclusive categories—is a spectre still haunting twentieth-century theorists. (The concept of genre has also been prominent in film studies: but the commercial motivation of cinematic genres make these a different proposition from the genres of dramatic theory.) Do the old distinctions of mood, ethos, and story type still make any sense after the creation of the *drame* in the eighteenth century as a new kind of play designed precisely to escape the old generic strait jacket? Is it meaningful to continue talking about drama in different aesthetic compartments? To which genre should we assign *Hedda Gabler*, *The Cherry Orchard*, or *Who's Afraid of Virginia Woolf*? Yet we find a modern playwright like Dürrenmatt, with his theoretical cap on, arguing in the middle of the twentieth century in genre terms—admittedly recognizing their inadequacy.[3] The old genre question was still uppermost in his mind, even if his answer was not the classical one. The fact is, of course, that Aristotle had stated many of the basic problems of dramatic theory, even though some of his answers may fail to satisfy today.

Problems of genre apart, the vision of the Greek theatre as a lost ideal has been haunting the European imagination ever since the Renaissance. How could such an exemplary ingathering of national energies which combined different arts be recovered by means appropriate to the modern age? This aspiration can be traced in the theorizing of various writers, notably Richard Wagner of course. (Theory apart, Greek drama persists in modern guise: ancient myths have again been dramatized, particularly by twentieth-century French playwrights like Cocteau, Anouilh, and Sartre.) Antiquity, then, has been a continuing influence into the twentieth century, even if only as something to be opposed. Brecht formulated his dramaturgy in explicitly anti-Aristotelian terms: he saw in the concept of catharsis a wasteful expenditure of social energy. His concept of an Epic Theatre provocatively combined the separate and distinct Aristotelian categories of Epic and Drama. (He nevertheless concurred with the Greek philosopher's insistence on the primacy of

---

[1] George Saintsbury, *A History of English Criticism* (Edinburgh: Blackwood, rev. edn., 1936), 244.
[2] See pp. 108–11.  [3] See pp. 50–4.

plot in drama—and he was to write his own adaptation of Sophocles' *Antigone*.) Augusto Boal, too, has seen the Aristotelian approach to drama as negative in that he sees it as anti-revolutionary.

But prescriptiveness has not followed an exclusively neoclassical line. The 'laws' of the well-made play were held in high esteem in the nineteenth century as a guide to playwriting.[4] The German novelist/playwright Gustav Freytag's *Technique of Drama* (1863) tempered Aristotelian maxims with insights drawn from more recent playwrights like Lessing and Schiller. His theory of the 'pyramidal structure' of the most effective drama, consisting of five parts and three crises, served as a guide to budding playwrights well into the twentieth century. Georges Polti's *Les 36 situations dramatiques* (The Thirty-Six Dramatic Situations, 1894) analysed plays ancient and modern in order to give the working playwright the basic tools for constructing as many as 1,332 different new scenarios.[5] His compatriot Étienne Souriau improved on that dazzling offer in *Les deux cent mille situations dramatiques* (The 200,000 Dramatic Situations, 1950). This latter breakdown of all the possible motifs of drama in various combinations was designed to produce not just the 200,000 situations of the book's title but a full complement of 210,141 such situations. Playwriting manuals continue to be produced up to the present, based on different theoretical precepts.

Instead of being conservative, dramatic theories may be *polemical*. Playwrights with a stake in their own products are prominent in tearing down old structures and building new ones. In the heat of argument, fairness is not always to be expected. Here, as a fresh programme is mapped out, theory may be ahead of the actual output of drama designed to illustrate it; alternatively, it may coincide with it, or else it may come later. For instance, Artaud formulated his concept of the Theatre of Cruelty before he had actually created any such thing. On the other hand, Shaw as he went along justified his ideas (and the dramatic form in which he expressed them) in numerous prefaces and articles. Brecht fought theoretically for his plays at the time of their appearance in print or on the stage; but he made the full and comprehensive statement of his dramatic doctrine only late in his career: *A Short Organon for the Theatre*.[6] Not surprisingly, politics looms large in theoretical polemics. (The term 'politics' includes gender and ethnic as well as ideological and class struggles.[7])

Dramatic theories may be *analytical*: assessing and offering a new reading of that which already exists. In this guise they tend to be the (by no means exclusive) domain of academia. The main aim is to change the intellectual landscape in which drama is received. An analytical approach may nevertheless have an effect on practice. The revaluation of the classical past has often indirectly coloured the reading of the present. This was the case with Nietzsche's *The Birth of Tragedy* (1872), which pointed out the Dionysian (i.e.

---

[4] For Shaw's dismissal of the well-made play, see pp. 102–4.    [5] See pp. 12–18.
[6] See pp. 232–46.    [7] See Michelene Wandor, pp. 261–5.

irrational) alongside the Apollonian (rational) element as a constituent feature of Greek tragedy. This eccentric work of scholarship was an oblique polemic in support of Wagnerian music-drama. Cornford's and Murray's tracing the origins of Greek comedy and tragedy respectively back to a supposed communal ritual has to some extent strengthened the contemporary longing for a return to ritualized forms of drama.

Twentieth-century analytical theories are not autonomous. They interact with related disciplines—with linguistics in the case of semiology, with anthropology in the case of structuralism, with sociology in the case of reception theory, to give a few examples. Some of the more recent theories abound in specialized concepts and technical terminology. The rigour they aspire to is miles away from the liberal-humanist tone that used to dominate theoretical discourse. They appeal to an intellectually alert, generally an academic, readership rather than to the general public. Diagrams as well as mathematical and quasi-scientific formulae are the order of the day. Some of this work may risk flying off into airless regions remote from the theatre as it is or is ever likely to be. However, there are analytical theorists, like the American academic Richard Schechner, who have sought to keep at least one foot on the ground, combining speculations with field research and practical stage experience.

The present anthology offers specimens of all three types of theory, drawn from various sources: manifestos, prefaces, or essays by playwrights, by theatre practitioners as well as by scholars. It offers a mixture of pieces reproduced previously, which could not be omitted in a general overview, and some less well known but nevertheless significant items. It is, of course, not possible for a work of this modest size to cover the period from the middle of the nineteenth to the latter part of the twentieth century, an era of restless productivity in every field (including that of dramatic theory) with anything approaching completeness.

The categorization employed calls for a word of explanation. It is thematic rather than chronological; a broad time sequence has been observed within each of the five subject headings, allowing for some thematic subgroupings under each heading. A few items might arguably have appeared under a different heading, according to what weight one might choose to give to different aspects of a complex argument.

The first section, 'General Theory', features pieces which do of course come out of particular historical situations (how could they not?); but they float free of the more specific arguments made in the following four sections. They deal with problems of genre or such broad matters as what constitutes comedy: hence, excerpts from Bergson's *Laughter* are included.

The second section is advisedly headed, 'Varieties of Realism'. Like most of the critical terms employed in this section, and indeed elsewhere too, 'realism' is a slippery concept which means different things in different contexts. If it is merely to hold the mirror up to nature (itself a concept open to many readings), does it amount to more than the sensible demand Hamlet put to the players at Elsinore? Should it give a photographic rather than an idealized reproduction of behaviour? If so, was Zola right to demand a naturalistic setting—since the environment largely conditions the way real men and women actually feel and act? Does realism imply a 'missing fourth wall', the device Strindberg, for instance, uses in a modified form in *Miss Julie*,[8] which turns the audience into fascinated voyeurs? Is the articulation of unspoken thoughts, O'Neill's device in *Strange Interlude*, a 'truer' kind of realism? Should realism imply a seemingly tape recorder-like rendering of ordinary speech, in the manner of some Pinter plays? Or should realism give us a *model* rather than a photograph of the workings of society, an uncovering of its hidden mechanics, as Brecht sets out to do? In one or another of these different meanings, realism has been the accepted convention of Western drama for the greater part of the nineteenth and the twentieth centuries. It largely reflects a positivist outlook, a belief in science and technology, a materialistic, urban, industrial culture. The naturalism, that out-and-out form of realism which revolutionized the stage towards the latter end of the nineteenth century and which has come under endless theoretical attack ever since, still continues to flourish as an important, arguably as the dominant, mode to this day—certainly in the cinema and on television if not in the theatre. In whatever interpretation of the word, realism implies staging methods claiming near-parity of esteem with the dramatic text. Production becomes a vital aspect of the playscript, as can be seen in the detailed stage directions of countless plays.

'Anti-Naturalism', the title of the third section, covers a great variety of reactions against this realistic/naturalistic mainstream. In fact, no sooner had realism in some form or other apparently conquered the stage in the final years of the nineteenth century than a counter-movement set in. Much of this was a displaced religious emotion in search of secular outlets. A romantic impulse, seemingly banished from the rationalistic stage, was to return time and again in a blizzard of different movements: symbolism, theatricalism, expressionism, futurism, dadaism, surrealism, the Theatre of Pure Form, the Theatre of Cruelty, the Theatre of the Absurd, Environmental Theatre and Happenings (the list is not exhaustive). These labels are no less deceptive than that of 'realism'. Calling all the different movements simply anti-realistic or anti-naturalistic may veil significant differences. Thus, the Italian futurists under Marinetti's leadership extolled modernity, speed, and war; the German expressionists, who did not rally under any one leader, tended to exalt humanity and peace. The hectic proliferation of objects in Ionesco's drama is utterly unlike the minimalism of Beckett's plays: yet both authors have been classified by Martin Esslin as absurdists. Some forms of anti-naturalism, like dada for instance, were politically provocative; others, like the American Happenings of the 1960s, were basically anodyne. That said, there *are* considerable links both personal and ideological between the various movements, and they have

---

[8] See pp. 96–7.

many aims in common. Freedom of the imagination is generally celebrated, rationality derided, and causality abandoned. Psychology becomes meaningless. The juxtaposition of essays and manifestos in this section reveals some continuities: thus, in France Jarry is followed by Apollinaire, who in turn is followed, in a darker vein, by Artaud, with Ionesco bringing up the theatrically more successful rear quite some time later. Increasingly the non-literary aspect of performance comes to the fore. This is partly a function of the growing distrust of rationality, of the word. It is also the result of theatre research: the commedia dell 'arte is rediscovered, European and exotic masks exert a new fascination.[9] The breakdown of old barriers in a society in flux reinstates the prestige of previously undervalued popular entertainments. The crumbling of a Eurocentric world picture opens Western eyes to the enchantments of Asian theatre: Yeats is inspired by Japanese Noh,[10] Artaud by Cambodian and Balinese dancers. More and more attention is paid to theatrical signifiers: set, costumes, and particularly light, which with the coming of electric stage lighting has become vastly more flexible and sophisticated, supplement or replace the text.

The next section, 'Political Theatre', is perhaps the most contentious—contentious not so much in the nature of its material as in terms of definition. What is it that belongs properly under this heading? Surely we all know nowadays that everything (including the personal) is political? Don't we all know that any play that avoids controversy is, by that very fact, an endorsement of the status quo? In fact, doesn't every portrayal of human conduct have ideological implications? Yes, all this is true enough. But there *is* a difference between drama whose politics are coded and veiled, and drama that wears its committed heart on its sleeve. When we speak of political theatre we tend to mean revolutionary, or at any rate Marxist-inspired, theatre; the status quo doesn't as a rule choose or indeed need to be openly on the theatrical agenda. At the same time, a common left-wing platform should not blind us to the ideological as well as formal differences within political theatre. We remember that Marx himself, commenting on French Marxists of the 1870s, said, 'I am not a Marxist.' Revolutionary doctrine has kept evolving according to the specific conditions of time and place. The theoretical debate between Brecht and Lukász in the 1930s revealed a gulf between two Marxist thinkers: the German playwright's formally innovative attitude clashed with the Hungarian scholar's formal traditionalism. Political theatre has ranged all the way from straight agit-prop exhortation, a style popular in the 1920s and revived in the 1960s, to the rigorously documentary theatre advocated by Peter Weiss[11]—with a great many variants in between. In the hands of the Brazilian Boal[12] and activists elsewhere it has transcended the limits of professional, and indeed

---

[9] For Yeats, *Certain Noble Plays of Japan*, Meyerhold, *The Fairground Booth* and O'Neill, *Memoranda on Masks*, see pp. 128–9, 133, and 153–7 respectively in this book.

[10] See pp. 126–31.    [11] See pp. 247–53.    [12] See pp. 254–60.

theatre-bound, drama altogether. It has gone out into the street and the workplace, blurring the boundary between the scripted play and the semi-improvised event.

The final section does not attempt to give a complete overview of the various analytical theories which have mushroomed—particularly in France but also in Germany and the United States—since the 1960s. Some of these will prove to have been ephemeral. Deconstruction—the 'oppositional' reading of a text, finding in it what the author had *not* intended to say—has itself begun to be deconstructed. The text has been radically devalued in the last few decades of the twentieth century: but performance theories which dispense with it altogether are beyond the scope of this book. So the last section concentrates on the one discipline which has attracted a great deal of academic attention since the 1960s: semiotics. There has been truly innovative work done in this area; some of it umbilically linked with earlier theories (according to Umberto Eco, 'semiotics is a very young discipline, only two thousand years old'[13]); some of it breaking new ground. Semiotics, the study of signs as the producers of meaning, covers a very wide range of fields other than just literature. It began with the work of the Prague School of structuralists in the 1930s and 1940s. This in turn had taken its inspiration from the work of the Swiss linguist Ferdinand de Saussure and the American philosopher Charles Sanders Pierce as well as the Russian formalists, notably Bogatyrev. After a period of dormancy the discipline was taken up again in the 1960s and developed in France, Italy, Germany, the (then) Soviet Union, the United States, and to a lesser extent in Britain. Viewing drama as a 'language' has been a basic tenet of theatrical semiotics. It goes beyond the study of the dramatic text and takes for its province all aspects of performance, in which a complex sign system, or rather interacting sign systems, are deployed so as to generate meaning. A central insight is the realization that anything that happens or appears on a stage *ipso facto* becomes a sign. The deciphering of signs has produced a great many insights on a theoretical level; the practical application of these insights is perhaps still open to question. Tadeusz Kowzan attempted in 1976 to do an exhaustive listing of all the signifying units of a theatrical performance; but how applicable are they in practice? To quote Keir Elam: 'these rules are not usually strong or explicit enough to bear analogy with those regulating correct sentence-formation in language.'[14] Indeed, the appropriateness of the linguistic model itself has been challenged by Georges Mounin, since drama, unlike language, is not a full two-way communication. Some theorists have argued for 'non-semiotic performance', i.e. the total abandonment of rationality and meaning. But this takes us to the borderline where the remit of this book ends.

---

[13] For Umberto Eco, *Semiotics of Theatrical Performance*, see p. 279–87 in this book.
[14] Keir Elam, *The Semiotics of Theatre and Drama* (London: Routledge, 1994), 51.

In any case, it is safe to say that whichever way the theatrical kaleidoscope turns, some link with the social perception of reality will inform drama in the future as it has done in the past. Drama and its reflection in theory will continue to evolve, its elements making an infinity of fresh patterns. And the debate will continue. There is no end in sight, no final resting point when the last word will have been spoken.

# PART I

## General Theory

# The Work of Art of the Future (1849)

## Richard Wagner

Richard Wagner (1813–83) had the widest international impact of any nineteenth-century German man of the theatre—an artistic (though one would hope not an ideo-logical) influence felt to this day—being in his own person a composer, a librettist, a conductor, a producer, and a festival organizer. In addition, he was a voluminous writer on dramatic and musical theory. In this latter aspect of his work, he was driven by impatience with the existing state of art rather than a desire to shine as a theorist as such. His wide-ranging, ponderous prose writings, often sharply polemical in tone, did not always express a single unchanging point of view: thus, his position evolved over time from a democratic to a pro-aristocratic stance. However, a constant factor was his opposition to the commercialization of art; he addressed himself, at least in theory, to the national community, the 'folk', rather than to the (money-minded, bourgeois) 'public'. Seeing ancient Greece as the summit of European civilization, much as Goethe and Schiller had done before him, he sought to create a new drama necessarily different in kind from that of antiquity but serving much the same high communal ambitions. Classical Greek tragedy having combined the arts of poetry, music, and dance in expressing the national spirit, Wagner wished to replace con-ventional opera, which he considered an obsolete and ridiculous form of art, with a new lyric drama in which dramatic, musical, and plastic values would once again be inextricably linked so as to serve the same communal ends. He saw the giants of modern art, Shakespeare and Beethoven, as having fallen short of the highest pos-sible achievement precisely because of the partial, unintegrated nature of their endeavours. The emphasis of the music-drama which Wagner advocated was to be on its *dramatic* value, superseding the type of (French or Italian) opera, in which the text was a mere pretext for music divided up into arias and interspersed with recitat-ives. Pursuing this ideal which he had defined in his theoretical writings, Wagner was

Richard Wagner, *Das Kunstwerk der Zukunft*, ch. 4, in *Sämtliche Schriften und Dichtungen*, vol. iii (Leipzig: Breitkopf & Härtel et al., 5th edn., n.d.), 148–60. Translated from the German by George Brandt.

to create music-dramas with an 'endless melody' studded with *Leitmotive* ('leading motives'—a word which incidentally he did not use himself). In his work, the words and the music were designed to be a seamless unity, doing far more than merely illustrating each other.

Key works among Wagner's theoretical writings were *Art and Revolution* (1849), *The Work of Art of the Future* (1849), and *Opera and Drama* (1851). These essays were all written—significantly *after* the composition of *Lohengrin*, the last of his works he called an 'opera'—during the years of his exile from Germany (1849–61), the consequence of his involvement in the revolutionary events of 1848 in Saxony. Together these three essays served the purpose of defining, and at the same time arguing the case for, the music-drama of the future which he was engaged in creating.

A crucial aspect of this drama was the concept of the *Gesamtkunstwerk* (the 'total' or 'integrated' work of art). The following excerpt from *The Work of Art of the Future* foreshadows Wagner's subsequent practice in many ways, a task he was uniquely qualified to carry out in that, unlike other composers, he was his own librettist. He polemically overstated his case: the claim that the new 'total work of art' would subsume all its separate constituent elements—poetry, music, the visual arts—and thereby make them individually redundant is clearly absurd. It is worth noting that even at this early stage he anticipated some features of the Bayreuth Festival Playhouse which his friend Gottfried Semper was later to design (following Wagner's ideas) and which did not open until 1876. Notable among these architectural ideas are the placing of the audience on one single, 'classless' level rather than above each other in the traditional tiers mirroring social divisions, and the concealment of the orchestra in a 'mystic gulf' between the auditorium and the actual stage with the aim of increasing its oneiric potential.

William Ashton Ellis's monumental English version of Wagner's prose works (1892–9) having dated rather badly, the passage quoted below is a new translation.

[…] The artist can only find full satisfaction by uniting every branch of art in the *conjoint* work of art: in every *separation* of his artistic faculties he is *not free*, not fully that which he is capable of being; whereas in the *conjoint* work of art he is *free*, and fully that which is capable of being.

The *true* endeavour of art is therefore *all-embracing*: anyone inspired with a true *artistic instinct* wishes, by the highest development of his own particular faculty, to attain not the glorification of this special faculty but the glorification *of mankind as such in art*.

The highest conjoint work of art is the *drama*: it can only exist in all its *potential completeness* when there exists in it each *separate branch of art* in *its own utmost completeness.*

True drama is only conceivable as proceeding from *a common tendency of every art* towards the most direct communication with a *common public*: each separate art, *to be fully intelligible*, can only communicate with the common public through a mutual interaction with the other arts in drama; for the purpose of each separate branch of art can only be fully attained by the reciprocal agreement and enlightening co-operation of all the branches of art.—

*Architecture* can have no higher aim than to provide a fellowship of artists, each of whom is productive in his own sphere, with the spatial environment necessary for the manifestation of the human work of art. Only that edifice is reared according to necessity which most effectively answers to a human aim: the highest human aim is the artistic aim; the highest artistic aim is drama. In the ordinary utilitarian building, the builder has only to answer to the basest human aim; in it, beauty is a luxury. In the luxury building he is forced to satisfy an unnecessary and unnatural need: his creation is therefore capricious, unproductive, and unlovely. On the other hand, in the construction of a building every part of which is to answer solely to a common artistic aim—that is, in the building of the *theatre*, the architect needs only to act as an *artist*, with the *work of art* as his objective. In a perfect theatre building the requirement of art alone gives measure and law, down to the smallest detail. This requirement is twofold, that of *giving* and that of *receiving*, which reciprocally penetrate and govern one another. The *stage* has first of all the task of meeting all the spatial conditions for the conjoint dramatic action to be represented on it: in the second place, it has to fulfil these conditions with the object of presenting this dramatic action to the eye and ear of the audience in an intelligible fashion. In ordering the *audience space*, the need for understanding the work of art will, optically and acoustically, provide the necessary law which can only be served, in addition to practicality, by a beautiful arrangement; for the desire of the collective spectator is the desire for the *work of art*, to whose understanding he must be led by everything that meets his eye.[1] So, by seeing and hearing, he is transported altogether onto the stage; the performer becomes an artist only by being completely absorbed into the audience. Everything that breathes and moves upon the stage, breathes and moves only from an eloquent desire to communicate, to be seen and heard within a space which, however circumscribed, seems to the actor from his scenic point of view to embrace the whole of mankind; whereas the audience, that representative of public life, forgets itself in the auditorium; it only lives and breathes in the work of art which

---

[1] The problem of the theatre building of the future cannot by any means be regarded as solved by our modern theatre buildings: they are laid out in accord with traditional assumptions and laws which have nothing in common with the requirements of pure art. Where speculation for profit, on the one hand, joins with luxurious ostentation on the other, the absolute interest of art is bound to be severely compromised; hence no architect anywhere will be able to raise to a law of beauty the stratification and fragmentation of our auditoria—dictated by the separation of our audience into the most diverse categories of class and civic status. When one envisions the spaces of the communal theatre of the future, one realizes readily enough what an undreamt-of, rich field for invention lies open there. [Wagner's note.]

seems to it to be Life itself, and upon the stage which seems to it to be the universe.

Such marvels spring from the edifice of the architect, to such enchantments he can give a solid foundation when he makes the purpose of man's highest work of art his own, when he summons forth the conditions of its coming into existence from his own special artistic capabilities. On the other hand, how cold, immobile, and dead does his edifice appear when, without following any higher aim than that of luxury, without the artistic necessity which leads him in the theatre to arrange and invent each detail with the greatest sense of fitness, he is forced to act according to every speculative whim of his self-glorifying caprice, to pile up and multiply masses and ornamentation, in order to give body to the honour of an insolent plutocrat today, or that of a modernized Jehovah tomorrow!²

But neither the fairest form nor the richest masonry are by themselves enough for the dramatic work of art to have a perfectly appropriate spatial setting. The stage which is to present to the spectator the picture of the life of man must also, for a thorough understanding of this life, be able to present a lively counterfeit of nature, in which alone the artist can fully display himself. The walls of this stage which stare coldly and dispassionately down at the artist and out at the audience, must deck themselves with the fresh tints of nature, with the warm light of heaven's ether, so as to be worthy to participate in the human work of art. Plastic *architecture* here feels its limitations, its own lack of freedom, and flings itself, thirsting for love, into the arms of painting which shall redeem it for the fairest union with nature.

Here *landscape painting* comes in, summoned by a shared need that only it can satisfy. What the painter's perceptive eye has seen in nature, what he, as an artist, wishes to display to the whole community for its artistic delight, he adds here as his own rich contribution to the combined work of all the arts. Through him the scene takes on complete artistic truth: his draughtsmanship, his colour, his warmly animating use of light compel nature to serve the highest artistic intentions. That which the landscape painter, in his urge to impart what he had seen and understood, had formerly squeezed into the narrow frame of the panel picture—that which he had hung up *on* the wall of the egoist's solitary chamber or put away in the isolated, incoherent, and disfiguring stacks of a picture store—*with that* he will fill the ample framework of the tragic stage from now on, shaping the whole scenic space to bear witness to his ability to recreate nature. The illusion which he could only hint at, only get close to, by means of his brush and the most subtle blend of colours, he will here bring to its illusive consummation by the artistic employment of all the optical devices at his command and the artistic use of light. He will not take

---

² This would seem to be a coded denunciation of Jewish participation in German culture. Although Wagner did not publish (under an assumed name) his notorious essay, *Judaism in Music*, until 1850, i.e. the year after the publication of *The Work of Art of the Future*, he already held anti-Semitic views at the time of writing this essay. He was to republish *Judaism in Music* in 1869, this time under his own name.

umbrage at the apparent crudity of his tools, the seeming grotesqueness of his procedure in so-called scene-painting; for he will reflect that even the finest brush is but a humbling instrument in relation to the completed work of art; and that the artist has a right to be *proud* only when he is *free*, i.e. when his work of art is finished and alive, and *he* has, with all his helping tools, been absorbed into it. But the finished work of art that confronts him from the *stage*, framed thus and in the full gaze of the public, will satisfy him infinitely more than had his earlier work, carried out with more delicate tools; he will in truth not regret having the use of scenic space for the sake of such a work of art merely because of his earlier command over a smooth piece of canvas: for, seeing that at the very worst his work remains the very same, no matter what frame it is viewed in, as long as it gives its subject an intelligible shape: so in any case his work of art will in *this* frame produce a livelier impression, a greater and more general understanding than his earlier landscape picture had done.

The organ for all understanding of nature is man: not only did the landscape painter have to impart this understanding to his fellow-men, but he also had to make it vivid for them by the depiction of man within his picture of nature. By setting his work of art within the frame of the tragic stage, he will extend the person being addressed to man in general as a member of the public, and will enjoy the satisfaction of having extended the latter's understanding and made him a sharer in his joy. However, he will only achieve this public understanding by allying his work with a shared, most lofty, and universally intelligible artistic purpose, this purpose being unmistakably disclosed to the common understanding by an actual physical person, with all the warmth of his being. The universally intelligible thing is the dramatic action, precisely because it is not artistically complete until every artificial prop in the drama has been cast aside as it were, and real life most truthfully and concretely attains its immediate presentation. Every branch of art addresses the *understanding* only to the extent that its core—only the relation of which to man or its derivation from man can animate and justify the work of art—is maturing towards *drama*. All artistic creativity becomes universally intelligible, wholly understood and justified to the extent that it passes over into drama, that it is inwardly illuminated by drama.[3]

---

[3] It cannot be a matter of indifference to the modern landscape painter to note by how few people his work is really understood today, and with what dull mindless complacency his nature paintings are merely stared at by the Philistine world that pays him; how the so-called 'charming scenery' is capable merely of satisfying the idle unthinking visual gluttony of these same people, *devoid* of real need, whose sense of hearing is worked up no less to that idiotic joy by our vapid modern music-making which to the *artist* is as nauseating a recompense for his labours as indeed it fully answers the intentions of the *industrialist*. There is a sad affinity between the 'charming scenery' and the 'tuneful music' of our times, the connecting link of which assuredly is not any profound thought but that blubbery, debased *sentimentality* which selfishly draws back from the spectacle of human suffering in its vicinity in order to hire for itself a private little paradise in the vapourings of a generalized nature. These sentimental folk like to hear and see anything except *Man true and undistorted* who stands ominously by the exit of their dreams. *But the latter is precisely what we must put into the foreground.* [Wagner's note.]

*Man the artist* now steps onto the architect's and the painter's stage, just as natural man steps onto the stage of nature. What the *sculptor* and the *historical painter* endeavoured to shape in *stone* or on *canvas,* they now shape to conscious artistic life upon *themselves,* their figure, the limbs of their bodies, their facial features. The same sense that led the sculptor in his understanding and rendering of the human figure, now guides the *performer* in the handling and bearing of his actual body. The same eye which taught the historical painter, in drawing and in colour, in the arrangement of drapery and the composition of groups, to discover whatever is beautiful, graceful, and characteristic, now orders the whole range of *actual human presence.* Sculptor and painter once upon a time freed the Greek tragic actor from the *buskin* and the *mask,* upon and under which the real person could only move according to a certain religious convention. Both these figurative arts quite properly swept away this last disfigurement of man the pure artist, thus prefiguring in stone and canvas the tragic actor of the future. As they once descried him in his undistorted truth, they are now to allow him to present himself in reality and to bring his form, which they as it were had described, to dynamic bodily portrayal.

Thus the illusion of figurative art will turn to truth in drama: the figurative artist will hold out his hand to the *dancer,* to the *actor,* so as to lose himself in them and thus himself be both a dancer and an actor.—So far as lies within his power, he will have to convey to the eye the inner man, his feeling and his will. The fullest breadth and depth of the scenic space belong to him for the plastic manifestation of his figure and his motion, singly or in unison with his fellow performers. But where his power ends, where the fullness of his will and feeling impels him to the *expression* of the inner man by means of *speech,* the word will proclaim his clearly conscious purpose: he becomes a *poet,* and in order to be a poet, a *musician.* But as dancer, musician, and poet he is still one and the same thing: nothing other than the *performing, artistic human being who, according to the fullest measure of his faculties, communicates with the highest receptivity.*

It is in him, the immediate performer, that the three sister arts unite in one collective operation in which the highest faculty of each reaches its highest manifestation. By working together, each one of them attains the power to be and to achieve the very thing which it longs to be and to achieve according to its innermost essence. By virtue of the fact that each can be absorbed, where its own power ends, within the other whose power begins at that point, it keeps itself pure, free and independent as *that* which it is. The *mimetic dancer* sheds his powerlessness as soon as he can sing and speak; the creations of *music* attain all-explaining interpretation through the actor as well as through the poet's word, and that exactly to the extent that it is able to be absorbed into the movement of the actor and the word of the poet. The *poet* in turn only becomes truly human through his passing into the flesh and blood of the *performer;* if he assigns to each artistic factor the purpose which binds them and guides them all towards a common goal, this purpose is only transformed from a wish to an achievement *by the poet's will being subsumed in the actor's accomplishment.*

Not *any one* richly developed faculty of the separate arts will remain unused in the integrated work of art (*Gesamtkunstwerk*) of the future; only in it will each attain its full potential. Thus music, in particular, with its remarkably complex developments in instrumental music, will be able to be deployed in this work of art in accordance with its richest powers; nay, it will incite the mimetic art of dance to entirely new discoveries and similarly expand the afflatus of poetry to unsuspected amplitude. For in its solitude music has fashioned for itself an organ capable of the utmost expressiveness: this is the *orchestra*. The tone-speech of Beethoven, introduced into drama by the orchestra, marks an entirely new departure for the dramatic work of art.[4] If architecture and, more especially, scenic landscape painting are able to place the performing dramatic artist in the setting of physical nature, giving him out of nature's inexhaustible store an ever variegated and significant background—so in the orchestra, that vital body of immeasurably varied harmony, the individual performer is given for support an unending spring of, as it were, a natural, artistic as well as human, element. The orchestra, so to speak, is the basis of infinite universal emotion from which the individual emotion of the single performer may grow to its fullest height: in a sense it dissolves the hard motionless basis of the actual scene into a fluent and soft, elastic, impressionable ethereal plane whose measureless bottom is the sea of feeling itself. Thus the orchestra resembles the *earth* from which *Antaeus*, as soon as his foot had grazed it, drew fresh undying vitality. By its essence diametrically opposed to the performer's scenic natural surroundings and therefore, in its location, quite properly placed in the sunken foregound outside the scenic frame, it forms at the same time the perfect complement to these surroundings of the performer, inasmuch as it extends the inexhaustible *physical* element of nature to the no less inexhaustible *emotional* element of man the artist—which jointly enclose the performer as with an atmospheric ring of the elements of nature and art, in which, like a heavenly body, he moves in splendid security, and from which he is able to radiate all at once his feelings and his views in every direction, extending to infinity, into the measureless distances, like those to which the heavenly body sends forth its rays of light.

Thus, complementing one another in their changeful dance, the united sister arts—now all together, now in pairs, now singly—will come forward and take the lead according to the requirement of the only source of measure and purpose, the dramatic action. Now plastic mimicry will listen to the dispassionate reflections of thought; now the will of resolute thought will flow into the direct expression of gesture; now music alone will have to articulate the flow of feeling, the tremors of deep emotion; but soon, in a mutual embrace, all three will raise the will of the drama to immediate and powerful action. For there is one thing for them all, the arts united here, for which they must find

[4] Wagner here refers to the intervention of the choir in the final movement of Beethoven's Ninth Symphony when it joins the orchestra to sing Schiller's 'Ode to Joy'.

the will in order to be free in action, and that one thing is precisely the drama: the attainment of the aim of drama must be their common goal. Provided they are mindful of this aim, provided they direct all their will to the execution of this, they will then gain the power to lop off the selfish shoots of their particularity from their own trunk so that the tree may grow, not randomly in all directions but upward towards its proud top of branches, boughs and leaves, towards its crown.

The nature of man, as of any branch of art, is exceedingly rich and varied as such: but the *soul* of each individual, his most fundamental bent, his most urgent impulse is but *one thing*. When this one thing has been recognized by him as his basic nature, then, in order to reach this one indispensable thing, he is able to ward off every weaker subordinate appetite, every feeble longing the satisfaction of which would prevent the attainment of that one thing. Only the weak and impotent man knows no imperious, mighty longing of the soul: at any moment accidental, externally aroused appetites sway him which, being but appetites, he can never allay; and hence, hurled capriciously from one thing to another, he can never attain any real enjoyment. But if this man of weak impulse has the power stubbornly to pursue the satisfying of fortuitous appetites, there arise just those horrid unnatural phenomena in life and art which, as products of mad selfish frenzy, as the despot's murderous lust, or as lascivious modern opera music, fill us with such unspeakable disgust. But if the individual feels in himself a mighty longing, an impulse that drives back all other desires, that is to say the necessary inner drive which is the essence of his soul, his very being, and if he puts forth all his strength to satisfy it, then he will raise his strength as well as his own particular ability to whatever power and pitch he is capable of reaching.

But the individual man, in full possession of health of body, heart and mind, can experience no need higher than that which is common to all of his kind; for, to be a *true* need, it is bound to be one that he can satisfy only in the community. Indeed, the most imperious and strongest longing of the complete artist is to communicate to the highest level of his being with the most comprehensive community, and this he reaches with the necessary general breadth of understanding only in the *drama*. In drama he extends his own particular self to a universal human being by the representation of an individual personality other than himself. He must completely transcend himself in order to grasp the inner nature of another's personality with the completeness needed to portray it; this he will only attain when he so exhaustively analyses, so vividly comprehends this individual in his contact with, his penetration of, and his completion by other individuals—and thus the nature of these other individuals as well—that he is able to experience empathy in his own person through this contact, penetration and completion; and thus the perfect artist-performer is the individual expanded to the *nature of the human species* by the utmost development of his own particular nature. The space in which this marvellous process takes place is the *theatrical stage*; the integrated work of art which it produces is the *drama*. But in order to force his own particular nature to the highest flowering of its contents in this *one* supreme work of art, each individual artist, like each single branch of art, must repress in himself each and every arbitrary selfish bent toward an ill-timed expansion detrimental to the whole, so as to be able to collaborate all the more vigorously in reaching the highest common purpose, which indeed cannot be realized without the individual contribution, nor without the restriction for the time being of the individual contribution.

This purpose of drama is, however, the only true artistic purpose that can ever be fully *realized*: whatever deviates from it must necessarily lose itself in the ocean of things indefinite, unintelligible, unfree. This purpose, however, will never be reached by *any one branch of art by itself alone*[5] but only by *all together*; and therefore the most *universal* work of art is at the same time the only real, free, that is to say the only *intelligible*, work of art.

[5] The modern *playwright* will be most reluctant to concede that drama should not exclusively belong to *his* branch of art, that of *writing*; above all he will not be able to overcome his reluctance to share with the composer, or as he sees it, to let drama be swallowed up by opera. True enough, as long as opera lives on, so must drama live on, and indeed mime too; but as long as any dispute about this is conceivable, the drama of the future itself remains inconceivable. If, however, the dramatist's doubts go deeper and consist in his not being able to conceive how *song* is to usurp entirely and in every case the place of spoken dialogue, then he must take for rejoinder that he is not yet quite clear about the character of the work of art of the future in two respects. First, he fails to consider that in this work of art, music is to be given a role different from that in modern opera; that it is to be deployed in full strength only wherever it is the *most effective* device but in places where, say, dramatic speech is that which is *most necessary*, it has to be fully subordinated to the latter; but that it is precisely music that has the faculty, without remaining altogether silent, of adapting itself to the thinking aspect of language so imperceptibly as to give it almost total latitude while yet supporting it. If the playwright grants this, then he has to recognize in the second place that such thoughts and situations to which even the softest and most restrained musical support would seem importunate and burdensome, could only be such as derive from the spirit of modern drama, for which there will be no breathing space whatever in the work of art of the future. The person on display in the work of art of the future will have nothing at all in common with the knotty tangle of prosaic plotting or fashionable manners which our modern writers are forced to tie and untie in a play in the most elaborate manner. Inspired by nature, his deeds and words will be: Yea, yea! and Nay, nay; and all else is evil, i.e. modern and superfluous. [Wagner's note.]

# The Thirty-Six Dramatic Situations (1895)

## Georges Polti

This proto-structuralist attempt by Georges Polti (b. 1868) to uncover the hidden mechanics of the drama was designed not merely to help the understanding and appreciation of the 'consumers' of theatre but actually to help its producers, i.e. contemporary authors. Polti chose the examples to illustrate his thesis from a wealth of dramatic traditions and periods—ranging from the ancient Greeks, Hindus, and Chinese to the modern Russians, from medieval to Renaissance drama, from the Elizabethans to Spanish Golden Age authors, and especially from French playwrights of the Grand Siècle down to the eighteenth and nineteenth centuries. Polti's thirty-six situations, which, with a large number of subgroups, were intended to catalogue exhaustively all conceivable plot lines, fell under the following headings which are neither, strictly speaking, comparable in kind nor mutually exclusive: (1) supplication; (2) deliverance; (3) crime pursued by vengeance; (4) vengeance taken for kindred upon kindred; (5) pursuit; (6) disaster; (7) falling prey to cruelty or misfortune; (8) revolt; (9) daring enterprise; (10) abduction; (11) the enigma; (12) obtaining; (13) enmity of kinsmen; (14) rivalry of kinsmen; (15) murderous adultery; (16) madness; (17) fatal imprudence; (18) involuntary crimes of love; (19) slaying of a kinsman unrecognized; (20) self-sacrifice for an ideal; (21) self-sacrifice for kindred; (22) all sacrificed for a passion; (23) necessity of sacrificing loved ones; (24) rivalry of superior and inferior; (25) adultery; (26) crimes of love; (27) discovery of the dishonour of a loved one; (28) obstacles to love; (29) an enemy loved; (30) ambition; (31) conflict with a god; (32) mistaken jealousy; (33) erroneous judgement; (34) remorse; (35) recovery of a lost one; (36) loss of loved ones.

The insight that there are constant recurrences in dramatic plots was sound; but it is doubtful whether such a classification ever helped any playwright to 'invent' a new plot line.

Translated from the French by Lucille Ray (Cincinnati: Writer's Digest, 1931), 7–12; 119–31; first published Paris: Mercure de France, 1895.

# Introduction

> Gozzi maintained that there can be but thirty-six tragic situations.
> Schiller took great pains to find more, but he was unable to find even so
> many as Gozzi.[1]

Thirty-six situations only! To me there is something tantalizing about the
assertion, unaccompanied as it is by any explanation either from Gozzi, or
from Goethe and Schiller, and presenting a problem which it does not solve
[...]

The Venetian's exuberance would have made me doubtful of him since,
once having launched at us this number 36, he kept silence. But Schiller, rigid
and ardent Kantian, prince of modern aestheticians, master of true historic
drama—had he not in turn, before accepting this rule, 'taken great pains' to
verify it (and the pains of a Schiller!), thereby giving it the additional authority of his powerful criticism and rich memory? And Goethe, his opposite in all
things save for a strong taste for the abstract—Goethe, who throughout his life
seems to have considered the subject, adds his testimony years after Schiller's
death, years after their fruitful conversations, at the very time when he was
completing *Faust*, that supreme combination of contrasting elements.

In France, Gérard de Nerval alone had grasped and presented briefly the
totality of all dramatic production, in an article upon Soumet's *Jane Grey*, in
'L'Artiste',[2] written unfortunately with what dandyism of style! Having early
desired to know the exact number of actions possible to the theatre, he found,
he tells us, twenty-four. His basis is, however, far from satisfactory. Falling back
upon the outworn classification of the seven capital sins, he finds himself
obliged at the outset to eliminate two of them, gluttony and sloth, and very
nearly a third, lust (this would be Don Juan perhaps). It is not apparent what
manner of tragic energy has ever been furnished by avarice, and the divergence
between pride (presumably the spirit of tyranny) and danger does not
promise well for the contexture of drama, the manifestations of the latter
being too easily confounded with those of envy. [...]

Since Nerval, no one has dealt in Gozzi's genuinely technical manner with
the secrets of invention, unless it be relevant to mention in this connection
Sarcey's celebrated theory of the 'scène-à-faire'[3] [...]; some intimate notes of

---

[1] This is a loose translation of the comments Goethe made on 14 February 1830 in talking to J. P.
Eckermann, as recorded by the latter. See John Oxenford (trans.), *Conversations of Goethe with Ecker-
mann and Soret* (Everyman's Library no. 851, London: Dent, 1930), 350. Goethe did not actually say that
Schiller had 'taken great pains' to discover more tragic situations than Gozzi.

[2] Gérard de Nerval (1808–55), writing in *L'Artiste* of 7 Apr. 1844, on Soumet's tragedy *Jane Grey*,
which had been performed at the Odéon, did indeed comment on the paucity of motives in the whole
history of tragedy.

[3] Franciscque Sarcey (1828–99), the most influential French critic in the second half of the nineteenth century, championed the 'well-made play'; an important aspect of this, according to him, was
the *scène à faire*—the obligatory scene without which the overall structure of a play would be left
incomplete.

Dumas *fils*[4] which were published against his wishes, if my youthful memories are correct, in the 'Temps' some years ago, and which set forth that double plot of Corneille and Racine, a heroine disputed by two heroes, and a hero disputed by two heroines and lastly, some works here and there by Valin upon composition. And that is all, absolutely all.

Finally, in brief, I rediscovered the thirty-six situations as Gozzi doubtless possessed them and as the reader will find them in the following pages; for there were indeed, as he had indicated, thirty-six categories which I had to formulate in order properly to distribute among them the innumerable dramas awaiting classification. There is, I hasten to say, nothing mystic or cabbalistic about this particular number; it might perhaps be possible to choose one a trifle higher or lower, but this one I consider the most accurate.

Now, to this declared fact that there are no more than thirty-six dramatic situations[5] is attached a singular corollary, the discovery that there are in life but thirty-six emotions. A maximum of thirty-six emotions—and therein we have all the savour of existence; there we have the unceasing ebb and flow which fills human history like tides of the sea; which is indeed the very substance of history since it is the very substance of humanity itself [...]; since it is with these thirty-six emotions—no more—that we colour, nay, we comprehend, the cosmic mechanism, and since it is from them that our theogonies and our metaphysics are and ever will be constructed; all our dear and fanciful 'beyonds';—thirty-six situations, thirty-six emotions, and no more.

It is then comprehensible that in viewing upon the stage the ceaseless mingling of these thirty-six emotions, a race or nation arrives at the beginning of its definite self-consciousness; the Greeks, indeed, began their towns by laying the foundations of a theatre. It is equally natural that only the greatest and most complete civilizations should have evolved their own particular conception of the drama, and that one of these conceptions should be revealed by each new evolution of society, whence arises the dim but faithful expectation of our own age, waiting for the manifestation of its own dramatic ideals [...]

These thirty-six facets, which I have undertaken to recover, should obviously be simple and clean and of no far-fetched character; of this we shall be convinced after seeing them repeated, with unfailing distinctness, in all epochs and in all genres. The reader will find in my brief exposition but twelve hundred examples cited, of which about a thousand are taken from the stage; but in this number I have included the most dissimilar and the most celebrated works, nearly all others being but mosaics of these. [...]

---

[4] Alexandre Dumas *fils* (1814–95) put forward his ideas on drama, which were largely coloured by the notion of social usefulness, in numerous prefaces and articles. See p. 84, n. 3.

[5] I have replaced the word 'tragic,' used in the quotation, with 'dramatic'. Those familiar with Goethe know that for him—one of the 'classic' Germans—the two terms were synonymous in this passage. [Polti's note.]—Actually, it is by no means certain that Goethe intended the word 'tragic' to be interpreted in the wider sense suggested by Polti. See n. 1.

It may here be allowable to ask, with our theory in mind, a number of questions which to us are of primary importance.

Which are the dramatic situations neglected by our own epoch, so faithful in repeating the few most familiar ones? Which, on the other hand, are most in use today? Which are the most neglected, and which the most used, in each epoch, genre, school, author? What are the reasons for these preferences? The same questions may be asked before the classes and sub-classes of the situations.

Such an examination, which requires only patience, will show first the list of combinations (situations and their classes and sub-classes) at present ignored and which remain to be exploited in contemporary art, second, how these may be adapted. On the way it may chance that we shall discern, hidden within this or that of our thirty-six categories, a unique case—one without analogue among the other thirty-five, with no immediate relationship to any other, the product of a vigorous inspiration. But in carefully determining the exact position of this case among the sub-classes of the situation to which it belongs, we shall be able to form, in each of the thirty-five others, a sub-class corresponding to it; thus will be created thirty-five absolutely new plots. These will give, when developed according to the taste of this or that school or period, a series of thirty-five 'original imitations', thirty-five new scenarios, of a more unforeseen character, certainly, than the majority of our dramas, which, whether inspired by books or realities, when viewed in the clear light of the ancient writings revealed to us only their reflections, so long as we had not for our guidance the precious thread which vanished with Gozzi. [...]

## Conclusion

To obtain the nuances of the thirty-six situations I have had recourse almost constantly to the same method of procedure; for example, I would enumerate the ties of friendship or kinship possible between the characters; I would also determine their degree of consciousness, of free-will and knowledge of the real end toward which they were moving. And we have seen that when it is desired to alter the normal degree of discernment in one of the two adversaries, the introduction of a second character is necessary, the first becoming the blind instrument of the second, who is at the same time invested with a Machiavellian subtlety, to such an extent does his part in the action become purely intellectual. Thus, clear perception being in the one case excessively diminished, it is, in the other, proportionately increased. Another element for modifying all the situations is the energy of the acts which must result from them. Murder, for instance, may be reduced to a wound, a blow, an attempt, an outrage, an intimidation, a threat, a too-hasty word, an intention not carried out, a temptation, a thought, a wish, an injustice, a destruction of a cherished object, a refusal, a want of pity, an abandonment, a falsehood. If the author so desires, this blow (murder or its diminutives) may be aimed, not at the object of hatred in person, but at one dear to him. Finally, the murder may be multiple and aggravated by circumstances which the law has foreseen. A third method of varying the situations: for this or that one of the two adversaries whose struggle constitutes our drama, there may be substituted a group of characters animated by a single desire, each member of the group reflecting that desire under a different light. There is, moreover, [...] no situation which may not be combined with any one of its neighbours, nay, with two, three, four, five, six of them and more! Now, these combinations may be of many sorts; in the first case, the situations develop successively and logically one from another; in the second case they form a dilemma, in the midst of which the distracted hero hesitates; in the third case, each one of them will appertain to a particular group or a particular role; in the fourth, fifth, sixth cases, etc., they are represented according to two, or according to all three of the cases already brought together in one situation, and together they escape from it, but the majority of them fall therefrom into a position no less critical, which may even offer but a choice between two equally painful courses; after finding a way between this Scylla and Charybdis, the very leap by which they escape precipitates them into a final situation resulting from the preceding ones, and which sweeps them all away together ... This, be it understood, is but one combination among a thousand, and I cannot here elaborate the system by which this study of the thirty-six situations may be continued, and by means of which they may be endlessly multiplied [...]

Aristotle has taught us to distinguish between 'simple' tragedy (in which superiority remains upon the same side until the end, and in which consequently there is no sudden change of fortune, no surprise) and 'complex' tragedy (the tragedy of surprise, of vicissitude) wherein this superiority passes from one camp to the other.[6] Our dramatists have since refined upon the latter; in those of their pieces which are least complicated, they double the change of fortune, thus leading ingeniously to the return of the opposed powers, at the moment of the spectator's departure, to the exact positions which they occupied when he entered the auditorium; in their plays of complicated plot, they triple, quadruple, quintuple the surprise, so long as their imaginations and the patience of the public permit. We thus see in these vicissitudes of struggle the first means of varying a subject. It will not go very far, however, since we cannot, however great our simplicity, receive from the drama, or from life, more than one thousand three hundred and thirty-two surprises.—One thousand three hundred and thirty-two? Obviously; what is any keen surprise if not the passing from a state of calm into a dramatic situation, and from one situation into another, or again into a state of calm? Perform the multiplication; result, one thousand three hundred and thirty-two.

---

[6] This reading of the *Poetics* is not quite correct. According to Aristotle, there *is* a change of fortune even in a simple plot, without which there would indeed not be any dramatic storyline; but this change of fortune comes about without a reversal or discovery, the latter characterizing a complex plot.

Shall we now enquire whence arise these vicissitudes, these unexpected displacements of equilibrium? Clearly in some influence, proceeding from a material object, a circumstance, a third personage. Upon this third actor—whose introduction into drama was the triumph of Sophocles—must rest what is called the plot. He is the unforeseen element, the ideal striven for by the two parties and the surrounding characters; he is fantastically divided and multiplied, by two, by three, by ten, by even more, to the point of encumbering the scene; but he is always himself, always easily recognizable. Some of his fragments become 'instruments', some, 'disputed objects', some, 'impelling forces'; they range themselves sometimes beside the protagonist, sometimes near the antagonist, or, moving here and there, they provoke that downfall the incessant avoidance of which is called—for events as for mankind—progress. [...]

But it is not possible to detail in these pages, even if I so desired, the second part of the art of combination; that which we in France call by the somewhat feeble term (as Goethe remarked), 'composition'.[7] All that I have here undertaken to show is, first, that a single study must create, at the same time, the episodes or actions of the characters, and the characters themselves: for upon the stage what the latter are may be known only by what they do; next, how invention and composition, those two modes of the art of combination (not imagination, empty word!) will, in our works to come, spring easily and naturally from the theory of the thirty-six situations.

[...] But I hear myself being accused, with much violence, of an intent to 'kill the imagination'. 'Enemy of fancy!'—'Destroyer of wonders!'—'Assassin of prodigy!' ... These and similar titles cause me not a blush.

A singular history, in truth, is that of the 'imagination'.

[...] We are not unaware of the importance, in the perfecting of Greek art, of the fact that it was circumscribed and restricted to a small number of legends (Oedipus, Agamemnon, Phaedra, etc.), which each poet had in his turn to treat, thus being unable to escape comparison, step by step, with each of his predecessors, so that even the least critical of spectators could see what part his personality and taste had in the new work. The worst that may be said of this tradition is that it rendered originality more difficult. By a study of the thirty-six situations and their results, the same advantage may be obtained without its accompanying inconvenience. Thenceforth proportion alone will assume significance.

By proportion I mean, not a collection of measured formulae which evoke familiar memories—but the bringing into battle, under the command of the writer, of an infinite army of possible combinations ranged according to their probabilities. Thus, to make manifest the truth or the impression which until now has been perceptible to him alone, the author will have to give a rapid overview of the field before him and to choose such of the situations and such

---

[7] A more common English term for 'composition' in this sense would be 'construction'.

of the details as are most appropriate to his purpose. This method—or, if you will, this freedom and this power—he will use not only in the choice, the outlining and fleshing out of his subject, but in his observation and meditation. And he will no more run the risk of falsifying, through preconceived ideas, the vision of reality than does the painter, for example, in his application of equally general laws which are likewise controlled by constant experimentation—the divine laws of perspective!

Proportion, finally realizable in the calm bestowed by complete possession of the art of combining, and recovering the supreme power long ago usurped by 'good taste' and by 'imagination', will bring about the recognition of that quality more or less forgotten in modern art—'beauty'. By this I mean, not the skilful selection of material from nature but the skilful and exact representation—with no groping, no uncertainty, no hanging on to what is superfluous—of the particular bit of nature under observation.

[…] In literature, in dramatic literature which is the special subject under consideration, the investigation of proportion of which I have spoken above will show us the various general methods of presenting any situation whatever. Each one of these general methods, containing a sort of canon applicable to all situations, will constitute for us an order analogous to the orders of architecture and which, like them, will take its place with other orders in a dramatic system. But the systems in their turn will come together under certain yet more general rubrics, comparisons of which will furnish us many a subject for reflection. […]

It will be remembered that when we were cataloguing dramatic production in its thirty-six classes, an assiduous effort to establish for every exceptional case found in one of them, symmetrical cases in the other thirty-five caused unforeseen subjects to spring up under our very feet. Likewise, when we shall have analysed these orders, systems and groups of systems, when we shall have measured with precision their resemblances and their differences, and classified them, or, one by one, according to the questions considered, shall have brought them together or separated them,—we shall necessarily observe that numerous combinations have been forgotten. Among these the New Art will choose. […]

# The Law of the Drama
## (1894)

### Ferdinand Brunetière

Ferdinand Brunetière (1849–1906)—an influential literary theorist and critic, not a practising playwright—was a man of deeply conservative and Catholic sympathies. He wrote extensively about French classical and nineteenth-century drama as well as other aspects of French literature and history. He taught French language and literature at the École Normale and at the Sorbonne; he also served on the staff of the prestigious *Revue des deux mondes*, first as contributor, then as secretary and sub-editor and, from 1893 onwards, as editor. In the same year he became a member of the French Academy. The theory quoted below, for which he became famous outside France, especially perhaps in the United States, stresses—more than previous writers had done—volition as the main driving force of dramatic conflict; it was published as the preface to *Les Annales du théâtre et de la musique* for 1894, and it was addressed in the form of a letter to one of the editors, Noël. The insight conveyed in it arose out of a series of lectures Brunetière had delivered in 1891–2 in which he examined and analysed the masterpieces of the French dramatic tradition.

[…] The fifteen lectures which I delivered at the Odéon, nearly three years ago, on the *Époques du Théâtre francais*[1] left me sated, saturated, wearied with the subject,—gorged if I may say so. But they were not without their usefulness for me. […] I had to try to grasp the essence and the connection of the works in the history of our stage, and to deduce from them, if I could, the theory or, to

Translated by Philip M. Hayden (New York: Dramatic Museum of Columbia University, 1914); repr. in Barrett H. Clark, *European Theories of the Drama* (New York: Crown Publishers, 1918), 404–10.

[1] The series of lectures on the evolution of French drama, which Brunetière delivered at the Odéon in 1891–2, was published under this title in 1892.

speak more modestly, *a* theory of dramatic action. [...] The theory, uncertain and still vague in my lectures, had taken definite form. It had become broader, it seems to me, by becoming more simple. A child could understand it. And do not tell me that you are tempted to mistrust it, precisely because of this simplicity! On the contrary, my dear friend, it is not art, science nor life that are complex, it is the ideas about them that we form for ourselves with regard to them. Whoever grasps a principle, grasps all its applications. But the very diversity, multiplicity, perversity and apparent contradiction of these applications prevent one from seeing the principle. Will any argument, however ingenious, alter the fact that all poetry is either lyric, epic or dramatic?[2] Certainly not. And if *Le Cid*,[3] if *Phèdre*,[4] if *Tartuffe*,[5] if *Le Légataire universel*,[6] if *Le Barbier de Séville*,[7] if *La Camaraderie*,[8] if *Le Demi-monde*,[9] if *Célimare le Bien-aimé*[10] are dramatic, does it not follow that all these very different works must nevertheless have not merely a few points of contact or vague resemblance but an essential characteristic in common? What is this characteristic? That is what I shall try to explain.

Observe, if you please, that I ask only one—no more—and that I leave the dramatist complete freedom in development. That is where I depart from the old school of criticism that believed in the mysterious power of the 'Rules' in their inspiring virtues; and consequently we see the critics of the old school struggling and striving, exercising all their ingenuity to invent additional rules [...]. But the truth is that there are no rules in that sense; there never will be. There are only conventions which are necessarily variable, since their only object is to fulfil the essential aim of the dramatic work, and the means of accomplishing this vary with the piece, the time and the man. Must we, like Corneille, regularly subordinate character to situation; invent, construct the situations first and then, if I may so express it, put the characters inside? We may do so certainly since he did it [...] Or shall we, like Racine, subordinate situation to character, find the characters first, study them, master them, and then seek the situations which will best bring out their different aspects? We may do so, and that is what he did [...] Take another rule. Shall we oblige the

---

[2] This classification of the branches of literature goes back of course to Aristotle's *Poetics*.

[3] Pierre Corneille first termed his play *Le Cid* (1637) a tragicomedy, but later reclassified it as a tragedy. It gave rise to a bitter literary controversy about the 'correct' way to write drama.

[4] Jean Racine's version (1677) of the myth of Phaedra which had been dramatized earlier by Euripides and Seneca.

[5] This comedy (1669) by Molière, earlier versions of which (that of 1664 and that of 1667) had been suppressed for offending religious sensibilities, at times comes close to being a tragicomedy.

[6] *The Residuary Legatee* (1708), a comedy by Jean Regnard.

[7] Beaumarchais's comedy, *The Barber of Seville* (1775), better known outside the French-speaking world in Rossini's operatic version.

[8] *La Camaraderie, ou la Courte Echelle* (Favouritism, or the Climb up, 1837), by Eugène Scribe (1791–1861), satirized political fraud.

[9] In the title of this play premiered in 1855, Dumas fils coined an expression which was to gain general currency for 'women of doubtful reputation'.

[10] *Célimare the Beloved* (1863), a comedy by Labiche.

dramatic author to observe the Three Unities? I reply that he will not be hampered by them if he can choose, like Racine, subjects which properly or necessarily adjust themselves of their own accord, so to speak, to the rule [...] But if he chooses, like Shakespeare, subjects which are checked by it in their free development, or diverted merely, we will relieve him of the rule [...] Or again, shall we mingle tragedy and comedy, tears and laughter, terror and joy, the sublime and the grotesque [...]? Shakespeare and Hugo have done it, but Euripides and Sophocles seem to have carefully avoided it; and who will deny that they were both right? [...] Evidently, all these alleged rules effect or express only the most superficial characteristics of the drama. Not only are they not mysterious, they are not in the least profound. Whether we observe them or not, drama is drama with them or without them. They are only devices which may at any time give place to others. It all depends on the subject, the author and the public. This is the point to add that there is something which does *not* depend on them.

To convince ourselves of that fact, let us examine more carefully two or three works whose dramatic value is universally recognized, and let us take them from species as different as *Le Cid*, *L'École des femmes*[11] and *Célimare le Bien-aimé*. Chimène *wants* to avenge her brother; and the question is how she will succeed. Arnolphe *wants* to marry Agnès whose stupidity will guarantee her fidelity; and the question is whether he will succeed. Célimare *wants* to get rid of the widowers of his former mistresses; and the question is what means he will employ. But, Célimare is hampered in the execution of his *will* by the fear of the vengeance of his friends. Arnolphe is disturbed in the execution of his *will* by the young madcap Horace who arouses love, and with love a *will*, in Agnès' heart. Chimène is betrayed in the execution of her *will* by the love she feels for Rodrigue. On the other hand, Chimène's *will* is checked and broken by the insurmountable obstacle which she encounters in a *will* superior to her own. Arnolphe, who is far from being a fool, sees all the plans of his *will* undone by the conspiracy of youth and love. And Célimare, by the power of his *will*, triumphs over the widowers of his mistresses. Nothing would be easier than to multiply examples. [...] Is it not easy now to draw the conclusion? In drama or farce, what we ask of the theatre is the spectacle of a *will* striving towards a goal, and conscious of the means which it employs.

This essential characteristic of dramatic composition distinguishes it, in the first place, from lyric composition [...] and from the composition of the novel with which, especially in our day, it has so often been confused. [...] The drama and the novel are not the same thing; or rather, each is exactly the opposite of the other. Read *Gil Blas* again, or go again to see *Le Mariage de Figaro*.[12]

---

[11] Molière's *The School for Wives*, a comedy considered highly controversial when it was first staged in 1662.

[12] *Gil Blas de Santillane* (1715–35), the picaresque novel by Alain René Lesage which traces its chameleon-like Spanish hero's numerous adventures in society.—Beaumarchais's *The Marriage of Figaro* (1784), better known in its operatic version by Mozart, describes the fight of the servant Figaro

The setting and the character are the same. Beaumarchais made a trip to Spain, but Lesage's novel was none the less his principal model. I have shown elsewhere that we find in the monologue of Figaro whole sentences from *Gil Blas*. Only, whereas nothing happens to Gil Blas that he has actually willed, it is on the contrary Figaro's *will* that conducts the plot of his marriage. Let us pursue this point of comparison.

Gil Blas, like everybody else, wants to live, and if possible to live agreeably. That is not what we call having a will. But Figaro wants a certain definite thing, which is to prevent Count Almaviva from exercising on Susanne the seigneurial privilege. He finally succeeds [...] He had not ceased to devise means of attaining it, and when these means have failed he has not ceased to invent new ones. That is what may be called *will*, to set up a goal and to direct everything toward it, to strive to bring everything into line with it. Gil Blas really has no goal. Highway robber, doctor's assistant, servant to a canon, to an actress or to a nobleman, all the positions which he occupies one after another come to him by fortune or chance. He has no plan because he has no particular or definite aim. He is subject to circumstances; he does not try to dominate them. He does not *act*; he is *acted upon*. Is not the difference obvious? The proper aim of the novel as of the epic—of which it is only a secondary and derived form, what the naturalists call a sub-species or a variety—[...] is to give us a picture of the influence which is exercised upon us by all that is outside of ourselves. The novel is therefore the contrary of the drama; and if I have successfully set forth this opposition, do you not see the consequences which result from it?

It is thus that one can distinguish action from motion or agitation; and that is certainly worth while. Is it action to move about? Certainly not, and there is no true action except that of a will conscious of itself, conscious as I was saying of the means which it employs for its fulfilment, one which adapts them to its goal, and all other forms of action are only imitations, counterfeits or parodies. The material or the subject of a novel or of a play may therefore be the same at bottom; but they become drama or novel only by the manner in which they are treated; and the manner is not merely different, it is opposite. One will never be able therefore to transfer to the stage any novels except those which are already dramatic; and note well that they are dramatic only to the extent to which their heroes are truly the architects of their destiny. [...] The general law of the theatre, thus defined, gives us then in the first place a sure means of perceiving what in any subject there is of the novel or the drama. The fact is that people do not know this well enough; and the Naturalist school in France has committed no worse error than confusing the conditions of the two species.

The same law provides, further, the possibility of defining with precision the dramatic species—roughly as one does the biological species; and for that

to protect his bride-to-be from being sexually harassed by the Count his master. His famous monologue in Act V has always been seen as a powerful challenge to the aristocratic values of the *ancien régime*.

it is only necessary to consider the particular obstacle against which the will struggles. If these obstacles are recognized to be insurmountable or reputed to be so, as were for example in the eyes of the ancient Greeks the decrees of Fate; or in the eyes of the Christians the decrees of Providence; as are for us the laws of nature, or the passions aroused to frenzy and becoming thus the internal fatality of Phaedra or of Roxane,[13] of Hamlet or of Othello—it is tragedy. The incidents are generally terrifying and the conclusion sanguinary, because in the struggle which man undertakes to wage against fate he is vanquished in advance and must perish. Suppose now that he has a chance of victory, just one, that he still has in himself the power to conquer his passion; or suppose that, the obstacles which he is striving to overcome being the work of his fellow men, as prejudice for example or social conventions, a man is for that very reason capable of surmounting them—that is the drama properly speaking, romantic drama or social drama [...] Change once more the nature of the obstacle, equalize at least in appearance the conditions of the struggle, bring together two opposing wills, Arnolphe and Agnès, Figaro and Almaviva, Suzanne d'Ange and Olivier de Jalin,[14]—this is comedy. [...] But instead of locating the obstacle in an opposing will, conscious and master of its acts, in a social convention or in the fatality of destiny, let us locate it in the irony of fortune, or in the ridiculous aspect of prejudice, or again in the disproportion between the means and the end—that is farce, that is *Le Légataire universel* or *Un Chapeau de paille d'Italie*.[15]

I do not say after that that the types are always pure. In the history of literature or of art, as in nature, a type is almost never anything but an ideal and consequently a limit. Where is the man among us, where is the woman who embodies the perfection of the sex and of the species? There is moreover a natural relationship, we might say a consanguinity, between adjoining species. Is a mulatto or a quadroon white or black? They are related to both. Likewise there may be an alliance or mixture of farce and comedy, of drama and tragedy. [...] It is nevertheless useful to have carefully defined the species; and if the law should only teach authors not to treat a subject of comedy by the devices of farce, that would be something. The general law of the theatre is defined by the action of a will conscious of itself; and the dramatic species are distinguised by the nature of the obstacles encountered by this will.

And the quality of will measures and determines, in its turn, the dramatic value of each work in its species. Intelligence rules in the domain of speculation, but the will governs in the field of action, and consequently in history. It is the will which gives power; and power is hardly ever lost except by a failure or

---

[13]  In Racine's tragedy *Bajazet* (1672), the Turkish sultana Roxane's frustrated love for the eponymous hero brings about the play's multiple calamities.

[14]  The antagonists of Molière's *The School for Wives*; of Beaumarchais's *The Marriage of Figaro*; and of Dumas fils's *Le Demi-Monde*, respectively.

[15]  For *Le Légataire universel* see n. 6.—Labiche's *An Italian Straw Hat* (1851), though labelled a comedy, is really a farce.

relaxation of the will. But that is also the reason why men think there is nothing grander than the development of the will, whatever the object, and that is the reason for the superiority of tragedy over the other dramatic forms. One may prefer for one's own taste a farce to a tragedy; one ought even to prefer a good farce to a mediocre tragedy, that goes without saying; and we do it every day. (But) one cannot deny that tragedy is superior to farce […] Another reason sometimes given is that it implies indifference to death, but that is the same reason if the supreme effort of the will is to conquer the horror of death. But shall we say that comedy is superior to farce, and why? We will say that and for the same reason […] And we will say in conclusion that one drama is superior to another drama according as the quantity of will exerted is greater or less, as the share of chance is less and that of necessity greater.

I will not continue. But I cannot refrain from noting the remarkable confirmation that this law finds in the general history of the theatre. As a matter of fact, it is always at the exact moment of its national existence when the will of a great people is exalted, so to speak, within itself, that we see its dramatic art, too, reach the highest point of its development and produce its masterpieces. Greek tragedy is contemporary with the Persian wars. […] Consider the Spanish theatre: Cervantes, Lope de Vega, Calderón belong to the time when Spain was extending the domination of her will all over Europe as well as over the New World, or rather, as great causes do not always produce their literary effects at once, they are of the time immediately following. And what about France in the seventeenth century? The greatest struggle that our fathers made to maintain the unity of the French nation, internally as well as externally, or to bring it to pass was at the end of the sixteenth century, and it took place under Henry IV, under Richelieu, under Mazarin. The development of the theatre followed immediately. I see indeed that great strengthenings of the national will have not always been followed by a dramatic renaissance, in England in the eighteenth century, for example, or in Germany today; but what I do not see is a dramatic renaissance whose dawn has not been announced, as it were, by some progress or some arousing of the will. Think of the theatre of Lessing, of Schiller, of Goethe and remember what Frederick the Great had done a few years before, without knowing it perhaps, to give to the Germany of the eighteenth century a consciousness of herself and of her national genius. The converse is no less striking. If it is extremely rare that a great development of the novel is contemporary even with a great development of the theatre—[…]—it is because in literature as in nature, the competition is always keenest between the neighbouring species; and the soil is rarely rich enough for two rival varieties to prosper, develop and multiply in peace. But it is also because, being as we have seen the contrary each of the other, drama and the novel do not answer to the same conception of life. […] The belief in determinism is more favourable to the progress of the novel, but the belief in free will is more favourable to the progress of dramatic art. Men of action, Richelieu, Condé, Frederick, Napoleon have always been fond of the theatre.

# The Comic in Situations
## (1900)

## Henri Bergson

Comedy down the ages has aroused rather less theoretical interest than has tragedy: partly because of comedy's supposedly inferior literary standing and partly because the very act of analysis is always in danger of killing its subject, that elusive will-o'-the-wisp, stone dead. The study of the comic in life and art constituted only a small part of the work of the French philosopher Henri Bergson (1859–1941); it was nevertheless a matter to which he devoted a good deal of thought. He first broached the subject of what makes us laugh in a series of lectures given at the Lycée of Clermont Ferrand in 1884; in 1899, he published the three articles in the *Revue de Paris* which, in the following year, were then turned into a book—*Laughter*. This analysis attracted very much more general attention than his other, more technical, philosophical writings. Indeed, *Laughter* proved to be one of his most famous books, second only to *Creative Evolution* (1907).

*Laughter*, a broad speculation about the nature of the comic impulse, was not *exclusively* preoccupied with comedy in the theatre. Nevertheless, Bergson quoted a great many examples from (predominantly French) comic drama both classical and modern, notably from Molière, in order to illustrate his thesis that laughter is aroused by our perception of the clash between something living and something mechanical. He claimed that this was the fundamental trigger of laughter, seeing automatism not only as derogatory to human dignity but also as a drawback in evolutionary terms, in that it showed insufficient adaptability to changing circumstances. In other words, he considered laughter—a physiological reaction confined to human beings as a species, specifically to human beings *in a group*—to be a corrective designed to punish social inadequacy and deviancy.

It is not surprising, then, that his analysis of the different types of laughter-provoking attitudes, words, and actions had a melancholy undertone. His speculations

Translated from the French by Cloudesley Brereton and Fred Rothwell, in Henri Bergson, *Laughter: An Essay on the Meaning of the Comic* (London: Macmillan, 1911; first published in French 1900), 68–101.

ended with the observation that laughter was 'a froth with a saline base' and that the philosopher might 'find that the substance is scanty, and the after-taste bitter'.

Bergson was received into the French Academy in 1918 and was awarded the Nobel Prize for Literature in 1928.

Comedy is a game, a game that imitates life. And if in the child's game when he is manipulating dolls and puppets, everything is done by strings, should we not find the same strings, somewhat the worse for wear, in the threads that tie up comedy situations? Let us then start with a child's games. Let us follow the imperceptible process by which he makes his puppets grow, animates them, and at last brings them to that ambiguous state in which, without ceasing to be puppets, they have nevertheless become human beings. So we obtain characters of a comedy type. And upon them we can test the law [...] in accordance with which we will define all broadly comic ('vaudeville') situations in general: *Any arrangement of acts and events is comic which, interlinked, gives us the illusion of life and the distinct impression of a mechanical arrangement.*

1. *The Jack-in-the-box.*—As children we have all played with the little man who springs out of his box. You squeeze him flat, he jumps up again. Push him lower, and he shoots up still higher. Crush him down beneath the lid, and often he will send everything flying. [...] It is a struggle between two stubborn elements, one of which, being purely mechanical, generally ends up by giving in to the other which treats it as a plaything. [...]

Many a comic scene may be referred to this simple type. For instance, in the scene of *Le Mariage forcé* between Sganarelle and Pancrace,[1] all the comedy derives from the conflict between the idea of Sganarelle, who wishes to make the philosopher listen to him, and the obstinacy of the philosopher, a regular talking-machine working automatically. As the scene progresses, the image of the jack-in-the-box becomes more apparent, so that at last the characters themselves adopt its movements,—Sganarelle pushing Pancrace, each time he shows himself, back into the wings, Pancrace returning to the stage after each repulse to continue his patter. And when Sganarelle finally manages to drive Pancrace back and shut him up inside the house—I nearly said inside the box—a window suddenly flies open and the head of the philosopher appears again as though it had burst open the lid of the box.

The same business occurs in *Le Malade imaginaire*. The outraged medical profession, through the mouth of Monsieur Purgon, pours out upon Argan threats of every kind of disease. And every time Argan rises from his seat as

---

[1] Molière wrote *The Forced Marriage* as a one-act comedy-ballet in 1664, the role of Sganarelle being designed to be played by himself (in this as in other plays of his where the same character occurs). The dispute described by Bergson between Sganarelle and Pancrace takes place in Scene iv.

though to silence Purgon, we see the latter disappear for a moment, being as it were thrust into the wings, then, as though impelled by a spring, rebound on to the stage with a fresh curse.[2] The same ceaselessly repeated exclamation, 'Monsieur Purgon!' punctuates this little scene.

Let us scrutinize more closely the image of the spring which is tightened, released and tightened again. Let us disentangle its central element, and we shall hit upon one of the usual processes of classical comedy,—*repetition*.

Why is there something comic in the repetition of a word on the stage? We shall look in vain for any theory of comedy offering a satisfactory answer to this very simple question. Nor can any answer be found so long as we look for the explanation of an amusing trait in the thing itself, isolated from all it suggests to us. [...] It makes us laugh only because it symbolizes a special play of moral elements, itself symbolizing an altogether material play. It is [...] the play of the child again and again pushing back the jack-in-the-box to the bottom of his box,—but refined, distilled and transferred to the realm of feelings and ideas. Let us then state the law which we think defines the main comic effects of word repetition on the stage: *In a comic repetition of words there are generally present two terms: a repressed feeling which goes off like a spring, and an idea that delights in repressing the feeling again.*

When Dorine is telling Orgon of his wife's illness and the latter keeps interrupting her with enquiries about the health of Tartuffe,[3] the recurrent question, 'And Tartuffe?' gives us the distinct feeling of a spring being released. This is the spring Dorine delights in pushing back each time she resumes her account of Elmire's illness. And when Scapin informs old Géronte that his son has been taken prisoner on the famous galley and that a ransom must be paid without delay,[4] he is playing with Géronte's avarice exactly as Dorine does with Orgon's infatuation. His avarice is no sooner repressed than it springs up again automatically, and it is this automatism that Molière tries to indicate by the mechanical repetition of a sentence expressing regret at the money that will have to be paid out: 'What the deuce did he go in that galley for?' [...]

True, this mechanism is at times less easy to detect, and here we encounter a fresh difficulty in the theory of the comic. There are cases where the whole interest of a scene lies in one character playing a double part, the interlocutor acting as a mere prism, so to speak, through which the dual personality is developed. [...] For instance, when Alceste stubbornly repeats the words, 'I don't say that!' on Oronte asking him if he thinks his poetry bad,[5] the

[2] In Molière's last play, *The Imaginary Invalid* (1673), a satire on the medical profession and its victims, Dr Purgon threatens Argan, the eponymous 'hero' of the play, in Act III, Scene v.

[3] The scene between the Parisian bourgeois Orgon and his daughter's maid-servant Dorine takes place in Act I, Scene iv of Molière's *Tartuffe* (third version, 1669).

[4] In Molière's *The Cheats of Scapin* (1672), the wily servant Scapin manipulates the old men Géronte and Argante for the benefit of their lovelorn and penniless sons.

[5] Alceste, the hero of Molière's *Misanthrope* (1666), avoids complimenting Oronte on the mediocre sonnet he has just read him, in Act I, Scene ii.

repetition is laughable though evidently Oronte is not here playing with Alceste the sort of game we have just described. But we must be careful: for in reality we have two men in Alceste—on the one hand, the 'misanthropist' who has vowed henceforth to call a spade a spade, and on the other the gentleman who cannot unlearn in a trice the usual forms of politeness, or perhaps just the honest fellow who, when called upon to put his theory into practice, shrinks from wounding another man's self-esteem or hurting his feelings. So the real scene is not between Alceste and Oronte, it is between Alceste and himself. The one Alceste would like to blurt out the truth, and the other stops his mouth as he is on the point of speaking out. Each ' I don't say that!' represents a growing effort to repress something that strives and struggles to get out. And so the tone in which the phrase is uttered grows more and more violent, Alceste get-ting more and more angry—not with Oronte as he thinks, but with himself. The tension of the spring is continually being renewed, continually being rein-forced until at last it goes off with a bang. Here we still have the same mech-anism of repetition.

For a man to resolve never again to say what he does not mean, even though he 'openly defy the whole human race', is not necessarily laughable; it is only an aspect of life at its best. For another man, through amiability, selfishness or disdain, to prefer to flatter people is only another aspect of life; there is noth-ing in that to make us laugh. Indeed, you may combine these two men into one and make that person waver between hurtful frankness and deceitful polite-ness, even then this duel between opposing feelings will not be comic; it will appear serious if these two feelings through their very opposition complement each other, develop side by side and make up a composite mental condition, adopting in short a *modus vivendi* which merely gives us the complex impres-sion of life. But now imagine a really living man harbouring these two unvary-ing and *inelastic* feelings, make him oscillate from one to the other; above all, ensure that this oscillation becomes entirely mechanical by adopting the form of some habitual, simple, childish contrivance: you will then get [...] *some-thing mechanical in something living*; in fact, something comic.

We have dwelt on this first image, that of the jack-in-the-box, in order to show how the comic imagination gradually converts a material mechanism into a moral one. Now we will consider one or two other games, confining our-selves to their most striking aspects.

2. *The String-puppet.*—There are innumerable comedy scenes in which one of the characters thinks he is speaking and acting freely, and consequently retains all the essentials of life, whereas viewed from a certain standpoint he ap-pears as a mere toy in the hands of another who is playing with him. The tran-sition is easily made from a puppet which a child works with a string to Géronte and Argante manipulated by Scapin. Listen to Scapin himself: 'The *engine* is all there'; and again: 'Providence has brought them into my net,' etc.[6] [...]

---

[6]   This again refers to *The Cheats of Scapin.*

All that is serious in life comes from our freedom. The feelings we have matured, the passions we have brooded over, the actions we have weighed, decided upon and carried out, these are the things that give life its sometimes dramatic and generally serious aspect. What then is needed to turn all this into a comedy? Merely to fancy that our seeming freedom conceals the strings of a puppet. [...] So that there is not any real, serious or even dramatic scene that fancy cannot render comic by simply conjuring up this image. Nor is there any game for which a wider field lies open.

3. *The Snowball.* The further we proceed in this investigation into the methods of comedy, the more clearly we see the part played by childhood memories. [...] Take for instance the rolling snowball, which gets bigger as it rolls along. We might also think of toy soldiers lined up behind one another: push the first and it tumbles down on the second, which knocks down a third, and things go from bad to worse until they all lie on the floor. [...] These instances [...] suggest the same abstract vision, that of an effect which grows by arithmetical progression so that the cause, trifling at the outset, culminates by a necessary evolution in a result as significant as it is unexpected. [...] Let us now turn to comedy. Read the speech of Chicanneau in the *Plaideurs* once again:[7] there are lawsuits within lawsuits, and the mechanism works faster and faster (Racine gives us this feeling of increasing acceleration by crowding his legal terms closer and closer together) until the lawsuit over a truss of hay costs the plaintiff the better part of his fortune. [...] Finally, let us pass to the vaudeville of today.[8] Need we call to mind all the forms in which this same combination appears? There is one that is employed rather frequently: that is making a certain thing, say a letter, to be so vitally important to some persons that it has got to be recovered at all costs. This object, which always vanishes just when you think you have caught it, runs through the entire play picking up more and more serious, more and more unexpected incidents on its way. [...] Once more the effect produced is that of the snowball.

It is the characteristic of a mechanical combination to be generally *reversible.* A child is delighted when he sees the ball in a game of ninepins knocking down everything in its way and spreading havoc in all directions; he laughs even more when the ball, after twists and turns and hesitations of every kind, returns to its starting-point. In other words, the mechanism just described is laughable even when rectilinear; it is more so on becoming circular and when every effort the player makes, by a fatal interaction of cause and effect, merely results in bringing it back to the same spot. Now a considerable number of vaudevilles turn on this idea. An Italian straw hat has been eaten by a horse.[9]

[7] Chicanneau is one of the characters in Jean Racine's only comedy, *The Litigants* (1668). The speech referred to occurs in Act I, Scene vii.

[8] The French vaudeville, a genre of plays of a light or satiric nature interspersed with songs, must not be confused with American vaudeville, a variety show comparable to the English music-hall.

[9] *An Italian Straw Hat* (1851) by Eugène Labiche (1815–88) was one of that prolific comic author's most popular plays.

There is only one other hat like it in the whole of Paris; it *must* be found at any cost. This hat, which always slips away the moment it is about to be got hold of, keeps the principal character on the run, and through him all the others who hang on to his coat tails. [...] And when at last, after all sorts of incidents, the goal seems in sight, it turns out that the ardently desired hat is the very one that has been eaten. [...]

But why do we laugh at this mechanical arrangement? The fact that the story of a person or of a group should sometimes appear like a game worked by gearings, strings or springs is undoubtedly strange; but where does the special character of this strangeness come from? What is it that makes it laughable? To this question [...] our answer must always be the same. The rigid mechanism which we occasionally detect, as a foreign body, in the living continuity of human affairs is of very special interest to us as being a kind of *absentmindedness* on the part of life. Were events unceasingly mindful of their own course, there would be no coincidences, no conjunctures, no circular series; everything would evolve and progress continuously. And were all men always attentive to life, were we constantly to keep in touch with others as well as with ourselves, nothing within us would ever appear as due to the working of strings or springs. The comic is that side of a person which reveals his likeness to a thing, that aspect of human events which through its particular inelasticity conveys the impression of pure mechanism, of automatism, in short of movement without life. It therefore expresses an individual or collective imperfection which calls for an immediate corrective. This very corrective is laughter. Laughter is a kind of social gesture that singles out and represses a special kind of absentmindedness in men and events. [...]

Let us now attempt to frame a full and methodical theory by seeking at the fountain-head the changeless and simple archetypes of the manifold and variable practices of the comic stage. Comedy, we said, combines events so as to introduce a mechanism into the outer forms of life. Let us now ascertain in what essential characteristics life, when viewed from without, seems to contrast with mere mechanism. We shall only have to turn then to the opposite characteristics in order to discover the abstract formula, this time a general and complete one, for every real and possible method of comedy.

Life presents itself to us as a kind of evolution in time and a kind of complexity in space. Considered in time, it is the continuous progression of a being constantly growing older; that means it never goes backwards and never repeats itself. Viewed in space, it exhibits certain coexisting elements so closely interdependent, so exclusively made for one another, that not one of them could at the same time belong to two different organisms: each living being is a closed system of phenomena incapable of interfering with other systems. A continual change of aspect, the irreversibility of phenomena, the perfect individuality of a self-contained series: these are the outward characteristics (whether real or apparent is of little moment) which distinguish the living from the merely mechanical. Let us take their counterpart: we shall obtain three processes which might be called *repetition, inversion* and *interference of series*. It is easy to see that these are also the methods of vaudeville, and that no others are possible. [...]

1. *Repetition*. It is no longer a question as before of a word or a sentence repeated by somebody but rather of a situation, that is to say a combination of circumstances which recurs several times in its original form and thus contrasts with the changing flow of life. Everyday experience supplies us with this type of the comic but only in a rudimentary state. Thus, I meet a friend in the street whom I have not seen for a long time; there is nothing comical in that situation. But if I meet him again the same day, and then a third and a fourth time, we shall end up laughing at the 'coincidence'. Now picture to yourself a series of imaginary events which affords a tolerable illusion of life, and within this ever-moving series imagine one and the same scene reproduced either by the same characters or by different ones: again you will have a coincidence but a more extraordinary one. Such are the repetitions produced on the stage. They are the more laughable in proportion as the scene repeated is more complex and introduced more naturally—two conditions which seem mutually exclusive and which the playwright must manage to reconcile.

Contemporary vaudeville employs this method in every shape and form. One of the best known of these consists in bringing a group of characters, act after act, into the most varied surroundings so as to reproduce under ever fresh circumstances one and the same series of incidents or mishaps which correspond to one another symmetrically.

In several of Molière's plays we find the same arrangement of events repeated right through the comedy from beginning to end. Thus, the *École des femmes*[10] does nothing more than reproduce and repeat a single incident in three beats: first beat, Horace tells Arnolphe of his plan to deceive Agnès's guardian who turns out to be Arnolphe himself; second beat, Arnolphe thinks he has checkmated the move; third beat, Agnès contrives that Horace gets all the benefit of Arnolphe's precautions. There is the same symmetrical repetition in the *L'École des maris*, in *L'Étourdi* and above all in *George Dandin*,[11] where the same three-beat effect is again met with: first beat, George Dandin discovers that his wife is unfaithful; second beat, he summons his father- and mother-in-law to his assistance; third beat, it is George Dandin himself who has to apologize.

At times the scene is reproduced with groups of different characters. As often as not the first group consists of masters and the second of servants. The servants repeat in another key, transposed into a less refined style, a scene already played by the masters. A part of the *Le Dépit amoureux* is constructed on this plan, as is also *Amphitryon*[12] [...]

---

[10]  Molière's *The School for Wives* (1662), regarded as one of the most perfect of French classical comedies, aroused a great deal of hostility when it was first staged.

[11]  *The School for Husbands* (1661), *The Blunderer* (1655), and *George Dandin* (1668).

[12]  *The Amorous Quarrel* (1656) and *Amphitryon* (1668)—likewise comedies by Molière.

But irrespective of the characters who serve as pegs for the arrangement of symmetrical situations, there seems to be a wide gulf between classical comedy and the theatre of today. Both aim at introducing a certain mathematical order into events while none the less maintaining their appearance of verisimilitude, that is to say of life. But the means they employ are different. The majority of vaudevilles of our day seek to work on the mind of the spectator directly. However extraordinary the coincidence, it becomes acceptable from the very fact of its being accepted; and we do accept it if we have been gradually prepared for its reception. That is how contemporary authors tend to proceed. In Molière's plays, on the contrary, it is the disposition of the persons on the stage rather than that of the audience that makes repetition seem natural. Each of the characters represents a given force applied in a given direction, and it is because these forces, constant in direction, necessarily combine together in the same way, that the same situation is reproduced. Thus interpreted, the comedy of situation is akin to the comedy of character. It deserves to be called classical if classical art is indeed that which does not claim to derive from the effect more than it has put into the cause.

2. *Inversion.*—This second method has so much analogy with the first that we will merely define it without insisting on illustrations. Picture to yourself certain characters in a certain situation: you obtain a comic scene by reversing the situation and inverting the roles. The double rescue scene in *Le Voyage de M. Perrichon* belongs to this class.[13] But there is not even any need for both the symmetrical scenes to be acted out before us. We may be shown only one provided the other one is really in our minds. [...]

Comedy often places before us a character who sets the snare in which he will be caught himself. The plot of the villain who is the victim of his own villainy, of the cheat cheated, forms the stock-in-trade of a good many plays. We find this even in old farces. The lawyer Pathelin suggests to his client a trick to outwit the magistrate; the client employs the same trick to avoid paying the lawyer.[14] A termagant of a wife insists upon her husband doing all the housework; she has put down each item on a rota.[15] But when she falls into a washtub, her husband refuses to pull her out, for 'that is not down on his rota.' In modern literature we meet with a good many variations on the theme of the robber robbed. The root idea is always an inversion of roles, and a situation which recoils on the head of its author. [...]

---

[13] *Monsieur Perrichon's Journey* (1860), a comedy (not a vaudeville) by Labiche. One of the suitors for the hand of M. Perrichon's daughter rescues him on an Alpine glacier, the other—more calculating—suitor allows himself to be rescued by his intended father-in-law so as to appeal to the latter's vanity.

[14] The medieval farce, *Master Pierre Pathelin* (written around 1464, published in 1490), has retained its popularity to this day.

[15] This is the plot of the medieval French farce, *Le Cuvier* (The Washtub), first published around 1545 but probably a good deal older.

3. [...] We come now to the *interference of series*.[16] This is a comic effect, the formula of which is difficult to disentangle by reason of the extraordinary variety of forms in which it appears on the stage. Perhaps it might be defined as follows: *A situation is always comical when it belongs simultaneously to two altogether independent series of events and is capable of being interpreted in two entirely different meanings at the same time.*

You will at once think of an *equivocal situation*. And the equivocal situation is indeed one which permits of two different meanings at the same time, the one merely plausible which is put forward by the actors, the other the real one which is given by the audience. [...] It is natural that certain philosophers should have been specially struck by this mental seesaw, and that some of them should regard the very essence of the comic as consisting in the collision or coincidence of two judgements that contradict each other. But their definition is far from meeting every case; and even when it does, it defines not the principle of the comic but only one of its more or less distant consequences. Indeed it is easy to see that the dramatic misunderstanding is only the particular instance of a more general phenomenon, the interference of independent series, and that moreover it is not laughable in itself but only as a *sign* of such an interference of series.

[...] The proof of this lies in the fact that the author must be constantly taxing his ingenuity to recall our attention to the double fact of independence and coincidence. This he generally manages to do by ceaselessly renewing the false threat of the two coinciding series coming unstuck. At every moment the whole thing is about to break down but it gets patched up again: this is the business that makes us laugh, far more than the oscillation in our minds between two contradictory statements. And it makes us laugh because it reveals to us the interference of two independent series, the real source of the comic effect. [...]

Labiche has made use of this method in every shape or form. Sometimes he begins by building up the independent series and then delights in making them interfere with one another: he will take a closed group—a wedding party for instance—[17] and will throw them into altogether unconnected surroundings where certain coincidences will give him a chance for a temporary overlap. Sometimes he will keep one and the same set of characters throughout the play but will contrive that some of these characters have something to conceal, have a secret understanding among themselves, in short play a lesser comedy in the midst of the principal one: at any moment one of the two comedies is on the point of upsetting the other; then everything comes right and the coincidence between the two series is restored. Sometimes he introduces into the

---

[16] The word 'interference' has here the meaning given to it in optics, where it indicates the partial superposition and neutralization, by each other, of two series of light waves. [Bergson's note.]

[17] The irruption of a wedding party into different scenes is indeed one of the comic devices used in *An Italian Straw Hat*.

actual series a purely notional series of events, for example a past one would rather hide which keeps cropping up in the present but which is every time brought into line with situations which it seemed bound to upset. But in every case we find the two independent series and in every case their partial co-incidence.

[...] Whether we find reciprocal interference of series, inversion or repetition, we see that the objective is always the same—to obtain what we have called a *mechanization* of life. You take a set of actions and relations and you repeat it as it is, or you turn it upside down, or you transfer it bodily to another set with which it partially coincides: all processes that consist in looking upon life as a repeating mechanism, with reversible action and interchangeable parts.

# Melodrama (1966)

## Eric Bentley

Eric Bentley (born in England in 1916) has been a seminal influence in the academic study and indeed in the general understanding of drama not only in the United States, where he has spent the greater part of his life, but also in other English-speaking countries. He has taught at Columbia University, at Harvard, Buffalo, Maryland, and elsewhere. He has written extensively on theatre as a theorist, a critic, and a reviewer; he has made a wide range of world drama available in English as a translator and an anthologist: a full bibliography of his works would number over 400 items. In the English-speaking world he pioneered the knowledge of, and the vogue for, Bertolt Brecht, with whom he had been personally acquainted during the latter's stay in America; he is also well known as an expert on Shaw and Pirandello. He is himself a playwright and he has directed for the stage: hence his approach to drama has been informed by first-hand knowledge of the practicalities of theatre.

The following essay, which takes a fresh look at the frequently derided genre of melodrama, is a good example of Professor Bentley's thoughtful but accessible style.

## In Praise of Self-Pity

What does it mean: to weep? Laughter has engaged the attention of many brains, among them some of the best. A brief search in book indexes and library catalogues calls attention to an extensive literature. Tears are a relatively unexplored ocean.

One reason why laughter has had a better press must be the obvious one: that laughter is (or is held to be) pleasant, whereas weeping is (or is held to be) unpleasant. Laughter is also something one gets a good mark for. What tired

From Eric Bentley, *The Life of the Drama* (London: Methuen, 1966), 195–218 orator does not expatiate on the benefits of a sense of humour? To weep, on the other hand, is something that little boys are assiduously taught not to do. Women are greater realists: they will speak of having a good cry. The phrase points to perhaps the commonest function of tears: they are a mechanism for working off emotion—commonly, quite superficial emotion. But there are tears and tears. Crying your heart out is a matter of deep emotion. Then there are tears of joy. 'Excess of sorrow laughs,' says Blake, 'excess of joy weeps.' Shaw put it this way:

Tears in adult life are the natural expression of happiness as laughter is at all ages the natural recognition of destruction, confusion, and ruin.

The tears shed by the audience at a Victorian melodrama come under the heading of a good cry. They might be called the poor man's catharsis, and as such have a better claim to be the main objective of popular melodrama than its notorious moral pretensions. Besides referring to superficial emotion, the phrase 'having a good cry' implies feeling sorry for oneself. The pity is self-pity. But, for all its notorious demerits, self-pity has its uses. E. M. Forster even says it is the only thing that makes bearable the feeling of growing old—in other words, that it is a weapon in the struggle for existence. Self-pity is a very present help in time of trouble, and all times are times of trouble.

Once we have seen that our modern antagonism to self-pity and sentiment goes far beyond the rational objections that may be found to them, we realize that even the rational objections are in some measure mere rationalization. Attacks on false emotion often mask a fear of emotion as such. Ours is, after all, a thin-lipped, thin-blooded culture. Consider how, in the past half-century, the prestige of dry irony has risen, while that of surging emotion has fallen. This is a cultural climate in which a minor writer like Jules Laforgue can rate higher than a major one like Victor Hugo. Or think of our changed attitude to death. [...] Is lamenting something we can imagine ourselves doing? On the contrary we modernize the Greek tragedies by deleting all variants of 'woe is me.' If Christ and Alexander the Great came back to life, we would teach them to restrain their tears. [...]

## Pity and Fear

I have been defending melodrama in its weakest link, for certainly self-pity is only valuable up to a point in life and only tolerable up to a point on the stage. Pity for the 'hero' is the less impressive half of melodrama; the other and more impressive half is fear of the villain. Pity and fear: it was Aristotle in his *Poetics* who coupled them and tried to give an account of the total effect of tragedy in these terms. It seems an oversimplification. In tragedy, most of us now feel, more is involved. Is more involved in melodrama? Is not working on the audience's capacity for pity and fear the alpha and omega of the melodramatist's job? In his *Rhetoric*, Aristotle explains that pity and fear have an organic relation to each other. An enemy or object of terror is presupposed in both cases. If it is we who are threatened, we feel fear for ourselves; if it is others who are threatened, we feel pity for them. One might wish to carry this analysis a little further in the light of the fact that most pity is self-pity. We are identified with those others who are threatened; the pity we feel for them is pity for ourselves; and by the same token we share their fears. We pity the hero of a melodrama because he is in a fearsome situation; we share his fears; and, pitying ourselves, we pretend that we pity him. To rehearse these facts is to put together the dramatic situation of the characteristic popular melodrama: goodness beset by badness, a hero beset by a villain, heroes and heroines beset by a wicked world.

Pity represents the weaker side of melodrama, fear the stronger. Perhaps the success of a melodramatist will always depend primarily upon his power to feel and project fear. Feeling it should be easy, for fear is the element we live in. 'We have nothing to fear but fear itself'[1] is not a cheering slogan because fear itself is the most indestructible of obstacles. Therein lies the potential universality of melodrama.

Human fears are of two kinds. One belongs to the common-sense world: it is reasonable in the everyday sense to fear that one might slip on ice or that an airplane might crash. The other kind of fear—perhaps none too rationally— is called irrational. Savage superstitions, neurotic fantasies and childhood imaginings spring to mind, and equally outside the bounds of common sense is the fear of God. Superstition and religion, neurosis and infantility are in the same boat.

Melodrama sometimes uses the 'irrational' type of fear in such a direct form as that of Frankenstein's monster or Dracula. More often it lets irrational fear masquerade as the rational: we are given reasons to fear the villain, but the fear actually aroused goes beyond the reasons given. Talent in melodramatic writing is most readily seen in the writer's power to make his human villain seem superhuman, diabolical. Historically the villains in our tradition stem from the archvillain Lucifer, and a good deal of recent Shakespeare scholarship has been illustrating in detail the possible derivation of *Richard III* from the medieval Vice. The illustrations are nice to have; the principle was clear in advance. But where the villains stem from is relatively unimportant. What matters is whether a given writer can actually endow his villain with some of the original energy. We must catch a glimpse of hell flame, a whiff of the sulphur. [ … ]

It is amazing what the nineteenth-century stage could do in the presentation of raging seas, mountains, glaciers, frozen lakes, and the like, yet there were always much narrower limits than in a novel, and the playwright had to reinforce the hostility of landscape with other hostilities. 'Melodramatic'

---

[1] This slogan was coined by President Franklin Delano Roosevelt.

artifices of plot come under this head, and particularly that notorious device: outrageous coincidence. It is often by virtue of this feature that melodrama is differentiated from tragedy, the argument being that the melodramatic procedure is too frivolous. Yet there are some particularly gross examples in the supreme tragedies, and, in general, outrageous coincidence, when not frivolously used, has no frivolous effect. It intensifies the effect of paranoia. It enlists circumstances in the enemy's ranks—as Strindberg did in real life when several little incidents conspired to deprive him of his absinthe on several occasions. It represents a projection of 'irrational' fear.

## Exaggeration

The long arm of coincidence is a freakish thing. Mention it and within a minute someone will use the word exaggeration. This brings us back both to the prejudice against melodrama and to the essence of melodrama itself. Like farce, this genre may be said, not to tumble into absurdity by accident but to revel in it on purpose. To question the absurd in it is to challenge, not the conclusion but the premise. In both genres, the writer enjoys a kind of *Narrenfreiheit*—the fool's exemption from common sense—and what he writes must be approached and judged accordingly.

We are accustomed to acknowledge only a slight degree of exaggeration in the artistic reproduction of life—just enough, we tell ourselves, to sharpen an outline. The image in our minds is of portraits in which the painter renders the appearances much as we think we have seen them ourselves, though we permit him a ten per cent deviation because he's an artist. But suppose the deviation from common sense grows much greater? Is the picture necessarily getting worse all the time? No, but for exaggerations which are no longer slight but gross, we require another criterion. A difference of degree turns into a difference of kind. Of a melodramatist whom we disapprove, we must not say: 'You have exaggerated too much,' but: 'You have exaggerated awkwardly, mechanically.' We might even have to say: 'You have exaggerated too little,' for in an age of Naturalism a writer's courage sometimes fails him and he tries to pass off a tame duck as a beast of the jungle.

The exaggerations will be foolish only if they are empty of feeling. Intensity of feeling justifies formal exaggeration in art, just as intensity of feeling creates the 'exaggerated' forms of childhood fantasies and adult dreams. It is as children and dreamers—one might melodramatically add: as neurotics and savages too—that we enjoy melodrama. Exaggeration of what? Of the facts as seen by the sophisticated, scientific, adult mind. The primitive, neurotic, childish mind does not exaggerate its own impressions.

What is a giant? A man, eighteen feet high. An exaggeration surely? Someone has multiplied by three. What is a giant? A grownup as seen by a baby. The baby is two feet high, the grownup, six. The ratio *is* one to three. There is no exaggeration. [...]

# Zola and after

[…] The most pointed and prolonged polemic ever conducted against melodrama is to be found in the works of Bernard Shaw, prefaces and plays alike. *The Devil's Disciple* is the obvious, crude example, but in the preface to *Saint Joan,* nearly thirty years later,[2] Shaw is still hammering away at the same point and arguing that the merit of his new play lies in its avoidance of melodrama. Notably, he has changed the character of the historical Bishop Cauchon so that the latter will no longer remind anyone of a stage villain.

Now Shaw's Cauchon is certainly at some distance from the snarling, gloating, swaggering villain of vulgar melodrama, but, for all Shaw's propaganda against the idea of villains, is he not still a villain, and even a traditional one? It was scarcely a new idea to make the devil witty, genial and sophisticated. Actors take to the role of Cauchon, just because, if they are experienced, they have played it many times before. One *may* smile and smile and be a villain: one often does.

If Shaw hated the morals of melodrama—the projection upon the world of our irresponsible narcissistic fantasies—he loved its manners. Maybe any man only parodies what he is secretly fond of; maybe he is envious of the parodied author's prowess; or maybe he thinks he could outdo him. In any case, Shaw did not rest content with parody. After firing salvos at melodrama, he went on to steal its ammunition. As well as illustrating the limitations of melodrama, *The Devil's Disciple* exemplifies its merits, and, in the critical writings of Shaw, though we do not find the *name* of melodrama held in honour, we find the melodramatic element honoured under other names: such as opera. […]

Since *Man and Superman* (1903) we have had various modernist schools of drama and various individual departures or one-man schools. The result of action and reaction, they represent themselves as battling factions of contrasting conviction, yet it is impossible to mention one innovator of the period who was not trying to reintroduce the melodramatic. German Expressionism can be interpreted as the search for a modern dress for melodrama, Brecht's Epic Theatre as an attempt to use melodrama as a vehicle for Marxist thought. Cocteau, Anouilh and Giraudoux have put the Greek myths to melodramatic use. Of the three, the most concentratedly melodramatic is Cocteau, perhaps because fear of persecution is his strongest emotion; in his *Orpheus*, the maenads are the hostile world of all melodrama.

What of Eugene O'Neill? Some think he revived tragedy. Those who disagree have usually spoken only of a failure. But if he often failed to achieve tragedy, O'Neill succeeded as often in achieving melodrama. […]

It was the melodramatic touch that O'Neill brought to the American theatre already in the twenties, that Lillian Hellman and Clifford Odets brought to it in the thirties, and that Tennessee Williams and Arthur Miller brought in the

---

[2] The first production dates of *The Devil's Disciple* and *Saint Joan* were 1897 and 1923 respectively.

late forties. In the nineteen fifties, one of the most striking new presences in world theatre was Eugene Ionesco.[3] His play *The Lesson* is about a mild-seeming teacher who murders forty pupils a day. Ionesco uses Grand Guignol as a vehicle for a vision of modern life. [...]

## The Quintessence of Drama

As modern persons we are willy-nilly under the spell of Naturalism. However often we tell ourselves the contrary, we relapse into assuming the normal and right thing to be a subdued tone, small human beings, a milieu minutely reproduced. Indeed a tremendous amount of energy goes into keeping up this illusion of the monotonous mediocrity of everyday life: otherwise how could the genteel tradition have survived the discoveries of modern physics and the atrocities of modern behaviour? I am arguing, then, up to a point, that melodrama is actually more natural than Naturalism, corresponds to reality, not least to modern reality, more closely than Naturalism. Something has been gained when a person who has seen the world in monochrome and in miniature suddenly glimpses the lurid and the gigantic. His imagination has been reawakened.

The melodramatic vision is in one sense simply normal. It corresponds to an important aspect of reality. It is the spontaneous, uninhibited way of seeing things. Naturalism is more sophisticated but Naturalism is not more natural. The dramatic sense is the melodramatic sense, as one can see from the play-acting of any child. Melodrama is not a special and marginal kind of drama, let alone an eccentric or decadent one; it is drama in its elemental form; it is the quintessence of drama. The impulse to write drama is, in the first instance, the impulse to write melodrama, and conversely, the young person who does not wish to write melodrama, does not write drama at all but attempts a non-dramatic genre, lyric, epic, or what not. [...]

Though melodramatic vision is not the worst, it is also not the best. It is 'good up to a point,' and the point is childhood, neuroticism, primitivity. Melodrama is human but it is not mature. It is imaginative but it is not intelligent. If again, for the sake of clarity, we take the most rudimentary form of melodrama, the popular Victorian variety, what do we find but the most crass of immature fantasies? The reality principle is flouted right and left, one is oneself the supreme reality, one's innocence is axiomatic, any interloper is a threat and a monster, the ending will be happy because one feels it has to be. [...]

Am I speaking now of all melodrama or just the vulgar melodrama of Victorian popular theatres? It is hard to draw such a line, as it is hard to draw a line between melodrama and tragedy. Rather than separate blocks, the reality

---

[3] For Ionesco's view of drama, see pp. 210–12.

seems to be a continuous scale with the crudest melodrama at one end and the highest tragedy at the other. In tragedy the reality principle is not flouted, one is not oneself the sole reality to be respected, one's guilt is axiomatic, other people may or may not be the threats or monsters, the ending is usually unhappy.

Yet the idea of such a scale is misleading if it suggests that tragedy is utterly distinct from melodrama. There is a melodrama in every tragedy, just as there is a child in every adult. It is not tragedy but Naturalism that tries to exclude childish and melodramatic elements. William Archer, a Naturalist, defined melodrama as 'illogical and sometimes irrational tragedy.' The premise is clear: tragedy is logical and rational. Looking for everyday logic and reasonableness in tragedy, Archer remorselessly drew the conclusion that most of the tragedy of the past was inferior to the middle-class drawing-room drama of London around 1910. Had he been consistent he would even have included Shakespeare in the indictment. [ ... ]

# For a Theatre of Situations
## (1947)

### Jean-Paul Sartre

The question of freedom, in the philosophical as well as the political sense, was a lifelong preoccupation of Jean-Paul Sartre (1905–80). A philosopher, essayist, novelist, and political activist of the left as well as playwright, he formulated a brand of existentialism which stressed the possibility of choice, however stark, for the individual, in spite of the Bad Faith concealing this possibility from his or her own consciousness. In other words, what Sartre endeavoured to show was man inventing himself through his actions. In the article quoted below in full, which first appeared in *La Rue* (November 1947), he rejected psychology, i.e. the dramatic element carrying the weight of the past with its constraints on freedom of action, in favour of the borderline situation in which the hero is able to define himself by an existential choice. Not surprisingly, this aligns Sartre's thinking with (some) traditional notions of (certain kinds of) classical tragedy. In fact, there was a gap between the theory he propounded here and his actual plays. It is worth pointing out that, challenging as Sartre's plays often were in terms of ideas, they were structurally conventional.

The chief source of great tragedy—the tragedy of Aeschylus and Sophocles, of Corneille—is human freedom. Oedipus is free; Antigone and Prometheus are free. The fate we think we find in ancient drama is only the other side of freedom. Passions themselves are freedoms caught in their own trap.

Translated from the French by Richard McLeary, in *The Writings of Jean-Paul Sartre*, vol. 2, ed. Michel Contat and Michel Rybalka (Evanston, Ill.: Northwestern University Press, 1972), 185–6.

Psychological theatre—the theatre of Euripides, Voltaire and Crébillon *fils*[1] announces the decline of tragic forms. A conflict of characters, whatever turns you may give it, is never anything but a composition of forces whose results are predictable. Everything is settled in advance. The man who is led inevitably to his downfall by a combination of circumstances is not likely to move us. There is greatness in his fall only if he falls through his own fault. The reason why we are embarrassed by psychology in the theatre is not by any means that there is too much greatness in it but too little, and it's too bad that modern authors have discovered this bastard form of knowledge and extended it beyond its proper range. They have missed the will, the oath, and the folly of pride which constitute the virtues and vices of tragedy.

But if we focus on these latter, our plays will no longer be sustained primarily by character—depicted by calculated 'theatrical expressions' and consisting in nothing other than the total structure of our oaths (the oath we take to show ourselves irritable, intransigent, faithful, and so on)—but by situation. Not that superficial imbroglio that Scribe and Sardou[2] were so good at staging and that had no human value. But if it's true that man is free in a given situation and that in and through that situation he chooses what he will be, then what we have to show in the theatre are simple and human situations and free individuals in these situations choosing what they will be. The character comes later, after the curtain has fallen. It is only the hardening of choice, its arteriosclerosis; it is what Kierkegaard called *repetition*. The most moving thing the theatre can show is a character creating himself, the moment of choice, of the free decision which commits him to a moral code and a whole way of life. The situation is an appeal: it surrounds us, offering us solutions which it's up to us to choose. And in order for the decision to be deeply human, in order for it to bring the whole man into play, we have to stage limit situations, that is, situations which present alternatives one of which leads to death. Thus freedom is revealed in its highest degree, since it agrees to lose itself in order to be able to affirm itself. And since there is theatre only if all the spectators are united, situations must be found which are so general that they are common to all. Immerse men in these universal and extreme situations which leave them only a couple of ways out, arrange things so that in choosing the way out they choose themselves, and you've won—the play is good. It is through particular situations that each age grasps the human situation and the enigmas human freedom must confront. Antigone, in Sophocles' tragedy, has to choose between civic morality and family morality. This dilemma scarcely makes sense today. But we have our own problems: the problem of means and

---

[1]  Sartre seems to have confused the novelist Claude-Prosper Jolyot de Crébillon (1707–77) with his father, Prosper Jolyot de Crébillon (1674–1762), the author of nine plays which combined pathos with horror.

[2]  The French playwrights Eugène Scribe (1791–1861) and Victorien Sardou (1831–1908), both of them immensely prolific and popular in their day, have since come to be regarded as exponents of highly ingenious but mechanical playmaking. See p. 102, n. 9 and p. 104, n. 10.

ends, of the legitimacy of violence, the problem of the consequences of action, the problem of the relationships between the person and the collectivity, between the individual undertaking and historical constants, and a hundred more. It seems to me that the dramatist's task is to choose from among these limit situations the one that best expresses his concerns, and to present it to the public as the question certain free individuals are confronted with. It is only in this way that the theatre will recover its lost resonance, only in this way that it will succeed in *unifying* the diversified audiences who are going to it in our time.

# Theatre Problems (1954–5)

## Friedrich Dürrenmatt

The essay, substantial excerpts from which are quoted below, was only one, albeit the longest and most important, of the numerous theoretical and critical writings that constituted one aspect of the work of the versatile Swiss playwright Friedrich Dürrenmatt (1921–90). Painter and illustrator, journalist as well as television director (among many other activities), Dürrenmatt in his literary capacity wrote in a wide variety of forms: fiction (much of it in the form of thrillers), stage, radio and television plays as well as film scripts. His essays dealing with literary and theatrical matters were given added authority by his other creative output, notably his more than twenty stage plays, among which *The Visit* (1956) and *The Physicists* (1962) in particular had worldwide success. Dürrenmatt has frequently been compared and contrasted with his older contemporary, fellow playwright-cum-theoretician Brecht. Like Brecht's, much of his drama is in parable form and shows critical concern with the state of the world; it is highly theatrical and non-naturalistic in form; but unlike Brecht, Dürrenmatt, no Marxist, had no ideological solution to offer to the problems he depicted in his plays. By its occasionally bantering tone of voice, *Theatre Problems* reveals its origin of being based on a lecture which the author had given in various Swiss and West German cities in the autumn of 1954 and the spring of 1955. Notable among the many points he makes in it is the justification of a comic, or rather a tragicomic, stance as the only appropriate one for the latter part of the twentieth century.

[…] The stage represents for me not a field for theories, ideologies and messages but an instrument whose potentialities I try to get to know by playing with it. Of course, characters do appear in my plays who have a faith or a

Translated from the German by H. M. Waidson, in Friedrich Dürrenmatt, *Writings on Theatre and Drama* (London: Jonathan Cape, 1976), 59–91.

philosophy of life [...]. But the problems I confront as a playwright are practical working problems which present themselves to me not before but while I am working, in fact to be precise, mostly after the work is finished, out of a kind of curiosity as to how I've actually done it. I should like to say something about these problems, even at the risk of not paying sufficient heed to the general yearning for profundity and the impression being created that it's a tailor who is speaking. Actually, I have no idea how I could do it differently, how one goes about talking about art in an un-tailorlike manner, and so I can only speak to those who fall asleep over Heidegger.

It is all about the empirical rules, about the potentialities of theatre; but since we live in an age in which literary studies and literary criticism are flourishing, I cannot altogether resist the temptation of casting a few side glances at dramatic theory. It's true the artist doesn't need any scholarship. Scholarship deduces its laws from something that exists, otherwise it wouldn't be scholarship, but the laws discovered in this way are useless for the artist even when they are correct. He cannot take over any law he hasn't found for himself; if he doesn't find one, not even scholarship can help him if it has found such a law; and if he has found one, he doesn't care whether or not it's been discovered by scholarship too. Nevertheless scholarship if denied stands like a threatening ghost behind him, always ready to appear whenever he wants to talk about art. So it is here. Talking about questions of drama is just an attempt to stand up to literary scholarship. But I begin my undertaking with misgivings. For academic literary studies, drama is an object; for the playwright it is never a purely objective thing separated from himself. He is involved. It is true that his activity makes drama into something objective (represented in fact by his work), but he destroys this created object again for himself, he forgets, denies, despises, overestimates it in order to make room for something new. Scholarship only sees the result: the dramatist cannot forget the process which has led to this result. [...] Literary scholarship without an inkling of the difficulties of writing and the hidden sandbanks (which direct the current of art into often unsuspected directions) runs the risk of becoming mere assertion, an obstinate proclamation of laws which are no laws.

Thus there is no doubt that the unities of place, time and action which Aristotle, as has long been thought, deduced from classical tragedy, have been postulated as an ideal of stage action. This statement is unchallengeable from the logical, and hence the aesthetic, point of view, so unchallengeable that the question arises whether the system of co-ordinates by which all playwrights must be guided has not been laid down once and for all. The Aristotelian unities call for the greatest precision, the greatest density and the greatest simplicity of dramatic means. The unities of place, time and action would basically be an imperative which literary theory ought to put to the playwright and which it does not put only because nobody has followed the law of Aristotle for ages; out of a necessity which best illustrates the relationship between the art of playwriting and the theories about it.

The fact is that the unities of place, time and action assume Greek tragedy as a precondition. It is not the Aristotelian unities that make Greek tragedy possible but Greek tragedy that makes the Aristotelian unities possible. However abstract an aesthetic rule may seem to be, the work of art from which it was inferred is actually contained in it. If I set about writing a plot which, let us say, is meant to develop and unfold within two hours in the same place, then this plot must have some antecedents, and these antecedents will have to be all the greater the fewer characters there are at my disposal. This is an experience of practical playwriting, an empirical rule. By antecedents I mean the story preceding the action on the stage, a story which makes the stage action possible in the first place. [...] Furthermore, the stage action is usually shorter than the event it portrays, it often begins in the middle of the event, often not until towards the ending. [...] The stage action concentrates an event the more it corresponds to the Aristotelian unities: the antecedents therefore become all the more important if one retains the Aristotelian unities.

Now antecedents can of course be invented and with them a plot which seems particularly well suited to the Aristotelian unities, but here the rule applies that the more fictitious or the more unknown to the audience a subject is, the more careful its exposition, the development of its antecedents, has to be. Now Greek tragedy lives off the opportunity of not having to invent its antecedents: the spectators knew the myths the theatre dealt in, and since the myths were familiar, something existent, something religious, the never-again-achieved audacities of the Greek tragic poets became possible, their abbreviations, their linearity, their stychomythias and their choruses and with them the Aristotelian unities. The audience knowing what it was all about was curious not so much about the subject as about the treatment of the subject. As the unities presuppose the universal character of the subject [...] and hence a religious, mythical theatre, the Aristotelian unities just had to be reinterpreted or dropped as soon as the theatre lost its religious, mythical significance. An audience confronted with unfamiliar subject matter pays more attention to the subject than the treatment of the subject, and hence such a play must of necessity be richer, more detailed than one with a familiar action. The audacities of the one are not the audacities of the other. [...] But the Aristotelian unities have not thereby been rendered obsolete: what once was the rule now becomes an exception, something that can occur time and again. The one-act play, too, obeys them, even though in a different context. Instead of the antecedents the situation dominates, and as a result the unities become possible again.

But what holds good for the dramatic theory of Aristotle, its being linked to a particular world and its merely relative validity, also holds good for any other dramatic theory. Brecht is only being consistent when he builds into his dramatic theory the ideology to which he thinks he belongs, Communism, though this writer is actually cutting off his nose to spite his face. Thus his plays often appear to signify the opposite of what they claim to be signifying, but this misreading cannot always be ascribed to the capitalist audience, it is often simply that the poet Brecht runs away with the dramatic theorist Brecht, a wholly legitimate case which only becomes dangerous when it stops happening.[1] [...]

The immediate impact every stage play aims at, the visibility into which it seeks to transform itself, takes for granted audience, theatre and stage. So it is as well for us to take a look at the theatre, too, for which plays have to be written. We know all about these deficit-burdened institutions. They are, like many of today's organizations, only still justifiable on an ideal basis: meaning, not at all any longer. Their architecture, their auditorium and their stage have developed out of the court theatre, or to put it more accurately have remained stuck in it.[2] The theatre of today is, if only for that reason, not a theatre of today. Thus, in contrast to the primitive platform stage of the age of Shakespeare, in contrast to this 'scaffolding', to use Goethe's words, 'where there was little to be seen, where everything merely stood for something', the court theatre set out to yield to the demand for naturalness, although this brought about a much greater unnaturalness. Instead of being prepared to suggest that the king's room was behind a 'green baize curtain', one now went about actually showing the room. The characteristic of this theatre is the tendency to separate audience and stage by means of the curtain and by the fact that the spectators are sitting in the dark facing an illuminated stage, probably the most disastrous innovation since only in this way has the reverential mood become possible in which our theatres are being stifled. The stage became a peep-show. Better and better lighting and the revolving stage were invented, as allegedly has a revolving auditorium. The courts have gone but the court theatre has remained. It is true that the present age has also found its own form of theatre, the cinema. However much the differences are emphasized and however important it is to emphasize them, we must none the less point out that film has developed out of drama and is able to do precisely that which was to remain a dream for the court theatre with its machines, revolving stages and other effects: to present an illusion of reality. [...]

But what is the theatre of today? [...] Today it has largely become a museum, there's no getting around that, in which the art treasures of bygone theatrical epochs are put on display. There is nothing whatever to be done about this. In our backward-looking era which seems to possess everything but its own present time this is only natural. [...]

If the present-day theatre is partly a museum this has a particular effect on the actors employed in it. They have become civil servants, often with pension

---

[1] An outstanding example of such a 'misreading' of a Brecht play was *Mother Courage and Her Children*, in which the 'heroine', guilty of profiting from the Thirty Years War, tended to attract more unqualified audience sympathy than the author had intended.

[2] This bird's-eye view of theatre history applies more particularly, for specific historical reasons, to the theatres of Germany and Austria.

rights,[3] in so far as film work still lets them act on the stage, as indeed the formerly despised profession, happily from the human but dubiously from the artistic point of view, has long since joined the middle class and is situated in the social pecking order somewhere between doctors and minor captains of industry; in the realm of the arts overtaken only by Nobel Prize winners, pianists and conductors. Some are visiting professors or independent scholars of sorts who take their turn to appear in museums or arrange exhibitions. This also provides the guidelines for management which increasingly adapts its repertoire to the guest actors: what is to be played if this or that star in this or that line of business is available at this or that time? Furthermore, actors are compelled to deport themselves in the various styles, now in a baroque, now in a classical, now in a naturalistic style and tomorrow in the manner of Claudel, something an actor in say Molière's time wasn't required to do. The director has become important, dominant as never before, the equivalent of the conductor in music. The demand for a correct interpretation of historical works has arisen, rightly so, though in the theatre fidelity to the work itself hasn't yet advanced to the point which some conductors take for granted. The classics are not so much interpreted as all too often executed, the lowered curtain covering a mutilated corpse. [...]

But the very multiplicity of styles which the present-day theatre has to master does have one good feature. This good feature appears at first sight to be something negative. Every great epoch in the theatre was possible because a certain theatrical form had been found, a certain theatrical style, in and by means of which plays were written. You can follow this in the case of the English and the Spanish stages, or the Viennese popular theatre, that most wonderful phenomenon in the German-language theatre. This is really the only way to account for the large number of plays Lope de Vega was able to write. In terms of style the stage play was no problem for him. But in so far as there isn't any longer, nor can there be, any homogeneous theatrical style, to that extent writing for the theatre has become a problem and hence more difficult. So the present-day theatre is two different things, on the one hand a museum, but on the other hand a field for experiments, so much so that every play confronts the author with new tasks, new questions of style. Style today is no longer a general but a personal matter, indeed it has become something to be decided on a case-by-case basis. There is no longer any one style but there are only styles, a statement which defines the situation in contemporary art generally, for that consists of experiments and nothing else, as does the contemporary world itself.

If there are only styles, there are only dramatic theories and no longer any one dramatic theory: the dramatic theory of Brecht, the dramatic theory of Eliot, that of Claudel, of Frisch, of Hochwälder, a dramatic theory from one case to another: and yet a dramatic theory is perhaps conceivable, meaning a

---

[3] This is truer of Continental theatres subsidized by municipality, region, or state, than of the commercial theatres which are the norm in the English-speaking world.

dramatic theory of all possible cases, just as there is a geometry which includes all possible dimensions. The dramatic theory of Aristotle would be only one of the possible dramatic theories in this dramatic theory. It would be a question of a dramatic theory which would have to investigate the possibilities not of any one stage but of *the* stage, a dramaturgy of experiment. [...]

Now I cannot conceal the fact that I am at war with the concept of dramatic craftsmanship. The view that art can in the end be learnt by anyone who gives himself with sufficient diligence and persistence to the task of producing it seems to have been discarded a long time ago, but it is evidently still found in those judgments made about the art of playwriting. This is taken to be something solid, something decent and honest. So the relationship a dramatist has with his art is regarded as a marriage in which everything takes place legitimately, provided with the sacraments of aesthetics. This is presumably the reason why here more than anywhere else critics speak of a craft which in any given case has or has not been mastered; but when we examine more closely what they actually understand by craft it turns out that it is nothing but the sum total of their prejudices. [...] Dramatic craftsmanship is an optical illusion. It is a much more Utopian undertaking to talk about dramas, about art, than those who do most of the talking believe.

By means of this non-existent craft we set about depicting a certain subject matter. It usually presents a core element, the hero. Dramatic theory distinguishes between a tragic hero, the hero of tragedy, and a comic hero, the hero of comedy. The qualities a tragic hero must have are well known. He must be capable of arousing our pity. His guilt and his innocence, his virtues and his vices must appear to be blended in the most pleasant and exact manner and doled out according to certain rules, in such a way for instance that if I choose a villain as hero I must add to his wickedness an equally large portion of wit, a rule which has had the effect of at once making the devil the most likeable stage figure in German literature.[4] Things have remained the same. All that has changed is the social status of the person who arouses our pity.

In classical tragedy and Shakespeare the hero belongs to the highest social class, the aristocracy. The audience sees a hero suffering, acting, raging, who has a higher social position than it occupies itself. That is still highly impressive for any audience.

Now when middle-class tragedy is introduced with Lessing and Schiller, the audience comes to see itself as the suffering hero on the stage. Then things were to go still further. Büchner's Woyzeck is a primitive proletarian who, viewed socially, represents less than the average playgoer.[5] The audience is

---

[4] Dürrenmatt is referring here to the wittily cynical figure of Mephistopheles in Goethe's *Faust* (Parts 1 and 2).

[5] Georg Büchner's *Woyzek*, though written in 1836–7 shortly before the author's untimely death, remained virtually unknown for many years afterwards; it was not staged until 1913. The theatrical influence of this episodic play which featured, perhaps for the first time, a lower-class hero was consequently not fully felt until the twentieth century.

meant to see mankind, i.e. itself, in this extreme form of existence, in this final, most pitiable form. […]

Now in earlier ages too the theatre dealt not only with kings and generals, since time immemorial comedy has known the peasant, the beggar, the citizen as hero, but that's just it—comedy. A comic king does not appear anywhere in Shakespeare; his age could indeed show a ruler as a monster dripping with blood but never as a fool. In his plays it is the court flunkeys, the mechanicals, the workers who are comical. So in the evolution of the tragic hero a turning towards comedy can be shown. The same thing can be demonstrated in the case of the fool who increasingly becomes a tragic figure. This stage of affairs is not, however, without significance. The hero of a play not only propels forward a plot or suffers a certain fate, he also represents a world. We must therefore ask ourselves how our endangered world has to be represented, by means of what heroes, what the mirrors for imaging this world must be like and how they are to be polished.

To put the question concretely, can today's world for example be portrayed by Schiller's dramatic method as some writers maintain, since Schiller after all still grips audiences? Of course, in art anything is possible as long as it works, the only question being whether an art that worked once upon a time is still possible today. Art can never be repeated, if it could it would be foolish not simply to write now by Schiller's rules.

Schiller wrote the way he did because the world in which he lived could still be reflected in the world he wrote about, which he created for himself as an historian. But only just. Napoleon was perhaps the last hero in the old sense after all. By way of contrast, the world of today as it appears to us can hardly be mastered in the form of Schiller's historical drama, for the simple reason that we encounter not any tragic heroes but only tragedies staged by universal butchers and executed by means of chopping machines. Wallensteins can no longer be made out of Hitler and Stalin. Their power is so gigantic that they themselves are only random external expressions of this power, replaceable at will, and the disaster associated especially with the former and to a considerable degree with the latter has become too far-reaching, too confused, too cruel, too mechanical and often simply all too senseless as well. The power of Wallenstein is still a visible power, power today is visible only to the smallest extent, as the greater part of an iceberg is submerged in faceless abstraction. Schiller's drama presupposes a visible world, genuine state transactions as in the case of Greek tragedy. What is visible in art is that which is capable of being open to view. But the present-day state has become impenetrable to view, anonymous, bureaucratic, and this is the case not only in say Moscow or Washington but even in Berne, and today's state transactions are satyr plays which serve as after-pieces to tragedies performed in silence. Genuinely representative figures are absent, and the tragic heroes are without names. The world of today can be represented much better by a petty crook, by a clerk, by a policeman than by a Federal Councillor or by a Federal Chancellor. Art only reaches out to the victims if it reaches out to any human beings at all, it no longer touches the powers that be. Creon's secretaries settle the Antigone case. Just as physics can now picture the world only by means of mathematical formulae, the state, having lost its form, can now be only represented statistically. Power today becomes visible and takes shape perhaps only where it explodes, in the atom bomb, in this wonderful mushroom that rises up and spreads, immaculate as the sun, uniting mass murder with beauty. It is no longer possible to depict the atom bomb since it has become possible to produce it. [...]

But the task of art, in so far as it can have any task at all, and hence the task of present-day drama, is the creation of form, of that which is concrete. This is something that comedy can do above all. Tragedy as the most rigorous genre assumes a world that possesses form; comedy [...] a world shapeless, in process of becoming, of upheaval, a world which is packing up like ours. Tragedy overcomes distance. It renders present to the men of Athens myths that go back to the dawn of history. Comedy creates distance [...]

Now the means by which comedy creates distance is the flash of inspiration. Tragedy is without any such flashes. That is why there are not many tragedies whose subject matter has been invented. I don't mean to say that the tragic poets of antiquity didn't have any inspired ideas such as may occur today, but their unique art consisted in not needing to have any. That makes a difference. Aristophanes on the other hand lives on flashes of inspiration. [...] Now that doesn't mean that a drama of today can only be comic. Tragedy and comedy are formal concepts, dramatic types of conduct, fictional figures of aesthetics able to encompass the same sort of thing. Only the conditions in which they arise differ, and these conditions are based only to a minor extent on art.

Tragedy presupposes guilt, suffering, balance, insight, responsibility. In the muddle of our century, in this last dance of the white race, no one is guilty and no one is responsible any longer. Nobody could help it and nobody wanted it to happen. Everybody is really dispensable. Everybody is dragged along and gets stuck in some sort of a rake. We are too collectively guilty, too collectively embedded in the sins of our fathers and forefathers. We are mere descendants now. That's our bad luck, not our guilt: guilt now only exists as a personal achievement, as a religious deed. Only comedy is appropriate for us. [...]

But the tragic element is still possible even if pure tragedy is no longer possible. We can produce the tragic out of comedy, produce it as a terrible moment, a chasm opening up [...]

Now it would be easy to conclude that comedy is the expression of despair, but this is not an inevitable conclusion. To be sure, anyone seeing the senselessness, the hopelessness of this world may well despair; however, this despair is not a consequence of this world but a response he gives to this world, and another response would be his non-despair, such as a decision to stand up to the world in which we often live like Gulliver among the giants. [...] It is still possible to show the person of courage. [...]

Finally: it is only through the flash of inspiration, through comedy that the anonymous audience again becomes possible as an audience, a reality to be reckoned with but also one to be precalculated. The flash of inspiration very easily transforms the crowd of playgoers into a mass ready to be attacked, seduced, outwitted into listening to things it would not otherwise listen to so easily. Comedy is a mousetrap in which the audience keeps getting caught and will continue to get caught. Tragedy on the other hand postulates a community which nowadays cannot always be pretended to without embarrassment [...]

Our unformed, unshaped present is characterized by being surrounded by shapes, by forms which make of our period a mere result, or even less, a transitional stage, and which lend a greater weight to the past as something completed and to the future as something possible. This remark could also be readily applied to politics; applied to art it means that the artist is not only hemmed in by opinions about art and by demands derived not from himself but from something historical, already existing, but also by subject matters which no longer are subject matters, i.e. possibilities, but are already figures, i.e. something formed: Caesar is no longer pure subject matter for us but a Caesar whom scholarship has made the object of its research. [...] Shakespeare's *Julius Caesar* was possible on the basis of Plutarch who was not yet an historian in our sense but a story-teller, an author of 'lives'. If Shakespeare had known Mommsen he would not have written *Julius Caesar* because at that moment he would inevitably have lost the detachment with which he wrote about his subject matter. The same thing is true even of the Greek myths which for us (since we no longer experience them but give expert opinions and investigate them, recognizing them precisely as myths and thus destroying them) have turned into mummies which, festooned with philosophy and theology, all too often act as a substitute for living material.

It is for this reason that the artist must diminish the figures he meets and comes across everywhere if he wishes once again to turn them into subject matter, hoping that he may succeed: he parodies them, i.e. he depicts them in deliberate contrast to what they have become. But by this means, by this act of parody he regains his freedom and thereby his subject matter which is no longer to be found but must be invented, for every parody presupposes invention. The dramaturgy of available subject matter is replaced by the dramaturgy of invented subject matter. Man's freedom is manifested in laughter, his necessity in weeping; today we have to prove freedom. This planet's tyrants are unmoved by the works of the poets, they yawn at their lamentations, they consider their heroic lays to be silly fairy tales, they fall asleep over their religious poems, there's only one thing that scares them: their mockery. So parody has crept into all genres, into the novel, into drama, into lyrical poetry. Wide swathes of painting and music have been conquered by it, and alongside parody the grotesque has turned up, often in disguise, overnight: all at once it is simply there.

But our super-subtle age can cope with this too and will not be got at by anything: it has educated the public to see in art something solemn, holy and full of pathos. The comic element is considered inferior, dubious, improper, it is only admitted if it makes one feel as snug as a bug in a rug. But the moment when comedy is recognized as dangerous, revealing, demanding and moral, it is dropped like a hot potato, for art is allowed to be anything it pleases as long as it remains cosy. [...]

Mankind today resembles a woman driver. She drives along ever faster, ever more recklessly. But she doesn't like it when the alarmed passenger shouts, 'Look out!' and 'Here is a warning sign', 'Now you should brake' or even 'Don't run over that child'. She hates it when someone asks who paid for the car or who provided the petrol and the oil for her mad journey, or when he goes so far as to ask to see her driving-licence. Uncomfortable truths might come to light. The car might perhaps have been purloined from a relative, the petrol and the oil pressed from the fellow passengers themselves, and indeed not oil and petrol but the blood and sweat of all of us, and the driving-licence might possibly not exist at all; it could turn out it that it was the first time she'd driven. So it would be embarrassing to enquire about such personal matters. She therefore prefers one to praise the beauty of the scenery she is driving through, the silver of a river and the glow of the glaciers in the distance, she also likes to have amusing stories whispered in her ear. For a writer today, however, whispering these stories and praising the scenery are no longer really compatible, as a rule, with a clear conscience. Unfortunately he cannot get out either in order to satisfy the demand for pure poetry which is being put forward by all non-poets. Fear, worry and, above all, anger force open his mouth.

# Theatre without a Conscience (1990)

## Howard Barker

In his dramatic output of over fifty works for stage, radio, television, and film, the English author Howard Barker (b. 1946) occupies a singular niche. Though originally taking a left-wing satirical stance he has come to advocate a morally and politically ambiguous 'Theatre of Catastrophe'; this aggressively black viewpoint he has defended in a collection of essays, *Arguments for a Theatre*. The following piece from that book was first delivered as a paper at the University College of Wales, Aberystwyth, in 1990. Barker's plays present striking but ambiguous images rather than conventionally readable plots and refuse to give any easy guidelines for deciphering the action. In order to force audiences to do their own thinking, Barker uses disjunctions of every kind—abrupt changes of character, multivalent time and place, sudden switches of tone. Since the British theatre and broadcast media have not proved wholly sympathetic to this difficult genre, a company—the Wrestling School—began work in 1988 with the sole aim of staging his plays.

There is a type of theatre which has dominated us for the last two or three decades which takes as its starting point, its inspiration, even, the apparently selfless desire to make people better. It is the kind of theatre which begins, long before the process of writing or rehearsal, with the question, 'What do people need?' When this need has been identified, the search for the subject begins. The insatiable appetite for improving other people can be detected in the way in which writers and directors justify and advertise their efforts. If a writer is asked why he wrote a particular play he or she invariably replies, 'I wanted people to understand such and such a thing better', or 'I wanted people to

From Howard Barker, *Arguments for a Theatre* (Manchester University Press, 1993), 72–8.

know how such and such a person feels', or 'I wanted to heighten their perception of such and such an issue', and even, at its most shamelessly ambitious, 'I
wanted to improve the quality of people's lives.' In all these responses there is a
passion to enlighten, a paternalistic beneficence, from the one who knows to
the many who do not, the largesse of perception dished out in the palaver of
dramatic form. This is the social hygiene of the gifted aching to illuminate the
ungifted, the above-prejudice correcting the prejudiced, and the artist
instructing the herd. It is the essential manner of the humanist play, which has
as its project the strictly utilitarian end of making us good and happy (happiness supposed to be derived from 'understanding one another') and turning
theatre into sticking plaster for the wounds of social alienation. This is the theatre of daylight, clarity and dubious truths, behind which lies the critical consensus that art is somehow to do with 'informing'. Who hasn't read again and
again the satisfied reviewer announcing in these terms why he had a good
night out—'I left the theatre knowing more about this subject than when I
went in …', 'I was enlightened about …', 'The play made me realize', etc., the
clucking of customers who have got their fistful of knowledge, the sort of
accolade that is the erosion of theatre as art and the triumph of a theatre of
social correction. And of course, because the desire to correct and be corrected
is an irrepressible human drive, the demand for such a theatre is continuous.
We have had for some decades now the spectacle of dramatists who haunt the
newspapers for their inspiration, indeed are wholly dependent on it, as well as
theatre companies of some distinction whose most significant activity is what
they call 'researching material', an activity closely related to the business of
'dramatizing' things. Theatre has no business with research, and things are not
dramatized: they are either drama or they are something else. They come into
existence as art, or they are not art at all, and research is something carried out
by specialists called academics or non-specialists called journalists. The verb
'to dramatize' is part of the kitsch vocabulary of the theatre of issues, in which
actors are employed as a means to a didactic end, the education of the ignorant
audience, and by 'research' we are threatened with the spurious legitimacy of
so-called facts. 'It's all right,' the actors seem to tell you in researched plays,
'everything we demonstrate has occurred', is in effect 'true'. But the theatre is
not true, it is not a true action, its very power, its whole authority comes from
the fact that it is not true, and the idea of accuracy, or reference to a source outside the theatre walls, is fatal to its particular unsettling and revolutionary
power. The moment that an action on the stage asserts its veracity by reference
to known and proven action elsewhere, theatre is overwhelmed by the world,
the world reclaims it. It is a symptom of the lost faith in theatre as an art form
that its practitioners require the credentials of authenticity. It is the poverty of
the journalist that he must provide evidence for his assertions, the frailty of the
academic that he must prove and counter-prove. The theatre is without evidence, it 'makes believe', it forces belief. The audience of the theatre comes for
what it cannot obtain elsewhere in any other forum. In other words, it comes

for the false, it comes for the speculative and the unproven. The researched theatre says, the informative theatre says, 'We have demonstrated such and such a fact, and it will make you better to know it', a sham democracy behind which lies a repugnant arrogance. The imaginative theatre says, 'We prove nothing, we assert that nothing can be proved by the actor.'

Let us not pretend, however, that the Theatre of Conscience does not have its attractions in the contemporary world. There is an obvious base pleasure to be had in enlightenment of this kind, a gratifying trade-off between customer and performer. You pay £5 or £10 for a seat and you are sent home with an item of sympathy or knowledge, you grasp what you are intended to grasp, some facts about a researched subject, some insight into the social conditions of somebody, you are officially encouraged to extend sympathy to a chosen group of fellow human beings, which is easily done in art if not in life, and your conscience is effectively massaged. If a theatre of entertainment is a deal, so is the theatre of enlightenment. As the writer says in his interview, 'I wanted people to understand such and such a thing better', and he cannot fail as long as he contains his efforts within the limits of popular conscience. People find it reassuring to be made to care about what they thought they already cared about. It is the fertile land of shared perceptions. The Theatre of Conscience is essentially a mass declaration of loyalty to moral principles. But it is not, as I believe art has to be, promiscuous. It is an activity that never sins.

Let me suggest that the theatre is literally a box, physically and morally a box. What occurs in the box is infinite because the audience wishes it to be infinite—there is no burden of proof at any moment. It is a black box, when the lights are off, because, as we all know, darkness permits the criminal and the promiscuous act. I wrote a play called *The Bite of the Night*.[1] Darkness permits the thought, darkness licenses, it bites, and sometimes you can be bitten by love and sometimes by fear. When Brecht commanded that the box be filled with light[2] he was driven by the passion for enlightenment, and he knew instructions require light just as the imagination hates light and flees from it. Imagination also flees its neighbours. In light you are only half-conscious of the stage and half-conscious of your neighbour. In all collective culture your neighbour controls you by his gaze. In darkness he is eliminated and you are alone with the actor. That is why the didactic play occurs in the street[3]—street theatre is about teaching, black box theatre is about imagination. In the black box you are trusted to be free, to be solely responsible. To enter it is to be engulfed by the possibility of freedom through the powers of the actor and the

---

[1] This drama, subtitled 'An Education', which was first produced at the Pit, Barbican Centre, London in 1988, plays variations on the theme of Troy—Paper Troy, Laughing Troy, The Poets' Troy, etc.—in defiance of any consistency of plot, character, place, or time.

[2] For Brecht's suggestions on how to stage his plays, see pp. 227–9, 245–6.

[3] For some ideas on street theatre in the literal sense, see p. 256 (Boal's 'Poetics of the Oppressed'). Brecht used the image of the Street Scene as a way of illustrating his ideas on 'estrangement' in acting style; see John Willett (ed.), *Brecht on Theatre* (London: Eyre Methuen, 1964), 121–9.

dramatist, the onus is placed on the audience not as a collectivity, but as individuals. No disciplines, no recall to conscience. Because the box is hidden from the world, it owes as little as it wishes to the world, the rules in the box are different from the rules outside it. What else can explain the residual excitement we still experience in dark theatres? Why are we still a little half-afraid? Is it because we are about to watch an actor? Yes, because actors are not entirely human, but more, it is the sense of attending on a sin, the possibility of witnessing a transgression, the freedom to part with the necessary disciplines of the street, the possibility of acquiring that criminal perspective— not more enlightenment, but less. And of course, it is not you who sins, the actors sin for you. The box is a dangerous place, but you are not yourself physically in danger—all theatre that affronts or offends the audience by direct engagement wrecks that sacred compact between actor and witness that is older than history. To insult the audience for the paltry gratification of the actors destroys theatre, erodes its authority as an art,[4] just as all invitations to debate what has been witnessed diminish its beauty. The great play is immune to discussion, the play eliminates debate, it is not about arguments, it replaces arguments.

A drama teacher, a pacifist, visited me. He told me of his production of *Antigone*, in which instead of a set he hung a massive map of the world on which every war currently being fought was illuminated by flaming red light. Of course, there were lots of these, and the actors played in the glare of them. At the end, he flung on the house lights and dragged chairs on to the stage, obliging the audience to engage in a debate on the so-called issues the production had raised. He therefore succeeded in eliminating the entire experience of the drama, humiliated the text by using it as a means to an end, a starting point for the endless curse of debating things, wrecked the invention of his actors, turning them into mere didactic instruments, and liquidated any possibility in the audience that their structure of feeling and thought could be inflamed by what they had witnessed—he had reduced the non-cerebral event of a play into a pack of arguments.

I repeat that the play is not a debate, it is literally 'play', and like children's play it is 'world-inventing', requiring no legitimation from the exterior. It is about impossibilities, and takes its immense spiritual authority from the simple question 'what if …?' not from the banal 'did you know …?' The question 'What if …?' immunizes the theatre from its worst enemies, the material researchers, who can devastate a documentary by flourishing a single fact. In black box theatre nothing can be challenged on the ground that it did not occur, or has no precedent. The response to the plaintive cry, 'This could never happen!' is 'Precisely, we are playing a play!' And play is dangerous, of course, it goes where it is not expected to go, it is quite simply immoral. When

---

[4] This is precisely what the Austrian playwright Peter Handke set out to do in *Publikumsbeschimpfung* (Offending the Audience, 1966).

Hochhuth wrote his notorious play on Winston Churchill,[5] the work was obscured—or it was intended to be—by a massive correspondence about the Churchillian archives. Hochhuth had 'researched' his play, but never well enough. By his meticulous realist method, he robbed his chosen art form of its major resource, and the whole event shifted from inside the theatre to outside it, to the columns of newspapers. If writers use theatre only as a means to get access to newspaper columns—what they call initiating debate—they vandalize theatre, they tear gaping holes in its walls through which a miserable daylight streams, showing us that actors are, after all, only people with painted faces.

It is my contention that theatre's power in the contemporary world ought to be much greater than it is, but that it has wilfully chosen to emasculate itself by imitating the habits of its rivals. Its writers are smitten with the idea of themselves as educators, and have subordinated actors to their wishes. They have made a theatre of morals almost as rigid as the medieval stage and have contributed to a new style of social conformism. They have told what they know, and have not dared to tread where they do not know, which is the authentic territory of black box theatre. I also am a moralist, but not a puritan. By moralist I mean one who is tough with morality, who exposes it to risk, even to oblivion, and it is not for nothing that I chose the theatre as my field because in essence the theatre is not a moral place, as our ancestors knew well when they intermittently banned it. It is a long time since anyone wanted to ban the theatre in this country, and that is itself suggestive. It is responsible, it is loyal, it is a willing collaborator in the enforcing of moral regulations. Let me for the last time return to the writer who thinks the purpose of his life and art is 'to make people understand one another'. I must admit that for many years when people asked me why I wrote, I resorted to such dismal platitudes myself, though with a deep sense of bad faith. I had a sense that art was a luxury and needed to be defended against charges of indulgence or privilege. In fact, I wrote because I needed to. I wrote for myself. But that seemed unforgivable. Only more recently did I understand that in writing for myself I also served others, and that, in not serving myself, I could not serve others. The more self-limiting an artist is, the less useful to his fellow human beings; the more he dares, the more he explores, and the more immoral he is, the better he serves. Then he or she becomes the enemy of collective lying. Then he or she runs the risk of seeing the work denied. Great art lives outside the moral system, and its audience, consciously or unconsciously, demands it, particularly in theatre whose very darkness is the condition of a secret pact, the pact of wilful infringement, of the suspension of conscience, between actor and audience. And the actor, as I suggested earlier, is not entirely human, nor do we wish him

---

[5] Rolf Hochhuth's play, *Soldiers: An Obituary for Geneva* (premiered in Berlin in 1967), was originally banned in Britain because it accused Churchill of having connived at the murder of the Free Polish leader General Sikorsky. In this, as in other plays, Hochhuth provided a wealth of documentation.

to be. He is not—and here as in most ways I totally reject the principle of community theatre—merely someone who might be in the audience on another night, the grocer in a funny hat, or your uncle pretending to be your ancestor—but quite other than us, gifted in special ways, not least in body and speech, particularly in speech; he has the gift of seducing—after all, dance is permitted everywhere, dance is the conformist act and ironically, repressive—but speech, that is the lost secret, and poetic speech is nearly religious in its power: not the humdrum repetition of naturalistic drama, but the rhythmic, undulating journey of the articulated form known as 'the speech'. On the stage the actor is licensed to do the undoable, and he or she 'takes us out of ourselves'—a strangely accurate phrase that, like most common expressions, hides as much as it reveals. To be 'taken out of yourself'—the very thing demanded of the actor—is to be like the dog let off its lead, the lead being conscience, the lead being responsibility and loyalty. Like the dog, the actor experiences an atavistic moment of relief, wildness and barbarism, and even fear—for he is domesticated, after all—so we glimpse, with fear and delight, the landscape of a premoral world and are allowed to run in it. And what is the form of this landscape, for there is only one? It is tragedy. Impossible in comedy, for comedy is the suspension, the denial of emotion. The artist who dares to be tragic, the actor who is unafraid of tragedy, lives at the expense of his conscience, lives outside conscience. He sins for the audience, living on the very fringes of morality. This is the reason the actor in historic periods was banned, even in death, from hallowed ground—he was the player of the forbidden action, the manifestation of forbidden life. In a conscience-free theatre, there is, of course, no 'telling'. It is the farthest reach from the Brechtian demonstration. There is no 'telling' because the writer had nothing to tell—his play was a journey to him as it is a journey to the actor, the outcome of which was unknown at its beginning. It was for the writer a journey without maps whose destination might be an intemperate zone, a place of fear and little comfort. This is the very act of honouring I have described elsewhere[6]—the honouring of an audience by refusing the simple fact of reiteration, affirmations, congratulation—the sort of theatre in which the morality was fixed in advance, and the writing, and the narrative was a means to an end. I repeat that the theatre tells nothing, and in a society where telling never stops, where news, political comment, advertising, the social debate, are a deafening cacophony, an orchestra of claims and counter-claims, all subject to the moral consensus of humanism, the theatre's sole and riveting power lies in its barbarism. Against the walls of the theatre there washes continuously the sea of morality and debate. The walls protect the actor and the audience not only from the racket of the street but also from its morality. Inside the black box, the imagination is wild and tragic and its criminality unfettered. The unspeakable is

---

[6] e.g. in 'Honour thy audience', first published in *City Limits* on 25 Feb. 1988 and repr. in *Arguments for a Theatre* (45–7) under the title, 'Honouring the Audience'.

spoken. Here alone is the audience trusted with the full burden of what it has witnessed and liberated from the ideology of redemption, it witnesses in silence, a silence of pain, the terrible ambitions of the human spirit. Cruelty. Magnificence. Wrong actions. Instinct. Horror. Love beyond legality. When an audience witnesses such things beyond the structures of redemption or education, ideology or affirmation, it has recourse only to silence, a pathos which is perhaps a kind of self-pity permitted to a hero who finds himself, at last, alone.

# Are There Universals of Performance in Myth, Ritual, and Drama? (1989)

## Victor Turner

Victor Turner (1920–83), an anthropologist and comparative symbologist with a strong interest in ritual and theatre, began his fieldwork among the Ndembu of Uganda. Later he travelled to India, Israel, Mexico, Ireland, and Japan. He was the William R. Kenan Professor of Anthropology and Religion at the University of Virginia from 1977 until the time of his death. A number of his books were concerned with the ritual aspects of theatre, and he laid the groundwork in practical workshops for what he called 'performing ethnography'. He was associated in this endeavour with Professor Richard Schechner, Professor of Performance Studies at the Tisch School of the Arts, New York University, with whom he collaborated on several interdisciplinary conferences.

In this essay I will discuss what I think is a characteristic developmental relationship from ritual to theatre, and I will lay out the relationship of both to social drama. [...] I have argued that every major socioeconomic formation has its dominant form of cultural-aesthetic 'mirror' in which it achieves a certain degree of self-reflexivity. Nonindustrial societies tend to stress immediate context-sensitive ritual; industrial pre-electronic societies tend to stress theatre, which assigns meaning to macroprocesses—economic, political, or generalized familial problems—but remains insensitive to localized, particularized contexts. Yet both ritual and theatre crucially involve liminal events and processes and have an important aspect of social metacommentary. In many field situations I have observed in markedly different cultures, in my

From Richard Schechner and Willa Appel (eds.), *By Means of Performance* (Cambridge University Press, 1990), 8–18.

experience of Western social life, and in numerous historical documents, I have clearly seen a community's movement through time taking a shape which is obviously 'dramatic'. It has a proto-aesthetic form in its unfolding— a generic form like the general mammalian condition that we still have with us throughout all the global radiation of specific mammalian forms to fill special niches. As detailed in my earlier writings, in the first stage, Breach, a person or subgroup breaks a rule deliberately or by inward compulsion, in a public setting. In the stage of Crisis, conflicts between individuals, sections, and factions follow the original breach, revealing hidden clashes of character, interest, or ambition. These mount towards a crisis of a group's unity and its very continuity unless rapidly sealed off by redressive public action, consensually undertaken by the group's leaders, elders, or guardians. Redressive action is often ritualized and may be undertaken in the name of law or religion. Judicial processes stress reason and evidence, religious processes emphasize ethical problems, hidden malice operating through witchcraft, or ancestral wrath against breaches or tabu or the impiety of the living towards the dead. If a social drama runs its full course, the outcome (…)—the fourth stage in my model—may be either (a) the restoration of peace and 'normality' among the participants, or (b) the social recognition of irremediable or irreversible breach of schism. Of course, this mode, like all models, is subject to manifold manipulations. For example, redressive action may fail, in which case there is *reversion* to the phase of crisis. If law and/or religious values have lost their cultural efficacy, endemic continuous factionalism may infect public life for long periods. Or redressive failure in a local community may lead to appeal to a higher court at a more inclusive level of social organization—village to district to province to nation. Or the *ancien régime* may be rejected altogether and revolution ensue. There may be a 'transvaluation of values'.

In that case the group itself may be radically restructured, including its redressive machinery. Culture obviously affects such aspects as the style and tempo of the social drama. Some cultures seek to retard the outbreak of open crisis by elaborate rules of etiquette. Others admit the use of organized ritualized violence (almost in the ethological sense) in crisis or redress, in such forms as the holmgang (island single-combat) of the Icelanders, the stick-fights of the Nuba of the Sudan, and the reciprocal head-hunting expeditions of the Ilongot hill people of Luzon in the Philippines. Simmel, Coser, Gluckmann and others have pointed out how conflict, if brought under gradual control, stopping short of massacre and war, may actually enhance a group's 'consciousness of kind,' may enhance and revive its self-image. For conflict forces antagonists to diagnose its source, and in so doing, to become fully aware of the principles that bond them beyond and above the issues that have temporarily divided them. As Durkheim said long ago, law needs crime, religion needs sin, to be fully dynamic systems, since without 'doing,' without the social friction that fires consciousness and self-consciousness, social life would be passive, even inert. These considerations, I think, led Barbara Myerhoff[1] to distinguish 'definitional ceremonies' as a kind of collective 'autobiography', by means of which a group creates its identity by telling itself a story about itself, in the course of which it brings to life 'its Definite and Determinate Identity' (to cite William Blake). [...] Some social dramas may be more 'definitional' than others, it is true, but most social dramas contain, if only implicitly, some means of *public reflexivity* in their redressive processes. For by their activation groups take stock of their own current situation: the nature and strength of their social ties, the power of their symbols, the effectiveness of their legal and moral controls, the sacredness and soundness of their religious traditions, and so forth. And this is the point I would make here: the world of theatre, as we know it both in Asia and America, and the immense variety of theatrical sub-genres derive not from imitation, conscious or unconscious, of the processual form of the complete or 'satiated' social drama—breach, crisis, redress, reintegration, or schism—but specifically from its third phase, the one I call redress, especially from redress as *ritual* process, rather than *judicial, political,* or *military* process, important as these are for the study of political or revolutionary action. Redressive rituals include divination into the hidden causes of misfortune, personal and social conflict, and illness (all of which in tribal societies are intimately interconnected and thought to be caused by the invisible action of spirits, deities, witches, and sorcerers); they include curative ritual (which may often involve episodes of spirit-possession, shamanic trance mediumship, and trance states among the patients who are subjects of ritual); and initiatory rites connected with these 'rituals of affliction'. Moreover, many of those rites that we call 'life-crisis ceremonies,' particularly those of puberty, marriage, and death, themselves indicate a major if not altogether unexpected breach in the orderly, customary running of group life, after which many relationships among its members must change drastically, involving much potential and even actual conflict and competition (for rights of inheritance and succession to office, for women, over the amount of bridewealth, over clan or lineage allegiance). Life-crisis rituals (and seasonal rituals, too, for that matter) may be called 'prophylactic', while rituals of affliction are 'therapeutic'. Life-crisis rituals portray and symbolically resolve archetypal conflicts in abstraction from the milling, teeming social life which characteristically and periodically throws up such conflicts. Society is, therefore, better equipped to deal with them concretely, having portrayed them abstractly.

All these 'third-phase' or 'first-phase' (if we are talking about life crisis) ritual processes contain within themselves what I have in several writings called a liminal phase, which provides a stage (and I use this term advisedly when thinking about theatre) for unique structures of experience [...], in

---

[1]  Barbara Myerhoff, *Number Our Days* (New York: Dutton, 1978), p. 22. [Turner's note.]

milieux detached from mundane life and characterized by the presence of ambiguous ideas, monstrous images, sacred symbols, ordeals, humiliations, esoteric and paradoxical instructions, the emergence of 'symbolic types' represented by maskers and clowns, gender reversals, anonymity, and many other phenomena and processes I have elsewhere described as liminal. The limen, or threshold, [...] is a no-man's-land betwixt-and-between the structural past and the structural future as anticipated by the society's normative control of biological development. It is ritualized in many ways, but very often symbols expressive of ambiguous identity are found cross-culturally: androgynes, at once male and female, theriomorphic figures, at once animals and men or women, angels, mermaids, centaurs, human-headed lions, and so forth, monstrous combinations of elements drawn from nature *and* culture. Some symbols represent both birth *and* death, womb *and* tomb, such as caverns or camps secluded from everyday eyes. I sometimes talk about the liminal phase being dominantly in the 'subjunctive mood' of culture, the mood of maybe, might-be, as-if, hypothesis, fantasy, conjecture, desire, depending on which of the trinity, cognition, affect, and conation (thought, feeling, or intention) is situationally dominant. [...] 'Ordinary' day-to-day life is in the indicative mood, where we expect the invariant operation of cause-and-effect, of rationality and commonsense. Liminality can perhaps be described as a fructile chaos, a fertile nothingness, a storehouse of possibilities, not by any means a random assemblage but a striving after new forms and structure, a gestation process, a fetation of modes appropriate to and anticipating postliminal existence. It is what goes on in nature in the fertilized egg, in the chrysalis, and even more richly and complexly in their cultural homologues.

Theatre is one of the many inheritors of that great multifaceted system of preindustrial ritual which embraces ideas and images of cosmos and chaos, interdigitates clowns and their foolery with gods and their solemnity, and uses all the sensory codes to produce symphonies in more than music: the intertwining of dance, body languages of many kinds, song, chant, architectural forms (temples, amphitheatres), incense, burnt offerings, ritualized feasting and drinking, painting, body painting, body marking of many kinds, including circumcision and scarification, the application of lotions and drinking of potions, the enacting of mythic and heroic plots drawn from oral traditions. And so much more. Rapid advances in the scale and complexity of society, particularly after industrialization, have passed this unified liminal configuration through the analytical prism of division of labour, with its specialization and professionalization, reducing each of these sensory domains to a set of entertainment genres flourishing in the leisure time of society, no longer in a central, driving place. The pronounced numinous supernatural character of archaic ritual has been greatly attenuated.

Nevertheless, there are today signs that the amputated specialized genres are seeking to rejoin and to recover something of the numinosity lost in their *sparagmos*, their dismemberment. Truly, [...] the aesthetic form of theatre is inherent in sociocultural life itself, in what I call 'social drama' [...], but the reflexive and therapeutic character of *theatre*, as essentially a child of the redressive phase of social drama, has to draw on power sources often inhibited or at least constrained in the cultural life of society's 'indicative' mood. The deliberate creation of a detached, still almost-sacred liminal space, allows a search for such sources. One source of this 'meta'-power is, clearly, the liberated and disciplined body itself, with its many untapped resources for pleasure, pain, and expression. Here, the experimental theatre of Jerzy Grotowski, Julian Beck and Judith Malina, Joseph Chaikin, Richard Schechner, Peter Brook, Suzuki Tadashi, and Squat Theatre in New York[2] has its growing importance. Another source draws on unconscious processes, such as may be released in trance foreshadowed by some of Antonin Artaud's theories.[3] This is akin to what I have often seen in Africa, where thin, ill-nourished old ladies, with only occasional naps, dance, sing, and perform ritual activities for two or three days and nights together. I think that a rise in the level of social arousal, however produced, is capable of unlocking energy sources in individual participants. [...]

My argument has been that what I would like to call the anthropology of experience (abolishing the sharp distinction between the classical study of culture and sociobiology) finds in certain recurrent forms of social experience (notably social dramas) sources of aesthetic form, including stage drama and dance. But ritual and its progeny, the performance arts among them, derive from the subjunctive, liminal, reflexive, exploratory heart of the social drama, its third, redressive phase, where the contents of group experiences [...] are replicated, dismembered, remembered, refashioned, and mutely or vocally made meaningful (even when, as so often in declining cultures, the meaning is that there is no meaning as in some Existentialist theatre). [...] True theatre 'at its height signifies complete interpenetration of self and the world of objects and events.' When this happens in performance, there may be produced in the audience and actors alike what d'Aquili and Laughlin[4] call in reference both to ritual and meditation a 'brief ecstatic state and sense of union (often lasting only a few seconds) and may often be described as no more than a shiver running down the back at a certain point.' A sense of harmony with the universe is made evident, and the whole planet is felt to be communitas. This shiver has to

---

[2]   For Jerzy Grotowski, see p. 200.—For Julian Beck and Judith Malina, co-founders of the Living Theatre, see p. 189, p. 309, n. 5.—Joseph Chaikin (b. 1935), American director, actor, and producer, whose Open Theatre was an influential Off-Off Broadway company between 1963 and 1973.—Richard Schechner (b. 1934), academic, editor of *Tulane Drama Review* and the *Drama Review*, director with a strong interest in ritual theatre, ran the Performance Group in New York City from 1967 to 1980.—For Peter Brook, see pp. 205.—Suzuki Tadashi (b. 1939), Japanese director, theorist, and leader of an actor-centred theatre group at the village of Toga, has taught and directed in Europe and America as well as Japan.—Squat Theatre: a fringe group that operated in New York City in the 1970s and 1980s in a private building, the store front of which incorporated random street events in their shows.

[3]   For Antonin Artaud, see pp. 188–99.

[4]   Eugene d'Aquili & Charles D. Laughlin, *The Spectrum of Rituals* (New York, Columbia University Press, 1979), p. 177. [Turner's note.]

be won, achieved, though, to be a consummation, after working through a tangle of conflicts and disharmonies. Theatre best of all exemplifies Thomas Hardy's dictum: 'If a way to the better there be, it exacts a full look at the worst.' Ritual or theatrical transformation can scarcely occur otherwise. Problems and obstacles (the 'crisis' stage of social dramas) challenge our brain neuro-biology into full arousal, and culture supplies that aroused activity with a store of preserved social experience which can be 'heated up' to supply the current hunger for meaning with reliable nutrients. [...]

Notice that the *manifest* social drama feeds into the latent realm of stage drama; its characteristic form in a given culture, at a given time and place, unconsciously, or perhaps preconsciously, influences not only the form but also the content of the stage drama of which it is the active or 'magic' mirror. The stage drama, when it is meant to do more than entertain—though enter-tainment is always one of its vital aims—is a metacommentary, explicit or implicit, witting or unwitting, on the major social dramas of its social context (wars, revolutions, scandals, institutional changes). Not only that, but its mes-sage and its rhetoric feed back into the *latent* processual structure of the social drama and partly account for its ready ritualization. Life itself now becomes a mirror held up to art, and the living now *perform* their lives, for the protagon-ists of a social drama, a 'drama of living,' have been equipped by aesthetic drama with some of their most salient opinions, imageries, tropes, and ideo-logical perspectives. Neither mutual mirroring, life by art, art by life, is exact, for each is not a planar mirror but matricial mirror; at each exchange some-thing new is added and something old is lost or discarded. Human beings learn through experience, though all too often they repress painful experience, and perhaps the deepest experience is through drama; not through social drama, or stage drama (or its equivalent) alone, but in the circulatory or oscillatory process of their mutual and incessant modification.

If one were to guess at origins, my conjecture would be that the genres of cultural performance, whether tribal rituals of TV specials, are not, as I have said, simply imitations of the overt form of the completed social drama. They are germinated in its *third*, redressive phase, the reflexive phase, the phase where society pulls meaning from that tangle of action, and, therefore, these performances are infinitely varied, like the result of passing light through a prism. The alternative versions of meaning that complex societies produce are innumerable. Within societies there are different classes, ethnicities, regions, neighbourhoods, and people of different ages and sexes, and they each pro-duce versions which try painfully to assign meaning to the particular crisis pattern of their own society. Each performance becomes a record, a means of explanation.

Finally, it should be noted that the interrelation of social drama to stage drama is not in an endless, cyclical, repetitive pattern; it is a spiralling one. The spiralling process is responsive to inventions and the changes in the mode of production in the given society. Individuals can make an enormous impact on the sensibility and understanding of members of society. Philosophers feed their work into the spiralling process; poets feed poems into it; politicians feed their acts into it; and so on. Thus the result is not an endless cyclical repetitive pattern or a stable cosmology. The cosmology has always been destabilized, and society has always had to make efforts, through both social drama and aesthetic dramas, to restabilize and actually *produce* cosmos.

# PART II

# Varieties of Realism

# The Relationship of Dramatic Art to its Age and Allied Matters: *The Preface to Mary Magdalene* (1844)

## Friedrich Hebbel

Friedrich Hebbel (1813–63) published this preface together with his third play, *Mary Magdalene*, in 1844. Since *Mary Magdalene*, then considered shocking for featuring an illegitimate pregnancy, was not to be performed until two years after publication of the text, the preface was a manifesto justifying the author's work. In an earlier polemic, *My Word about Drama* (1843), Hebbel had declared his intention of combining social, historical, and philosophical motives in his playwriting. This preface, not as well known to English readers as it deserves to be for its argument, is reproduced here in shortened form. It is more than the defence of just one particular play. Unfortunately it showed Hebbel's prose style at its most ponderous, in contrast to the highly speakable dialogue of the play itself; and it somewhat unfairly gained the author a reputation as a playwright inspired more by philosophical considerations than by living characters.

However, he made some important general points that anticipated major developments—not only in Germany but elsewhere too—in the dramaturgy of the later nineteenth and indeed the twentieth century. First, he related drama to its period: not in the obvious sense of advocating mere topicality but insisting that it reflect the *Zeitgeist* in its most significant historical conflictual currents; and second, he redefined bourgeois tragedy as going beyond the conventional clash between the aristocracy and the middle class, situating it instead within the divided psyche of the bourgeoisie itself—actually, in this particular instance, the lower middle class.

[…] Drama, as the highest of all arts, should illustrate the condition of the world and of humanity at any given time in its relation to the idea, i.e. to the

From Friedrich Hebbel, *Sämtliche Werke*, xi (Berlin: B. Behr's Verlag, 1904), 39–65. Translated from the German by George Brandt.

moral centre governing everything which we must assume [to exist] in the universal organism, if only for its own preservation. Drama, i.e. [that of] the highest epoch-making kind—for there are also a second and a third kind, a partial/national and a subjective/individual one, which in relation to the former are like single scenes and characters which stand for the entire play but which are a [mere] substitute for it until an all-embracing spirit appears and, if that fails to appear, take its place as *disjecti membra poetae*—drama is possible only when a decisive change is taking place in this condition [of the world]; hence it is wholly a product of its age, but to be sure only in the sense that such an age is itself the product of all preceding ages, the connecting link between a concatenation of centuries now concluded and a new one which is about to begin.

Hitherto history has had only two crises to show in which the highest drama could manifest itself, and indeed it has manifested itself only twice; once among the ancients, when the world view of antiquity passed from its original naivety to the at first disintegrating and then destructive momentum of reflection; and once among the moderns when the Christian world view underwent a similar internal conflict. Greek drama unfolded when paganism had outlived itself, and it devoured the latter; it laid bare the nerve of the idea running through all the colourful divinities of Olympus or, if you like, it created fate. Hence the immeasurable demotion of the individual as against the moral powers with which he sees himself engaged in a not at all fortuitous but inevitable struggle, which reaches its dizzying climax in *Oedipus*. Shakespeare's drama developed alongside Protestantism and emancipated the individual. Hence the fearful dialectic of his characters who, in so far as they are men of action, push aside whatever lives around them in the most inordinate expansion, and in so far as they live the life of the mind, like Hamlet, in an equally inordinate plunging into their own depths through the most audacious and dreadful questions, seek to drive God out of the world as out of a botched piece of work.

After Shakespeare, Goethe was the first in *Faust* and in *The Elective Affinities*, which are rightly called dramatic,[1] to lay another foundation stone for a great drama, and he did, or rather he set out to do, the only thing that had been left undone—he cast the dialectic directly into the idea itself, he sought to show up the contradiction, which Shakespeare only showed up in the individual, in the centre around which the individual revolves [...]

But Goethe only pointed the way, he can barely be said to have taken the first step, for in *Faust* he retraced his steps having climbed too high and got to the chilly region where one's blood begins to freeze[2] [...]

So Goethe [...] did enter upon but failed to make his own the great heritage of the age; he saw clearly enough that human consciousness was striving to

---

[1] Goethe's novel, *The Elective Affinities* (1809), dealt with problems of marriage in quasi-symbolical form; if it is dramatic as Hebbel claimed, it is so in the manner of the novel, not that of the theatre.

[2] The Second Part of *Faust* (1832) uses allegory more than the First Part. In the Catholic imagery of its conclusion (the salvation of Faust), which is somewhat reminiscent of Jesuit drama, it disappointed many admirers of the earlier work.

expand, to break yet another shackle, but he could not surrender himself to history in devout confidence; and since he did not know how to resolve the dissonances arising from the transitional conditions into which he had himself been violently dragged in his youth, he resolutely, or even with repugnance and disgust, turned his back on them.[3] But that did not remove those conditions, they have continued until the present day, indeed they have worsened, and all the fluctuations and divisions in our public as well as our private lives derive from them; nor are they by any means as unnatural or even as dangerous as people make out; for in this century man does not, as he is accused of doing, demand new and unprecedented institutions, he only wishes to have a better foundation for the existing ones so that they rest on nothing other than morality and necessity, which are the same thing, and thus exchange the external fixed point whereby they have hitherto been partially secured for an inner centre of gravity from which they can be derived entirely. This I am convinced is the world-historical process which is under way these days. Philosophy, disintegrating and dissolving, has been preparing for it from Kant and really from Spinoza onwards, and the art of drama, assuming that it has any function at all [...] is meant to help bring it to a conclusion; it is meant [...] to show in great and powerful images how the elements, not so far fully absorbed and integrated into a living organism but only partly ossified into a phantom body and now released by the latest great movement of history, are to produce, mingling their currents and fighting one another, the new form of humanity in which everything will once again find its place, in which woman will once again confront man, man [will confront] society and society [will confront] the idea. This of course carries with it the drawback that dramatic art will have to engage with controversial, indeed highly controversial matters, since the universal collapse can only be made manifest in terms of individual breakdowns; an earthquake cannot be represented other than by the collapse of churches and houses and the unstoppable inrush of the waters of the sea. [...] I say unto you who call yourselves dramatic authors, if you are content [merely] to put on the stage anecdotes (historical or other, it matters not which), or at best to dissect a character in his psychological mechanism, you are not one whit better, regardless of whether you choose to squeeze our tearducts or tickle our ribs, than our well known Thespian cousin who makes the puppets dance in his booth. Your art has no function except where there is a problem, but wherever such a one strikes you, wherever life in its fragmentation comes forward to meet you together with, in your minds (for both must coincide), the momentum of the idea in which it rediscovers its lost unity, then seize hold of it and ignore the mob of aesthetes who only wish to have good health demonstrated in the very disease. After all, you can only show the

---

[3] Goethe's early works, notably the play, *Götz von Berlichingen* (1773) and the novel, *Werther* (1774), were regarded as revolutionary literary innovations. The neoclassicism of many of his later works reflected the growing conservatism of the older Goethe.

transition to good health and are indeed unable to cure the fever without dealing with the fever, for this mob who wants to hold you accountable for the
paroxysms that you depict as if they were your own, should, if it were to be
consistent, also blame the judge who interrogates the felon about his crime, or
the priest who hears confession, for dabbling in filth. You are answerable for
nothing, nothing whatsoever, other than for the treatment which has to
demonstrate your subjective independence from the matter in hand and your
personal detachment from it, and for the end product; and even that product
need not culminate in a polemical point, it may present itself no less as the
starting point of a character than as the starting point of the whole play,
although to be sure if the latter is the case, the drama must formally attain a
higher degree of perfection. If you are forced to speak of things which are not
fully comprehensible to anyone without some inner experience, you cannot
help but protect yourself against being misinterpreted; so I explicitly add that
what one has to have in mind is not an allegorical, let alone a philosophical,
dressing-up of the idea but a dialectic planted right in the midst of life, and
that, if in a process in which, as in every creative act, all the elements entail and
imply one another with the same necessity, there can always be a question of
the before and after, the writer [...] will in any case be more conscious of the
characters than of the idea, or rather of the relationship of the characters to the
idea. But, I repeat, this is an altogether unacceptable way of looking at things
which, however, still seems to be widespread, since even judicious men [...]
will never stop taking the author to task about what they call his choice of subjects, thereby betraying the fact that they tend to regard creativity, the first
germinative stage of which lies deep below the level of consciousness and
sometimes goes back to the darkest recesses of childhood, as a kind of superior
manufacturing process, and that they regard a spiritual birth as an arbitrary
act such as they would never attribute to a physical birth, whose dependence
on nature is of course very much more self-evident. [...] The author must be
forgiven if he misses his aim, he has no choice in the matter, he has not even the
choice of whether or not he wants to produce a work at all, for whatever has
taken on a life of its own cannot be reabsorbed, it cannot be converted back
into blood but must come forth in free independence [...]

As I said, dramatic art is intended to help complete the world-historical
process which is taking place in our times and which aims not to overthrow the
existing institutions—political, religious, and moral—of the human race but
to give them a deeper foundation, thus actually securing them against revolution. In that sense, like all literature that seeks to be more than [mere] super-
fetation and arabesques, it ought to be in tune with the times, as is all genuine
literature in that and no other sense; and in that sense I have described my
plays as artistic offerings to the age in my preface to *Genevieve*,[4] knowing full
well that the individual life processes I have depicted and propose to depict are

---

[4] In the brief preface to his second tragedy, *Genevieve* (1841), Hebbel had stated that even plays

intimately connected with the general questions of principle discussed above. Although I was by no means displeased that reviewers have so far almost exclusively examined my characters and failed to consider the ideas they represent, in that I see this with some justification as the best proof of the true vitality of these characters, I would nevertheless wish that this [state of affairs] might end and some attention be paid to the second factor of my writings; obviously quite a different judgement concerning their plan and execution results from looking at them merely from the story point of view rather than assessing them according to the fundamental ideas treated, which make necessary a good many things that would be redundant for the former. [...]

Perhaps someone or other will say: these are all old, familiar, long-since-settled matters. Indeed they are. Actually I should be shocked if it were not so, since I am convinced we should not invent the eleventh commandment in aesthetics any more than in moral matters but obey the existing ten. Still, a man may yet claim some modest merit who once more wipes down the old tablets of the law with a sponge and erases the insolent chalked inscriptions with which various profane hands have bedaubed the underlying text. A highly suspect vocabulary has been built up. Poetry is not supposed to remain what it was and [still] is: the mirror of the century and the movement of humanity in general—it is supposed to turn into a mirror of the day, nay of the hour. The worst sufferer is drama, not because too many or the wrong things are demanded of it but because nothing whatever is demanded of it. It is merely meant to entertain, it is to present a thrilling story, sustained at a pinch for the sake of excitement by psychologically fascinating characters, but it must not on any account do any more [than that]. Whatever is not entertaining in Shakespeare (they have the audacity to invoke him) is damnable, in fact it has, looked at more closely, only been dreamt up by the enthusiasm of his interpreters, he never thought of it himself, he was a good lad who was happy when he drummed up a larger public than usual with his wild yarns [...] A famous, recently deceased actor added, according to his friends' testimony, the practical rider to the new gospel, claiming in all seriousness that the 'poet' should only supply the 'artist' with a scenario which the latter would flesh out by improvisation. This rigorous logic is praiseworthy as is all logic because you can see where the entertainment principle leads you, but the fact of the matter is as follows. A poem which claims to be a drama must be capable of being represented, but only because whatever the artist [i.e. that actor] cannot represent has not been represented by the author in the first place but has remained an embryo and a phantom idea. Now what can be represented is only action, not thought and emotion; there is no place for thought and emotion *per se* in drama but only to the extent that they translate directly into action. At the same time, actions are not actions, at least not dramatic ones, if they manifest

dealing with mythical themes must be relevant to contemporary concerns and express the spirit of the age in which they were written.

themselves in baldly uncontextualized form like natural phenomena, without being prepared for by thoughts and accompanied by emotions; otherwise a silently drawn sword would be the summit of all action. Nor should one overlook the fact that the gap between acting and suffering is by no means as wide as language makes it, for all action dissolves into suffering in the face of fate, i.e. the universal will, and it is precisely this that is shown in tragedy; but all suffering in the individual is action turned in upon itself; just as our interest dwells with equal satisfaction on the individual when in suffering he becomes mindful of himself, of what is eternal and imperishable in the crushed individual, thus making himself whole again, which happens in suffering, and when he affronts what is eternal and imperishable, within his individual limitations, and in return [...] receives a strict chastisement, then both the one and the other are equally capable of being represented [...] But this capacity for being represented is not to be measured by [criteria of] propriety or intellectual fashion which are in constant flux, and if it is to borrow its criteria from the real theatre it has to ask for the theatre of all ages and for not this or that special theatre [...] It becomes self-evident upon further reflection that the playwright must not [...] at the same time give a picture of the world and yet eliminate the contradictory elements out of all those that make up the world, but that he satisfies all legitimate claims when he assigns the right place to each of these elements and allows the subordinate ones, which after all exist in the organism like a network of nerves and arteries, to become apparent so that they may be subsumed in the higher ones. I cannot believe that the value and the significance of a drama depend on the question, governed by a myriad of fortuitous factors, of whether or not it gets to be staged, that is to say on its external fate, for if the theatre, which is to be very greatly valued as the intermediary organ between poetry and the public, possessed such miraculous powers, it should first of all keep alive whatever is committed to it body and soul. But where are they, the hundreds and thousands of 'stageworthy' plays that have 'numerous revivals with well merited applause'? Leaving the machine-made goods aside, do Shakespeare and Calderón, who after all were supposed to be not only great dramatic poets but also real working playwrights, get performed, has not the theatre dropped them long since, proving thereby that it cherishes excellence as little as it does triviality;[5] and does this not prove conclusively that it is not, contrary to the opinion of those who only half know what is important, the actual representation, which ceases sooner or later without setting any bounds to the author's effectiveness, that determines the value and significance of a drama but rather its capacity for being represented which I deduce from its form as the ineluctably necessary one [...]? [...] This shows that [...] the genuine process of representation, entirely by itself

---

[5] Whatever may have been true at the time Hebbel wrote the Preface to *Mary Magdalene*, there was to be no lack of Shakespearian productions in the German theatre of the second half of the nineteenth, nor indeed during the twentieth, century.

and without any side glances at actual performance, incarnates matters of the spirit, condenses into characters the dualistic ideational factors from the clash of which springs the spark that ignites the entire work of art, lets the inner event arrange itself according to all its developmental phases into an external story, an anecdote, and makes this anecdote [...] result in a climax, that is to say shaping it in an interesting and arresting manner and thus entertaining and satisfying that part of the reading or theatre-going public that has no inkling of the veritable action.

But I must not skirt the question of whether philosophy, far advanced as it is, cannot solve the great problem of the age by itself, and whether the point of view of art should not be regarded as superseded or at any rate something that should be superseded?[6] If art were only what most people see in it, a [...] continuation of the phenomenal world, a comedy of figures transferred as it were from the outer into the inner theatre, in which the disguised idea plays hide-and-seek with itself time and again, one would certainly have to reply in the affirmative [...] But art is not only infinitely more, it is something altogether different, it is philosophy realized, just as the world is the idea realized [...] A creative and original philosophy [...] has always known that it must not suppress a proof which the bare idea it has brought forth could not do without, and hence has never seen in art a mere point of view but its own goal and summit; however, it is characteristic of formal [philosophy] [...] that even when it has or should have taken on a living shape it cannot cease disintegrating [...] Such a philosophy fails to recognize itself in the higher code of art, it even considers it suspicious to find the code of nature unified which it has gone to so much effort and trouble to tear apart, and it does not know what to make of that; fortunately it encounters some particular passages in the work of art [...] which have been composed in the only style of expressing thought and reflection with which it is familiar, either because the spirit of the whole has not found its form there or because it was a matter of a link that did not require any form; these it takes to be the main thing, the result of the representation around which cluster the other flourishes of figures and characters as do the border decorations—Mercury and his kin–around the actual sum in a merchant's bill of exchange, and it eagerly and honestly threads together these pearls called maxims and aphorisms on a string [...] and evaluates them; but since the result is bound to turn out as miserable as if one were to assess philosophy according to its richness of life and form, it pronounces its final judgement with full conviction that art is a childish frivolity [...].

But if drama is to help solve no less a task than [the problem of] world history, if it is to mediate between the idea and the condition of the world and humanity, does it not follow that it must entirely devote itself to history, that is

---

[6] The idea that philosophy (or science) might have taken the place of art and thus rendered the latter obsolete was a commonplace view that had already been put forward in the eighteenth century. Cf. also Strindberg's 'Preface to *Miss Julie*', p. 90.

must be historical? I have elsewhere [...] made the point that drama is of its very nature and without any special tendency [...] historical and that art is the highest [kind of] historiography.[7] No one who knows how to look forwards or backwards will challenge this statement, for he will remember that we retain an image only of those nations of antiquity who have achieved artistic expression, who have documented their existence and their doings in imperishable form [...]. But he will also recognize the fact that the increasingly rigorous historical process of elimination which separates [...] the significant from the insignificant, that which is dead for us, however significant in itself, from that which is still operative in the historical process, is going to grow [...] so that later on he will retain only the general features of the nations and then finally only the most general developmental epochs of humanity brought about by the phases of religion and philosophy [...] But since the great achievements of art are much more uncommon than the rest [...] it follows that art [...] can transmit to posterity the general [...] contents of history in the guise of specific periods [...] and thus offer it if not the comprehensive and meaningless register of the gardeners who planted and fertilized the tree, at any rate the fruit with its flesh and its core, which is all that matters, and besides the aroma of the atmosphere in which it ripened. [...]

So much by way of general comment. Now for a word with reference to the play I am here submitting to the public. [...] It is a bourgeois tragedy. Bourgeois tragedy has fallen out of favour in Germany, mainly on account of two defects.[8] More than anything because it was built up not out of its inner elements peculiar to itself, out of the harsh isolation in which some individuals totally incapable of any dialectics were facing each other within an extremely narrow circle and out of the dreadful limitation of life in one-sidedness which springs from this, but because it was cobbled together out of all sorts of external matters, e.g. lack of money coupled with plentiful hunger, but above all out of the clash of the third estate with the second in matters of love. Now that undeniably produces much that is sad but nothing tragic, for the tragic must from the start appear as something based on necessity, as something like death which is inherent in life itself and in no way to be circumvented; as soon as one can console oneself with: if he (had only had thirty dollars, feeble sentimentality perhaps adding: if only he'd come to my place, I live at No. 32, you know), or with: if she (had only been a middle-class girl, etc.) the impression which should have been moving becomes trivial, and the effect, if it does not evaporate altogether, consists of the spectators paying their poor-rate with greater readiness than usual or treating their daughters more indulgently the following day, for which the guardians of the poor and the daughters respectively

---

[7] In *My Word about Drama* (1843), a polemic directed against the Danish critic and playwright J. L. Heiberg.

[8] What Hebbel had in mind was the sort of sentimental family drama written by the prolific actor-playwright August Wilhelm Iffland (1759–1814).

should be thankful—but not the art of drama. And then, too, [bourgeois tragedy is out of favour] because our playwrights, once they condescended to the people—having remembered that all that was required to have a destiny, perhaps an immense destiny, was to be a human being—always first ennobled the common folk, whom they dealt with in their idle moments, by means of fine speeches paid to them out of their own treasury, or else thought it necessary to depress them below their actual worldly status by making them stubbornly bone-headed, so that their characters emerged either as princes and princesses under a spell whom the magician had maliciously transformed not even into dragons and lions and other notabilities of the animal kingdom but into lowly bakery servant-girls and journeymen tailors, or else into animated blocks who amazed us if they were able to say as much as Yea or Nay. Now the latter was if anything worse, it added absurdity and ridiculousness to triviality, and in a highly conspicuous manner at that, since everybody knows that ordinary citizens and peasants do not pick their figures of speech, which they use every bit as well as the heroes of drawing-rooms and promenades, from the starry heavens nor do they fish them from out of the ocean, but that the artisan gathers them from out of his workshop, the ploughman from behind his plough; and a good many people may have discovered that these simple folk, even if they do not know how to converse, know quite well how to speak vividly and to put together and illustrate their ideas. These two defects make the prejudice against bourgeois tragedy understandable but they cannot justify it, because they are obviously the fault not of the genre [itself] but only of the hacks who have made a botch of it. It is by itself a matter of indifference whether the hand of the clock is made of gold or of brass, and it does not matter whether an action significant in itself, i.e. symbolical, takes place in a lower or a higher social sphere. But of course, while in heroic tragedy the gravity of the subject matter, the weight of the reflections directly arising out of it [may] reconcile us up to a point for the formal defects of the tragic form, in bourgeois tragedy everything depends on whether the circle of the tragic form has been closed, i.e. whether the point has been reached in which on the one hand we are no longer to be troubled by any miserable sympathy with the individual fate of a person arbitrarily picked by the author, but the latter has been resolved into a broadly human fate, even though it would manifest itself that drastically only in extreme cases, and where on the other hand [...] we are confronted, [...] together with the outcome [...] of the struggle, with the necessity of reaching it in this and no other way. [...]

Paris, 4 March 1844

# Naturalism (1881)

## Émile Zola

Émile Zola (1840–1902), now primarily remembered as a great novelist, also left his mark on the theatre—principally as the passionate advocate of the naturalist drama which was in process of being born in the latter part of the nineteenth century, in the face of much opposition. When he worked as a theatre critic for *L'Avenir national* (1873), *Le Bien public* (1876–8), *Le Voltaire* (1878–80), and *Le Figaro* (1880–1 and again 1895–6), he went beyond merely reviewing current productions of the Parisian stage and engaged in widely noticed theoretical arguments that attacked the old style of drama and called for something new. These polemics were sufficiently important for him to republish articles from *Le Bien public* and *Le Voltaire* in two volumes: *Le Naturalisme au théâtre* (Naturalism in the Theatre) and *Nos Auteurs dramatiques* (Our Playwrights, both 1881). The essay quoted below, which is taken from *Le Naturalisme au théâtre*, examines the subject-matter and style of classical, romantic, and naturalist theatre in turn and comes out in favour of the last-named as being the most appropriate form for the modern age. Other essays in the same volume deal with such extra-literary theatrical matters as settings, costumes, and acting style—all of them related to the question of how to bring the stage closer to real life. Zola's own plays made no great contribution towards this end, except for his own dramatization of his novel of lust and murder, *Thérèse Raquin* (1873), which is still revived occasionally; but the most successful stage adaptation of another of his novels, *L'Assommoir*, was undertaken in 1879 not by him but by Busnach and Gastineau. It is then as a theorist rather than as theatrical practitioner that he made his main contribution to drama. His most direct impact on the theatre of his day was to inspire André Antoine (1858–1943) to found the Théâtre Libre in Paris in 1887 as a platform for innovative playwrights, French as well as foreign.

A translation of Zola's Preface to *Thérèse Raquin* appeared in Barrett H. Clark (ed.), *European Theories of the Drama* (rev. edn., 1947), 400–2; a translation of his essay,

From Émile Zola, *Le Naturalisme au théâtre* (Paris: G. Charpentier, 1881), 3–25. Translated from the French by George Brandt.

'Naturalism on the Stage', taken from *Le Roman expérimental* (1880), can be found in Toby Cole (ed.), *Playwrights on Playwriting* (1961), 5–14.

**I**

Every winter, as the theatre season opens, I am haunted by the same thoughts. A hope springs up within me and I tell myself that perhaps by the time the first hot days of summer have emptied the playhouses, a playwright of genius may have appeared. Our theatre badly needs a new man to make a clean sweep of our blighted stage and to revive an art which mere hacks have brought down to the simple needs of the masses. Yes, what is wanted is a mighty talent with an imagination sufficiently innovative to overturn accepted conventions and to establish at last a human drama of truth instead of the ridiculous lies on offer today. [...]

Unfortunately this dream which I cherish every October has not yet come true and perhaps will not come true in the near future. Wait as I will, I am let down time and again. So is this just a poet's idle fancy? [...]

In order to grasp why a theatrical revolution is necessary, let us state our present position clearly. During the whole of our classical period, tragedy ruled supreme. Rigid and intolerant, it would not permit the slightest stirrings of freedom and it subjected the greatest minds to its inexorable laws. When an author tried to evade them, he was condemned as odd, cranky, and wayward; he was practically regarded as a dangerous fellow. However, even within this narrow formula, a genius would build his own monument in marble and bronze. The formula had been born in the revival of Greek and Latin literature, and the writers who had made it their own found it provided a sufficient pattern for [the creation of] great works. Only later, when imitators came along, a gaggle of increasingly lacklustre and feeble disciples, did the formula's shortcomings become apparent, and people noticed its absurdities and improbabilities, its dishonest uniformity, and its endless and insufferable declamation. Still, the authority of tragedy was such that it took all of two hundred years to go out of fashion. Step by step it had tried to adapt—unsuccessfully since the authoritarian principles on which it was based strictly forbade it, on pain of extinction, to make any concession to the new spirit. Only when it tried to accommodate itself was it overthrown, after a long and glorious reign.

Ever since the eighteenth century, romantic drama had been astir within tragedy. Sometimes the three unities were violated, scenery and extras were featured to a greater extent, violent crises were exhibited on stage, which tragedy had confined to speeches so as not to impair the majestic calm of psychological analysis. [...] A rebirth of drama under a new formula was becoming inevitable, and the romantic drama boisterously planted its flag in front of the prompter's box. Its hour had come, the ground had been well prepared, and the insurrection swarmed over a field ready for victory. Never was the word 'insurrection' more apt, since romantic drama fought tragedy at close quarters and, hating this now powerless queen, tried to smash everything that recalled her reign. Tragedy had eschewed action and observed a frigid majesty on her throne, acting by means of conversation and long speeches; romantic drama revelled in action, even action to excess, leaping around all over the stage, striking out left and right with never a rational or analytical thought, displaying the bloody horror of its catastrophes before the audience's eyes. Tragedy had chosen antiquity for its setting, never anything other than Greeks and Romans, and immobilized its action in a palace or the peristyle of a temple; romantic drama chose the Middle Ages, parading doughty knights and noble ladies, piling up strange scenery, hilltop castles that overlooked rivers, armouries packed with suits of armour, dripping underground dungeons, moonlight in ancient forests. And so the antagonism is found everywhere: romantic drama makes itself the armed foe of tragedy and fights it in total opposition to its formula.

It is necessary to note this furious hostility in the heyday of romantic drama, because there is a valuable clue here. No doubt the authors who led the movement spoke of putting authentic passions on the stage and called for a wider framework so as to show the whole of human life, with its conflicts and its contradictions; thus, we recall that romantic drama fought, above all, for the mixing of tears and laughter in the same play, arguing that joy and grief walk hand in hand in real life.[1] But truth and reality did not really matter much to these innovators, in fact it bothered them. They were intent on one thing only, and that was overturning the tragic formula which had held them back, smashing it noisily and routing it utterly. They did not want their medieval heroes to be any more real than the classical heroes of tragedy had been, but to make them passionate and sublime as the latter had been cold and correct. A simple war of costumes and rhetoric, nothing more, a mock battle in which peplums were torn up in favour of doublets and a lady would address her lover as 'My lion' intead of 'My lord'.[2] Both parties indulged equally in fantasy and moonshine, one as much as the other.

---

[1] The key manifesto of French romantic drama was the preface to the (unperformed) history play, *Cromwell* (1827), by Victor Hugo (1802–85). This outstanding figure in French nineteenth-century literature—poet and novelist as well as playwright—sided with Shakespearian rather than with neoclassicist drama in that he rejected the latter's strict adherence to the three unities of time, place, and action, and he called for a breaking down of genre boundaries, so that tragic and comic moments might occur in the same play; he championed the 'grotesque' as a potent literary device. He notably advocated a loosening up, both in terms of diction and prosody, of the over-regulated language of classical drama.

[2] In Victor Hugo's *Hernani*, Doña Sol addresses her lover, the eponymous hero, as 'my lion' (III. iv). The production of this play at the Comédie-Française in 1830 is generally regarded as the breakthrough of romantic drama in France.

Now I do not want to be unfair to the romantic movement. It was of the greatest, it was of decisive importance, it has made us what we are, i.e. free artists. It was, I repeat, a necessary revolution, a violent uprising which came along at the right time to sweep away the reign of a tragic drama which was in its second childhood. However, it would be absurd to make the evolution of drama stop at romantic drama. Especially today it is staggering to read certain prefaces, in which the movement of 1830 is represented as a glorious coming of human truth. Forty years later we can see clearly enough that the alleged truthfulness of the romantics is a continual, monstrous exaggeration of reality, fantasy pushed to extreme lengths. [...]

Without believing there is any progress in art, we can say that art is in a state of continual flux within civilizations, and that the phases of the human spirit are reflected in it. Genius manifests itself under any formula, even the most primitive and naive; but unquestionably the formulas change and follow the spread of civilizations. [...] There is no progress in human creativity as such but there *is* a logical succession of formulas, of ways of thinking and self-expression. [...]

Seen in this light it is certain that, starting out from tragedy, romantic drama was a first step towards the naturalistic drama which is our goal. Romantic drama cleared the ground and proclaimed artistic freedom. Its love of action, its mixture of laughter and tears, its search for exact costumes and settings show the forward movement towards real life. [But] don't things always happen like that in any revolution against a hoary regime? People start by breaking the windows, they sing and they shout, they smash up the emblems of the last regime. [...] Tomorrow's truths are lost sight of in the heat of battle. Only when everything has calmed down and the fever has abated do you regret the window-smashing and become aware of the job botched, of laws hastily cobbled together which are no better than those you have revolted against. [...]

Today, then, tragedy and romantic drama are equally old and worn out. And it must be said that that hardly speaks well for romantic drama, because in the space of half a century it has fallen into the same state of decrepitude that it took tragedy two centuries to reach. It has now gone down in its turn, toppled by the same passion it manifested in its [own] struggle. There is nothing left. It is simply a matter of guessing what is to follow. It is obvious that on the open terrain conquered in 1830, nothing but the naturalist formula can flourish.

## II

It seems inconceivable that the movement of enquiry and analysis, which is *the* movement of the nineteenth century, should have overturned all the sciences and all the arts but should have passed by and as it were left isolated the art of drama. The natural sciences date back to the end of the last century; chemistry and physics are barely a hundred years old; history and criticism have been overhauled, virtually recreated after the Revolution; a whole world has sprung up, we have thrown ourselves into the study of documents and into experimental science, realizing that in order to create afresh we had to start from scratch, to investigate man and nature and to find out the facts. Hence the great naturalist school which has spread silently, unstoppably, often travelling in the dark but nevertheless advancing, to triumph finally in the light of day. Writing the history of this movement, with the misunderstandings that seemed to halt it, the multiple causes that have speeded it up or slowed it down would be like writing the history of the century itself. An irresistible current has carried our society towards the study of the truth. In the novel, Balzac was the bold and powerful innovator who replaced the poet's imagination with the scholar's observation. But in the theatre the development seems slower. No famous writer has as yet formulated the new idea clearly.

Of course I don't say there have not been some excellent works in which we find carefully delineated characters or bold truths brought to the stage. Thus, let me mention certain plays by M. Dumas *fils*, whose talent I do not greatly care for, or by M. Émile Augier, who is more humane and stronger.[3] But they are pigmies compared to Balzac; they have lacked the genius to devise the (new) formula. It must be said that one never knows just when a movement begins, because it generally goes back quite a way and merges with the preceding movement from which it has sprung. The naturalist current has been there all along if you like. It has not brought anything absolutely new. But it has finally arrived at a time favourable to it, it is winning and spreading because the spirit of mankind has attained the necessary level of maturity. I do not disparage the past, I merely take note of the present. The strength of naturalism is precisely that it is rooted in our national literature which is full of good sense. [...]

## III

It already seems a long time ago that drama ruled supreme, that it boasted five or six flourishing theatres in Paris. The demolition of the old playhouses of the boulevard du Temple[4] was the first disaster. Theatres have had to go further afield, the public has changed, other fashions have arisen. But the disrepute into which drama has fallen is mainly due to the exhaustion of the genre, the absurd and boring plays which have gradually followed the powerful plays of 1830. [...]

---

[3] Alexandre Dumas *fils* (1824–95) was the immensely successful author of a great many plays that tackled contemporary, especially sexual, issues in a highly moralizing fashion. His *Lady of the Camellias* (1852) is still remembered in its own right, in addition to having provided the story for Verdi's opera, *La Traviata* (1853).—Émile Augier (1820–89) also dealt with modern problems in his numerous plays which reflected a bourgeois, republican point of view. Both writers were elected to the French Academy.

[4] The boulevard du Temple (colloquially referred to as the boulevard du Crime) had been an entertainment district in Paris, with theatres as well as sideshows, since the Revolution. It was torn down in 1862 as part of Haussmann's urban development project.

It is true, morale has risen with the odd success. But the slide is unstoppable, drama is slipping towards extinction; and if it occasionally halts in its fall it is only to tumble down even further. Of course, there are loud complaints. Latter-day romantics above all are desperate; they assert at the top of their voices that outside the *drame*—i.e. *their* drama—there is no salvation for our dramatic literature. I believe on the contrary that a new formula must be found to transform the *drame*, just as the writers of the first half-century transformed tragedy. That's what it's all about. Today's battle has to be between romantic and naturalist drama.

By romantic drama I mean any play which disregards the truth of circumstances and persons, which puts on the stage puppets full of sound and fury and which, inspired by goodness knows what ideal, wallows in pastiche Shakespeare and Hugo. Every epoch has its own formula, and our formula certainly isn't that of 1830. We live in an age of method, of experimental science, what we need above all is exact analysis. It would be to sell short the freedom we have won if we let ourselves be shut up in a new tradition. The ground has been cleared, we can once again deal with man and nature.

Great efforts have been made lately to revive the history play. That's fine. No critic can have anything to say against the choice of historic subjects, whatever preference he may have for modern ones. But I do have my suspicions. The pattern followed by plays of that sort frightens me from the start. We have to see how history is treated, what great persons are represented there under the name of kings, great captains, or great artists, in short what dreadful mishmash our chronicles are turned into. As soon as authors of such products dabble in the past they think anything is permissible, far-fetched events, cardboard figures, outrageous nonsense, all garishly bedaubed with false local colour. [...]

What amazes me is the fact that our playwrights don't seem even remotely aware that the history play is inevitably the hardest genre, for which research, intellect, a profound talent for intuiting and resurrecting the past are vitally necessary. I appreciate this sort of drama when it is written by poets of genius or by men of immense learning, capable of placing an entire epoch, with its particular atmosphere, its manners and its civilization, before an audience; in that event it is a most interesting work of empathy or criticism.

But unfortunately I know what the advocates of the history play want to revive: it's simply the play of plumes and old iron, the play of big stage effects and big words, the dishonest play that shows off to the crowd, in a crude way that is offensive to people of taste. And so I suspect the worst. [...]

## IV

All the ancient formulas—classical and romantic alike—are based on the manipulation and the systematic mutilation of the truth. The assumption is that the truth is sordid; and so one must attempt to extract its poetic essence, on the pretext that nature has to be cleaned up and elevated. Hitherto the different schools of literature have fought over the question of how to dress up reality lest it look too disreputable in public. The classicists had adopted the peplum, the romantics made a revolution in order to have a coat of mail and a doublet instead. Actually this costume change hardly matters; it puts nature in fancy dress anyway. But today the naturalists have come along, declaring that truth has no need for dressing up; it can walk naked. That, I repeat, is what the quarrel is about.

Of course, all knowledgeable writers know perfectly well that tragedy and the romantic drama are dead. But the greater number are deeply troubled thinking about the still uncertain formula for tomorrow. Does truthfulness demand that they sacrifice grandeur, poetry, and the epic touch they aspire to put in their plays? Does naturalism require them to shrink their horizons and not to venture any more on soaring flights of the imagination?

Let me try to give an answer. But first we must make clear by what means idealists seek to raise their works to the level of poetry. For a start, they thrust their chosen subject back into the distant past. That provides them with costumes and makes the framework vague enough to give them scope for all sorts of lies. Then they generalize instead of individualizing; their characters are not living beings but [mere] feelings, arguments, manufactured and dreamt-up emotions. The false setting implies heroes of marble or cardboard. A person of flesh and blood, with his own distinct character, would stick out like a sore thumb in the setting of the days of yore. So you see the characters of tragedy or romantic drama stride about in stiff attitudes, one representing duty, the other patriotism, a third superstition, a fourth mother love; and so on and so on, all the abstract ideas in procession. No person is fully analysed, there is no character whose mind and body function as they would in real life.

[...] Now this is where the naturalists come in, stating quite bluntly that poetry is to be found in anything, no matter where, in fact more in the present and in reality than in the past and in generalization. Any fact at any given time has its [own] splendid poetic aspect. We encounter in reality far greater and mightier heroes than the puppets turned out by romance writers. No playwright has created any figures of the stature of Baron Hulot, old Grandet, César Birotteau, and the rest of Balzac's other characters, so fully characterized and so alive. Compared to these towering and truthful creations, Greek and Roman heroes shake like jellies and medieval heroes topple over like so many toy soldiers.

[...] Poetry flows freely through whatever exists, all the more so for being alive. I wish to give the word poetry its full meaning [...]—the celebration and broadcasting of all that is true.

So take the contemporary scene and try to present living people in it: and you will be writing beautiful plays. No doubt it will require an effort, you will have to discover the simple formula of naturalism in the hurly-burly of life. That is the problem—how to give significance to subjects and persons whom our eyes, used to the daily round, have come to regard as trivial. I know it is easier to set a puppet before the public, call this puppet Charlemagne and blow it up with high-flown speeches for the audience to think they have seen a colossus; that is easier than taking an everyday citizen, a grotesque, ill-dressed fellow and make of him, say, a Father Goriot,[5] a father who gives his all to his daughters, a figure so rich in truthfulness and love that nothing in any literature can equal him.

There is nothing easier than working to a pattern with familiar formulas; and the classical or romantic-style heroes cost so little effort that they are turned out by the dozen. Our literature is clogged up with these standard articles. But it becomes hard work indeed if you want a genuine, sharply analysed, three-dimensional and living hero. That no doubt is why writers used to fishing for great men in the troubled waters of history are scared of naturalism. They would have to examine mankind too deeply, learn about life, aim at real greatness, and portray it powerfully. [...]

Of course, I cannot predict what form this drama of tomorrow will take; we must give genius the freedom to speak. But I shall make so bold as to point out which road I reckon our theatre is going to follow.

First of all, it will give up the romantic drama. It would be a disaster to take over its exaggerations, its rhetoric, its theory of action for action's sake at the expense of character analysis. The finest examples of the kind are, it has been said, merely spectacular operas. I believe that we have to go back to tragedy—not, for heaven's sake, in order to borrow its rhetoric, its system of confidants, of declamation, of interminable narrations; but to come back to its simple plotlines and the unique study of its characters' psychology and physiology. In this sense the tragic pattern is an excellent thing: an action unfolding in its real consequences and arousing in the characters passions and feelings, the analysis of which would constitute the sole interest of the play—and that in a contemporary setting with the sort of people we are familiar with.

My constant concern, my anxious expectation is therefore to speculate and ask myself which one of us will have the strength to stand up and prove to be that genius. If naturalist drama is to exist, only a man of genius can give it birth. Corneille and Racine produced tragedy. Victor Hugo created the romantic drama. And where is the as yet unknown writer who will create the naturalist drama? There have been a good many attempts made in the past few years. But either because the public wasn't ready or because none of the beginners had sufficient staying power, none of these attempts has as yet had any positive outcome.

In battles of this kind, small-scale victories mean nothing; what is needed are triumphs that overwhelm the enemy and win the crowd over to one's cause. In the face of a truly strong man the spectators would give in. Then this man would proclaim the watchword we have been waiting for, the solution to

---

[5] The self-sacrificing 'hero' of Balzac's novel, *Le Père Goriot* (1834–5).

the problem, the formula of actual life on the stage combined with the necessary theatrical perspective. He would achieve what the newcomers have as yet failed to do: to be skilful or strong enough to command attention, to remain sufficiently truthful to prevent mere skill turning into a lie.

What an immense place in our literature such an innovator would occupy! [...] Of all the ambitious dreams a writer of our time might cherish, surely none is greater. The field of the novel is crowded; that of the stage is wide open. At this hour, imperishable glory awaits the man of genius in France who, taking up the work of Molière, would find the living comedy, the true drama of modern society in the fullness of reality.

# Author's Preface to Miss Julie (1888)

## August Strindberg

It is paradoxical that this, perhaps the best known, manifesto of naturalism should have been issued by a writer who was not himself by any means a lifelong, all-or-nothing naturalist. In fact, August Strindberg (1849–1912), author of some sixty plays—as well as a vast output of novels, short stories, autobiographical writings, poems, and essays—did not follow any one literary theory throughout his career. Many of his later dramas, such as *To Damascus*, Parts I–III (1898, 1904), *A Dream Play* (1901) (see pp. 158–9) and *The Ghost Sonata* (1907) were trail-blazing examples of subjective drama—the very reverse of naturalism. The theory formulated in defence of *Miss Julie* applies then only to a portion, albeit an important portion, of his work.

The Preface, which he wrote some twelve days after finishing the play (itself composed in the short space of a fortnight, in 1888) is an argument flung aggressively in the reader's face. It is riddled with contradictions: drama as an art form is both decried and defended; Miss Julie's death is a matter both for sorrow and rejoicing; Jean is described as worthy both of respect and contempt; etc., etc. But this contrariness, which makes an alert and critical reading of the Preface essential, reflects a quality in the play itself. *Miss Julie* refuses to supply any easy answers to the questions it raises. This fascinatingly ambivalent quality helps to account for the play's continuing life in the theatre of many countries to this day. (*Miss Julie* has also been filmed at least five times, and it has been turned into a ballet.)

The Swedish playwright was inspired by the foundation, in 1887, of the Théâtre Libre by André Antoine in Paris, itself a response to Zola's call for a naturalist stage (see Zola, pp. 80–8). *Miss Julie* was in fact performed at Antoine's theatre in 1893. But Strindberg went beyond Zola's largely physiological approach to character, insisting—in addition to the required ingredients of race, environment, and the historic moment—on a new psychological complexity in motivating his dramatis personae.

Translated from the Swedish by Michael Meyer, in *Strindberg: The Plays*, i (London: Secker & Warburg, 1964), 99–112.

Indeed, one of the most remarkable aspects of the Preface was the stress on *multiple* motivation of action, a departure from the stereotypical depictions of character which had been common in drama (and other forms of literature) for centuries.

The other crucial point of the Preface, and one that foreshadowed much subsequent playwriting, was the approach to dialogue. Strindberg championed the illogicality and seeming randomness of real conversation as against the 'symmetrical, mathematically constructed dialogue' regarded as normal stage speech until then. He indicated, with much insight, the revolutionary consequences of this new dramaturgy for the art of acting. His naturalistic conception of theatre logically extended to other non-literary aspects of staging as well, such as stage décor, lighting, and make-up, which the Preface glances at very perceptively.

The theatre, and indeed art in general, has long seemed to me a *Biblia pauperum*, a Bible in pictures for the benefit of the illiterate; with the dramatist as a lay preacher hawking contemporary ideas in a popular form, popular enough for the middle classes, who comprise the bulk of playgoers, to be able to grasp without too much effort what the minority is arguing about. The theatre has always been a primary school for the young, the semi-educated, and women, all of whom retain the humble faculty of being able to deceive themselves and let themselves be deceived—in other words, accept the illusion, and react to the suggestion, of the author. Nowadays the primitive process of intuition is giving way to reflection, investigation and analysis, and I feel that the theatre, like religion, is on the way to being discarded as a dying form which we lack the necessary conditions to enjoy. This hypothesis is evidenced by the theatrical crisis now dominating the whole of Europe; and, not least, by the fact that in those cultural strongholds which have nurtured the greatest thinkers of our age, namely England and Germany, the art of writing plays is, like most of the other fine arts, dead.

In other countries, men have tried to create a new drama by pouring new ideas into the old forms. But this has failed, partly because the new thinkers have not yet had time to become popularized and thus educate the public to understand the issues involved; partly because polemical differences have so inflamed emotions that dispassionate appreciation has become impossible—the cheers and whistles of the majority exercise a pressure that upsets one's instinctive reaction—and partly also because we have not succeeded in adapting the old forms to the new content, so that the new wine has burst the old bottles.

In my previous plays, I have not tried to do anything new—for that one can never do—but merely to modernize the form so as to meet the demands which I supposed that the new men and women of today would make of this art. To this end I chose, or let myself be caught up by, a theme which may be said to lie outside current party conflicts. For the problem of social ascent and decline, of higher or lower, better or worse, man or woman, is, has been and will be of permanent interest. When I took this theme from an actual incident which I heard about some years ago, and which at the time made a deep impression on me, it seemed to me a suitable matter for tragedy; for it is still tragic to see one on whom fortune has smiled go under, much more to see a line die out. But the time may come when we shall have become so developed and enlightened that we shall be able to observe with indifference the harsh, cynical and heartless drama that life presents—when we shall have discarded all those inferior and unreliable thought-mechanisms called feelings, which will become superfluous and harmful once our powers of judgment reach maturity. The fact that the heroine arouses our sympathy is merely due to our weakness in not being able to resist a feeling of fear lest the same fate should befall us. Even so, the hyper-sensitive spectator may possibly even feel that sympathy is not enough, while the politically-minded will doubtless demand positive measures to remedy the evil—some kind of 'programme'. But there is no such thing as absolute evil, since the death of a family is good luck for some other family that will be able to take its place, and social change constitutes one of the main pleasures of life, happiness being dependent on comparison. As for the political planner, who wishes to remedy the regrettable fact that the bird of prey eats the dove, and the louse eats the bird of prey, I would ask him: 'Why should this state of affairs be remedied?' Life is not so foolishly and mathematically arranged that the great always devour the small. It happens equally often that a bee kills a lion, or at any rate drives it mad.

If my tragedy makes a tragic impression on people, they have only themselves to blame. When we become as strong as the first French revolutionaries, we shall feel uninhibited pleasure and relief at seeing our national forests thinned out by the removal of decayed and superannuated trees which have too long obstructed the growth of others with an equal right to live and fertilize their age—a relief such as one feels when one sees an incurable invalid at last allowed to die.

Recently, people complained of my tragedy *The Father* that it was too tragic—as though tragedies ought to be jolly. One hears pretentious talk about 'the joy of life',[1] and theatrical managers feverishly commission farces, as though joy consisted in behaving idiotically and portraying the world as though it were peopled by lunatics with an insatiable passion for dancing.[2] I find 'the joy of life' in life's cruel and mighty conflicts; I delight in knowledge and discovery. And that is why I have chosen a case that is unusual but from which one can learn much—an exception, if you like, but an important exception which proves the rule—though I dare say it will offend those people who

---

[1]  'The joy of life' (*livsglaede*) is a key-phrase in Ibsen's *Ghosts*, published seven years before Strindberg wrote *Miss Julie*. [Translator's note.]

[2]  This clearly refers to the type of French farce known as vaudeville. See also Bergson, p. 29, n. 8.

only love what is commonplace. Another thing that will offend simple souls is the fact that the motivation of my play is not simple, and that life is seen from more than one viewpoint. An incident in real life (and this is quite a new discovery!) is usually the outcome of a whole series of deep-buried motives, but the spectator commonly settles for the one that he finds easiest to understand, or that he finds most flattering to his powers of judgment. Someone commits suicide. 'Bad business!', says the business man. 'Unrequited love!', say the ladies. 'Bodily illness!', says the invalid. 'Shattered hopes!', says the man who is a failure. But it may be that the motive lay quite elsewhere, or nowhere, and that the dead man concealed his true motive by suggesting another more likely to do credit to his memory!

I have suggested many possible motivations for Miss Julie's unhappy fate. The passionate character of her mother; the upbringing misguidedly inflicted on her by her father; her own character; and the suggestive effect of her fiancé upon her weak and degenerate brain. Also, more immediately, the festive atmosphere of Midsummer Night; her father's absence; her menstruation; her association with animals; the intoxicating effect of the dance; the midsummer twilight; the powerfully aphrodisiac influence of the flowers; and, finally, the chance that drove these two people together into a private room—plus of course the passion of the sexually inflamed man.

I have therefore not suggested that the motivation was purely physiological, nor that it was exclusively psychological. I have not attributed her fate solely to her heritage, nor thrown the entire blame on to her menstruation, or her lack of morals. I have not set out to preach morality. This, in the absence of a priest, I have left to a cook.

This multiplicity of motives is, I like to think, typical of our times. And if others have done this before me, then I congratulate myself on not being alone in my belief in these 'paradoxes' (the word always used to describe new discoveries).

As regards characterization, I have made my protagonists somewhat lacking in 'character', for the following reasons:

The word 'character' has, over the years, frequently changed its meaning. Originally it meant the dominant feature in a person's psyche, and was synonymous with temperament. Then it became the middle-class euphemism for an automaton; so that an individual who had stopped developing, or who had moulded himself to a fixed role in life—in other words, stopped growing— came to be called a 'character'—whereas the man who goes on developing, the skilful navigator of life's river, who does not sail with a fixed sheet but rides before the wind to luff again, was stigmatized as 'characterless' (in, of course, a derogatory sense) because he was so difficult to catch, classify and keep tabs on. The *bourgeois* conception of the immutability of the soul became transferred to the stage, which had always been *bourgeois*-dominated. A character, there, became a man fixed in a mould, who always appeared drunk, or comic, or pathetic, and to establish whom it was only necessary to equip with some physical defect, such as a club-foot, a wooden leg or a red nose, or else some oft-repeated phrase, such as, 'Absolutely first-rate!', 'Barkis is willin'!', etc. This over-simplified view of people we find even in the great Molière. Harpagon is a miser and nothing else, although he might have been both miserly and a first-class financier, a loving father, a good citizen. And, what is worse, his 'defect' is in fact extremely advantageous to both his daughter and his son-in-law, who are his heirs and are thus the last people who ought to blame him if they have to wait a little before gathering the fruits of his parsimony. So I do not believe in 'theatrical characters'. And these summary judgments that authors pronounce upon people—'He is stupid, he is brutal, he is jealous, he is mean', etc.—ought to be challenged by naturalists, who know how richly complex a human soul is, and who are aware that 'vice' has a reverse image not dissimilar to virtue.

Since they are modern characters, living in an age of transition more urgently hysterical at any rate than the age which preceded it, I have drawn my people as split and vacillating, a mixture of the old and the new. And I think it not improbable that modern ideas may, through the media of newspapers and conversation, have seeped down into the social stratum which exists below stairs.

My souls (or characters) are agglomerations of past and present cultures, scraps from books and newspapers, fragments of humanity, torn shreds of once-fine clothing that has become rags, in just the way that a human soul is patched together. I have also provided a little documentation of character development, by making the weaker repeat words stolen from the stronger, and permitting the characters to borrow 'ideas', or, as the modern phrase is, accept suggestions from each other.

Miss Julie is a modern character—not that the half-woman, the man-hater, has not existed in every age, but because, now that she has been discovered, she has stepped forward into the limelight and begun to make a noise. The half-woman is a type that pushes herself to the front, nowadays selling herself for power, honours, decorations and diplomas, as formerly she used to for money. They are synonymous with corruption. They are a poor species, for they do not last, but unfortunately they propagate their like by the wretchedness they cause; and degenerate men seem unconsciously to choose their mates from among them, so that their number is increased. They engender an indeterminate sex to whom life is a torture, but fortunately they go under, either because they cannot adapt themselves to reality, or because their repressed instinct breaks out uncontrollably, or because their hopes of attaining equality with men are shattered. It is a tragic type, providing the spectacle of a desperate battle against Nature—and tragic also as a romantic heritage now being dissipated by naturalism, which thinks that the only good lies in happiness— and happiness is something that only a strong and hardy species can achieve.

But Miss Julie is also a relic of the old warrior nobility, which is now disappearing in favour of the new neurotic or intellectual nobility; a victim of the discord which a mother's 'crime' implanted in a family; a victim of the errors of her age, of circumstances, and of her own flawed constitution, all of which add up to the equivalent of the old concept of Destiny or the Universal Law. The naturalist has abolished guilt with God, but he cannot expunge the consequences of her action—punishment, and prison, or the fear of it—for the simple reason that, whether or not he acquits her, the consequences remain. One's injured fellow-beings are not as indulgent as outsiders who have not suffered can afford to be. Even if her father felt impelled to postpone the moment of Nemesis, vengeance would be taken on his daughter, as it is here, by that innate or acquired sense of honour which the upper classes inherit—from where? From barbarism, from their Aryan forefathers, from mediaeval chivalry. It is very beautiful, but nowadays it is fatal to the continuation of the species. It is the nobleman's *hara-kiri*, the Japanese law of inner conscience which commands a man to slit his stomach when another has insulted him, and which survives in a modified form in that ancient privilege of the nobility, the duel. Thus, the servant, Jean, lives; but Miss Julie cannot live without honour. The slave has this advantage over the knight, that he lacks the latter's fatal preoccupation with honour; but in all of us Aryans there is a little knight or Don Quixote who makes us sympathize with the man who kills himself because he has committed a dishonourable act and thereby lost his honour. [...] The servant Jean is the type who founds a species; in him, we trace the process of differentiation. He was the son of a poor peasant, and has now educated himself to the point where he is a potential gentleman. He has proved a quick student, possesses finely developed senses (taste, smell, sight), and an eye for beauty. He has already risen in the world, and is strong enough not to worry about using other people's shoulders to climb on. He has already reacted against his fellow servants, whom he despises as representing the world which he has left behind him; he fears them and shrinks from them because they know his secrets, sniff out his intentions, envy his rise and hopefully await his fall. Hence his dual, uncrystallized character, wavering between sympathy for the upper class and hatred of those who constitute it. He is, as he himself says, an aristocrat; he has learned the secrets of good society, is polished, but coarse underneath; he knows how to wear a tail-coat, but can offer us no guarantee that his body is clean beneath it.

He respects Miss Julie, but is afraid of Christine, because she knows his dangerous secrets; and he is sufficiently callous not to allow the events of the night to interfere with his future plans. With the brutality of a slave and the indifference of a tyrant he can look at blood without fainting and shake off misfortune [...]

I do not think that any 'love relationship' in the higher sense can exist between two spirits of such unequal quality, and I have therefore made Miss Julie imagine herself to be in love so as to excuse her action and escape her feeling of guilt; and I make Jean fancy that he might be able to fall in love with her, provided he could improve his social standing [...]

What of Christine? She is a female slave, utterly conventional, bound to her stove and stuffed full of religion and morality, which serve her as both blinkers and scapegoats. She goes to church in order to be able to shift the guilt of her domestic pilferings on to Jesus, and get herself recharged with innocence. She is a supporting character, and I have therefore deliberately portrayed her as I did the priest and the doctor in *The Father*; I wanted them to appear everyday human beings, as provincial priests and doctors usually are. And if these supporting characters seem somewhat abstract, that is because ordinary people are, to a certain degree, abstract in the performance of their daily work— conventional, and only showing one side of themselves—and as long as the spectator feels no need to see their other sides, my abstract portrayal of them will serve well enough.

Finally, the dialogue. Here I have somewhat broken with tradition by not making my characters catechists who sit asking stupid questions in order to evoke some witty retort. I have avoided the symmetrical, mathematically constructed dialogue of the type favoured in France, and have allowed their minds to work irregularly, as people's do in real life, when, in conversation, no subject is fully exhausted, but one mind discovers in another a cog which it has a chance to engage. Consequently, the dialogue, too, wanders, providing itself in the opening scenes with matter which is later taken up, worked upon, repeated, expanded and added to, like the theme in a musical composition.

The plot is, I fancy, passable enough, and since it really only concerns two persons I have confined myself to them, introducing but one minor character, a cook, and making the unhappy spirit of the father hover over and behind the whole of the action. I have done this because I believe that what most interests people today is the psychological process. Our prying minds are not content merely with seeing something happen—they must know why it happens. We want to see the wires, watch the machinery, examine the box with the false bottom, finger the magic ring to find the join, look at the cards to see how they are marked. [...]

On the question of technique, I have, by way of experiment, eliminated all intervals. I have done this because I believe that our declining capacity for illusion is possibly affected by intervals, which give spectators time to reflect and thereby withdraw from the suggestive influence of the author-hypnotist. My play will probably run for one and a half hours, and if people can listen to a lecture, a sermon or a parliamentary debate for that length of time, I think they should be able to endure a play for ninety minutes. [...] This form is by no means new, though it appears at present to be my monopoly, and perhaps, thanks to the changing laws of taste, it may prove appropriate to the spirit of our time. My ultimate hope would be to educate an audience to the point where they will be able to sit through a full evening in the theatre without an interval. But one would have to examine the matter first. Meanwhile, in order to provide short periods of rest for the audience and the actors, without allowing the former to escape from my world of illusion, I have used three art-forms all of which properly belong to the drama—namely, the monologue, mime, and ballet. These were originally a part of ancient tragedy, the monody having developed into the monologue and the Greek chorus into ballet.

The monologue is nowadays abominated by our realists as being contrary to reality, but if I motivate it I make it realistic, and can thus use it to advantage. It is after all realistic that a speaker should walk up and down alone in his room reading his speech aloud, that an actor should rehearse his part aloud, a servant-girl talk to her cat, a mother prattle to her child, an old maid jabber at her parrot, a sleeper talk in his sleep. And, to give the actor the chance for once to create for himself and get off the author's leash, it is better that monologues should be implied rather than specified. For, since it matters little what one says in one's sleep, or to one's parrot or cat (for it does not influence the action), so a talented actor, attuned to the atmosphere and situation, may be able to improvise better than the author, who cannot calculate in advance how much needs to be said, or for how long the audience will accept the illusion.

As is known, the Italian theatre has in certain instances returned to improvisation, and thereby created actors who themselves create, on the author's blueprint. This may well be a step forward or even a new species of art, of which we shall be able to say that it is an art that engenders art.

Where a monologue would seem unrealistic, I have resorted to mime, which leaves the player even more freedon to create, and so gain independent recognition. But in order not to make too great a demand upon the audience, I have allowed music, well motivated by the midsummer dance, to exercise its illusory power during the dumb show. [...]

The ballet which I have introduced must not be smudged into a so-called 'crowd scene', because crowd scenes are always badly acted, and a mob of buffoons would seize the chance to be clever and so destroy the illusion. [...] So there must be no chattering or clowning in what is, after all, a serious piece of action, no coarse sniggering in a situation which drives the nails into the coffin of a noble house.

As regards the décor, I have borrowed from the impressionist painters asymmetry and suggestion (i.e., the part rather than the whole), believing that I have thereby helped to further my illusion. The fact that one does not see the whole room and all the furniture leaves room for surmise—in other words, the audience's imagination is set in motion and completes its own picture. I have also profited by eliminating those tiresome exits through doors; for stage doors are made of canvas and flap at the slightest touch; they will not even allow an angry father to express his fury by stamping out after a bad dinner and slamming the door 'so that the whole house shakes'. (In the theatre, the door simply waves.) I have likewise confined myself to a single set, both to enable the characters to accustom themselves to their milieu, and to get away from the tradition of scenic luxury. But when one has only one set, one is entitled to demand that it be realistic—though nothing is more difficult than to make a room which looks like a room, however skilful the artist may be at creating fire-spouting volcanoes and waterfalls. Even if the walls have to be of canvas, it is surely time to stop painting them with shelves and kitchen utensils. We have so many other stage conventions in which we are expected to believe that we may as well avoid overstraining our imagination by asking it to believe in painted saucepans.

I have placed the rear wall and the table at an angle so that the actors shall be able to face each other and be seen in demi-profile when they sit opposite each other at the table. [...]

Another not perhaps unnecessary innovation would be the removal of the footlights. This illumination from below is said to serve the purpose of making the actors fatter in the face; but I would like to ask: 'Why should all actors be fat in the face?' Does not this bottom-lighting annihilate all subtle expressions in the lower half of the face, particularly around the mouth? Does it not falsify the shape of the nose, and throw shadows up over the eyes? Even if this were not so, one thing is certain: that pain is caused to the actors' eyes, so that any realistic expression is lost. For the footlights strike the retina on parts of it which are normally protected (except among sailors, who see the sun reflected from the water), so that one seldom sees any attempt at ocular expression other than fierce glares either to the side or up towards the gallery, when the whites of the eyes become visible. Perhaps this is also the cause of that tiresome habit, especially among actresses, of fluttering eyelashes. And when anyone on the stage wishes to speak with his eyes, he has no alternative but to look straight at the audience, thereby entering into direct contact with them outside the framework of the play—a bad habit which, rightly or wrongly, is known as 'greeting one's friends'.

Would not side-lights of sufficient power (with reflectors, or some such device) endow the actor with this new resource, enabling him to reinforce his mime with his principal weapon of expression, the movement of his eyes?

I have few illusions of being able to persuade the actor to play *to* the audience and not with them, though this would be desirable. I do not dream that I shall ever see the full back of an actor throughout the whole of an important scene, but I do fervently wish that vital scenes should not be played opposite the prompter's box as though they were duets milking applause. I would have them played at whatever spot the situation might demand. So no revolutions, but simply small modifications; for to turn the stage into a room with the fourth wall missing, so that some of the furniture would have its back to the audience, would, I suppose, at this juncture, simply serve as a distraction.

A word about make-up; which I dare not hope will be listened to by the ladies, who prefer beauty to truth. But the actor might well ponder whether it is to his advantage to paint an abstract character upon his face which will remain sitting there like a mask. Imagine a gentleman dipping his finger into soot and drawing a line of bad temper between his eyes, and suppose that, wearing this permanently fierce expression, he were called upon to deliver a line smiling? How dreadful would be the result! And how is this false forehead, smooth as a billiard ball, to wrinkle when the old man gets really angry?

In a modern psychological drama, where the subtler reactions should be mirrored in the face rather than in gesture or sound, it would surely be best to experiment with strong side-lights on a small stage and with the actor wearing no make-up, or at best a minimum.

If we could dispense with the visible orchestra with their distracting lamp-shades and faces turned towards the audience; if we could have the stalls raised so that the spectator's sightline would be above the actors' knees; if we could get rid of the side-boxes (my particular *bête noire*), with their tittering diners and ladies nibbling at cold collations, and have complete darkness in the auditorium during the performance; and, first and foremost, a *small* stage and a *small* auditorium—then perhaps a new drama might emerge, and the theatre might once again become a place for educated people. While we await such a theatre, one must write to create a stock of plays in readiness for the repertoire that will, some day, be needed.

I have made an attempt! If it has failed, there will, I hope, be time enough to make another!

# Against the Well-Made Play (1911)

## George Bernard Shaw

Among the numerous subjects that George Bernard Shaw (1856–1950) dealt with in the vast range of his writings which cover more than six decades, questions of drama and theatrical presentation as such occupy a *relatively* modest place. Even in the prefaces, independent literary efforts in their own right which he appended to many of his plays, Shaw expounded his views on such diverse matters of extra-dramatic interest as marital problems, Irish politics, medical ethics, phonetics, the pitfalls of democracy, Creative Evolution, and many other topics of current or more long-term concern; but more specifically theatrical matters—such as the Lord Chamberlain's censorship (which he opposed) or the current repertoire of the English theatre (much of which he deplored)—were infrequently the centre of interest; or if they did occur, did so, as often as not, as part of wider speculations. Shaw's most substantial critical works were *The Quintessence of Ibsenism* (1st edn., 1891—based on a course of lectures delivered to the Fabian Society the previous year) and *The Perfect Wagnerite* (1st edn., 1898—a detailed commentary on Wagner's *Ring* tetralogy): in both treatises he stressed those aspects most congenial to his own philosophical outlook and dramatic aims. When he worked as a theatre critic for the *Saturday Review* (1895–8), he presented, as he put it, 'not a series of judgments aiming at impartiality, but a siege laid to the theatre of the XIXth century by an author who had to cut his own way into it at the point of the pen.' To him, then and later, the task of theatre was to be 'a factory of thought, a prompter of conscience, an elucidator of social conduct, an armory against despair and dullness, and a Temple of the Ascent of Man'. The following excerpt from his preface to three plays by Eugène Brieux (1858–1932), the French author of socially committed plays, illustrates this emphasis on theatre being, at least potentially, much more than a mere place of entertainment. Shaw gives an amusingly dismissive account of the 'well-made play', then still regarded as the acid test of the playwright's craft.

From G. B. Shaw, Preface to *Three Plays by Brieux* (London: A. C. Fifield, 1911), pp. xv–xxvii.

## Zolaism as a Superstition

[…] Zola and Ibsen could not, of course be confined to mere reaction against taboo. Ibsen was to the last fascinating and full of a strange moving beauty; and Zola often broke into sentimental romance. But neither Ibsen nor Zola, after they once took in hand the work of unmasking the idols of the bourgeoisie, ever again wrote a happy or pleasant play or novel. Ibsen's suicides and catastrophes at last produced the cry of 'People don't do such things,' which he ridiculed through Judge Brack in Hedda Gabler.[1] This was easy enough: Brack was so far wrong that people do do such things occasionally. But on the whole Brack was right. The tragedy of Hedda in real life is not that she commits suicide but that she continues to live. If such acts of violent rebellion as those of Hedda and Nora and Rebecca[2] and the rest were the inevitable or even the probable consequences of their unfitness to be wives and mothers, or of their contracting repugnant marriages to avoid being left on the shelf, social reform would be very rapid; and we should hear less nonsense as to women like Nora and Hedda being mere figments of Ibsen's imagination. Our real difficulty is the almost boundless docility and submission to social convention which is characteristic of the human race. What baulks the social reformer everywhere is that the victims of social evils do not complain, and even strongly resent being treated as victims. The more a dog suffers from being chained the more dangerous it is to release him: he bites savagely at the hand that dares touch his collar. […] Nothing that is admittedly and unmistakeably horrible matters very much, because it frightens people into seeking a remedy: the serious horrors are those which seem entirely respectable and normal to respectable and normal men. Now the formula of tragedy had come down to the nineteenth century from days in which this was not recognized, and when life was so thoroughly accepted as a divine institution that in order to make it seem tragic, something dreadful had to happen and somebody had to die. But the tragedy of modern life is that nothing happens, and that the resultant dulness does not kill. Maupassant's Une Vie[3] is infinitely more tragic than the death of Juliet.

In Ibsen's works we find the old traditions and the new conditions struggling in the same play, like a gudgeon half swallowed by a pike. Almost all the sorrow and the weariness which makes his plays so poignant are the sorrow and the weariness of the mean dull life in which nothing happens; but none the less he provides a final catastrophe of the approved fifth-act-blank-verse type. Hedwig and Hedda shoot themselves: Rosmer and Rebecca throw themselves into the mill-race: Solness and Rubeck are dashed to pieces; Borkman

---

[1] This, the last line in Ibsen's play, is spoken immediately after Hedda's death by the corrupt and calculating Judge Brack, who had hoped to make her his mistress (Act IV).

[2] The eponymous heroine of *Hedda Gabler* (1891) shoots herself; Nora Helmer walks out on her marriage in *A Doll's House* (1879); and Rebecca West drowns herself, together with John Rosmer, at the end of *Rosmerholm* (1886).

[3] *Une vie* (1883), Guy de Maupassant's first large-scale novel, described an ordinary woman's life of constant disillusionment.

dies of acute stage tragedy without discoverable lesions.[4] I will not [...] say [...] that these catastrophes are forced, because a fortunate performance often makes them seem inevitable; but I do submit that the omission of them would leave the play sadder and more convincing.

## The Passing of the Tragic Catastrophe and the Happy Ending

Not only is the tradition of the catastrophe unsuitable to modern studies of life: the tradition of an ending, happy or the reverse, is equally unworkable. The moment the dramatist gives up accidents and catastrophes, and takes 'slices of life' as his material, he finds himself committed to plays that have no endings. The curtain no longer comes down on a hero slain or married: it comes down when the audience has seen enough of the life presented to it to draw the moral, and must either leave the theatre or miss its last train.

The man who faced France with a drama fulfilling all these conditions was Brieux. He was as scientific, as conscientious, as unflinching as Zola without being in the least morbid. He was no more dependent on horrors than Molière, and as sane in his temper. He threw over the traditional forced catastrophe uncompromisingly. You do not go away from a Brieux play with the feeling that the affair is finished or the problem solved for you by the dramatist. Still less do you go away in 'that happy, easy, ironically indulgent frame of mind that is the true test of comedy', as Mr. Walkley[5] put it in The Times of the 1st October 1909. You come away with a very disquieting sense that you are involved in the affair, and must find the way out of it for yourself and everybody else if civilization is to be tolerable to your sense of honour. [...]

## Brieux and the Boulevard

[...] Up to quite recent times it was impossible for an Englishman to mention Brieux to a Parisian as the only French playwright who really counted in Europe without being met with astonished assurances that Brieux is not a playwright at all; that his plays are not plays; that he is not (in Sarcey's[6] sense of the phrase) 'du théâtre'; that he is a mere pamphleteer without even literary style. And when you expressed your natural gratification at learning that the

---

[4] Hedwig Ekdal is the 14-year-old girl in The Wild Duck (1885) who kills herself after being rejected by her supposed father; Solness, the protagonist of The Master Builder (1892), falls to his death from a tower; the sculptor Rubeck perishes in the mountains at the end of When We Dead Awaken (1899); the eponymous hero of John Gabriel Borkman (1896) dies of exposure to the wintry cold out of doors, after having been confined to his room for eight years.

[5] The well-known drama critic Alfred Bingham Walkley (1855–1926) was more concerned with the literary than the performance aspects of the plays he reviewed. He wrote for The Times from 1900 to 1926. Shaw prefaced his Man and Superman (1905) with an Epistle Dedicatory to Walkley.

[6] Francisque Sarcey (1827–99), the French dramatic critic, was essentially conservative in his tastes, seeing the critic as the spokesman for public opinion. See p. 13, n. 3.

general body of Parisian dramatists was so highly gifted that Brieux counted for nothing in Paris—when you respectfully asked for the names of a few of the most prominent of the geniuses who had eclipsed him, you were given three or four of which you had never heard, and one or two known to you as those of cynically commercial manipulators of the *ménage à trois*, the innocent wife discovered at the villain's rooms at midnight (to beg him to spare the virtue of a sister, the character of a son, or the life of a father), the compromising letter, the duel, and all the rest of the claptraps out of which dramatic playthings can be manufactured for the amusement of grown-up children. Not until the Académie Française elected Brieux[7] did it occur to the boulevardiers that the enormous difference between him and their pet authors was a difference in which the superiority lay with Brieux.

## The Pedantry of Paris

Indeed it is difficult for the Englishman to understand how bigotedly the Parisians cling to the claptrap theatre. The English do not care enough about the theatre to cling to its traditions or persecute anyone for their sake; but the French do. [...] Racine and Corneille, who established the alexandrine tradition,[8] deliberately aimed at classicism, taking the Greek drama as their model. Even a foreigner can hear the music of their verse. Corneille wrote alexandrines as Dryden wrote heroic couplets, in a virile, stately, handsome and withal human way; and Racine had tenderness and beauty as well. This drama of Racine and Corneille, with the music of Gluck, gave the French in the XVII and XVIII centuries a body of art which was very beautiful, very refined, very delightful for cultivated people, and very tedious for the ignorant. When, through the spread of elementary education, the ignorant invaded the theatre in overwhelming numbers, this exquisite body of art became a dead body [...]

Commercially, the classic play was supplanted by a nuisance which was not a failure: to wit, the 'well made play' of Scribe[9] and his school. The manufacture of well made plays is not an art: it is an industry. It is not at all hard for a literary mechanic to acquire it: the only difficulty is to find a literary mechanic who is not by nature too much of an artist for the job; for nothing spoils a well made play more infallibly than the least alloy of high art or the least qualm of conscience on the part of the writer. 'Art for art's sake' is the formula of the well made play, meaning in practice 'Success for money's sake.' Now great art is

---

[7]  This event took place in 1909.

[8]  This is not strictly speaking true: the 12-syllable alexandrine as the appropriate metre for tragedy had been introduced during the sixteenth century by Étienne Jodelle (1532–73), long before Corneille and Racine. The work of these two classical playwrights did, however, represent the high point of the tradition within which they were working.

[9]  Eugène Scribe (1791–1861), the French playwright who wrote more than 400 pieces, alone or in collaboration, is generally credited with having been the originator of the well-made play.

never produced for its own sake. It is too difficult to be worth the effort. All the great artists enter into a terrible struggle with the public, often involving bitter poverty and personal humiliation, because they believe they are apostles doing what used to be called the Will of God, and is now called by many prosaic names, of which 'public work' is the least controversial. And when these artists have travailed and brought forth, and at last forced the public to associate keen pleasure and deep interest with their methods and morals, a crowd of smaller men—art confectioners, we may call them—hasten to make pretty entertainments out of scraps and crumbs from the masterpieces. [...] And these confectioners are by no means mere plagiarists. They bring all sorts of engaging qualities to their work: love of beauty, desire to give pleasure, tenderness, humour, everything except the high republican conscience, the identification of the artist's purpose with the purpose of the universe, which alone makes an artist great.

But the well made play was not confectionery: it had not even the derived virtue of being borrowed from the great playwrights. Its formula grew up in the days when the spread of elementary schooling produced a huge mass of playgoers sufficiently educated to want plays instead of dog-fights, but not educated enough to enjoy or understand the masterpieces of dramatic art. Besides, education or no education, one cannot live on masterpieces alone, not only because there are not enough of them, but because new plays as well as great plays are needed, and there are not enough Molières and Shakespears in the world to keep the demand for novelty satisfied. Hence it has always been necessary to have some formula by which men of mediocre talent and no conscience can turn out plays for the theatrical market. [...]

## How to Write a Popular Play

The formula for the well made play is so easy that I give it for the benefit of any reader who feels tempted to try his hand at making the fortune that awaits all successful manufacturers in this line. First, you 'have an idea' for a dramatic situation. If it strikes you as a splendidly original idea whilst it is in fact as old as the hills, so much the better. For instance, the situation of an innocent person convicted by circumstances of a crime may always be depended on. If the person is a woman, she must be convicted of adultery. If a young officer, he must be convicted of selling information to the enemy, though it is really a fascinating female spy who has ensnared him and stolen the incriminating document. If the innocent wife, banished from her home, suffers agonies through her separation from her children, and, when one of them is dying (of any disease the dramatist chooses to inflict), disguises herself as a nurse and attends it through its dying convulsions until the doctor, who should be a serio-comic character, and if possible a faithful old admirer of the lady's, simultaneously announces the recovery of the child and the discovery of the wife's innocence, the success of the play may be regarded as assured if the writer has any sort of knack for his work. Comedy is more difficult, because it requires a sense of humour and a good deal of vivacity; but the process is essentially the same: it is the manufacture of a misunderstanding. Having manufactured it, you place its culmination at the end of the last act but one, which is the point at which the manufacture of the play begins. Then you make your first act out of the necessary introduction of the characters to the audience, after elaborate explanations, mostly conducted by servants, solicitors, and other low life personages (the principals must all be dukes and colonels and millionaires), of how the misunderstanding is going to come about. Your last act consists, of course, of clearing up the misunderstanding, and generally getting the audience out of the theatre as best you can.

Now please do not misunderstand me as pretending that this process is so mechanical that it offers no opportunity for the exercise of talent. On the contrary, it is so mechanical that without very conspicuous talent nobody can make much of a reputation by doing it, though some can and do make a living at it. And this often leads the cultivated classes to suppose that all plays are written by authors of talent. As a matter of fact the majority of those who in France and England make a living by writing plays are unknown and, as to education, all but illiterate. Their names are not worth putting on the playbill, because their audiences neither know nor care who the author is, and often believe that the actors improvise the whole piece, just as they in fact do sometimes improvise the dialogue. To rise out of this obscurity you must be a Scribe or a Sardou,[10] doing essentially the same thing, it is true, but doing it wittily and ingeniously, at moments almost poetically, and giving the persons of the drama some touches of real observed character.

## Why the Critics are always Wrong

Now it is these strokes of talent that set the critics wrong. For the talent, being all expended on the formula, at last consecrates the formula in the eyes of the critics. Nay, they become so accustomed to the formula that at last they cannot understand or relish a play that has grown naturally, just as they cannot admire the Venus de Milo because she has neither a corset nor high heeled shoes. [...]

No writer of the first order needs the formula any more than a sound man needs a crutch. In his simplest mood, when he is only seeking to amuse, he does not manufacture a plot: he tells a story. He finds no difficulty in setting people on the stage to talk and act in an amusing, exciting or touching way. His characters have adventures and ideas which are interesting in themselves, and need not be fitted into the Chinese puzzle of a plot. [...]

---

[10]   Victorien Sardou (1831–1908), the very popular French playwright now chiefly remembered as the author of the play on which Puccini's *Tosca* is based. In his column in the *Saturday Review* Shaw frequently attacked Sardou's type of playwriting as 'Sardoodledom'.

# How the Great Dramatists torture the Public

Now if the critics are wrong in supposing that the formula of the well made play is not only an indispensable factor in playwriting, but is actually the essence of the play itself—if their delusion is rebuked and confuted by the practice of every great dramatist even when he is only amusing himself by story-telling, what must happen to their poor formula when it impertinently offers its services to a playwright who has taken on his supreme function as the Interpreter of Life? Not only has he no use for it; but he must attack and destroy it; for one of the very first lessons he has to teach to a play-ridden public is that the romantic conventions on which the formula proceeds are all false, and are doing incalculable harm in these days when everybody reads romances and goes to the theatre. Just as the historian can teach no real history until he has cured his readers of the romantic delusion that the greatness of a queen consists in her being a pretty woman and having her head cut off; so the playwright of the first order can do nothing with his audiences until he has cured them of looking at the stage through the keyhole and sniffing round the theatre as prurient people sniff around the divorce court. The cure is not a popular one. The public suffers from it exactly as a drunkard or a snuff taker suffers from an attempt to conquer the habit. The critics especially, who are forced by their profession to indulge immoderately in plays adulterated with falsehood and vice, suffer so acutely when deprived of them for a whole evening that they hurl disparagements and even abuse and insult at the merciless dramatist who is torturing them. To a bad play of the kind they are accustomed to they can be cruel through superciliousness, irony, impatience, contempt, or even a Rochefoucauldian pleasure in a friend's misfortune.[11] But the hatred provoked by deliberately inflicted pain, the frantic denials as of a prisoner at the bar accused of a disgraceful crime, the clamour for vengeance thinly disguised as artistic justice, the suspicion that the dramatist is using private information and making a personal attack: all these are to be found only when the playwright is no mere *marchand de plaisir*, but, like Brieux, a ruthless revealer of hidden truth and a mighty destroyer of idols.

[11] The French moral philosopher La Rochefoucauld (1613–80) put forward a sceptical view of human nature as being essentially self-centred, as for instance in the following of his *Maxims*: 'If we had no faults we should not take so much pleasure in observing the faults of others' (31); or 'The ruin of one's neighbour pleases both his friends and his enemies' (521).

# *Death of a Salesman*: **A Modern Tragedy?** (1958)

## Arthur Miller

Undoubtedly the most eminent American playwright since Eugene O'Neill, Arthur Miller (b. 1915) has shown considerable technical variety in his dramatic output, from the Ibsen-type 'retrospective' structure of *All My Sons* (1947), to the near-expressionism of *Death of a Salesman* (1949), the quasi-Greek structure, complete with Chorus, of *A View from the Bridge* (rev. version, 1956), the tightly classical structure of *The Price* (1968) or the lyrical and dreamlike duet, *Elegy for a Lady* (1982). Although profoundly American, he has perhaps been appreciated more in Europe than in the United States, at any rate as far as theatrical performance is concerned. Miller has also spoken and written extensively on drama, neither seeking nor avoiding controversy: his consistently undoctrinaire, humanist viewpoint emerges clearly from the collection, *The Theatre Essays of Arthur Miller* (London: Methuen, 2nd edn. 1994). A continuing thread running through his thinking has been the linking of the private and the public, the psychological and the social. It was perhaps this dual aspect of his work that gave rise to the critical controversy, in 1949, over *Death of a Salesman*, which had far-reaching theoretical implications. Eric Bentley (see p. 35) attacked the play as falling between the stools of tragedy (with an Aristotelian catharsis) and social drama (with its claim to remedying the conditions pilloried on stage). Miller's own summing-up of the controversy, given below, places the concept of tragedy in a modern context and distances his playwriting from any overtly propagandizing aim.

[…] A great deal has been said and written about what *Death of a Salesman* is supposed to signify, both psychologically and from the socio-political viewpoints. For instance, in one periodical of the far Right it was called a 'time

From Arthur Miller, Introduction to *The Collected Plays* (London: Cresset Press, 1958), 27–38.

bomb expertly placed under the edifice of Americanism,' while the *Daily Worker* reviewer thought it entirely decadent. [...]

On the psychological front the play spawned a small hill of doctoral theses explaining its Freudian symbolism, and there were innumerable letters asking if I was aware that the fountain pen which Biff steals is a phallic symbol. Some, on the other hand, thought it was merely a fountain pen and dismissed the whole play. [...] Probably the most succinct reaction to the play was voiced by a man who, on leaving the theatre, said, 'I always said that New England territory was no damned good.' This, at least, was a fact.

That I have and had not the slightest interest in the selling profession is probably unbelievable to most people, and I very early gave up trying even to say so. And when asked what Willy was selling, what was in his bags, I could only reply, 'Himself.' I was trying neither to condemn a profession nor particularly to improve it, and, I will admit, I was little better than ignorant of Freud's teachings when I wrote it. There was no attempt to bring down the American edifice nor to raise it higher, to show up family relations or to cure the ills afflicting that inevitable institution. The truth, at least of my aim—which is all I can speak of authoritatively—is much simpler and more complex.

The play grew from simple images. [...]

The image of aging and so many of your friends already gone and strangers in the seats of the mighty who do not know you or your triumphs or your incredible value. [...]

The image of people turning into strangers who only evaluate one another.

Above all, perhaps, the image of a need greater than hunger or sex or thirst, a need to leave a thumbprint somewhere on the world. A need for immortality, and by admitting it, the knowing that one has carefully inscribed one's name on a cake of ice on a hot July day. [...]

It came from structural images. The play's eye was to revolve from within Willy's head, sweeping endlessly in all directions like a light on the sea, and nothing that formed in the distant mist was to be left uninvestigated. [...]

There were two undulating lines in mind, one above the other, the past webbed to the present moving on together in him and sometimes openly joined and once, finally, colliding in the showdown which defined him in his eyes at least—and so to sleep.

Above all, in the structural sense, I aimed to make a play with the veritable countenance of life. To make one the many, as in life, so that 'society' is a power and a mystery of custom and inside the man and surrounding him, as the fish is in the sea and the sea inside the fish, his birthplace and burial ground, promise and threat. To speak commonsensically of social facts which every businessman knows and talks about but which are too prosaic to mention or are usually fancied up on the stage as philosophical problems. When a man gets old you fire him, you have to, he can't do the work. To speak and even to celebrate the common sense of businessmen, who love the personality that wins the day but know you've got to have the right goods at the right price, handsome and well-spoken as you are. (To some, these were scandalous and infamous arraignments of society when uttered in the context of art. But not to the businessmen themselves; they knew it was all true and I cherished their clear-eyed talk.)

The image of a play without transitional scenes was there in the beginning. There was too much to say to waste precious stage time with feints and preparations, in themselves agonizing 'structural' bridges for a writer to work out since they are not why he is writing. [...]

The play was always heroic to me, and in later years the academy's charge that Willy lacked the 'stature' for the tragic hero seemed incredible to me. I had not understood that these matters are measured by Greco-Elizabethan paragraphs which hold no mention of insurance payments, front porches, refrigerator fan belts, steering knuckles, Chevrolets, and visions seen not through the portals of Delphi but in the blue flame of the hot-water heater. How could 'Tragedy' make people weep, of all things?

I set out not to 'write a tragedy' in this play, but to show the truth as I saw it. However, some of the attacks upon it as a pseudo-tragedy contain ideas so misleading, and in some cases so laughable, that it might be in place here to deal with a few of them.

Aristotle having spoken of a fall from the heights, it goes without saying that someone of the common mould cannot be a fit tragic hero. It is now many centuries since Aristotle lived. There is no more reason for falling down in a faint before his *Poetics* than before Euclid's geometry, which has been amended numerous times by men with new insights; nor, for that matter, would I choose to have my illnesses diagnosed by Hippocrates rather than the most ordinary graduate of an American medical school, despite the Greek's genius. Things do change, and even a genius is limited by his time and the nature of his society.

I would deny, on grounds of simple logic, this one of Aristotle's contentions if only because he lived in a slave society. When a vast number of people are divested of alternatives, as slaves are, it is rather inevitable that one will not be able to imagine drama, let alone tragedy, as being possible for any but the higher ranks of society. There is a legitimate question of stature here, but none of rank, which is so often confused with it. So long as the hero may be said to have had alternatives of a magnitude to have materially changed the course of his life, it seems to me that in this respect at least, he cannot be debarred from the heroic role.

The question of rank is significant to me only as it reflects the question of the social application of the hero's career. There is no doubt that if a character is shown on the stage who goes through the most ordinary actions, and is suddenly revealed to be the President of the United States, his actions immediately assume a greater magnitude, and pose the possibilities of much greater meaning, than if he is the corner grocer. But at the same time, his stature as a hero is not so utterly dependent upon his rank that the corner grocer cannot outdistance him as a tragic figure—providing, of course, that the grocer's career engages the issues of, for instance, the survival of the race, the relationships of man to God—the questions, in short, whose answers define humanity and the right way to live so that the world is a home, instead of a battleground or a fog in which disembodied spirits pass each other in an endless twilight.

In this respect *Death of a Salesman* is a slippery play to categorize because nobody in it stops to make a speech objectively stating the great issues which I believe it embodies. If it were a worse play, less closely articulating its meanings with its actions, I think it would have more quickly satisfied a certain kind of criticism. But it was meant to be less a play than a fact; it refused admission to its author's opinions and opened itself to a revelation of process and the operations of an ethic, of social laws of action no less powerful in their effects upon individuals than any tribal law administered by gods with names. I need not claim that this play is a genuine solid gold tragedy for my opinions on tragedy to be held valid. My purpose here is simply to point out a historical fact which must be taken into account in any consideration of tragedy, and it is the sharp alteration in the meaning of rank in society between the present time and the distant past. More important to me is the fact that this particular kind of argument obscures much more relevant considerations.

One of these is the question of intensity. It matters not at all whether a modern play concerns itself with a grocer or a president if the intensity of the hero's commitment to his course is less than the maximum possible. It matters not at all whether the hero falls from a great height or a small one, whether he is highly conscious or only dimly aware of what is happening, whether his pride brings the fall or an unseen pattern written behind clouds; if the intensity, the human passion to surpass his given bounds, the fanatic insistence upon his self-conceived role—if these are not present there can only be an outline of tragedy but no living thing. I believe, for myself, that the lasting appeal of tragedy is due to our need to face the fact of death in order to strengthen ourselves for life, and that over and above this function of the tragic viewpoint there are and will be a great number of formal variations which no single definition will ever embrace.

Another issue worth considering is the so-called tragic victory, a question closely related to the consciousness of the hero. One makes nonsense of this if a 'victory' means that the hero makes us feel some certain joy when, for instance, he sacrifices himself for a 'cause,' and unhappy and morose because he dies without one. To begin at the bottom, a man's death is and ought to be an essentially terrifying thing and ought to make nobody happy. But in a great variety of ways even death, the ultimate negative, can be, and appear to be, an assertion of bravery, and can serve to separate the death of a man from the death of animals; and I think it is this distinction which underlies any conception of a victory in death. For a society of faith, the nature of the death can prove the existence of the spirit, and posit its immortality. For a secular society it is perhaps more difficult for such a victory to document itself and to make itself felt, but conversely, the need to offer greater proofs of the humanity of man can make the victory more real. It goes without saying that in a society where there is basic disagreement as to the right way to live, there can hardly be agreement as to the right way to die, and both life and death must be heavily weighted with meaningless futility.

It was not out of any deference to a tragic definition that Willy Loman is filled with a joy, however broken-hearted, as he approaches his end, but simply that my sense of his character dictated his joy, and even what I felt was an exultation. In terms of his character, he has achieved a very powerful piece of knowledge, which is that he is loved by his son and has been embraced by him and forgiven. In this he is given his existence, so to speak—his fatherhood, for which he has always striven and which until now he could not achieve. That he is unable to take this victory thoroughly to his heart, that it closes the circle for him and propels him to his death, is the wage of his sin, which was to have committed himself so completely to the counterfeits of dignity and the false coinage embodied in his idea of success that he can prove his existence only by bestowing 'power' on his posterity, a power deriving from the sale of his last asset, himself, for the price of his insurance policy.

I must confess here to a miscalculation, however. I did not realize while writing the play that so many people in the world do not see as clearly, or would not admit, as I thought they must, how futile most lives are; so there could be no hope of consoling the audience for the death of this man. I did not realize either how few would be impressed by the fact that this man is actually a very brave spirit who cannot settle for half but must pursue his dream of himself to the end. Finally, I thought it must be clear, even obvious, that this was no dumb brute heading mindlessly to his catastrophe.

I have no need to be Willy's advocate before the jury which decides who is and who is not a tragic hero. I am merely noting that the lingering ponderousness of so many ancient definitions has blinded students and critics to the facts before them, and not only in regard to this play. Had Willy been unaware of his separation from values that endure he would have died contentedly while polishing his car, probably on a Sunday afternoon with the ball game coming over the radio. But he was agonized by his awareness of being in a false position, so constantly haunted by the hollowness of all he had placed his faith in, so aware, in short, that he must somehow be filled in his spirit or fly apart, that he staked his very life on the ultimate assertion. That he had not the intellectual fluency to verbalize his situation is not the same thing as saying that he lacked awareness, even an overly intensified consciousness that the life he had made was without form and inner meaning.

To be sure, had he been able to know that he was as much the victim of his beliefs as their defeated exemplar, had he known how much of guilt he ought to bear and how much to shed from his soul, he would be more conscious. But it seems to me that there is of necessity a severe limitation of self-awareness in any character, even the most knowing, which serves to define him as a character, and more, that this very limit serves to complete the tragedy and, indeed, to make it at all possible. Complete consciousness is possible only in a play about forces, like *Prometheus*, but not in a play about people. I think that the point is whether there is a sufficient awareness in the hero's career to make the audience supply the rest. Had Oedipus, for instance, been more conscious and more aware of the forces at work upon him he must surely have said that he was not really to blame for having cohabited with his mother since neither he nor anyone else knew she was his mother. He must surely decide to divorce her, provide for their children, firmly resolve to investigate the family background of his next wife, and thus deprive us of a very fine play and the name for a famous neurosis. But he is conscious only up to a point, the point at which guilt begins. Now he is inconsolable and must tear out his eyes. What is tragic about this? Why is it not even ridiculous? How can we respect a man who goes to such extremities over something he could in no way help or prevent? The answer, I think, is not that we respect the man, but that we respect the Law he has so completely broken, wittingly or not, for it is that Law which, we believe, defines us as men. The confusion of some critics viewing *Death of a Salesman* in this regard is that they do not see that Willy Loman has broken a law without whose protection life is insupportable if not incomprehensible to him and to many others; it is the law which says that a failure in society and in business has no right to live. Unlike the law against incest, the law of success is not administered by statute or church, but it is very nearly as powerful in its grip upon men. The confusion increases because, while it is a law, it is by no means a wholly agreeable one even as it is slavishly obeyed, for to fail is no longer to belong to society, in his estimate. Therefore, the path is opened for those who wish to call Willy merely a foolish man even as they themselves are living in obedience to the same law that killed him. Equally, the fact that Willy's law—the belief, in other words, which administers guilt to him—is not a civilizing statute whose destruction menaces us all; it is, rather, a deeply believed and deeply suspect 'good' which, when questioned as to its value, as it is in this play, serves more to raise our anxieties than to reassure us of the existence of an unseen but humane metaphysical system in the world. My attempt in the play was to counter this anxiety with an opposing system which, so to speak, is in a race for Willy's faith, and it is the system of love which is the opposite of the law of success. It is embodied in Biff Loman, but by the time Willy can perceive his love it can serve only as an ironic comment upon the life he sacrificed for power and for success and its tokens.

A play cannot be equated with a political philosophy, at least not in the way a smaller number, by simple multiplication, can be assimilated into a larger. I do not believe that any work of art can help but be diminished by its adherence at any cost to a political programme, including its author's, and not for any other reason than that there is no political programme—any more than there is a theory of tragedy—which can encompass the complexities of real life. Doubtless an author's politics must be one element, and even an important one, in the germination of his art, but if it is art he has created it must by definition bend itself to his observation rather than to his opinions or even his hopes. If I have shown a preference for plays which seek causation not only in psychology but in society, I may also believe in the autonomy of art, and I believe this because my experience with *All My Sons* and *Death of a Salesman* forces the belief upon me. [...]

The most decent man in *Death of a Salesman* is a capitalist (Charley), whose aims are not different from Willy Loman's. The great difference between them is that Charley is not a fanatic. Equally, however, he has learned how to live without that frenzy, that ecstasy of spirit which Willy chases to his end. And even as Willy's sons are unhappy men, Charley's boy, Bernard, works hard, attends to his studies, and attains a worthwhile objective. These people are all of the same class, the same background, the same neighbourhood. What theory lies behind this double view? None whatever. It is simply that I knew and know that I feel better when my work is reflecting a balance of the truth as it exists. A muffled debate arose with the success of *Death of a Salesman* in which attempts were made to justify or dismiss the play as a Left-Wing piece, or as a Right-Wing manifestation of decadence. The presumption underlying both views is that a work of art is the sum of its author's political outlook, real or alleged, and more, that its political implications are valid elements in its aesthetic evaluation. I do not believe this, either for my own or other writers' works. [...]

By the evidence of his plays, Shaw, the socialist, was in love not with the working class, whose characters he could only caricature, but with the middle of the economic aristocracy, those men who, in his estimate, lived without social and economic illusions. There is a strain of mystic fatalism in Ibsen so powerful as to throw all his scientific tenets into doubt, and a good measure besides of contempt—in this radical—for the men who are usually called the public. The list is long and the contradictions are embarrassing until one concedes a perfectly simple proposition. It is merely that a writer of any worth creates out of his total perception, the vaster part of which is subjective and not within his intellectual control. For myself, it has never been possible to generate the energy to write and complete a play if I know in advance everything it signifies and all it will contain. The very impulse to write, I think, springs from an inner chaos crying for order, for meaning, and that meaning must be discovered in the process of writing or the work lies dead as it is finished. To speak, therefore, of a play as though it were the objective work of a propagandist is an almost biological kind of nonsense, provided, of course, that it is a play, which is to say a work of art. [...]

# PART III

## Anti-Naturalism

# The Tragical in Daily Life
## (1894)

## Maurice Maeterlinck

The following essay by the playwright, poet, and essayist Maurice Maeterlinck (1862–1949) was first published in *Le Figaro* in 1894. This manifesto, widely noted at the time and frequently quoted since, called for a new type of drama, a drama of *stasis*. The theory came on the heels of the success of Maeterlinck's early plays—e.g. *The Blind* and *The Intruder* (both 1890)—which had death at the centre of the action, or rather inaction, and which had caused the young author to be hailed by one French critic as the 'Belgian Shakespeare'. With their emphasis on stillness and inwardness, these plotless 'death dramas' were like motionless tableaux rather than dramatic events in the conventional sense. They set out to capture a timeless moment which would invite the spectators to contemplate ineffable mysteries in a meditative frame of mind. While the 'soulful', 1890-ish style of the essay may well strike the modern reader as dated; while Maeterlinck's approach to dramatic structure was diametrically opposed to what, from Aristotle onwards, had always been regarded as the one essential ingredient of drama, viz. inner or outer development of situation if not of character; while, moreover, the author himself was to declare later (in 1913, by which time his own playwriting style had altered drastically): 'You must not attach too great importance to the expression *Static*; it was an invention, a theory of my youth, worth what most literary theories are worth—that is, almost nothing'[1]—it is nevertheless a fact that the principles of non-action and the 'second-degree dialogue' championed below were echoed, in the early years of the twentieth century, in the work of several notable symbolist playwrights such as Yeats and late Strindberg. Comparable if not identical principles can even be traced—whether or not owing to any direct influence of Maeterlinck—in some authors in the second half of the twentieth century, whose tone of voice differs fundamentally from his, writers such as Beckett and Pinter: for example in plays like *Krapp's Last Tape* in the case of the former or *Landscape* and *Silence* in the case of the latter.

From Maurice Maeterlinck, *Le Trésor des humbles* (The Treasure of the Humble) (Paris: Société du Mercure de France, 1898), 179–201. Translated from the French by George Brandt.

[1] Barrett H. Clark, *European Theories of the Drama* (rev. edn., New York, Crown Publishers, 1947), 411.

There is a tragic element in daily life that is far more real, far deeper, and far more consistent with our true self than the tragedy of great adventures. This is easy to feel but hard to show because the essential tragic element is not merely material or psychological. It is not a matter of the unflinching struggle of one person against another, the struggle of one desire against another, nor the eternal conflict of passion and duty. It is more a matter of revealing what is so astonishing about the mere act of living. It is more a matter of revealing the existence of the soul itself, in the midst of an immensity that is never at rest. It is more a matter of allowing to be heard, above the ordinary dialogue of reason and the feelings, the more solemn and uninterrupted dialogue of man and his destiny. It is more a matter of making us follow the uncertain and painful steps of someone approaching or retreating from his own truth, his beauty, or his God. And it is a matter of showing us and making us hear a thousand similar things which the tragic poets have given us brief glimpses of in passing. But here is the essential point: could not that which they have given us brief glimpses of in passing be shown before anything else? That which we hear underlying King Lear, Macbeth, and Hamlet for instance, the mysterious chant of the infinite, the ominous silence of souls or of the gods, the rumble of eternity on the horizon, the destiny or fatality one senses inwardly without being able to say by what signs one perceives it—could one not by I know not what interchange of roles bring them closer to us while putting the actors at a greater distance? Is it then too bold to maintain that the authentic tragic element of life, normal, deep-rooted and universal tragedy, only begins at the moment when so-called adventures, sorrows, and dangers are over? Is not the arm of happiness longer than that of sorrow, and do not some of its forces come closer to the soul? Must we really shriek like the Atrides before an eternal god will reveal himself in our life, and will he never sit down with us in the calm light of our lamp? Is not tranquillity, watched over by the stars, a terrible thing when you consider it; and does our sense of life grow in tumult or in silence? Is it not when we are told at the end of a story, 'They were happy,' that a great unease should come upon us? What is going on while they are happy? Does not happiness or a simple moment of rest reveal more of what is serious and changeless than does the whirlwind of passion? Is it not then that the progression of time and other more secret progressions at last become visible and the hours go rushing forward? Does not all this touch deeper chords than the dagger-thrust of ordinary drama? Is it not just when a man thinks he is secure from death threatening from without that the strange and silent tragedy of being and of the immensities does indeed throw open the doors of his drama? While I am fleeing before a naked sword, does my existence reach its most interesting point? Is it always at its most sublime in a kiss? Are there not other moments when one hears more lasting and purer voices? Does your soul only burst into flower during stormy nights? This seems to have been the general opinion until now. Almost all our tragic authors only see the life of violence, the life of the past; and one may say that all our theatre is out of date and that the art of drama is as many years behind the times as is sculpture. It is a different story with, for instance, good painting and good music which have managed to tease out and reproduce the most hidden but none the less serious and astonishing features of the life of today. They have noted that what life has lost by way of surface decoration it has gained in depth, in intimate meaning and spiritual weight. [...]

But our tragic authors, just like the mediocre artists who have not gone beyond history painting, make the violence of the story they are telling carry all the interest of their plays. And they set about entertaining us with the same kind of deeds that delighted barbarians who were used to crimes, murders, and treasons. But we spend most of our lives far away from blood, shouting, and swords, and the tears of mankind have become silent, invisible, and almost spiritual ...

When I go to the theatre I feel as if I were back for a few hours among my ancestors whose idea of life as something simple, arid, and brutal I have all but forgotten and which I can no longer share. There I see a betrayed husband kill his wife; a woman poison her lover, a son avenge his father, a father butcher his children, children cause the death of their father, murdered kings, ravished virgins, citizens in gaol, and all the traditional sublime, but alas! so superficial and so crude—blood, unfelt tears, and death. What do these creatures, who have but one fixed idea and no time to live because they must put to death a rival or a mistress, mean to me?

I had come in the hope of seeing something of life connected to its sources and its mysteries by links which my daily routine gives me neither the opportunity nor the power to observe. I had come in the hope of glimpsing for a moment the beauty, the grandeur, and the gravity of my humble everyday existence. I was hoping that I should be shown I know not what presence, what power or what god living with me in my room. I was expecting I know not what meaningful moments which I experience unperceived amid my most wretched hours; and all too often I was to discover a man who told me at length why he was feeling jealous, why he was administering poison or why he was committing suicide.

I admire Othello, but he does not seem to me to be living the sublime daily life of a Hamlet who has time to live because he does not act. Othello is admirably jealous. But is it not perhaps a long-standing error to think that it is at moments when such a passion or other equally violent ones possess us that we are truly alive? I have come to think that an old man, seated in his armchair, simply waiting underneath his lamp, listening unawares to all the eternal laws that reign about his house, interpreting uncomprehendingly what there is in the silence of the doors and the windows and the quiet voice of the light, submitting to the presence of his soul and his destiny with his head slightly inclined, never suspecting that all the powers of this world are acting and watching in the room like so many attentive servants, not realizing that the very sun is supporting above the abyss the little table on which his elbows are resting, and that there is not a star in the heavens nor a power of the soul that are indifferent to the movement of a drooping eyelid or of a rising thought—I have come to think that this motionless old man was actually living a deeper, more human and more general life than the lover who strangles his mistress, the captain who wins a victory or 'the husband who avenges his honour.'[2]

I shall perhaps be told that a motionless life would scarcely be visible, that it has to be animated with some movements and that these varied movements, in order to be acceptable, can only be found in the small number of passions employed hitherto. I do not know whether it is true that a static theatre is impossible. But it actually seems to me to exist already. Most of the tragedies of Aeschylus are motionless tragedies. I do not mean *Prometheus* and *The Suppliants* in which there is no action; but the entire tragedy of *The Libation Bearers*, which is surely the most terrible drama of antiquity, errs like a nightmare around Agamemnon's tomb until murder springs forth like lightning from the accumulation of prayers which keep gathering there. Consider a few more of the finest ancient tragedies from this point of view: *The Eumenides, Antigone, Electra, Oedipus at Colonus.* 'People have admired,' Racine says in his preface to *Bérénice,* 'people have admired Sophocles' *Ajax* which is about nothing else but Ajax killing himself out of regret for the fury into which he had fallen after being denied the arms of Achilles. People have admired *Philoctetes* whose sole subject is Ulysses coming to seize the arrows of Hercules. Even *Oedipus,* though full of recognitions, contains less subject matter than the simplest tragedy of our days.'

Is this anything other than a life almost without motion? Usually there is not even any psychological action, which is a thousand times better than physical action and which seems indispensable but which has nevertheless been suppressed or wonderfully reduced in such a way as to leave as the only interest that which arises out of the situation of man in the universe. Here we are no longer among barbarians, and man is no longer driven by those crude passions which are not the only interesting things about him. We have time to observe him at rest. We are dealing not with an exceptional violent moment in life but with life itself. There are thousands and thousands of laws mightier and more venerable than the laws of passion; but these slow-moving, discreet and silent laws, like all things endowed with irresistible strength, are not seen and heard except in the twilight and the serenity of the quiet moments of life.

When Ulysses and Neoptolemus come to Philoctetes to ask him for the arms of Hercules, their action in itself is as simple and as ordinary as that of a man of our time who enters a house to visit an invalid, of a traveller who knocks at the door of an inn or of a mother by the fireside who waits for her child to come home. Sophocles swiftly sketches in the character of his hero.

---

[2] This image seems vaguely to be based on the Grandfather in Maeterlinck's *The Intruder*—a blind old man who senses more clearly than the rest of his spiritually obtuse family the approach of Death to the house.

But can we not say that the main interest of the tragedy does not lie in the struggle we see there between cunning and loyalty, between love of one's homeland, rancour, and stubborn pride? There is something else; it is man's higher existence that is shown to us. The poet adds to ordinary life something that is the secret of poets, and all of a sudden it is revealed in its astonishing grandeur, its subordination to unknown powers, its unending affinities and its awesome misery. A chemist lets fall but a few mysterious drops into a vessel that seems to contain nothing but clear water: and all at once a whole world of crystals will rise up to the rim and reveal to us what was latent in the vessel where our flawed vision had not perceived anything. Similarly in *Philoctetes*, the sketchy characterization of the three main actors would seem to be merely the sides of the vessel containing the clear water which is ordinary life, into which the poet lets fall the revealing drops of his genius ...

So it is not in the actions but in the words that the beauty and the greatness of beautiful and great tragedies lie. Are they found only in the words which accompany and explain the actions? No, something is needed other than the outwardly necessary dialogue. It is the words which at first seem redundant that matter in a play. It is in them that its soul lies. Side by side with the necessary dialogue there is almost always a dialogue that seems superfluous. Examine it carefully and you will see that that is the only one to which the soul will listen profoundly because it is only here that it is being addressed. You will also become aware that the quality and the scope of this dialogue determine the quality and the ineffable range of the play. It is a fact that in the ordinary drama the indispensable dialogue does not reflect reality at all; and what constitutes the mysterious beauty of the most beautiful tragedies are those very words which are spoken beside what seems to be the strict truth. It is found in the words that conform to a truth deeper and incomparably closer to the invisible soul which breathes through the poem. One may even affirm that the poem comes closer to beauty and a higher truth to the extent that it does away with the words which explain the action and substitutes for them words which explain, not what is called a 'state of the soul' but I know not what intangible and unceasing striving of souls towards their beauty and towards their truth. To that extent also it comes closer to the true life. It is a common experience in daily life that one has to resolve a very serious situation by means of words. Just think about it. At these moments, or indeed ordinarily, is what you say or what is said to you always that which matters most? Are not other powers, other words that one cannot hear brought into play that determine the event? What I say often counts for little; but my presence, the attitude of my soul, my future and my past, that which will be born in me, that which has died in me, a secret thought, the friendly stars, my destiny, the thousands and thousands of mysteries that surround me and envelop you, that is what speaks to you at that tragic moment and that is what responds to me. All this underlies each of my words and each of yours, and it is chiefly this we see, and it is chiefly this we hear in spite of ourselves. If you have come, you 'the outraged husband', the 'deceived lover', the 'abandoned wife' intending to kill me, your arm will not be stayed by my most eloquent pleas. But it may be that you will then encounter one of those unexpected forces and that my soul, knowing that they are watching over me, may speak a secret word which will disarm you. These are the spheres where adventures are resolved, this is the dialogue the echo of which should be heard. And it is this echo that one hears—exceedingly attenuated and variable, it is true—in some of the great plays I have just spoken of. But could we not try to draw closer to these spheres where everything happens 'in reality'?

It seems to me that the attempt is being made. Some time ago, dealing with Ibsen's play where this 'second-degree' dialogue is heard at its most tragic, dealing with *The Master Builder* I endeavoured, unskilfully enough, to prize open its secrets. These are still gropings very much like the same blind man's hand on the same wall striving towards the same light. 'What is it,' I said, 'that in *The Master Builder* the author has added to life in order to make it appear so strange, so profound and so disquieting beneath its trivial surface? It is not easy to make out, and the old master has kept more than one secret from us. It would even seem that what he wanted to say was but little compared to what he *had* to say. He has set free certain powers of the soul which had never been free before, and he may have been possessed by them. 'Do you see, Hilde,' exclaims Solness, 'do you see! There is sorcery in you just as there is in me. It is this sorcery that causes the outside powers to act. And we *have* to yield to it. Whether we like it or not, we *have* to.'[3]

There is sorcery in them as there is in all of us. Hilde and Solness are, I believe, the first dramatic characters who feel for an instant that they are living in the atmosphere of the soul, and this essential life they have discovered within themselves, beyond their everyday life, terrifies them. Hilde and Solness are two souls who have caught a glimpse of their situation in the true life. There is more than one way of getting to know a person. Let me take, for instance, two or three people whom I see almost every day. Probably for a long time I shall distinguish them only by their gestures, their outer or inner habits, their manner of feeling, acting, and thinking. But there comes a mysterious moment in any friendship of some duration in which we become aware, so to speak, of our friend's exact relationship to the unknown that surrounds him and the attitude destiny has assumed towards him. It is from this moment onwards that he truly belongs to us. [...]

I believe that Hilde and Solness are in this state and perceive each other in this fashion. Their conversation is unlike anything we have ever heard before because the poet has endeavoured to blend inner and outer dialogue in one

---

[3] A somewhat more accurate translation of this speech from Act II of Ibsen's *The Master Builder* (1892) would read: 'There you are! There you are, Hilde! There's a troll in you, too. Just as in me. And it's the troll in us, you see, that calls on the powers outside. Then we *have* to give in—whether we like it or not.' Translation by James Walter McFarlane, in *The Oxford Ibsen*, vol. vii (Oxford: Oxford University Press, 1966), 413. Note the specific use of the word 'troll' rather than the more general 'sorcery'.

expression. There reign in this somnabulistic drama I know not what novel powers. All that is said in it at once conceals and uncovers the sources of an unknown life. And if we are bewildered at times, we must not lose sight of the fact that our soul often appears to our poor eyes a most demented force, and that there are in mankind many more fruitful, more profound, and more interesting regions than those of reason or intelligence …

# The Theatre (1899)

## William Butler Yeats

William Butler Yeats (1865–1939), recipient of the Nobel Prize for Literature in 1923, is very much better known and appreciated as a poet than as a playwright. However, he devoted much of his life to drama and in particular to the creation of an Irish theatre. The thematic and stylistic range of his plays was wide—from symbolist verse dramas, many of them concerned with the deeds of the mythical Irish hero Cuchulain, to prose plays situated in the present; but the underlying tone was consistently non-rhetorical and informed with an awareness of mystical powers. In their revulsion against the prosiness of naturalism, Yeats's efforts had their visual correlative in Gordon Craig (see pp. 138–44), who designed special screens for the Abbey Theatre in 1911. But this Irish National Theatre, which Yeats helped to found, was never to become the powerhouse for a new poetic drama that he had dreamt it would. The two essays quoted below are from different periods of his work as a playwright and theorist of drama, but both reveal a persistent attitude: a preference for poetic otherworldliness, to be conveyed by actors skilled above all in verse-speaking. The first essay dates from the time of the foundation of the Irish Literary Theatre, which was the forerunner of the Abbey; the second from his discovery of Noh, towards which his attention had been drawn relatively late in life by his friend Ezra Pound: it was in fact his introduction to the latter's translation of a number of Noh plays. Yeats saw in this traditional Japanese form—an amalgam of poetry, song, instrumental music, and dance—guidelines for what he had himself been trying to accomplish in the theatre for many years. His understanding of Noh was not altogether correct, nor did he follow it in pedantic detail in his Plays for Dancers and other works broadly inspired by Noh. But if there was a cultural misunderstanding at work here it was on the whole a productive one. Another of Yeats's theoretical essays worth noting was *The Tragic Theatre* (1910).[1]

From W. B. Yeats, *Essays and Introductions* (London: Macmillan, 1961), 165–70.

[1] See *Essays and Introductions*, 238–45.

I remember, some years ago, advising a distinguished, though too little recognized, writer of poetical plays to write a play as unlike ordinary plays as possible, that it might be judged with a fresh mind, and to put it on the stage in some little suburban hall, where a little audience would pay its expenses. I said that he should follow it the year after, at the same time of the year, with another play, and so on from year to year; and that the people who read books, and do not go to the theatre, would gradually find out about him. I suggested that he should begin with a pastoral play, because nobody would expect from a pastoral play the succession of nervous tremors which the plays of commerce, like the novels of commerce, have substituted for the purification that comes with pity and terror to the imagination and the intellect. He followed my advice in part, and had a small but perfect success, filling his small theatre for twice the number of performances he had announced; but instead of being content with the praise of his equals, and waiting to win their praise another year, he hired immediately a well-known London theatre, and put his pastoral play and a new play before a meagre and unintelligent audience. I still remember his pastoral play with delight, because, if not always of a high excellence, it was always poetical; but I remember it at the small theatre, where my pleasure was magnified by the pleasure of those about me, and not at the big theatre, where it made me uncomfortable, as an unwelcome guest always makes one uncomfortable.

Why should we thrust our works, which we have written with imaginative sincerity and filled with spiritual desire, before those quite excellent people who think that Rossetti's women are 'guys,' that Rodin's women are 'ugly,' and that Ibsen is 'immoral,' and who only want to be left at peace to enjoy the works so many clever men have made especially to suit them? We must make a theatre for ourselves and our friends, and a few simple people who understand from sheer simplicity what we understand from scholarship and thought. We have planned the Irish Literary Theatre[2] with this hospitable emotion, and that the right people may find out about us, we hope to act a play or two in the spring of every year; and that the right people may escape the stupefying memory of the theatre of commerce which clings even to them, our plays will be for the most part remote, spiritual, and ideal.

A common opinion is that the poetic drama has come to an end, because modern poets have no dramatic power; and Mr. Binyon seems to accept this opinion when he says: 'It has been too often assumed that it is the manager who bars the way to poetic plays. But it is much more probable that the poets have failed the managers. If poets mean to serve the stage, their dramas must be dramatic.' I find it easier to believe that audiences, who have learned, as I think, from the life of crowded cities to live upon the surface of life, and actors

---

[2] The opening seasons (1899–1901) of the Irish Literary Theatre, which had been founded by Yeats, Lady Gregory, and Edward Martyn, led directly to the creation of the Irish National Theatre Society; this found its permanent home in Abbey Street, Dublin, and hence became known as the Abbey Theatre.

and managers, who study to please them, have changed, than that imagination, which is the voice of what is eternal in man, has changed. The arts are but one Art; and why should all intense painting and all intense poetry have become not merely unintelligible but hateful to the greater number of men and women, and intense drama move them to pleasure? The audiences of Sophocles and of Shakespeare and of Calderón were not unlike the audiences I have heard listening in Irish cabins to songs in Gaelic about 'an old poet telling his sins,' and about 'five young men who were drowned last year,' and about 'the lovers that were drowned going to America,' or to some tale of Oisin and his three hundred years in Tir na nOg.[3] [...]

Blake has said that all art is a labour to bring again the Golden Age, and all culture is certainly a labour to bring again the simplicity of the first ages, with knowledge of good and evil added to it. The drama has need of cities that it may find men in sufficient numbers, and cities destroy the emotions to which it appeals, and therefore the days of the drama are brief and come but seldom. It has one day when the emotions of cities still remember the emotions of sailors and husbandmen and shepherds and users of the spear and the bow; as the houses and furniture and earthen vessels of cities, before the coming of machinery, remember the rocks and the woods and the hillside; and it has another day, now beginning, when thought and scholarship discover their desire. In the first day, it is the art of the people; and in the second day, like the dramas acted of old times in the hidden places of temples, it is the preparation of priesthood. It may be, though the world is not old enough to show us any example, that this priesthood will spread their religion everywhere, and make their Art the Art of the people.

When the first day of the drama had passed by, actors found that an always larger number of people were more easily moved through the eyes than through the ears. The emotion that comes with the music of words is exhausting, like all intellectual emotions, and few people like exhausting emotions; and therefore actors began to speak as if they were reading something out of the newspapers. They forgot the noble art of oratory, and gave all their thought to the poor art of acting, that is content with the sympathy of our nerves; until at last those who love poetry found it better to read alone in their rooms what they had once delighted to hear sitting friend by friend, lover by beloved. I once asked Mr. William Morris if he had thought of writing a play, and he answered that he had, but would not write one, because actors did not know how to speak poetry with the half-chant men spoke it with in old times. [...]

As audiences and actors changed, managers learned to substitute meretricious landscapes, painted upon wood and canvas, for the descriptions of poetry, until the painted scenery, which had in Greece been a charming

---

[3] The legendary Gaelic warrior and bard Oisin (more commonly known as Ossian), son of Finn MacCoul, was the subject of Yeats's poem, *The Wanderings of Oisin* (1899). Tir na nOg is the mythical land of eternal youth beyond the sea.

explanation of what was least important in the story, became as important as the story. It needed some imagination, some gift for day-dreams, to see the horses and the fields and flowers of Colonus as one listened to the elders gathered about Oedipus, or to see 'the pendent bed and procreant cradle' of the 'martlet' as one listened to Banquo before the castle of Macbeth; but it needs no imagination to admire a painting of one of the more obvious effects of nature painted by somebody who understands how to show everything to the most hurried glance. At the same time the managers made the costumes of the actors more and more magnificent, that the mind might sleep in peace, while the eye took pleasure in the magnificence of velvet and silk and in the physical beauty of women. These changes gradually perfected the theatre of commerce, the masterpiece of that movement towards externality in life and thought and art against which the criticism of our day is learning to protest.

Even if poetry were spoken as poetry, it would still seem out of place in many of its highest moments upon a stage where the superficial appearances of nature are so closely copied; for poetry is founded upon convention, and becomes incredible the moment painting or a gesture reminds us that people do not speak verse when they meet upon the highway. The theatre of art, when it comes to exist, must therefore discover grave and decorative gestures, such as delighted Rossetti and Madox Brown, and grave and decorative scenery that will be forgotten the moment an actor has said, 'It is dawn,' or 'It is raining,' or 'The wind is shaking the trees'; and dresses of so little irrelevant magnificence that the mortal actors and actresses may change without much labour into the immortal people of romance. The theatre began in ritual, and it cannot come to its greatness again without recalling words to their ancient sovereignty.

It will take a generation, and perhaps generations, to restore the theatre of art; for one must get one's actors, and perhaps one's scenery, from the theatre of commerce, until new actors and new painters have come to help one; and until many failures and imperfect successes have made a new tradition, and perfected in detail the ideal that is beginning to float before our eyes. If one could call one's painters and one's actors from where one would, how easy it would be! [...]

# Certain Noble Plays of Japan (1917)

## William Butler Yeats

**I**

I am writing with my imagination stirred by a visit to the studio of Mr. Dulac, the distinguished illustrator of the *Arabian Nights*. I saw there the mask and the head-dress to be worn in a play of mine by the player who will speak the part of Cuchulain,[1] and who, wearing this noble, half-Greek, half-Asiatic face, will appear perhaps like an image seen in a reverie by some Orphic worshipper. I hope to have attained the distance from life which can make credible strange events, elaborate words. I have written a little play that can be played in a room for so little money that forty or fifty readers of poetry can pay the price. There will be no scenery, for three musicians, whose seeming sunburned faces will, I hope, suggest that they have wandered from village to village in some country of our dreams, can describe place and weather, and at moments action and accompany it all by drum and gong or flute and dulcimer. Instead of players working themselves into a violence of passion indecorous in our sitting-room, the music, the beauty of form and voice all come to climax in a pantomimic dance.

In fact, with the help of Japanese plays 'translated by Ernest Fenollosa and finished by Ezra Pound,'[2] I have invented a form of drama, distinguished, indirect, and symbolic, and having no need of mob or Press to pay its way—an aristocratic form. When this play and its performance run as smoothly as my

From W. B. Yeats, *Essays and Introductions* (London: Macmillan, 1969), 221–37.

[1] What Yeats had in mind here were the preparations for his first play inspired by the Noh style, *At the Hawk's Well*; this was first performed on 2 Apr. 1916 in Lady Cunard's drawing-room in London, Henry Ainley playing the part of the legendary hero Cuchulain.

[2] *Certain Noble Plays of Japan, from the Manuscripts of Ernest Fenollosa, Chosen and finished by Ezra Pound, with an introduction by William Butler Yeats* (Dundrum: Cuala Press, 1916). This is a not altogether reliable guide to Noh since Ezra Pound, who edited the late E. Fenollosa's fragmentary and less than accurate papers at the request of the latter's widow, himself had no first-hand knowledge of the subject.

skill can make them, I shall hope to write another of the same sort and so complete a dramatic celebration of the life of Cuchulain planned long ago.[3] Then having given enough performances for, I hope, the pleasure of personal friends and a few score people of good taste, I shall record all discoveries of method and turn to something else. It is an advantage of this noble form that it need absorb no one's life, that its few properties can be packed up in a box or hung upon the walls where they will be fine ornaments.

## II

[…] I love all the arts that can still remind me of their origin among the common people, and my ears are only comfortable when the singer sings as if mere speech had taken fire, when he appears to have passed into song almost imperceptibly. I am bored and wretched, a limitation I greatly regret, when he seems no longer a human being but an invention of science. To explain him to myself I say that he has become a wind instrument and sings no longer like active men, sailor or camel-driver, because he has had to compete with an orchestra, where the loudest instrument has always survived. The human voice can only become louder by becoming less articulate, by discovering some new musical sort of roar or scream. As poetry can do neither, the voice must be freed from this competition and find itself among little instruments, only heard at their best perhaps when we are close about them. It should be again possible for a few poets to write as all did once, not for the printed page but to be sung. But movement has also grown less expressive, more declamatory, less intimate. When I called the other day upon a friend I found myself among some dozen people who were watching a group of Spanish boys and girls, professional dancers, dancing some national dance in the midst of a drawing-room. Doubtless their training had been long, laborious, and wearisome; but now one could not be deceived, their movement was full of joy. They were among friends, and it all seemed but the play of children; how powerful it seemed, how passionate, while an even more miraculous art, separated from us by the footlights, appeared in the comparison laborious and professional. It is well to be close enough to an artist to feel for him a personal liking, close enough perhaps to feel that our liking is returned.

My play is made possible by a Japanese dancer whom I have seen dance in a studio and in a drawing-room and on a very small stage lit by an excellent stage-light.[4] In the studio and in the drawing-room alone, where the lighting was the light we are most accustomed to, did I see him as the tragic image that has stirred my imagination. There, where no studied lighting, no stage-picture made an artificial world, he was able, as he rose from the floor, where he had been sitting cross-legged, or as he threw out an arm, to recede from us into

---

[3] Earlier plays in the Cuchulain cycle were *On Baile's Strand* (1904) and *The Green Helmet* (1910).

[4] Michio Ito (1893–1961), who performed the role of the Guardian of the Well in the original production of *At the Hawk's Well*, was an accomplished dancer but not a trained Noh actor at all.

some more powerful life. Because that separation was achieved by human means alone, he receded but to inhabit as it were the deeps of the mind. One realized anew, at every separating strangeness, that the measure of all arts' greatness can but be in their intimacy.

# III

All imaginative art remains at a distance and this distance, once chosen, must be firmly held against a pushing world. Verse, ritual, music and dance in association with action require that gesture, costume, facial expression, stage arrangement must help in keeping the door. Our unimaginative arts are content to set a piece of the world as we know it in a place by itself, to put their photographs as it were in a plush or a plain frame, but the arts which interest me, while seeming to separate from the world and us a group of figures, images, symbols, enable us to pass for a few moments into a deep of the mind that had hitherto been too subtle for our habitation. As a deep of the mind can only be approached through what is most human, most delicate, we should distrust bodily distance, mechanism, and loud noise.

It may be well if we go to school in Asia, for the distance from life in European art has come from little but difficulty with material. [...] The spiritual painting of the fourteenth century passed on into Tintoretto and that of Velázquez into modern painting with no sense of loss to weigh against the gain, while the painting of Japan, not having our European moon to churn the wits, has understood that no styles that ever delighted noble imaginations have lost their importance, and chooses the style according to the subject. In literature also we have had the illusion of change and progress, the art of Shakespeare passing into that of Dryden, and so into the prose drama, by what has seemed when studied in its details unbroken progress. Had we been Greeks, and so but half-European, an honourable mob would have martyred, though in vain, the first man who set up a painted scene, or who complained that soliloquies were unnatural, instead of repeating with a sigh, 'We cannot return to the arts of childhood however beautiful.' Only our lyric poetry has kept its Asiatic habit and renewed itself at its own youth, putting off perpetually what has been called its progress in a series of violent revolutions.

Therefore it is natural that I go to Asia for a stage convention, for more formal faces, for a chorus that has no part in the action, and perhaps for those movements of the body copied from the marionette shows of the fourteenth century.[5] A mask will enable me to substitute for the face of some commonplace player, or for that face repainted to suit his own vulgar fancy, the fine invention of a sculptor, and to bring the audience close enough to the play to hear every inflection of the voice. A mask never seems but a dirty face, and no

---

[5] Here Yeats confused Noh, which has not been influenced by the puppet theatre, with Kabuki which has.

matter how close you go is yet a work of art; nor shall we lose by stilling the movement of the features, for deep feeling is expressed by a movement of the whole body. In poetical painting and in sculpture the face seems the nobler for lacking curiosity, alert attention, all that we sum up under the famous word of the realists, 'vitality.' [...]

## IV

Realism is created for the common people and was always their peculiar delight, and it is the delight today of all those whose minds, educated alone by schoolmasters and newspapers, are without the memory of beauty and emotional subtlety. [...]

Let us press the popular arts on to a more complete realism—that would be their honesty—for the commercial arts demoralize by their compromise, their incompleteness, their idealism without sincerity or elegance, their pretence that ignorance can understand beauty. In the studio and in the drawing-room we can found a true theatre of beauty. Poets from the time of Keats and Blake have derived their descent only through what is least declamatory, least popular in the art of Shakespeare, and in such a theatre they will find their habitual audience and keep their freedom. Europe is very old and has seen many arts run through the circle and has learned the fruit of every flower and known what this fruit sends up, and it is now time to copy the East and live deliberately.

## V

[...] The Noh theatre of Japan became popular at the close of the fourteenth century, gathering into itself dances performed at Shinto shrines in honour of spirits and gods, or by young nobles at the Court, and much old lyric poetry, and receiving its philosophy and its final shape perhaps from priests of a contemplative school of Buddhism.[6] A small *daimio* or feudal lord of the ancient capital of Nara, a contemporary of Chaucer, was the author, or perhaps only the stage-manager, of many plays.[7] He brought them to the Court of the Shogun at Kyoto. From that on the Shogun and his Court were as busy with dramatic poetry as the Mikado and his with lyric. [...] Some of the old noble families are today very poor, their men, it may be, but servants and labourers, but they still frequent these theatres. 'Accomplishment' the word Noh means, and it is their accomplishment and that of a few cultivated people who understand the literary and mythological allusions and the ancient lyrics quoted in

---

[6]  Zen Buddhism was indeed a strong influence on the development of Noh.

[7]  Kanze Kan'ami Kiyotsugu (1333–84), the creator of Nohgaku (i.e., Noh drama in the narrow sense which developed out of earlier types of Noh-related performance) was no mere stage-manager, even in the sense of director: he was both an author and a performer of distinction.

speech and chorus, their discipline, a part of their breeding. The players themselves, unlike the despised players of the popular theatre, have passed on
proudly from father to son an elaborate art, and even now a player will publish
his family tree to prove his skill.[8] One player wrote in 1906 in a business circular—I am quoting from Mr. Pound's redaction of the Notes of Fenollosa—
that after thirty generations of nobles a woman of his house dreamed that a
mask was carried to her from Heaven, and soon after she bore a son who
became a player and the father of players. His family, he declared, still possessed a letter from a fifteenth-century Mikado conferring upon them a
theatre-curtain, white below and purple above.

There were five families of these players.[9] [...] The white and purple curtain
was no doubt to hang upon a wall behind the players or over their entrance-
door, for the Noh stage is a platform surrounded upon three sides by the audience[10]. No 'naturalistic' effect is sought. The players wear masks. [...] They
sing as much as they speak, and there is a chorus which describes the scene and
interprets their thought and never becomes as in the Greek theatre a part of
the action. At the climax, instead of the disordered passion of nature, there is a
dance, a series of positions and movements which may represent a battle, or a
marriage, or the pain of a ghost in the Buddhist Purgatory. I have lately studied
certain of these dances, with Japanese players, and I notice that their ideal of
beauty, unlike that of Greece and like that of pictures from Japan or China,
makes them pause at moments of muscular tension. The interest is not in the
human form but in the rhythm to which it moves, and the triumph of their art
is to express the rhythm in its intensity. There are few swaying movements of
arms or body such as make the beauty of our dancing. They move from the
hip, keeping constantly the upper part of their body still, and seem to associate
with every gesture or pose some definite thought. They cross the stage with a
sliding movement, and one gets the impression not of undulation but of continuous straight lines. [...]

## VI

[...] In the plays themselves I discover a beauty or a subtlety that I can trace
perhaps to their threefold origin. The love-sorrows—the love of father and
daughter, of mother and son, of boy and girl—may owe their nobility to a
courtly life, but he to whom the adventures happen, a traveller commonly
from some distant place, is most often a Buddhist priest; and the occasional
intellectual subtlety is perhaps Buddhist. The adventure itself is often the

---

[8] The beginnings of the popular Kabuki theatre—in the early years of the seventeenth century—
were considerably later than those of Noh. The performance skills of Kabuki also tend to be passed
down from father to son, very much like those of Noh.

[9] There are still five family-based Noh companies to this day, viz., Kanze, Komparu, Hōshō, Kongō,
and Kita.

[10] Actually, the audience sits on two, not three, sides of the Noh stage.

meeting with ghost, god, or goddess at some holy place or much-legended tomb; and god, goddess or ghost reminds me at times of our own Irish legends and beliefs which once, it may be, differed little from those of the Shinto worshipper. […]

I wonder am I fanciful in discovering in the plays themselves […] a playing upon a single metaphor, as deliberate as the echoing rhythm of line in Chinese or Japanese painting. In the *Nishikigi*[11] the ghost of the girl-lover carries the cloth she went on weaving out of grass when she should have opened the chamber door to her lover, and woven grass returns again and again in metaphor and incident. The lovers, now that in an aery body they must sorrow for unconsummated love, are 'tangled up as the grass patterns are tangled.' Again they are like an unfinished cloth; 'these bodies, having no weft, even now are not come together; truly a shameful story, a tale to bring shame to the gods.' Before they can bring the priest to the tomb they spend the day 'pushing aside the grass from the overgrown ways in Kefu,' and the countryman who directs them is 'cutting grass on the hill'; and when at last the prayer of the priest unites them in marriage the bride says that he has made 'a dream-bridge over wild grass, over the grass I dwell in'; and in the end bride and bridegroom show themselves for a moment 'from under the shadow of the love-grass.' […]

One half remembers a thousand Japanese paintings, or whichever comes first into the memory: that screen painted by Korin, let us say, shown lately at the British Museum, where the same form is echoing in wave and in cloud and in rock. […] In neglecting character, which seems to us essential in drama, as do their artists in neglecting relief and depth, whether in their paintings or in arranging flowers in a vase in a thin row, they have made possible a hundred lovely intricacies. […]

---

[11] *Nishikigi* (The Decorated Tree), a play by Kanze Zeami Motokiyo (1363–1443), was to be one of the sources for Yeats's *The Dreaming of the Bones* (1919) shortly after the above essay was written. See F. A. C. Wilson, *Yeats's Iconography* (London: Gollancz, 1960), 213–23.

# On the Theatre: The Fairground Booth (1913)

## Vsevolod Emilievich Meyerhold

The Russian director Vsevolod Emilievich Meyerhold (1874–1942) had been a theatrical innovator long before he was to become the dominant (though never uncontroversial) director in the Soviet theatre of the 1920s and early 1930s. He began his career in 1897 with the Moscow Art Theatre, but broke away from Stanislavsky as early as 1902 to seek out his own defiantly anti-naturalistic path. In his quest for a pure theatricalism unclogged by over-elaborate psychology, Meyerhold looked to older forms of theatre such as the *commedia dell'arte*, to popular entertainments such as circus and fairground, and to exotic types of performance such as Japanese Kabuki. Some of these different strands came together in 1906 when he directed the first production of *The Fairground Booth* (also known as *The Puppet Show* or *The Farce*) by the Russian symbolist poet-playwright Alexander Blok (1880–1921), which combined commedia motifs with touches of the grotesque. Meyerhold's pre-war battle to reform the theatre, in parallel with similar efforts by other innovators such as the Englishman Gordon Craig (see pp. 138–44), the Swiss Adolphe Appia (see pp. 145–52), the German Georg Fuchs, and the Russian Nikolai Evreinov, was carried on into the Soviet period under drastically altered auspices, when the ideological superstructure of his post-revolutionary work was to be thoroughly reformulated as he became an advocate of a communist theatre. The following essay, excerpts from which are given below, sums up Meyerhold's strivings before the First World War; it was first published in his book *O Teatre* (On the Theatre, 1912).

[…] The public comes to the theatre to see the art of man, but what art is there in walking about the stage as oneself? The public expects invention, play-acting and skill. But what it gets is either life or a slavish imitation of life. Surely

From Edward Braun (trans. and ed.), *Meyerhold on Theatre* (London: Methuen, rev. edn., 1991), 119–42.

the art of man on the stage consists in shedding all traces of environment, carefully choosing a mask, donning a decorative costume, and showing off one's brilliant tricks to the public—now as a dancer, now as the intrigant at some masquerade, now as the fool of old Italian comedy, now as a juggler.

If you examine the dog-eared pages of old scenarios such as Flaminio Scala's anthology, you will discover the magical power of the mask.[1]

Arlecchino, a native of Bergamo and the servant of the miserly Doctor, is forced to wear a coat with multicoloured patches because of his master's meanness. Arlecchino is a foolish buffoon, a roguish servant who seems always to wear a cheerful grin. But look closer! What is hidden behind the mask? Arlecchino, the all-powerful wizard, the enchanter, the magician; Arlecchino, the emissary of the infernal powers.

The mask may conceal more than just two aspects of a character. The two aspects of Arlecchino represent two opposite poles. Between them lies an infinite range of shades and variations. How does one reveal this extreme diversity of character to the spectator? With the aid of the mask.

The actor who has mastered the art of gesture and movement (herein lies his power!) manipulates his masks in such a way that the spectator is never in any doubt about the character he is watching: whether he is the foolish buffoon from Bergamo or the Devil.

This chameleonic power, concealed beneath the expressionless visage of the comedian, invests the theatre with all the enchantment of chiaroscuro. Is it not the mask which helps the spectator to fly away to the land of make-believe?

The mask enables the spectator to see not only the actual Arlecchino before him but all the Arlecchinos who live in his memory. Through the mask the spectator sees every person who bears the merest resemblance to the character. [...]

The theatre of the mask has always been a fairground show, and the idea of acting based on the apotheosis of the mask, gesture and movement is indivisible from the idea of the travelling show. Those concerned in reforming the contemporary theatre dream of introducing the principles of the fairground booth into the theatre. However, the sceptics believe that the revival of the principles of the fairground booth is being obstructed by the cinematograph.

Far too much importance is attached to the cinematograph, that idol of the modern city, by its supporters. The cinematograph is of undoubted importance to science as a means of visual demonstration; it can serve as an illustrated newspaper depicting 'the events of the day'; for some people it might even replace travel (horror of horrors!). But there is no place for the cinematograph in the world of art, even in a purely auxiliary capacity. And if for some reason or other the cinematograph is called a theatre, it is simply because

---

[1] Flaminio Scala, director and writer of the commedia dell'arte group of I Confidenti from 1612 to 1621, published the first ever collection of scenarios, *Il teatro delle favole rappresentative* (1611); this contained as many as fifty pieces.

during the period of total obsession with naturalism (an obsession which has already cooled off considerably) everything mechanical was enrolled in the service of the theatre.

This extreme obsession with naturalism, so characteristic of the general public at the end of the nineteenth and the beginning of the twentieth century, was one of the original reasons for the extraordinary success of the cinematograph. [...]

Whilst reproaching the classicists and the romantics with their obsession with form, the naturalists themselves set about perfecting form and in so doing transformed art into photography. [...]

Just as all the theatres which are still trying to propagate naturalistic drama and plays fit only for reading cannot stay the growth of truly theatrical and totally non-naturalistic plays, so the cinematograph cannot stifle the spirit of the fairground booth.[2]

At the present time, when the cinematograph is in the ascendant, the absence of the fairground booth is only apparent. The fairground booth is eternal. Its heroes do not die; they simply change their aspects and assume new forms. The heroes of the ancient Atellanae, the foolish Maccus and the simple Pappus,[3] were resurrected almost twenty centuries later in the figures of Arlecchino and Pantalone, the principal characters of the *commedia dell'arte*, the travelling theatre of the late Renaissance. Their audience came not so much to listen to dialogue as to watch the wealth of movement, cudgellings, dizzy leaps, and all the whole range of tricks native to the theatre.

The fairground booth is eternal. Even though its principles have been banished temporarily from within the walls of the theatre, we know that they remain firmly embedded in the lines of all true theatrical writers. [...]

Banished from the contemporary theatre, the principles of the fairground booth found a temporary refuge in the French cabarets, the German Überbrettl, the English music halls and the ubiquitous 'variétés'. If you read Ernst von Wolzogen's Überbrettl manifesto,[4] you will find that in essence it is an apologia for the principles of the fairground booth.

The manifesto stresses the significance of the art of the variétés, whose roots extend far below the surface of our age, and which it is wrong to regard as 'a temporary aberration of taste'. [...]

Wolzogen's manifesto contains an apologia for the favourite device of the fairground booth—*the grotesque*.[5] [...]

---

[2] Meyerhold was to modify his rejection of the cinema shortly afterwards—in fact he directed several films between 1915 and 1917.

[3] The comic slave Maccus and the testy old man Pappus were stock characters of the *fabula Atellana*, the type of farce which flourished in Campania from the 3rd century BC or earlier.

[4] The aristocratic poet Ernst von Wolzogen (1855–1934) founded the *Überbrettl* (or Supercabaret) in Berlin in 1901—the first of a series of literary cabarets that were to spring up in Germany at that time.

[5] The idea of the 'grotesque' as a weapon against fossilized aesthetic concepts had been put forward as early as in 1827 by Victor Hugo, in the famous preface to his play, *Cromwell*.

Grotesque (Italian—grottesca) is the title of a genre of low comedy in literature, music and the plastic arts. Grotesque usually implies something hideous and strange, a humorous work which with no apparent logic combines the most dissimilar elements by *ignoring their details and relying on its own originality, borrowing from every source anything which satisfies its joie de vivre and its capricious, mocking attitude to life.*[6]

This is the style which reveals the most wonderful horizons to the creative artist. 'I', my personal attitude to life, precedes all else. Everything which I take as material for my art corresponds not to the truth of reality but to the truth of *my* personal artistic whim.

Art is incapable of conveying the sum of reality, that is, all concepts as they succeed one another in time. Art dismantles reality, depicting it now spatially, now temporally. [...] *The impossibility of embracing the totality of reality justifies the schematization of the real (in particular by means of stylization).*[7]

Stylization involves a certain degree of verisimilitude. In consequence, the stylizer remains an analyst *par excellence* [...]

'Schematization'—the very word seems to imply a certain impoverishment of reality, as though it somehow entailed the reduction of its totality. The grotesque is the second stage in the process of stylization, when the final link with analysis has been severed. Its method is strictly synthetical. Without compromise, the grotesque ignores all minor details and creates a totality of life 'in stylized improbability' (to borrow Pushkin's phrase). Stylization impoverishes life to the extent that it reduces empirical abundance to typical unity. The grotesque mixes opposites, consciously creating harsh incongruity and *relying solely on its own originality.*

In Hoffmann,[8] ghosts take stomach pills, a bunch of flaming lilies turns into the gaudy dressing-gown of Lindhorst, the student Anselmus is fitted into a glass bottle. In Tirso de Molina,[9] the hero's monologue has no sooner attuned the spectator to an air of solemnity—as though with the majestic chords of a church organ—than it is followed by a monologue of the *gracioso*[10] whose comic twists instantly wipe the devout smile from his face and make him guffaw like some mediaeval barbarian.

---

[6] *Bolshaya Entsiklopdeia*, 1902. [Meyerhold's note.]

[7] Andrei Bely, *Simvolism* (Moscow, 1910), section 2, 'Formy iskusstva'.

[8] Many of the fantastic tales of the German author Ernst Theodor Amadeus Hoffmann (1776–1822) combined macabre with comical elements. Multi-talented, Hoffmann was also a composer and conductor, a stage director, scenic designer and scene painter, a cartoonist and muralist. His influence extended all over Europe; his image has been immortalized in Offenbach's opera, *The Tales of Hoffmann* (1880).—The archivist Lindhorst and student Anselmus are characters in Hoffmann's story, *The Golden Pot*.

[9] Tirso de Molina was the pseudonym of the Spanish monk and playwright Gabriel Téllez (*c.*1579–1648). The best remembered of his approximately 300 plays is the first dramatic treatment of the Don Juan theme, *El burlador de Sevilla y convidado de piedra* (The Trickster of Seville and the Stone Guest, 1630).

[10] The *gracioso* (the amusing one) was the stereotypical comic servant of Spanish Golden Age drama. If Meyerhold had Tirso de Molina's Don Juan play in mind here, the comic servant referred to would be the *gracioso* Catalinón.

On a rainy autumn day a funeral procession creeps through the streets, the gait of the pall-bearers conveys profound grief. Then the wind snatches the hat from the head of one of the mourners; he bends down to pick it up, but the wind begins to chase it from puddle to puddle. Each jump of the staid gentleman chasing his hat lends his face such comic grimaces that the gloomy funeral procession is suddenly transformed by some devilish hands into a bustling holiday crowd. If only one could achieve an effect like that on the stage![11]

*Contrast.* Surely the grotesque is not intended simply as a means of creating or heightening contrasts! Is the grotesque not an end in itself? Like Gothic architecture, for example, in which the soaring bell-tower expresses the fervour of the worshipper whilst its projections decorated with fearsome distorted figures direct one's thoughts back towards hell. [...] Just as in Gothic architecture a miraculous balance is preserved between affirmation and denial, the celestial and the terrestrial, the beautiful and the ugly, so the grotesque parades ugliness in order to prevent beauty from lapsing into sentimentality (in Schiller's sense).[12]

The grotesque has its own attitude towards the outward appearance of life. The grotesque deepens life's outward appearance to the point where it ceases to appear merely natural.

Beneath what we see of life there are vast unfathomed depths. In its search for the supernatural, the grotesque synthesizes opposites, creates a picture of the incredible, and invites the spectator to solve the riddle of the inscrutable.

Blok (in Acts One and Three of *The Unknown Woman*), Fyodor Sologub (*Vanka the Steward and Jehan the Page*) and Wedekind (*Earth Spirit, Pandora's Box, Spring's Awakening*) have all succeeded in remaining within the bounds of realistic drama whilst adopting a new approach to the portrayal of life.[13] They have achieved unusual effects within the bounds of realistic drama by resorting to the grotesque.

The realism of these dramatists in the plays mentioned is such that it forces the spectator to adopt an ambivalent attitude towards the stage action. Is it not the task of the grotesque in the theatre to preserve this ambivalent attitude in the spectator by switching the course of the action with strokes of contrast?

---

[11] While the comic funeral here wished-for by Meyerhold has not become a stage convention, the cinema has attempted it more than once, e.g. René Clair in *Entr'acte* (1924) and Fellini in *The Clowns* (1970).

[12] This reference to Schiller's famous essay, *Über naive und sentimentalische Dichtung* (On Naive and Sentimental Poetry) is perhaps less than fair to Schiller, who employed the concept of 'sentimentality' not in the current derogatory sense of the word but rather to denote the poetic self-consciousness of the modern age as against the spontaneous (naive) productivity of earlier periods.

[13] Alexander Blok (1880–1921), Russian poet and playwright, used grotesque juxtapositions in his later plays, foreshadowing the Theatre of the Absurd. His play, *The Unknown Woman*, was staged by Meyerhold in 1914.—The play, *The Triumph of Death* (1907) by the Russian symbolist playwright, Fyodor Sologub (1863–1927), was also produced by Meyerhold.—Many of the plays of the German dramatist Frank Wedekind (1864–1918) contained some grotesque elements.

The basis of the grotesque is the artist's constant desire to switch the spectator from the plane he has just reached to another which is totally unforeseen.

'Grotesque is the title of a genre of low comedy in literature, music and the plastic arts.' Why '*low* comedy? And why only 'comic'? It is not only humorous artists who for no apparent reason have synthesized the most diverse natural phenomena in their works. The grotesque [...] can as easily be tragic, as we know from the drawings of Goya, the horrific tales of Edgar Allen Poe, and above all, of course, from E. T. A. Hoffmann. [...]

The art of the grotesque is based on the conflict between form and content. The grotesque aims to subordinate psychologism to a decorative task. That is why in every theatre which has been dominated by the grotesque the aspect of design in its widest sense has been so important (for example, the Japanese theatre). Not only the settings, the architecture of the stage, and the theatre itself are decorative, but also the mime, movements, gestures and poses of the actors. Through being decorative they become expressive. For this reason the technique of the grotesque contains elements of the dance; only with the help of the dance is it possible to subordinate grotesque conceptions to a decorative task. It was no coincidence that the Greeks looked for elements of the dance in every rhythmical movement, even in the march. It is no coincidence that the Japanese actor offering a flower to his beloved recalls in his movements the lady in a Japanese quadrille with her torso swaying, her head turning and slightly inclining, and her arms gracefully outstretched first to the left, then to the right.

'*Cannot the body, with its lines and its harmonious movements, sing as clearly as the voice?*'

When we can answer this question (from Blok's *Unknown Woman*) in the affirmative, when in the art of the grotesque form triumphs over content, then the soul of the grotesque and the soul of the theatre will be one. The fantastic will exist in its own right on the stage; *joie de vivre* will be discovered in the tragic as well as in the comic; the demonic will be manifested in deepest irony and the tragi-comic in the commonplace; we shall strive for 'stylized improbability', for mysterious allusions, deception and transformation; we shall eradicate the sweetly sentimental from the romantic; the dissonant will sound as perfect harmony, and the commonplace of everyday life will be transcended.

# On the Art of the Theatre: The First Dialogue (1905)
## *An Expert and a Playgoer are Conversing* (1911)

## Edward Gordon Craig

The practical amount of stage work—as actor, director, and designer—that Edward Gordon Craig (1872–1966) accomplished in a lifetime dedicated to the theatre was actually quite modest; the influence of his ideas, however, has been immense. He tirelessly argued that the theatre was more than just an interpretative enterprise and claimed for it the status of an autonomous art form in its own right. This was to be craft-based and integrated (as the music-drama had been in Wagner's hands) by the dominant figure of the all-powerful stage-director. Craig spread his anti-naturalist message in the quarterly magazine, *The Mask*, which he edited virtually single-handed from 1908 to 1929, as well as in his books, often lavishly illustrated by himself—notably in *The Art of the Theatre* (1905) and its revised version, *On the Art of the Theatre* (1911). In close contact, during the earlier part of his career, with outstanding men of the theatre in different parts of Europe, from Reinhardt in Germany to Yeats in Ireland and Stanislavsky in Russia, he supplied a theoretical foundation for the notion of a *director's theatre*, which had in any case been taking root in the nineteenth and which was to become the dominant mode in the twentieth century. Craig's theoretical view of the theatre was, if only negatively, a contribution to the theory of drama as well. This emerges clearly enough in the following excerpt from a Dialogue between a Stage-Director (Craig himself in thin disguise) and a somewhat naive Playgoer who is content to ask all the right questions. The downgrading of the literary text advocated here, from having been the mainspring of the whole theatrical phenomenon to constituting no more than one of its several ingredients (and not necessarily the most important one at that), was an early articulation of a tilt, characteristic of a good deal of twentieth-century theatre, in the balance between its literary and the non-literary aspects.

From Edward Gordon Craig, *On the Art of the Theatre* (London: Heinemann, 1911), 171–81.

**Stage-Director**

[...] It will not be difficult for you to understand that a theatre in which so many hundred persons are engaged at work is in many respects like a ship, and demands like management. And it will not be difficult for you to see how the slightest sign of disobedience would be disastrous. Mutiny has been well anticipated in the navy, but not in the theatre. The navy has taken care to define, in clear and unmistakable voice, that the captain of the vessel is the king, and a despotic ruler into the bargain. Mutiny on a ship is dealt with by a court-martial and is put down by a very severe punishment, by imprisonment, or by dismissal from the service.

**Playgoer**

But you are not going to suggest such a possibility for the theatre?

**Stage-Director**

The theatre, unlike the ship, is not made for purposes of war, and so for some unaccountable reason discipline is not held to be of such vital importance, whereas it is of as much importance as in any branch of service. But what I wish to show you is that until discipline is understood in the theatre to be willing and reliant obedience to the manager or captain no supreme achievement can be accomplished.

**Playgoer**

But are not the actors, scene-men, and the rest all willing workers?

**Stage-Director**

Why, my dear friend, there never were such glorious-natured people as these men and women of the theatre. They are enthusiastically willing, but sometimes their judgement is at fault, and they become as willing to be unruly as to be obedient, and as willing to lower the standard as to raise it. As for nailing the flag to the mast—this is seldom dreamed of—for *compromise* and the vicious doctrine of compromise with the enemy is preached by the officers of the theatrical navy. Our enemies are vulgar display, the lower public opinion, and ignorance. To these our 'officers' wish us to knuckle under. What the theatre people have not yet quite comprehended is *the value of a high standard and the value of a director who abides by it.*

**Playgoer**

And that director, why should he not be an actor or a scene-painter?

**Stage-Director**

Do you pick your leader from the ranks, exalt him to be captain, and then let him handle the guns and the ropes? No; the director of a theatre must be a man apart from any of the crafts. He must be a man who knows but no longer handles the ropes.

**Playgoer**
But I believe it is a fact that many well-known leaders in the theatres have been actors and stage-managers[1] at the same time?

**Stage-Director**
Yes, that is so. But you will not find it easy to assure me that no mutiny was heard of under their rule. Right away from all this question of positions there is the question of the art, the work. If an actor assumes the management of the stage, and if he is a better actor than his fellows, a natural instinct will lead him to make himself the centre of everything. He will feel that unless he does so the work will appear thin and unsatisfying. He will pay less heed to the play than he will to his own part, and he will, in fact, gradually cease to look upon the work as a whole. And this is not good for the work. This is not the way a work of art is to be produced in the theatre.

**Playgoer**
But might it not be possible to find a great actor who would be so great an artist that as manager he would never do as you say, but who would always handle himself as actor, just the same as he handles the rest of the material?

**Stage-Director**
All things are possible, but, firstly, it is against the nature of an actor to do as you suggest; secondly, it is against the nature of the stage-manager to perform; and thirdly, it is against all nature that a man can be in two places at once. Now, the place of the actor is on the stage, in a certain position, ready by means of his brains to give suggestions of certain emotions, surrounded by certain scenes and people; and it is the place of the stage-manager to be in front of this, that he may view it as a whole. So that you see even if we found our perfect actor who was our perfect stage-manager, he could not be in two places at the same time. [...]

**Playgoer**
I understand, then, that you would allow no one to rule on the stage except the stage-manager?

**Stage-Director**
The nature of the work permits nothing else.

---

[1] The word 'stage manager' is here used not in the current sense of the person in charge of the technical aspects of running a show, but in the sense of what is now called a 'director'.

**Playgoer**
Not even the playwright?

**Stage-Director**
Only when the playwright has practised and studied the crafts of acting, scene-painting, costume, lighting, and dance, not otherwise. But playwrights, who have not been cradled in the theatre, generally know little of these crafts. Goethe, whose love for the theatre remained ever fresh and beautiful, was in many ways one of the greatest of stage-directors. But when he linked himself to the Weimar theatre, he forgot to do what the great musician who followed him remembered. Goethe permitted an authority in the theatre higher than himself, that is to say, the owner of the theatre.[2] Wagner was careful to possess himself of his theatre and become a sort of feudal baron in his castle.

**Playgoer**
Was Goethe's failure as a theatre director due to this fact?

**Stage-Director**
Obviously, for had Goethe held the keys of the doors that impudent little poodle would never have got as far as the dressing-room; the leading lady would never have made the theatre and herself immortally ridiculous; and Weimar would have been saved the tradition of having perpetrated the most shocking blunder which ever occurred inside a theatre.[3]

**Playgoer**
The traditions of most theatres certainly do not seem to show that the artist is held in much respect on the stage.

**Stage-Director**
Well, it would be easy to say a number of hard things about the theatre and its ignorance of art. But one does not hit a thing which is down, unless perhaps with the hope that the shock may cause it to leap to its feet again. And our Western theatre is very much down. The East still boasts a theatre.[4] Ours here in the West is on its last legs. But I look for a Renaissance.

**Playgoer**
How will that come?

---

[2] A somewhat one-sided presentation of the case. After Duke Karl August set up his own theatre in Weimar in 1791 and appointed Goethe to run it for him, there was no possibility of the latter ever taking it over as if he were its owner.

[3] Goethe's dismissal from the direction of the Weimar Court Theatre on 13 April 1817 was due in the first instance to his objecting, contrary to Karl August's wishes, to a spectacle being staged which featured a trained dog; the indirect cause was the opposition of the company's leading actress, Karoline Jagemann, who was the Duke's mistress, to Goethe's management style.

[4] For Yeats's—somewhat later—admiration for Japanese Noh plays, see pp. 126–31.

**Stage-Director**

Through the advent of a man who shall contain in him all the qualities which go to make up a master of the theatre, and through the reform of the theatre as an instrument. When that is accomplished, when the theatre has become a masterpiece of mechanism, when it has invented a technique, it will without any effort develop a *creative art* of its own. [...] There are already some theatre men at work on the building of the theatres; some are reforming the acting, some the scenery. And all of this must be of some small value. But the very first thing to be realized is that little or no result can come from the reforming of a single craft of the theatre without at the same time, in the same theatre, reforming all the other crafts. *The whole Renaissance of the Art of the Theatre depends upon the extent that this is realised.* The Art of the Theatre [...] is divided up into so many crafts: acting, scene, costume, lighting, carpentering, singing, dancing, etc., that it must be realized at the commencement that ENTIRE, not PART reform is needed; and it must be realized that *one* part, one craft has a *direct* bearing upon each of the other crafts in the theatre, and that no result can come from fitful, uneven reform, but only from a systematic progression. Therefore, the reform of the Art of the Theatre is possible to those men alone who have studied and practised all the crafts of the theatre.

**Playgoer**

That is to say, your ideal stage-manager.

**Stage-Director**

Yes. [...] I told you my belief in the Renaissance of the Art of the Theatre was based in my belief in the Renaissance of the stage-director, and that when he had understood the right use of actors, scene, costume, lighting, and dance, and by means of these had mastered the crafts of interpretation, he would then gradually acquire the mastery of action, line, colour, rhythm, and words, this last strength developing out of all the rest ... Then I said the Art of the Theatre would have won back its rights, and its work would stand self-reliant as a creative art, and no longer be an interpretative craft.

**Playgoer**

[...] I do not quite in my mind's eye see the stage without its poet.

**Stage-Director**

What? Shall anything be lacking when the poet shall no longer write for the theatre?

**Playgoer**

The play will be lacking.

**Stage-Director**

Are you sure of that?

**Playgoer**
Well, the play will certainly not exist if the poet or playwright is not there to write it.

**Stage-Director**
There will not be any play in the sense in which you use the word.

**Playgoer**
But you propose to present something to the audience, and I presume before you are able to present them with that something you must have it in your possession.

**Stage-Director**
Certainly; you could not have made a surer remark. Where you are at fault is to take for granted, as if it were a law for the Medes and Persians, that that *something* must be made of words.

**Playgoer**
Well, what is this something which is not words, but for presentation to the audience?

**Stage-Director**
First tell me, is not an idea something?

**Playgoer**
Yes, but it lacks form.

**Stage-Director**
Well, but is it not permissible to give an idea whatever form the artist chooses?

**Playgoer**
Yes.

**Stage-Director**
And is it an unpardonable crime for the theatrical artist to use some different material to the poet's?

**Playgoer**
No.

**Stage-Director**
Then we are permitted to attempt to give form to an idea in whatever material we can find or invent, provided it is not a material which should be put to a better use?

**Playgoer**
Yes.

**Stage-Director**
Very good. […] Since you have granted all I asked you to permit, I am now going to tell you out of what material an artist of the theatre of the future will create his masterpieces. Out of ACTION, SCENE and VOICE. Is it not very simple?

And when I say *action*, I mean both gesture and dancing, the prose and poetry of action.

When I say *scene*, I mean all which comes before the eye, such as the lighting, costume, as well as the scenery.

When I say *voice*, I mean the spoken word or the word which is sung, in contradiction to the word which is read, for the word written to be spoken and the word written to be read are two entirely different things. […]

Berlin: 1905.

# Organic Unity (1921)

## Adolphe Appia

The life's work of the Swiss stage designer and theorist Adolphe Appia (1862–1928) paralleled that of the other great theatrical innovator, Gordon Craig. Both Appia and Craig undermined the supremacy of the scenic theatre which had dominated European staging methods since the Renaissance; their new thinking inevitably questioned conventional notions of drama as well. Like Craig, whom he knew but with whom he never collaborated, Appia called for the unifying artistic control of a director-designer. Like him, he felt that the illusionistic theatre—no matter whether romantic or naturalistic—had arrived at an artistic dead end. Like Craig, Appia sketched out a revolutionary approach to production but he, too—whether by reason of personality or unfavourable external circumstances—rarely had a chance to put his ideas into practice. The first impetus to his innovative vision came from thinking through the implications of Wagner's music-dramas. He saw that in staging terms Wagner had been too much of a traditionalist as a director to do full justice to his own works at Bayreuth. In *La Mise-en-scène du drame Wagnérien* (1895) and *Die Musik und die Inscenierung* (1899) Appia suggested replacing painted scenery with three-dimensional but non-naturalistic scenic units, thus creating an integrated acting area for musically inspired stage movement, the shape and atmospherics of which were to be defined by the (then still novel) electric lighting. Later, working with his compatriot Émile Jaques-Dalcroze, the creator of eurhythmics, Appia went even further in devising variable stage spaces for movement, increasing the subtlety of lighting and doing away with the division between performers and audiences. In the final phase of his speculations he worked on the concept of 'living art'. As the following chapter indicates, he saw the intimate link between performance spaces and dramatic texts: his call for new spaces implied a call for a new type of drama altogether. Wholly divorced by this time from any practical theatre work and inspired by philosophical idealism, Appia imagined a merging of performers and spectators— the creation, in fact, of a new spirit of community in a socially disrupted world.

Translated from the French by H. D. Albright, in *Adolphe Appia's 'The Work of Living Art'* (Coral Gables: University of Miami Press, 1960), 38–58.

Fantastic as some of his late ideas may have seemed, they foreshadowed a good deal of later theatre work of the second half of the twentieth century—performance art, improvisations, happenings, and other such non-text-based developments.

[…] The dramatic author never considers the stage, as it is offered to him, as definite technical material. He always agrees to accommodate himself to the stage; he even goes so far as to shape his artistic thought according to this sad model, and he does not suffer too much in the process, for this is apparently the only way he can achieve a minimum of harmony. His situation is like that of a painter who is allowed an insufficient number of colours and a canvas of fixed but ridiculous dimensions. It is really worse than that, for a painter of genius will always find the means to express himself, as long as the essential principles of his technique are not perverted; that is to say, as long as he can work with brush, colours, and plane surface. But our modern stage offers the dramatist nonsensical technical material; it is not a medium which can be truly dedicated to dramatic work—only through an inconceivable outrage are we obliged to accept it, or even to consider it, as such a medium. Unfortunately, the habit is formed. It is with this material that we evoke dramatic works and, what is worse, it is with this material that the dramatist conceives these works, fearing lest he be not 'theatrical'. The term is hallowed: it is never our stage that is accused of not being 'theatrical,' but always the dramatist himself. That is why he is an artist without a name: he does not dominate a technique; the technique of the stage dominates him. An artist must be free; the dramatist is enslaved. Today he is not—and cannot be—an artist. […]

Slavery, like all other habits, can become second nature; it has become that for the dramatist and for his public. This is a question of conversion, then, in the truest sense of the word. A function creates its organ. […] In our day, the function of the dramatist has not created its organ; that is, a work of dramatic art is not presented to our eyes *organically*, but through an artificial, exterior mechanism which does not belong to the dramatic organism. Hence, we must probably seek within the function itself the weak point which has placed the dramatist in dependence and which helps to keep him there. […]

Should not the dramatist himself have suggested the principles of our stage decoration from the very beginning? And is he not now in danger of further postponing this initiating impulse through sheer inertia and blundering? The indiscriminate use of painting is so characteristic of all our staging that painted canvases and stage decoration are almost synonymous to us. Now, all artists know that the aim of these canvases is not to present an expressive combination of colours and forms, but to 'indicate' […] a group of details and objects. We must suppose that a real need for showing us these objects accounts for the author's seeking help from the painter. The painter, of course, responds eagerly!

If we put ourselves in the place of the author at the moment he chooses his subject, it is evident that this is the precise moment in which his technical liberty or dependence is decided. If the author decides that he can free himself from the means imposed by the stage, he is immediately confronted by the necessity of determining *the essential nature of a subject intended for representation.* From his point of view, a subject is concerned with characters in conflict with one another; from this conflict arise particular circumstances that make the characters react; out of their way of reacting, dramatic interest is born. To a dramatic author, this is all; dramatic art, consisting entirely of such reactions, is apparently capable of infinite variety. But he soon perceives that such is not the case; that the reactions do not vary infinitely; on the contrary, they are repeated without change; that in this sense human nature is limited; and that each of our passions has a name. As a result, he seeks to vary the interest through diversity in character; and there begin his difficulties— difficulties of dimension. To present a character, one needs time on the stage, space on paper; thus the choice is limited. The novel and the psychological study have an indefinite space—on paper, of course—at their command; a play has but three or four hours.[1]

We must seek elsewhere for variety, then; here the influence of the setting comes into play. The setting is always geographical and historical, dependent on a climate and a culture which are indicated visually by a group of specific objects. Unless the audience can see these objects, the text of the play must convey a quantity of information that will completely paralyze the action. As a result we are forced to represent them in the stage decoration.

There is more to the problem of stage decoration than the mere question of whether or not a setting can be executed. In the theatre we are not at the cinema; the laws that rule the stage are, above all, technical ones. To wish to represent nearly everything on the stage, and to invoke on that account the so-called liberty of the artist, is deliberately to lead dramatic art beyond its own limits and consequently beyond the domain of art. As long as an author remains content to show characters and their reactions, he finds himself relatively independent as far as his work is concerned. But from the moment when he uses the influence of the setting to vary the motifs, he meets with problems of staging and must reckon with them. Under present conditions his only concern is the possibility of representing things on the stage. He will reject all projects that are too difficult to represent; in general, he will confine his choice to places and things that he knows are easy to realize in production and are suitable for maintaining the illusion which is so dear to him. Like the ostrich, he chooses to ignore danger. But how can he help perceiving that decorative

---

[1] To put on the stage a character whose description and development need a volume of 300 pages is one of the banal monstrosities of our theatre. [Appia's note.]

technique is regulated by laws other than those of possibility? If he has money to throw out of the window, an author can obtain anything on the stage. The Romans caused a river to pass through the Circus, in the midst of vegetation like that of a virgin forest. The Duke of Meiningen bought museums, apartments, and palaces in order to realize two or three scenes.[2] The results in both cases were artistically regrettable.

No; stage decoration is regulated by the presence of the living body. This body is the final authority concerning the possibility of realization; everything that is incongruous or inconsistent in relation to its presence is 'impossible' and suppresses the play.

In the choice of his subject, the author must question, not the director-designer but the actor. Such a generalization, of course, is not meant to suggest that he seek his advice from this actor or that. It is the Idea of the living actor—plastic and mobile—that must be his guide. For example, he must ask himself whether a certain setting is in keeping with the presence of the actor, and not merely whether its realization is 'possible'. From a technical point of view, his choice is concerned with the importance he wishes to—or must—give to the influence of the setting. From both points of view, he must choose with a full knowledge of conditions, and consequently must know perfectly the normal scenic hierarchy and its results.

His technique as an artist determines his choice. The painter is not irked by the fact that plastic relief is denied him; his technique simply does not permit such a possibility. So must it be for the dramatic author. He need not be distressed by the fact that he cannot place his character in a cathedral, but rather by the fact that he cannot free the character from conditions harmful to its full realization on the stage. The novelist and the epic poet can evoke their heroes by means of description; their work is a story that is told, and the action is placed *in* the story, since it is not living. But the dramatic author is not merely telling a story; his living action is free, stripped of all drapery. Every indication of specific place tends to bring it nearer to the novel or the epic, and to remove it further from dramatic art. The more 'indication' of place is necessary to the action—that is, to make the characters, the events, and the reactions plausible —the more the action will be estranged from *living* Art. *The reason is purely and simply a technical one, and no one can change it in any way.* [...]

For when anyone says 'Dramatist,' he says 'Stage-director' in the same breath; it is a sacrilege to specialize the two activities. We may set up as a rule, then, that if the dramatist does not insist on controlling both, he will be incapable of controlling either—since it is from their mutual correlation that *living* art must be born. Only in very rare exceptions do we yet have this supreme art or its artist. By misplacing the centre of gravity, so to speak, we divide our art; in one respect our dramatic art rests on the author, in another on the

---

[2] The company of George II, Duke of Meiningen (1826–1914), was noted throughout Europe for the elaborate historical detail of its productions between 1874 and 1890.

director-designer. Sometimes it relies more on the one, sometimes on the other; it should rest simply and clearly on the dramatist himself.

The technical synthesis of the elements of representation finds its source in the *initial idea* of dramatic art. It depends on the *attitude* of the author. This attitude frees him; without it, he is not an artist. [...]

The synthesis of the elements of production cannot be determined by and for itself. If we are familiar with these elements, if we know how to measure their power of expression and their respective limits, if we are able to place them in proper relation—then we possess the means to make their use depend exclusively on the author. That is why the idea of a subject now appears of *technical* importance. The unity of the elements will no longer be regulated in advance and imposed upon the dramatist, as it is by the stage of today; the whole responsibility will be his from the beginning. Consequently, he is obliged to be an artist.

However, although the elements he uses are henceforth at his disposal, yet they are not completely in his hands; to realize his artistic dreams, he doubtless needs collaborators. Will this be a new form of slavery? Barely promoted to the rank of an artist—through the complete possession of his own technique—is he going to fall back again into guardianship and lose all the advantages of his many sacrifices? What will be the character of such collaboration? Will this collaboration be merely assistance, or will it penetrate deeper—even to the choice of a subject? Let us put aside for the moment the material services that the electrician, the carpenter and other artisans will be prepared to offer; they go on by themselves, hierarchically concerned with the body of the actor which regulates them. Let us consider for the present only those elements which dictate to the life and the movement of that body. Then, afterwards, we shall turn to the body itself, that marvellous intermediary, dominated by the dramatist, but in its turn dominating space.

Our theatrical habits make it very difficult to imagine what freedom in staging could mean and to visualize a new handling of the elements of production. We cannot conceive of a theatre, it seems, except in terms of the present-day stage—a limited space filled with cut-out paintings, in the midst of which actors pace up and down, separated from us by a clear-cut line of demarcation. Further, the presence of plays and musical scores in our libraries is apparently enough to convince us that a work of dramatic art can exist without actual presentation. Reading the play, or playing over the score on the piano, we are convinced that they are living and that we possess them. Otherwise, how can we account for the renown of a Racine or a Wagner? Is it not evident that their work is on these sheets of paper? What does it matter whether we produce their work or not, since these texts in themselves can remain immortal? There we are! The dramatic author chooses a form of art that is visual, that is meant for our eyes; yet when he writes it down on paper its fame and glory are assured.

What would Rembrandt amount to, if we had only an account of his pictures? His treatment of colour cannot be adequately described, would you say? [...]

The theatre has become intellectualized. Today the body is nothing but the bearer and representative of a literary text; its gestures and movements are not *regulated* by the text but simply *inspired* by it. The actor interprets, according to his own liking, what the author has written; hence his personal importance on the stage is exclusively interpretative rather than technical, with the result that his role is developed according to one conception, while the settings are being painted according to another. Their union is therefore arbitrary and almost accidental. This procedure is repeated for each new play, and the principle remains the same, whatever care we take with the production in other respects.

It is characteristic of theatre reform that all serious effort is instinctively directed toward the *mise en scène*. As for the text of the play, fluctuations of taste result in classicism, romanticism, realism, etc., all of which encroach on each other, combine with each other, approve or disapprove of each other, and make a desperate appeal to the designer-technician without being heard. But in spite of so many varieties of text, we remain in the same place. The detailed scenic indications which the author sometimes adds to the text of his play always have a childish effect, like the little boy who is determined to enter his little countryside of sand and twigs. The presence of the actor overwhelms the artificial construction; the only contact between the two is grotesque since it accentuates the impotence of the author's effort.

But if one courageously directs one's efforts to the *mise en scène* itself, one is surprised to find that one is attacking the *whole dramatic problem*. To be precise: for what existing plays do we wish to reform the stage? What shall be our standard of values? When we consider the stage as something to be stared at, so to speak, as something quite distinct from the audience, it eludes us. What is the stage as a thing apart? Obviously nothing. It is precisely because of this desire to make the stage something in itself that we have strayed so far from Art. At the very start, then, we must clear the table; we must effect in our imagination this apparently difficult conversion, which consists of no longer looking upon our theatres, our stages, our halls, as necessarily existing for spectators. We must completely free the dramatic idea from any such apparently changeless law.

I spoke of halls for spectators. But dramatic art does not exist to present the human being for *others*. The human being is independent of the passive spectator; he is, or ought to be, *living*. And Life is concerned with the living. Our first move, then, will be to place ourselves imaginatively in a boundless space, with no witness but ourselves [...] To set definite proportions in this space, we must walk, then stop, then walk once more, only to stop again. These stopping places will create a sort of rhythm, which will be echoed in us and which will awaken there a need to possess Space. But Space is boundless; the only guide-mark is ourselves. Hence we are—and should be—its centre. Will its measure, then, exist in us? Shall we be the creators of Space? For whom? We are alone. Consequently it will be for ourselves alone that we will create space—that is to say, proportions to be measured by the human body in boundless space.

Soon the hidden rhythm, of which up to now we were unaware, is revealed. From whence does it spring? We know it is there: we even react to it. Under what compulsion? Our inner life grows and develops; it prescribes this gesture rather than another, this deliberate step rather than that uncertain pose. And our eyes are opened at last: they see the step and the gesture that grew out of an inner feeling: they *consider* it. The hand is advanced this far, the foot is placed there: these are the two portions of Space which they have measured. But have they measured these portions consciously and deliberately? No. Then, why just that far and no farther or no nearer? They have been led.

It is not merely mechanically that we possess Space and are its centre: it is because we are living. Space is our life; our life creates Space; our body expresses it. To arrive at that supreme conviction, we have had to walk and to gesticulate, to bend and to straighten up, to lie down and to rise again. In order to move from one point to another, we exerted an effort—however small— corresponding to the beatings of our heart. Those heart beats proportioned our gestures. In Space? No. In Time. In order to proportion Space, our body needs Time! The time duration of our movements, consequently, has determined their extent in space. Our life creates space and time, one through the other. Our living body is the expression of Space during Time, and of Time in Space. Empty and boundless Space—wherein we are placed at the start so that we may effect this essential transformation—no longer exists. We alone exist.

In dramatic art, too, we alone exist. There is no auditorium, no stage, without us and beyond us. There is no spectator, no play, without us, without us alone. We *are* the play and the stage, because it is our living body that creates them. Dramatic art is a spontaneous creation of the body; our body is the dramatic author.

The work of dramatic art is the only one that is truly identified with its author. It is the only art whose existence is certain *without spectators.* Poetry must be read; painting and sculpture, contemplated; architecture, surveyed; music, heard. A work of dramatic art is lived: it is the dramatic author who lives it. A spectator comes to be moved or convinced; therein is the limit of his role.

The work lives for itself—without the spectator. The author expresses it, possesses it, and contemplates it at the same time. A spectator's eyes and ears will never obtain anything but its reflection and echo. The framework of the stage is but a keyhole through which we overhear bits of life never intended for us. [...]

The writer has heard a renowned dramatist exclaim, after seeing a perfectly executed, but nonetheless simple, exercise in plastic rhythm: 'But now I no longer need to write plays!' Returning to his home, he may have continued to write them—but with a new *knowledge*, a knowledge of what he could and could not do, within his own art form. [...] Much the same might be true of the architect, whose visions of space and proportion would be subtly modified and clarified. No longer could he think in terms of mere walls and floors … From that time on, the living body would haunt him; henceforth, he would have to work for it alone—for the incomparable body.

# Memoranda on Masks (1932)

## Eugene O'Neill

Although Eugene O'Neill (1888–1953), author of more than sixty completed and partly written plays, has been described as a 'melodramatist', he was of all American playwrights the one most deeply dedicated to great themes in a theatre conceived as a temple of art. True, his language often prevented him from reaching the greatest heights; but as a tireless experimenter he tried to extend the language of the stage and to create, to use Cocteau's expression, a vivid 'poetry of the theatre'. In this endeavour his preoccupation with masks—either masks used literally, or actors adopting a masklike countenance—played an important role which he defended in a number of articles: a relatively rare effort at theorization on his part. Two of three articles in favour of the contemporary use of masks written for *The American Spectator* are quoted below, the second article in this series, entitled 'Second Thoughts' (December 1932), having been omitted. To O'Neill the mask offered contradictory possibilities: on the one hand, the opening up of the inner man and the revelation of secret motivations, on the other hand the depersonalization of the all too human actor. In this latter respect his thinking ran along broadly parallel lines to that of Gordon Craig, who had advocated an *Über-marionette* to replace the fallible human being on the stage, and of W. B. Yeats, who championed the mask as the engine of theatrical mystery and as a piece of fine art in its own right (see pp. 128–9).

## 1

Not masks for all plays, naturally. Obviously not for plays conceived in purely realistic terms. But masks for certain types of plays, especially for the modern play, as yet only dimly foreshadowed in a few groping specimens, but which

From: *The American Spectator* (Nov. 1932); repr. in Oscar Cargill, N. Bryllion Fagin, and William J. Fisher (eds.), *O'Neill and His Plays* (New York: New York University Press, 1961), 116–18.

must inevitably be written in the future. For I hold more and more surely to the conviction that the use of masks will be discovered eventually to be the freest solution of the modern dramatist's problem as to how—with the greatest possible dramatic clarity and economy of means—he can express those profound hidden conflicts of the mind which the probings of psychology continue to disclose to us. He must find some method to present this inner drama in his work, or confess himself incapable of portraying one of the most characteristic preoccupations and uniquely significant, spiritual impulses of his time. With his old—and more than a bit senile!—standby of realistic technique, he can do no more than, at best, obscurely hint at it through a realistically disguised surface symbolism, superficial and misleading. But that, while sufficiently beguiling to the sentimentally mystical, is hardly enough. A comprehensive expression is demanded here, a chance for eloquent presentation, a new form of drama projected from a fresh insight into the inner forces motivating the actions and reactions of men and women (a new and truer characterization, in other words), a drama of souls, and the adventures of 'Free wills,' with the masks that govern them and constitute their fates.

For what, at bottom, is the new psychological insight into human cause and effect but a study in masks, an exercise in unmasking? Whether we think the attempted unmasking has been successful, or has only created for itself new masks, is of no importance here. What is valid, what is unquestionable, is that this insight has uncovered the mask, has impressed the idea of mask as a symbol of inner reality upon all intelligent people of today; and I know they would welcome the use of masks in the theatre as a necessary, dramatically revealing new convention, and not regard them as any 'stunty' resurrection of archaic props.

This was strikingly demonstrated for me in practical experience by *The Great God Brown*,[1] which ran in New York for eight months, nearly all of that time in Broadway theatres—a play in which the use of masks was an integral part of the theme. [...]

I emphasize this play's success because the fact that a mask drama, the main values of which are psychological, mystical, and abstract, could be played in New York for eight months, has always seemed to me a more significant proof of the deeply responsive possibilities in our public than anything that has happened in our modern theatre before or since.

## 2

Looked at from even the most practical standpoint of the practising playwright, the mask *is* dramatic in itself, *has always* been dramatic in itself, *is* a proven weapon of attack. At its best, it is more subtly, imaginatively, suggest-

---

[1] In O'Neill's *The Great God Brown* (1926), masks were used to represent the divided self of the characters, as well as the personae they projected onto the people around them.

ively dramatic than any actor's face can ever be. Let anyone who doubts this study the Japanese Noh masks, or Chinese theatre masks, or African primitive masks—or right here in America the faces of the big marionettes Robert Edmond Jones made for the production of Stravinsky's *Oedipus*,[2] or Benda's famous masks, or even photographs of them.

# 3

*Dogma for the new masked drama.* One's outer life passes in a solitude haunted by the masks of others; one's inner life passes in a solitude hounded by the masks of oneself.

# 4

With masked mob a new type of play may be written in which the Mob as King, Hero, Villain, or Fool will be the main character—the Great Democratic Play!

# 5

Why not give all future Classical revivals entirely in masks? *Hamlet*, for example. Masks would liberate this play from its present confining status as exclusively a 'star vehicle'. We would be able to see the great drama we are now only privileged to read, to identify ourselves with the figure of Hamlet as a symbolic projection of a fate that is in each of us, instead of merely watching a star giving us his version of a great acting role. We would even be able to hear the sublime poetry as the innate expression of the spirit of the drama itself, instead of listening to it as realistic recitation—or ranting—by familiar actors. [...]

---

[2] Robert Edmond Jones (1887–1954) revolutionized American standards of stage design by bringing the 'New Stagecraft' of Europe over to the United States. His striking design for the staging of the Cocteau-Stravinsky *Oedipus Rex* at the Metropolitan Opera House, Philadelphia, in 1931 employed gigantic three-dimensional figures towering over the singers.

# A Dramatist's Notebook
## (1933)

### Eugene O'Neill

I advocate masks for stage crowds, mobs—wherever a sense of impersonal, collective mob psychology is wanted. This was one reason for such an extensive use of them in *Lazarus Laughed*.[1] In masking the crowds in that play, I was visualizing an effect that, intensified by dramatic lighting, would give an audience visually the sense of the Crowd, not as a random collection of individuals, but as a collective whole, an entity. When the Crowd speaks, I wanted an audience to hear the voice of the Crowd mind, Crowd emotion, as one voice of a body composed of, but quite distinct from, its parts.

And, for more practical reasons, I wanted to preserve the different crowds of another time and country from the blighting illusion-shattering recognitions by an audience of the supers on the stage. Have you ever seen a production of *Julius Caesar*? Did the Roman mob ever suggest to you anything more Roman than a gum-chewing Coney Island Mardi Gras or, in the case of a special all-star revival, a gathering of familiar-faced modern actors masquerading uncomfortably in togas? But with masks—and the proper intensive lighting—you would have been freed from these recognitions; you would have been able to imagine a Roman mob; you would not even have recognized the Third Avenue and Brooklyn accents among the supers, so effectively does a mask change the quality of a voice.

It was interesting to watch, in the final rehearsals of *The Great God Brown*, how after using their masks for a time the actors and actresses reacted to the demand made by the masks that their bodies become alive and expressive and participate in the drama. Usually it is only the actors' faces that participate. Their bodies remain bored spectators that have been dragged off to the theatre

From *The American Spectator* (Jan. 1933); repr. in Oscar Cargill, N. Bryllion Fagin, and William J. Fisher (eds.), *O'Neill and His Plays* (New York: New York University Press, 1961), 120–2.

[1] Masks helped to create the highly stylized form of *Lazarus Laughed* (1928), O'Neill's paean to life inspired by the New Testament.

when they would have much preferred a quiet evening in the upholstered chair at home.

Meaning no carping disrespect to our actors. I have been exceedingly lucky in having had some exceptionally fine acting in the principal roles in my plays, for which I am exceedingly grateful. Also some damned poor acting. But let that pass. Most of the poor acting occurred in the poor plays, and there I hold only myself responsible. In the main, wherever a part challenged the actors' or actresses' greatest possibilities, they have reacted to the challenge with a splendid creative energy and skill. Especially, and this is the point I want to make now, where the play took them away from the strictly realistic parts they were accustomed to playing. They always welcomed any opportunity that gave them new scope for their talents. So when I argue here for a non-realistic imaginative theatre I am hoping, not only for added scope for playwright and director and scenic designer, but also for a chance for the actor to develop his art beyond the narrow range to which our present theatre condemns it. Most important of all, from the standpoint of future American culture, I am hoping for added imaginative scope for the audience, a chance for a public I know is growing yearly more numerous and more hungry in its spiritual need to participate in imaginative interpretations of life rather than merely identifying itself with faithful surface resemblances of living.

I harp on the word 'imaginative'—and with intention! But what do I mean by an 'imaginative' theatre—(where I hope for it, for example, in the subtitle of *Lazarus Laughed*: A Play for an Imaginative Theatre)? I mean the one true theatre, the age-old theatre, the theatre of the Greeks and the Elizabethans, a theatre that could dare to boast—without committing a farcical sacrilege— that it is a legitimate descendant of the first theatre that sprang, by virtue of man's imaginative interpretation of life, out of his worship of Dionysus. I mean a theatre returned to its highest and sole significant function as a Temple where the religion of a poetical interpretation and symbolical celebration of life is communicated to human beings, starved in spirit by their soul-stifling daily struggle to exist as masks among the masks of the living!

But I anticipate the actors' objections to masks: that they would extinguish their personalities and deprive them of their greatest asset in conveying emotion by facial expression. I claim, however, that masks would give them the opportunity for a totally new kind of acting, that they would learn many undeveloped possibilities of their art if they appeared, even if only for a season or two, in masked roles. After all, masks did not extinguish the Greek actor, nor have they kept the acting of the East from being an art.

# Author's Note to *A Dream Play* (1901)

## August Strindberg

Just as Strindberg had written the definitive manifesto of naturalistic drama in his Preface to *Miss Julie* (see pp. 88–9), he put forward precisely the opposite doctrine in equally memorable terms at the turn of the century. The following note to *A Dream Play*—which was his own favourite among all of his plays—sums up in few words what was to become a major trend in twentieth-century drama: an irrationalism which, if not invariably indebted to the inner world of the dream, at any rate cut loose from the constraints of the everyday reality of naturalism and reinstated the unfettered imagination upon the stage. The essentially dark tone of *A Dream Play* anticipated much of the angst expressed in various kinds of irrationalist drama. Although this brief seminal statement by Strindberg has (deservedly) been reproduced quite a few times before, it simply cried out to be included here yet once again.

In this dream play the author has, as in his former dream play, TO DAMASCUS,[1] attempted to imitate the inconsequent yet transparently logical shape of a dream. Everything can happen, everything is possible and probable. Time and place do not exist; on an insignificant basis of reality the imagination spins, weaving new patterns; a mixture of memories, experiences, free fancies, incongruities and improvisations. The characters split, double, multiply, evaporate, condense, disperse, assemble. But one consciousness rules over

Translated from the Swedish by Michael Meyer, in *August Strindberg: The Plays*, ii (London: Secker & Warburg, 1975), 553.

[1] Strindberg's *To Damascus* trilogy, a fantasticated piece of autobiography, was not perhaps strictly speaking a series of 'dream plays'; but like *A Dream Play*, it can be seen as a forerunner of expressionism and other forms of theatrical non-realism. Parts I and II of *To Damascus* had been published in 1898; Part I was staged in Stockholm in 1900; but Part III did not appear until after *A Dream Play*, in 1904.

them all, that of the dreamer; for him there are no secrets, no illogicalities, no scruples, no laws. He neither acquits nor condemns, but merely relates; and, just as a dream is more often painful than happy, so an undertone of melancholy and of pity for all mortal beings accompanies this flickering tale. Sleep, the liberator, often seems a tormentor, but when the agony is harshest comes the awakening and reconciles the sufferer with reality—which, however painful, is yet a mercy, compared with the agony of the dream.

# On the Futility of the 'Theatrical' in the Theatre
## (1896)

### Alfred Jarry

This article by Alfred Jarry (1873–1907) was published in the September 1896 issue of the *Mercure de France*, shortly before the opening night of his play, *Ubu Roi* (King Ubu), which was about to be staged at the Théâtre de l'Œuvre by the avant-garde director Aurélien Lugné-Poe. Lugné-Poe published an article under the same title in the following month's issue of the *Mercure de France*, in which he referred to Elizabethan staging methods as a precedent for the non-naturalistic décor employed in the production. *Ubu Roi* was in fact only given twice (it has been revived many times since), but its sensational, scandal-raising performance constitutes a landmark in European theatre. Jarry's technical notes, which referred specifically to the forthcoming production, must be read as a practical expression of his dramaturgic innovations. His anti-bourgeois stance, formulated in the essay as an all-out attack on the theatre-going public, was embodied in the text in scabrous dialogue, primitive and blatantly two-dimensional characterization, a farcical approach to tragic material (King Ubu is a parody of sorts of *Macbeth*), and an overall defiance of decorum. This violently anti-classical play clearly implied a new form of staging, in provocative opposition to any romantic or naturalistic illusionism. It also meant a totally new, as it were dehumanized, approach to performance; Jarry's call for masked acting was not realized in the actual production, but its potential for depersonalization is one of the several sources of the twentieth-century theatre's return to the mask. Both the play and its theatrical realization were to have a long-term influence on many non-rationalist forms of theatre, especially in France (but elsewhere too)—an influence clearly traceable in the work of Apollinaire, Marinetti, and Ionesco (see pp. 165–70, 176–81, and 210–12).

I think the question of whether the theatre should adapt itself to the masses, or the masses to the theatre, has been settled once and for all. The masses only understood, or pretended to understand, the tragedies and comedies of

Translated from the French by Barbara Wright, in Alfred Jarry, *Ubu Roi* (London: Gaberbocchus Press, 1951), 177–82.

ancient Greece because their stories were known to everybody and were explained over and over again in every play anyway and, as often as not, set out by a character in the prologue. Just as nowadays they go to see the plays of Molière and Racine at the Comédie-Française because they are always being played. Besides it's a fact that most of them are over their heads. The theatre not yet having gained the freedom forcibly to chuck out anyone who doesn't understand, or to clear the auditorium at each interval before the shouting and smashing begins, we can be satisfied with the established truth that if people do fight in the theatre it will be over a work of popularization, one that is not in the least original and is therefore more readily accessible than the original; an original work will, at least on the first night, be greeted by a public that remains bemused and consequently dumb.

And the first-night public consists of the people who want to understand.

If we want to lower ourselves to the level of the public, there are two things we can do for them and which *are* being done for them: the first is to give them characters who think as they do (a Siamese or Chinese ambassador, seeing *The Miser*, bet that the miser would be outwitted and his money-box stolen),[1] and whom they understand perfectly thinking: 'I must be witty to laugh at all this wit'—which never fails to happen to Monsieur Donnay's audiences[2]—and thinking that they are doing their bit in creating the play, which cuts out the effort of anticipating what is going to happen; and in the second place, to give them a commonplace sort of plot—everyday events that happen any time to just anybody,[3] because the fact is that Shakespeare, Michelangelo, and Leonardo da Vinci are rather outsize figures whose diameter is somewhat hard to measure up to, because genius, intelligence, and even talent, are larger than life, and so beyond most people.

If in the whole universe there are five hundred people who, compared with infinite mediocrity, have a touch of Shakespeare and Leonardo in them, is it not right and proper to grant these five hundred healthy minds the same thing that is lavished on Monsieur Donnay's audiences—the relief of not seeing on the stage what they don't understand; the active pleasure of participating in creation, and of anticipation?

What follows is a list of a few things which are outstandingly horrifying and incomprehensible to these five hundred minds, and which clutter up the stage to no purpose; first and foremost, the *décor* and the *actors*.

A décor is a hybrid, neither natural nor artificial. If it were exactly like nature it would be a superfluous duplication ... [...] It isn't artificial, in the sense that it doesn't give the artist a chance to realize the outside world as he has seen it or rather as he has created it.

---

[1]   In this unpleasant racial aside Jarry seems to suggest that oriental observers would readily identify with the ethos if not the person of Harpagon, the pathological 'hero' of Molière's *L'Avare*.

[2]   Maurice Donnay (1859–1945), popular French playwright appreciated in his day for his witty and realistic dialogue.

[3]   A shaft obviously aimed at the contemporary vogue of naturalism.

Now it would be very dangerous for the poet to impose on a public of artists the décor as he himself might paint it. In a written work anyone who knows how to read sees the hidden meaning in it that makes sense to him [...]. But there is hardly anyone for whom a painted backcloth has two meanings, as it is far harder to extract the quality from a quality than the quality from a quantity. And every spectator has a right to see a play in a setting which suits his own view of it. For the general public, on the other hand, any 'artistic' décor will do, as the masses don't understand anything by themselves but wait to be told.

There are two sorts of décor; indoor and outdoor. Each is supposed to represent either rooms or the countryside. We shall not once more go over the question, which has been settled once and for all, of the stupidity of *trompe l'œil*. Let us state that the said *trompe l'œil* fools people who only see things crudely, that is to say, who don't see at all, and it shocks those who see nature intelligently and selectively, since it presents them with a caricature of it by someone who lacks all understanding. They say Zeuxis deceived the brute beasts, and Titian an innkeeper.[4]

A décor by someone who can't paint is nearer to an abstract décor, as it only gives the essentials, just as a simplified décor would pick out only the relevant aspects.

We tried *heraldic* décors, where a single shade is used to represent a whole scene or act, with the characters 'passant' harmonically against the blazon. That is rather stupid, as the said colour can only establish itself [...] against a colourless background. This can be achieved simply and in a way which is symbolically accurate by an unpainted backcloth or the reverse side of a set. Each spectator can then conjure up for himself the background he requires or, better still, if the author knew his business, the real scene, by a process of exosmosis.[5] The placard brought on to mark the changes in place[6] cuts out the intermittent appeal to mindlessness of a material change of scenery, which one becomes aware of especially at the moment of change.

In these conditions, any specially needed piece of scenery—a window to be opened or a door to be broken down—becomes a prop and can be brought on like a table or a torch.

The actor makes up his face according to his character, and should do as much to his body. The play of his features, his expressions, etc., are caused by various contractions and extensions of the muscles of his face. No one has realized that the muscles remain the same under the make-believe, made-up

---

[4] The Greek painter Zeuxis (*c*.420–390 BC) allegedly painted grapes so realistically in a picture as to attract birds to it. I have been unable to trace the Titian reference; did Jarry by any chance have some story about Caravaggio in mind?

[5] *Exosmosis*: the outward passage of a bodily fluid to mix with an external fluid, a concept here used metaphorically to represent the spectator's imagination filling the (empty) stage.

[6] Compare the use of placards in a good many Brechtian productions, as advocated for instance by Brecht in *The Literarization of the Theatre* (Notes to the *Threepenny Opera*), 1931: see John Willett (ed.), *Brecht on Theatre* (London: Eyre Methuen, 1964), 43–7.

face, and that Mounet and Hamlet[7] do not have the same zygomatics,[8] even though in anatomical terms we think they are the same man. Or else people say that the difference is negligible. The actor should use a *mask* to envelop his head, thus replacing it by the effigy of his CHARACTER. His mask should not, like those of antiquity, simply betoken tears or laughter, but should indicate the nature of the character: the Miser, the Waverer, the Covetous Man piling up crimes ...[9]

And if the eternal nature of the character is embodied in the mask, we can learn from the kaleidoscope, and particularly the gyroscope, a simple means of *highlighting* the critical moments, singly or several at a time.

With the old-style actor, masked only in thinly applied make-up, each facial expression is raised to a power by colour and particularly by relief, and then to cubes and higher powers by LIGHTING.

What we are about to describe was impossible in the Greek theatre as the light, vertical or at least never sufficiently horizontal, produced a shadow under every protuberance in the mask—but not sharply enough because the light was diffused.

Contrary to the deductions of rudimentary and imperfect logic, there is no clear shadow in those sunny countries, and in Egypt, under the Tropic of Cancer, there is hardly a trace of shadow left on the face; the light was reflected vertically as if by the face of the moon, and diffused both by the sand on the ground and the sand suspended in the air.

The *footlights* illumine the actor along the hypotenuse of a right-angled triangle, the actor's body forming one of the sides of the right angle. And as the footlights are a series of luminous points, that is to say a line which, in relation to the narrowness of the front view of the actor, extends indefinitely to right and left of its intersection with the actor's plane, they should be considered as a single point of light situated at an indefinite distance, as it were *behind* the audience.

It is true that the footlights are less than an infinite distance away, so that one cannot really regard all the rays reflected by the actor (or facial expressions) as travelling along parallel lines. In practice each spectator sees the character's mask *equally*, with differences which are certainly negligible compared to the idiosyncracies and different perceptive attitudes of the individual spectator, which cannot be attenuated—and which in any case cancel each other out in the audience *qua* herd, which is what an audience is.

By slowly nodding up and down and lateral movements of his head the actor displaces the shadows over the whole surface of his mask. And experience has shown that the six main positions (and the same number in profile,

---

[7] Jean Mounet-Sully (1841–1916)—the leading French tragic actor of the late nineteenth century and long-time member of the Comédie-Française—was a famous Hamlet.

[8] *Zygomatics*: configuration of the skull.

[9] In fact the ancient Greek theatre did have a number of different character masks.

though these are less clear) suffice for every expression. We shall not cite any examples, as they vary according to the nature of the mask and because everyone who has managed to watch a puppet show will have been able to observe this for himself.

They are simple expressions and therefore universal. Present-day mime has made the great mistake of ending up with a conventional, tiresome and incomprehensible mimed language. An example of this convention is the hand describing a vertical ellipse round the face and a kiss being implanted on this hand to suggest a beautiful woman and love.—An example of a universal gesture is the marionette displaying its bewilderment by starting back violently and banging its head against a flat.

Behind all these accidentals there remains the essential expression, and the finest thing in many scenes is the impassibility of the mask, whether it utters words grave or merry. This can only be compared with the solid structure of the skeleton, deep down under its surrounding animal flesh, the tragicomical qualities of which have always been acknowledged.

It goes without saying that the actor must have a special *voice*, which is the voice appropriate to the part, as if the cavity forming the mouth of the mask were incapable of uttering anything other than what the mask would say, if the muscles of its lips could move. And it is better for them not to move, and that the whole play should be spoken in a monotone.

And we have also said that the actor must take on the body appropriate to the part. [...]

# Preface and Prologue to
## *The Breasts of Tiresias*
## (1903)

### Guillaume Apollinaire

Guillaume Apollinaire (1880–1918), the half-Polish, half-Italian poet (whose medium of expression was French) is remembered less as a playwright than as a journalist, author and editor of erotica, art critic, and highly influential champion of cubism. His play, *The Breasts of Tiresias*, mostly written as early as 1903, only had one Sunday matinee performance in Paris during the First World War, in 1917; it never had any significant stage history. Nevertheless, it has come to occupy an important place in the formulation of an anti-naturalistic theory of drama, more for its preface and prologue than for the actual text of the play. Apollinaire, who had known Jarry personally, was obviously influenced in this play by *King Ubu*; like Jarry, he rejected naturalism in the theatre (though prepared to concede it to the cinema which he loved). Like Jarry, he advocated an imaginative freedom that was essentially joyous even when dealing with supposedly serious themes: in this particular instance, the problem of the nation's falling birth rate, a frequent French preoccupation during the twentieth century. It was Apollinaire who coined the term 'surrealism', to denote a style that was more impudently aggressive and less open to soulful interpretation than the other anti-naturalist trend, symbolism. But the new concept was to be modified shortly by André Breton in his first *Manifesto of Surrealism* (1924): this pushed it even further out of the range of rational control and in the direction of dreams and the subconscious.

## Preface (1916)

Without pleading for your indulgence, may I point out that this is a work of youth, for with the exception of the Prologue and the last scene of the second

Translated from the French by Louis Simpson, in Michael Benedikt and George E. Wellwarth (eds.), *Modern French Plays: An Anthology from Jarry to Ionesco* (London: Faber & Faber, 1964), 55–67.

act, which were added in 1916, this work was written in 1903, that is to say, fourteen years before it was put on the stage.

I have called it a drama, meaning an action, to make clear what distinguishes it from those comedies of manners, dramatic comedies, light comedies, which for over half a century have provided the stage with works many of which are excellent but of the second rank and simply called plays.

To characterize my drama I have used a neologism which, as I rarely use them, I hope will be excused: I have invented the adjective *surrealist*, which does not at all mean *symbolic*, as Mr. Victor Basch[1] has assumed in his article on the theatre, but defines fairly well a tendency in art which, if it is not the newest thing under the sun, at least has never been formulated as a credo, an artistic and literary faith.

The cheap idealism of the playwrights who followed Victor Hugo sought for verisimilitude in conventional local colour, which as 'photographic' naturalism produced comedies of manners the originals of which may be found long before Scribe,[2] in the sentimental comedies of Nivelle de la Chaussée.[3]

And in order to attempt, if not a renovation of the theatre, at least an original effort, I thought it necessary to come back to nature itself, but without copying it photographically.

When man wanted to imitate walking he created the wheel, which does not resemble a leg. In the same way he has created surrealism unconsciously.

However, I cannot possibly decide if this drama is serious or not. Its aim is to interest and entertain. That is the aim of every dramatic work. It also undertakes to emphasize a question of vital importance to those who understand the language in which it is written: the problem of repopulation.

I could have written on this subject, which has never been treated before, a play in the mock-melodramatic style which has been made fashionable by the writers of 'problem plays'. I preferred a less sombre style, for I don't think that the theatre ought to make anyone feel desperate.

I might also have written a play of ideas and flattered the taste of the contemporary public, which likes to think that it thinks. I have preferred to give free rein to the fantasy which is my way of interpreting nature, a fancy which, like life from day to day, is sometimes more and sometimes less melancholy, satiric, and lyrical, but always, and as much as lies within my power, showing a common sense in which there is sometimes enough novelty to shock and anger, but which will be convincing to those who are sincere. [...]

It has been said that I have used some of the techniques of vaudeville: I don't really see where. Anyway there is nothing in that criticism that disturbs me, for popular art is an excellent basis and I would congratulate myself for having

---

[1] Victor Basch (1863–1944), philosopher who worked in the field of aesthetics and politics.
[2] See George Bernard Shaw, p. 102, n. 9.
[3] Pierre Claude Nivelle de la Chaussée (1692–1754), the creator of the *comédie larmoyante* (weeping or pathetic comedy), a sentimental genre with a strong moralizing slant.

drawn on it if all my scenes followed the natural sequence of the fable I have imagined, of which the main idea, a man who makes children, is new to the theatre and to literature in general, but can be no more shocking than certain improbable inventions of novelists whose vogue depends on so-called science fiction.

Moreover, there is no symbolism in my play and it is transparent, but you are free to find in it all the symbols you want and to disentangle a thousand meanings, as with the oracles of the sybil.

Mr Victor Basch, who has not understood, or has not wanted to understand, that it was about repopulation, insists that my work is symbolic; he's free to think so! But he adds: 'The first requirement for a symbolic drama is that the relationship between the symbol, which is always a sign, and the thing signified shall be immediately apparent.'

Not always, however, and there are notable works in which the symbolism rightly has numerous interpretations which sometimes contradict one another.

I wrote my surrealist drama above all for the French as Aristophanes composed his comedies for the Athenians. I have warned them of the grave danger, recognized by everybody, that not making children holds for a nation that wishes to be prosperous and powerful, and to remedy the evil I have shown them what must be done [...]

To get back to dramatic art, you will find in the prologue to this work the essential characteristics of the drama I propose.

Let me add that in my opinion this art will be modern, simple, swift-paced, with the short cuts or expansions that are needed to move the spectator. The subject will be general enough so that the dramatic work of which it is the basis may influence minds and manners in the direction of duty and honour.

Depending on circumstances, tragedy will prevail over comedy or vice versa. But I do not think that from now on you will be able to endure, without impatience, a theatre piece in which these elements are not balanced against each other, for there is such an energy in mankind today and in the writing of the younger generation that the greatest misfortune immediately seems understandable, as though it may be considered not only from the viewpoint of a kindly irony which permits laughter, but also from the perspective of a true optimism which at once consoles us and makes way for hope.

After all, the stage is no more the life it represents than the wheel is a leg. Consequently, it is legitimate, in my opinion, to bring to the theatre new and striking aesthetic principles which accentuate the roles of the actors and increase the effect of the production, yet without modifying the pathos or comedy of the situations, which must be self-sufficient.

Finally, may I say that, in abstracting from contemporary literary movements a certain tendency of my own, I am in no way undertaking to form a school, but above all to protest against that 'realistic' theatre which is the predominating theatrical art today. This 'realism', which is no doubt suited to the cinema is, I believe, as far removed as possible from the art of drama.

I should like to add that, in my opinion, the only verse suitable for the theatre is a supple line based on rhythm, subject matter and breathing, and adaptable to all dramatic purposes. The dramatist will not scorn the music of rhyme, which in future must not be a constraint of which the author and the audience soon grow weary, but which may add beauty to the pathetic, the comic, in choruses, in certain cues, at the end of certain speeches, or to bring an act to a dignified conclusion.

Does not such a drama have infinite possibilities? It gives free play to the imagination of the dramatist who, while throwing off all the apparently necessary bonds or perhaps rediscovering a neglected tradition, does not think it useful to deny the greatest of his predecessors. Here he pays them the honour due to those who have raised humanity above the mere appearances of things, with which, left to itself, if it did not have geniuses who surpass it and point the way, it would have to be content. But these men reveal new worlds which, extending horizons, ceaselessly multiplying the vision of mankind, provide it with the joy and honour of advancing always toward the most astonishing discoveries. [...]

## Prologue

*In front of the lowered curtain The Director, in evening dress and carrying a swagger stick, emerges from the prompt box.*

DIRECTOR:  So here I am once more among you
　　I've found my ardent company again
　　I have also found a stage
　　But to my dismay found as before
　　The theatre with no greatness and no virtue
　　That killed the tedious nights before the war
　　A slanderous and pernicious art
　　That showed the sin but did not show the saviour
　　Then the hour struck the hour of men
　　I have been at war like all other men
　　[...]
　　So here I am once more among you
　　My troupe don't be impatient
　　Public wait without impatience

　　I bring you a play that aims to reform society
　　It deals with children in the family
　　The subject is domestic
　　And that is the reason it's handled in a familiar way

　　The actors will not adopt a sinister tone
　　They will simply appeal to your common sense

And above all will try to entertain you
So that you will be inclined to profit

From all the lessons that the play contains
And so that the earth will be starred with the glances of infants
Even more numerous than the twinkling stars
Hear O Frenchmen the lesson of war
And make children you that made few before

We're trying to bring a new spirit into the theatre
A joyfulness voluptuousness virtue
Instead of that pessimism more than a hundred years old
And that's pretty old for such a boring thing
The play was created for an antique stage
For they wouldn't have built us a new theatre
A circular theatre with two stages
One in the middle the other like a ring
Around the spectators permitting

The full unfolding of our modern art
Often connecting in unseen ways as in life
Sounds gestures colours cries tumults
Music dancing acrobatics poetry painting
Choruses actions and multiple sets[4]

Here you will find actions
Which add to the central drama and augment it
Changes of tone from pathos to burlesque
And the reasonable use of the improbable
And actors who may be collective or not[5]
Not necessarily taken from mankind
But from the universe

For the theatre must not be 'realistic'

It is right for the dramatist to use
All the illusions he has at his disposal
As Morgana did on Mount Gibel[6]
It is right for him to make crowds speak and inanimate things[7]
If he wishes
And for him to pay no more heed to time
Than to space

---

[4] Cf. Artaud's staging ideas, pp. 193, 198.

[5] e.g. the People of Zanzibar, represented in the play by a single actor—just as the entire Polish army had been in Jarry's *King Ubu*.

[6] The great magician Fata Morgana figured in several Charlemagne romances, such as Boiardo's *Orlando Innamorato* (1487) and Ariosto's *Orlando Furioso* (1532).

[7] e.g. a speaking Kiosk as one of the characters in *The Breasts of Tiresias*.

His universe is his stage
Within it he is the creating god
Directing at his will
Sounds gestures movements masses colours
Not merely with the aim
Of photographing the so-called slice of life[8]
But to bring forth life itself in all its truth
For the play must be an entire universe
With its creator
That is to say nature itself
And not only
Representation of a little part
Of what surrounds us or has already passed
[...]

[8] A common way of describing naturalistic drama; according to the critic and playwright Jean Jullien (1854–1919), a play was 'a slice of life artistically set on the stage' (1890). See also p. 101.

# Preface to *The Immortals*
## (1920)

### Yvan Goll

Born in Alsace-Lorraine of Jewish parentage, Iwan (or Yvan) Goll (1891–1950) was raised bilingually and wrote in German and French with equal facility. A poet of distinction in both languages (to which he added English during a wartime stay in the United States), he projected himself in the character of Landless John in his writings and borrowed much of the imagery of his late poetry from esoteric sources. His dramatic output was only a small part of his œuvre, but he represents a link between the French and the German avant-garde as well as a transition point between expressionism and surrealism in the theatre. Familiar with the work of Apollinaire in France—he wrote the latter's obituary in a German paper in 1919—he was the first German author to use the word 'surrealism' (*Überrealismus*). The prefaces to his surrealist works, *The Immortals* and *Methusalem, or The Eternal Bourgeois*, are perhaps more significant as resonant statements of principle than are the plays themselves *qua* plays. *Methusalem* shares its social satire with a good many German expressionist plays, but the theatrical devices used look forward to later developments, including absurdism. Although Goll's contribution to dramatic theory has not so far been given much attention in the English-speaking world, it is worth noting that Antonin Artaud took part in a production of *Methusalem* in Paris in 1927—and that when *The Bald Prima Donna* was premiered in Paris in 1950, some French critics regarded Goll's play as a clear forerunner of Ionesco's work.

A hard struggle has begun for a new drama, a superdrama. The first drama was that of the Greeks in which the gods tried conclusions with Man. An enormous thing: the god then deemed Man worthy of this, something that hasn't happened since. Drama meant an immense amplification of reality, a very deep, dark, Pythian immersion into boundless passion, into corrosive pain, all in superreal colours.

From Yvan Goll, *Dichtungen: Lyrik. Prosa. Dramen* (Darmstadt: Hermann Luchterhand Verlag, 1960), 64–6. Translated from the German by George Brandt.

Later there came the drama of man for man's sake. Inner conflict, psychology, problems, rationality. Account is taken of only one reality and one plane, and all dimensions are consequently restricted. Everything revolves around one man, not around Man. The life of the collective is barely developed: no crowd scene equals the impact of the chorus of antiquity. You can tell how wide the gap is by the useless dramas of the last century which aimed to be nothing more than interesting, forensically challenging or simply descriptive imitations of life, not creative.

Now the new dramatist feels that the final battle is at hand: the struggle of Man with whatever around him and in him partakes of object and animal. It is an invasion of the realm of the shades that cling to everything, that lie in wait behind all reality. Only after their defeat will liberation perhaps be possible. The poet must know again that there are worlds quite different from those of the five senses: a superworld. He has got to get to grips with it. This will in no way be a relapse into mysticism or romanticism or into the clowning of variety shows, although there is a common denominator—the supersensory.

First of all the whole outer form will have to be smashed: sensible conduct, conventionality, morality, all the formalities of our lives. Man and objects will be shown as nakedly as possible, and for a better effect always through a magnifying glass.

It's been forgotten altogether that the stage is nothing but a magnifying glass. Great drama has always known that: the Greek trod on buskins, Shakespeare spoke with the ghosts of the gigantic dead. It's been forgotten altogether that the first emblem of the theatre is the mask. The mask is fixed, unique and penetrating. It is unchangeable, inescapable, Fate. Every man wears his mask, what the ancients called his guilt. Children are afraid of it and they scream. Man, complacent and sober, must learn to scream again. That's what the stage is for. And doesn't a sublime work of art, a Negro divinity or an Egyptian king, very often seem like a mask to us?

There is a law inherent in the mask, and that is the law of drama. The unreal becomes fact. For a moment we have proof that the most banal thing can be unreal and 'divine', and that the greatest truth lies precisely in that. Truth is not contained in reason, it is discovered by the poet, not the philosopher. Life, not thought. And we are shown furthermore that any event, the most shattering as well as the unconscious opening and shutting of an eyelid, is of eminent importance for the total life of this world. The stage must not only operate with 'real' life, and it becomes 'superreal' when it shows itself aware of things beyond things. Pure realism has been the worst following of a false track in all literature.

The function of art is not to make life easy for the bloated bourgeois so that he can shake his head: 'Ah yes, that's how it is! Now let's go to the buffet!' Art, in so far as it aims to educate, ameliorate, or be somehow effective, has to kill off the everyday citizen, terrify him as the mask does the child, as Euripides did the Athenians who could only stagger on their way out. Art must turn man into a child again. The simplest means is the grotesque, but without causing any laughter. The drabness and stupidity of people are so enormous that only enormity will get to them. Let the new drama be one of enormity.

The new drama will therefore make use of all such technical devices as have the impact of the mask today. There is for instance the gramophone, the mask of the voice, electrical posters, or the megaphone. The performers must wear disproportionate facial masks in which character can be read by crude externals: an excessively big ear, white eyes, peg legs.[1] To these physiognomical exaggerations—which let us stress we do not ourselves regard as exaggerations —there correspond the inner ones of the action: let the situation stand on its head and, in order to sharpen it up, let an utterance often be expressed by its contrary. It will be just the same effect as if you were to take a long hard look at a chessboard, and soon the black squares appear to you white and the white ones black: concepts leapfrog when you get to the borders of truth.

We demand theatre. We demand unreal reality. We are looking for the superdrama.

---

[1] These suggestions for a highly theatricalized performance recall some of the devices used in Apollinaire's *The Breasts of Tiresias* (see pp. 169–70). Presumably the 'electric poster' would be something like a news-scanner.

# Preface to *Methusalem, the Eternal Bourgeois* (1922)

## Yvan Goll

Aristophanes, Plautus, Molière had an easy time of it: they achieved their greatest impact by the simplest means in the world: by cudgelling or symbolical bastinados. We have lost that sort of naivety. The clown in the circus and Chaplin in the cinema still box people's ears: but those are the moments when the audience laughs least. A basic naivety is lacking. Or is it due to our more refined sensibility? Surely it is; but what about that of the people? Even in army barracks, corporal punishment is now taboo: not so in Aristophanes' and Molière's day. Anyway, modern man carries a stick much less often than a revolver. But a pistol-shot is not so funny as a blow with a stick.

So the modern *satirist* has to look for new stimuli. He has found them in *superrealism* and *illogic*.

Superrealism is the strongest negation of realism. The reality of appearance is unmasked in favour of the truthfulness of being. 'Masks': coarse, grotesque like the feelings they express. No more 'heroes', but human beings, no more characters but naked instincts. Stark naked. In order to know an insect you've got to dissect it. The dramatist is a researcher, a politician, and a legislator; as a super-realist he sets down things from a distant realm of truth which he had heard by putting his ear against the world's closed walls.

*Illogic* is today's intellectual humour, hence the best weapon against the phrases that dominate all of life. People commonly only talk in order to set their tongues, not their minds, in motion. Why all that chatter, and taking it all so seriously! What's more, the average person is so over-sensitive that he feels offended by some foul-smelling word and throws death into the scales to have his revenge.

Dramatic illogic is intended to ridicule all our everyday phrases, strike out at mathematical logic and even dialectics in their most deep-seated inner mendacity. At the same time illogic will serve to show the tenfold oscillation of

From Yvan Goll, *Methusalem* (Berlin: Walter de Gruyter & Co., 1966), 7–8. Translated from the German by George Brandt.

the human brain which thinks one thing and says another and leaps about from thought to thought without the slightest apparent logical connection.

But so as not to be a crybaby, a pacifist, or a Salvation Army type, the author must perform a few somersaults for you so that you may become children again. What then is he aiming at? To give you some dolls, teach you how to play and then scatter the sawdust of the broken dolls in the wind again.

The plot of the play? Events are so strong in themselves that they are effective by themselves. A person gets knocked down in the road: a happening tossed hard and irrevocably into the life of the world. Why do they only call a person's death tragic? An exchange of five sentences with an unknown woman can turn out to be much more tragic for your eternity. The drama is meant to have no beginning and no end, like everything under the sun. Yet it does stop somewhere, why? No, life carries on, everybody knows that. But the drama stops because you've got tired, you've aged in a single hour, and because truth, the strongest poison for the heart of man, may only be swallowed in very small quantities.

# The Futurist Synthetic Theatre (1915)

## Filippo Tommaso Marinetti with Emilio Settimelli and Bruno Corra

The propagandist activities, before, during, and after the First World War, of the Italian poet, novelist, journalist, and playwright F. P. Marinetti (1876–1944) were essentially theatrical, although they were in fact directed at a total renewal not merely of the theatre but of all the arts. Marinetti's efforts to sweep the whole of traditional European culture (including classical, naturalist, and symbolist drama) into the dustbin of history in order to make room for the 'Futurism' which he was advocating and indeed helping to create together with like-minded friends, came in the form of public, highly staged provocations: *serate* (evenings) of mixed artistic events and *sintesi* (syntheses, i.e. extremely short performance pieces) designed to surprise and infuriate audiences. Marinetti's theories were stridently articulated in a series of manifestos on a variety of cultural themes. The first of these, the *Manifesto of Futurism* (written in French and published in 'Le Figaro', 20 February 1909) eulogized speed, technology, anti-feminism, violence, and war but did not specifically refer to the theatre. In *Futurism* (1911) Marinetti derided first-night audiences and called for a theatre of total originality which would discard history, love, and psychology as dramatic ingredients. His manifesto, *The Variety Theatre* (29 September 1913), demanded 'a theatre of amazement, record-setting, and body madness'—an anarchic, essentially popular performance art that would actively involve the audience as well. In *The Futurist Cinema* (11 September 1916—a manifesto signed jointly with several futurist colleagues), he endorsed the new medium of film, his suggestions for a radically experimental cinema anticipating many later actual developments. As for the theatre as such, Marinetti wrote the manifesto quoted below in the heady days before Italy joined the Entente Powers in the First World War—a step which he and Mussolini had been vigorously agitating to bring about: clear evidence, together with his later support of fascism, that avant-gardism was not necessarily synonymous with a progressive political stance.

Translated from the Italian by R. W. Flint, in *Marinetti, Selected Writings* (London: Secker & Warburg, 1972), 123–9.

As we await our much-prayed-for great war, we Futurists carry our violent anti-neutralist action from city square to university and back again, using our art to prepare the Italian sensibility for the great hour of maximum danger. Italy must be fearless, eager, as swift and elastic as a fencer, as indifferent to blows as a boxer, as impassive at the news of a victory that may have cost fifty thousand dead as at the news of a defeat.[1]

For Italy to learn to make up its mind with lightning speed, to hurl itself into battle, to sustain every undertaking and every possible calamity, books and reviews are unnecessary. They interest and concern only a minority, are more or less tedious, obstructive and relaxing. They cannot help chilling enthusiasm, aborting impulses and poisoning with doubt a people at war. War— Futurism intensified—obliges us to march and not to rot [*marciare, non marcire*] in libraries and reading rooms. THEREFORE WE THINK THAT THE ONLY WAY TO INSPIRE ITALY WITH THE WARLIKE SPIRIT TODAY IS THROUGH THE THEATRE. In fact 90 per cent of Italians go to the theatre, whereas only 10 per cent read books and reviews. But what is needed is a FUTURIST THEATRE, completely opposed to the passéist theatre that drags its monotonous, depressing processions around the sleepy Italian stages.

Not to dwell on the historical theatre, a sickening genre already abandoned by the passéist public, we condemn the whole contemporary theatre because it is too prolix, analytic, pedantically psychological, explanatory, diluted, finicking, static, as full of prohibitions as a police station, as cut up into cells as a monastery, as moss-grown as an old abandoned house. In other words it is a pacifistic, neutralist theatre, the antithesis of the fierce, overwhelming, synthesizing velocity of the war.

Our Futurist theatre will be

*Synthetic.* That is, very brief. To compress into a few minutes, into a few words and gestures, innumerable situations, sensibilities, ideas, sensations, facts and symbols.

The writers who wanted to renew the theatre (Ibsen, Maeterlinck, Andreyev, Claudel, Shaw) never thought of arriving at a true synthesis, of freeing themselves from a technique that involves prolixity, meticulous analysis, drawn-out preparation. Before the works of these authors, the audience is in the indignant attitude of a circle of bystanders who swallow their anguish and pity as they watch the slow agony of a horse that has collapsed on the pavement. The sigh of applause that finally breaks out frees the audience's stomach from all the indigestible time it has swallowed. Each act is as painful as having to wait patiently in an antichamber for the minister (*coup de théâtre*: kiss, pistol shot, verbal revelations, etc.) to receive you. All this passéist or semi-Futurist theatre, instead of synthesizing fact and idea in the smallest number of words and gestures, savagely destroys the variety of place (source

---

[1] Marinetti had praised war as 'the world's only hygiene' as early as the first Manifesto of Futurism. His wish to have Italy declare war on the Central Powers was fulfilled in May 1915.

of dynamism and amazement), stuffs many city squares, landscapes, streets, into the sausage of a single room. For this reason this theatre is entirely static.

We are convinced that mechanically, by force of brevity, we can achieve an entirely new theatre perfectly in tune with our swift and laconic Futurist sensibility. Our acts can also be moments [*atti—attimi*] only a few seconds long. With this essential and synthetic brevity the theatre can bear and even overcome competition from the *cinema*[2].

*Atechnical.* The passéist theatre is the literary form that most distorts and diminishes an author's talent. This form, much more than lyric poetry or the novel, is subject to *the demands of technique*: (1) to omit every notion that doesn't conform to public taste; (2) once a theatrical idea has been found (expressible in a few pages), to stretch it out over two, three or four acts; (3) to surround an interesting character with many pointless types: coat-holders, door-openers, all sorts of bizarre comic turns; (4) to make the length of each act vary between half and three quarters or an hour; (5) to construct each act taking care to (a) begin with seven or eight absolutely useless pages, (b) introduce a tenth of your idea in the first act, five tenths in the second, four tenths in the third, (c) shape your acts for rising excitement, each act being no more than a preparation for the finale, (d) always make the first act *a little boring* so that the second can be *amusing* and the third *devouring*; (6) to set off every *essential* line with a hundred or more insignificant *preparatory* lines; (7) never to devote less than a page to explaining an entrance or an exit minutely; (8) to apply systematically to the whole play *the rule of superficial variety*, to the acts, scenes and lines. For instance, to make one act a day, another an evening, another deep night; to make one act pathetic, another anguished, another sublime; when you have to prolong a dialogue between two actors, make something happen to interrupt it, a falling vase, a passing mandolin player. ... Or else have the actors constantly move around from sitting to standing, from right to left, and meanwhile vary the dialogue to make it seem as if a bomb might explode outside at any moment (e.g., the betrayed husband might catch his wife red-handed) when actually nothing is going to explode until the end of the act; (9) to be enormously careful about the *verisimilitude of the plot*; (10) to write your play in such a manner that *the audience understands in the finest detail the how and why of everything that takes place on the stage, above all that it knows by the last act how the protagonists will end up.*

With our synthetist movement in the theatre, we want to destroy the technique that from the Greeks until now, instead of simplifying itself, has become more and more dogmatic, stupid, logical, meticulous, pedantic, strangling.
THEREFORE:

---

[2] As stated above, Marinetti was to take a positive view of the cinema, and several futurist films were made.

1. *It's stupid to write one hundred pages where one would do*, only because the audience through habit and infantile instinct wants to see character in a play result from a series of events, wants to fool itself into thinking that the character really exists in order to admire the beauties of Art, meanwhile refusing to acknowledge any art if the author limits himself to sketching out a few of the character's traits.

2. *It's stupid* not to rebel against the prejudice of theatricality when life itself (which consists *of actions vastly more awkward, uniform and predictable* than those that unfold in the world of art) is for the most part *antitheatrical* and even in this offers *innumerable possibilities for the stage.* EVERYTHING OF ANY VALUE IS THEATRICAL.

3. *It's stupid* to pander to the primitivism of the crowd, which in the last analysis wants to see the bad guy lose and the good guy win.

4. *It's stupid* to worry about verisimilitude (absurd because talent and worth have little to do with it).

5. *It's stupid* to want to explain with logical minuteness everything taking place on the stage, when even in life one never grasps an event entirely in all its causes and consequences, because reality throbs around us, bombards us *with squalls of fragments of interconnected events, mortised and tenoned together, confused, mixed up, chaotic.* E.g., it's stupid to act out a contest between two persons *always* in an orderly, clear and logical way, since in daily life we nearly always encounter mere *flashes of argument* made *momentary* by our modern experience, in a tram, a café, a railway station, which remain cinematic in our minds like fragmentary dynamic symphonies of gestures, words, lights and sounds.

6. *It's stupid* to submit to obligatory *crescendi, prepared effects and postponed climaxes.*

7. *It's stupid* to allow one's talent to be burdened with the weight of a technique that *anyone* (even imbeciles) *can acquire by study, practice and patience.*

8. It's stupid to renounce the dynamic leap into the void of total creation, beyond the range of territory previously explored.

*Dynamic, simultaneous.* That is, born of improvisation, lightning-like intuition, from suggestive and revealing actuality. We believe that a thing is valuable to the extent that it is improvised (hours, minutes, seconds), not extensively prepared (months, years, centuries).

We feel an unconquerable repugnance for desk work, a priori, that fails to respect the ambience of the theatre itself. The greater number of our works have been written in the theatre. The theatrical ambience is our inexhaustible reservoir of inspirations: the magnetic circular sensation invading our tired brains during morning rehearsal in an empty gilded theatre; an actor's intonation that suggests the possibility of constructing a cluster of paradoxical thoughts on top of it; a movement of scenery that hints at a symphony of lights; an actress's fleshiness that fills our minds with genially full-bodied notions.

We overran Italy at the head of an heroic battalion of comedians who imposed on audiences *Elettricità*[3] and other Futurist syntheses (alive yesterday, today surpassed and condemned by us) that were revolutions imprisoned in auditoriums—from the Politeama Garibaldi of Palermo to the Dal Verme of Milan. The Italian theatres smoothed the wrinkles in the raging massage of the crowd and rocked with bursts of volcanic laughter. We fraternized with the actors. Then, on sleepless nights in trains, we argued, goading each other to heights of genius to the rhythm of tunnels and stations. Our Futurist theatre jeers at Shakespeare but pays attention to the gossip of actors, is put to sleep by a line from Ibsen but is inspired by red or green reflections from the stalls. We achieve an absolute dynamism through the interpenetration of different atmospheres and times. E.g., whereas in a drama like *Piu che l'amore* [D'Annunzio],[4] the important events (for instance, the murder of the gambling-house keeper) don't take place on the stage but are narrated with a complete lack of dynamism; in the first act of *La Figlia di Iorio* [D'Annunzio][5] the events take place against a simple background with no jumps in space or time; and in the Futurist synthesis, *Simultaneità*,[6] there are two ambiences that interpenetrate and many different times put into action simultaneously.

*Autonomous, alogical, unreal.* The Futurist theatrical synthesis will not be subject to logic, will pay no attention to photography; it will be *autonomous*, will resemble nothing but itself, although it will take elements from reality and combine them as its whim dictates. Above all, just as the painter and composer discover, scattered through the outside world, a narrower but more intense life made up of colours, forms, sounds and noises, the same is true *for the man gifted with theatrical sensibility, for whom a specialized reality exists that violently assaults his nerves*: it consists of what is called THE THEATRICAL WORLD.

THE FUTURIST THEATRE IS BORN OF THE TWO MOST VITAL CURRENTS in the Futurist sensibility, defined in the two manifestos 'The Variety Theatre' and 'Weights, Measures and Prices of Artistic Genius,'[7] which are: (1) our frenzied

---

[3] A play of Marinetti's, first produced in Paris in 1909 as *Poupées électriques* (Electrical Puppets), and then performed in Italy under various titles—*Elettricità* (Electricity), *Elettricità sessuale* (Sexual Electricity), and *Fantocci Elettrici* (Electrical Puppets).

[4] D'Annunzio's *Piu che l'amore* (More than Love) was premiered in 1906 and published in 1907. Marinetti at times opposed his literary rival D'Annunzio as being an essentially traditionalist writer.

[5] D'Annunzio wrote *La Figlia di Iorio* (The Daughter of Jorio) for his lover Eleonora Duse, who did not however star in it when it opened in 1904.

[6] *Simultaneity*, a playlet by Marinetti published in 1915, used two different spaces—i.e. two different worlds—occupying the stage at the same time. The idea of juxtaposing unrelated events in one single action was championed by the French avant-garde too.

[7] In *The Variety Theatre* (1913), Marinetti praised the anti-rational elements of speed, innovation, naivety, eroticism, dangerous acrobatics, absurdity, and audience participation—elements fundamental to his overall concept of theatre. *Weights, Measures and Prices of Artistic Genius*, a futurist manifesto issued in 1914 by Bruno Corradini and Emilio Settimelli, had no specific bearing on theatre but demanded, as a matter of principle, the elimination of traditional, subjective, or spiritual values from all the arts which were henceforth to become scientifically measurable in terms of the amount of energy invested in each individual work.

passion for real, swift, elegant, complicated, cynical, muscular, fugitive, Futurist life; (2) our very modern cerebral definition of art according to which no logic, no tradition, no aesthetic, no technique, no opportunity can be imposed on the artist's natural talent; he must be preoccupied only with creating synthetic expressions of cerebral energy that have THE ABSOLUTE VALUE OF NOVELTY.

The *Futurist theatre* will be able to excite its audience, that is, make it forget the monotony of daily life, by sweeping it through *a labyrinth of sensations imprinted on the most exacerbated originality and combined in unpredictable ways.*

Every night the *Futurist theatre* will be a gymnasium to train our race's spirit to the swift, dangerous enthusiasms made necessary by this Futurist year.

## Conclusions

1. TOTALLY ABOLISH THE TECHNIQUE THAT IS KILLING THE PASSÉIST THEATRE.

2. DRAMATIZE ALL THE DISCOVERIES (no matter how unlikely, weird and antitheatrical) THAT OUR TALENT IS DISCOVERING IN THE SUBCONSCIOUS, IN ILL-DEFINED FORCES, IN PURE ABSTRACTION, IN THE PURELY CEREBRAL, THE PURELY FANTASTIC, IN RECORD-SETTING AND BODY-MADNESS. (E.g., *Vengono*,[8] F. T. Marinetti's first drama of objects, a new vein of theatrical sensibility discovered by Futurism.)

3. SYMPHONIZE THE AUDIENCE'S SENSIBILITY BY EXPLORING IT, STIRRING UP ITS LAZIEST LAYERS BY EVERY MEANS POSSIBLE; ELIMINATE THE PRECONCEPTION OF THE FOOTLIGHTS BY THROWING NETS OF SENSATION BETWEEN STAGE AND AUDIENCE; THE STAGE ACTION WILL INVADE THE ORCHESTRA SEATS, THE AUDIENCE.

4. FRATERNIZE WARMLY WITH THE ACTORS WHO ARE AMONG THE FEW THINKERS WHO FLEE FROM EVERY DEFORMING CULTURAL ENTERPRISE.

5. ABOLISH THE FARCE, THE VAUDEVILLE, THE SKETCH, THE COMEDY, SERIOUS DRAMA AND TRAGEDY, AND CREATE IN THEIR PLACE THE MANY FORMS OF FUTURIST THEATRE, SUCH AS: LINES WRITTEN IN FREE WORDS, SIMULTANEITY, COMPENETRATION, THE SHORT ACTED-OUT POEM, THE DRAMATIZED SENSATION, COMIC DIALOGUE, THE NEGATIVE ACT, THE REECHOING LINE, EXTRALOGICAL DISCUSSION, SYNTHETIC DEFORMATION, THE SCIENTIFIC OUTBURST THAT CLEARS THE AIR.

6. THROUGH UNBROKEN CONTACT, CREATE BETWEEN US AND THE CROWD A CURRENT OF CONFIDENCE RATHER THAN RESPECTFULNESS, in order to instil in our audiences the dynamic vivacity of a new futurist theatricality. [...]

---

[8] This playlet (*They Are Coming*), in which inanimate objects—chairs—play the principal role, may have inspired Ionesco's much later play, *Les Chaises* (first staged in 1952).

# On a New Type of Play
## (1920)

### Stanisław Ignacy Witkiewicz

The widely travelled and eccentric Polish avant-garde artist Stanisław Ignacy Witkiewicz (1885–1930) was not only a playwright, novelist, and painter but also a photographer, aesthetician, philosopher, and an expert on narcotics. Author of over thirty plays (many of them unpublished and unperformed during his lifetime), he called himself 'Witkacy' to avoid being confused with his better known father, like himself a writer and painter. Witkacy's Theory of Pure Form in the Theatre was inspired as much by formalist innovations in painting and by post-Newtonian scientific concepts as by purely literary ideas. His radical attack on realism and psychological verisimilitude ran parallel to but was independent of and somewhat different from the theatrical avant-garde doctrines being formulated around that time in France and elsewhere in Western Europe. Witkacy criticized the futurists for their insufficient interest in creating large forms (see pp. 176–81). Unlike Artaud (see pp. 188–99), he upheld the supremacy of the dramatic text, highly though he valued the other elements that went into theatrical performance. Largely ignored during his lifetime, his real influence came posthumously, after the political changes in 1956 in Poland, when his plays came to loom large in the national repertoire and to attract attention abroad. His approach to drama—'comedies with corpses'—came to be seen as prophetic of the later Theatre of the Absurd. The essay given below is the last section of *An Introduction to the Theory of Pure Form in the Theatre*, which appeared in issues 1, 2, and 3 of the Polish magazine 'Skamander' (1920). A follow-up to this, *A Few Words about the Role of the Actor in the Theatre of Pure Form* appeared in the same publication in 1921.[1]

Translated from the Polish by Daniel Gerould and C. S. Durer, in Stanisław Ignacy Witkiewicz, *The Mother and Other Unsavoury Plays* (New York: Applause Books, 1966), 234–9.

[1] A translation of this essay by Daniel Gerould appeared in *Theatre Quarterly*, 5/18 (June–Aug. 1975), 66–8.

Theatre, like poetry, is a *composite art,* but it is made up of even more elements not intrinsic to it; therefore, it is much more difficult to imagine Pure Form on the stage, essentially independent, in its final result, of the content of human action.

Yet it is not perhaps entirely impossible.

Just as there was an epoch in painting and sculpture when Pure Form was identical with metaphysical content derived from religious concepts, so there was an epoch when performance on stage was identical with myth. Nowadays form alone is the only content of our painting and sculpture, and subject matter, whether concerned with the real world or the fantastic, is only the necessary pretext for the creation of form and has no direct connection with it, except as the 'stimulus' for the whole artistic machine, driving it on to creative intensity. Similarly, we maintain that it is possible to write a play in which the performance itself, existing independently in its own right and not as a heightened picture of life, would be able to put the spectator in a position to experience metaphysical feeling, regardless of whether the *fond* of the play is realistic or fantastic, or whether it is a synthesis of both, combining each of their individual parts, provided of course that the play as a *whole* results from a sincere need on the part of the author *to create a theatrical idiom capable of expressing* metaphysical feelings within purely formal dimensions. What is essential is only that the meaning of the play should not necessarily be limited by its realistic or fantastic content, as far as the totality of the work is concerned, but simply that the realistic element should exist for the sake of the purely formal goals—that is, for the sake of the synthesis of all the elements of the theatre: sound, décor, movement on the stage, dialogue, in sum, performance through time, as an uninterrupted whole—so transformed, when viewed realistically, that the performance seems utter non-sense. The idea is to make it possible *to deform either life or the world of fantasy with complete freedom so as to create a whole whose meaning would be defined only by its purely scenic internal construction, and not by the demands of consistent psychology and action according to assumptions from real life. Such assumptions can only be applied as criteria to plays which are heightened reproductions of life.* Our contention is not that a play should necessarily be non-sensical, but only that from now on the drama should no longer be tied down to pre-existing patterns based solely on life's meaning or on fantastic assumptions. The actor, in his own right, should not exist; he should be the same kind of part within a whole as the colour red in a particular painting or the note C-sharp in a particular musical composition. The kind of play under discussion may well be characterized by absolute freedom in the handling of reality, but what is essential is that this freedom, like 'non-sensicality' in painting, should be adequately justified and should become valid for the new dimension of thought and feeling into which such a play transports the spectator. At present we are not in a position to give an example of such a play, we are merely pointing out that it is possible if only foolish prejudices can be overcome. But let us assume that someone writes such a play: the public will have to get used to it, as well as to that deformed leg in the painting by Picasso. Although we can imagine a painting composed entirely of abstract forms, which will not evoke any associations with the objects of the external world unless such associations are self-induced, yet it is not even possible for us to imagine such a play, because pure performance in time is possible only in the world of sounds, and a theatre without characters who act, no matter how outrageously and improbably, is inconceivable; simply because theatre is a composite art, and does not have it own intrinsic, *homogeneous* elements, like the pure arts: Painting and Music.

The theatre of today impresses us as being something hopelessly bottled up which can only be released by introducing what we have called *fantastic psychology and action*. The psychology of the characters and their actions should only be the pretext for a pure progression of events: therefore, what is essential is that the need for a psychology of the characters and their actions to be consistent and lifelike should not become a bugbear imposing its particular construction on the play. We have had enough wretched logic about characters and enough psychological 'truth'—already it seems to be coming out of our ears. Who cares what goes on at 38 Wspólna Street, Apartment 10, or in the castle in the fairy tale, or in past times? In the theatre we want to be in an entirely new world in which the fantastic psychology of characters who are completely implausible in real life, not only in their positive actions but also *in their errors*, and who are perhaps completely unlike people in real life, produces events which by their bizarre interrelationships create a performance in time not limited by any logic except the logic of the form itself of that performance. What is required is that we accept as inevitable a particular movement of a character, a particular phrase having a realistic or only a formal meaning, a particular change of lighting or décor, a particular musical accompaniment, just as we accept as inevitable a particular part of a composition on a canvas or a sequence of chords in a musical work. We must also take into account the fact that such characters' thoughts and feelings are completely unfettered and that they react with complete freedom to any and all events, even though there is no justification for any of this. Still, these elements would have to be suggested on the same level of formal necessity as all the other elements of performance on the stage mentioned above. Of course, the public would have to be won over to this fantastic psychology, as with the square leg in the painting by Picasso. The public has already laughed at the deformed shapes on the canvases of contemporary masters; now they will also have to laugh at the thoughts and actions of characters on the stage, since for the time being these cannot be completely explained. We believe that this problem can be resolved in exactly the same way as it has been in contemporary painting and music: by understanding the essence of art in general and by growing accustomed to it. Just as those who have finally understood Pure Form in painting can no longer even look at other kinds of painting and cannot help understanding correctly paintings which they laughed at before as incomprehensible, so those who become used to the theatre we are proposing will not be able to stand any of the productions of today, whether realistic or heavily symbolic. As far as painting is concerned, we have tested this matter more than once on people who were apparently incapable of understanding Pure Form at the beginning, but who after receiving systematic 'injections' over a certain period of time reached a remarkably high level of perfection in making truly expert judgments. There may be a certain amount of perversity in all this, but why should we be afraid of purely artistic perversity? Of course, perverseness in life is often a sad affair, but why should we apply judgments which are reasonable in real life to the realm of art, with which life has essentially so little in common. Artistic perversity (for example, unbalanced masses in pictorial composition, perversely tense movements or clashing colours in a painting) is only a means, and not an end; therefore, it cannot be immoral, because the goal which it enables us to attain—unity within diversity in Pure Form—cannot be subjected to the criteria of good and evil. It is somewhat different with the theatre, because its elements are beings who act; but we believe that in those new dimensions which we are discussing even the most monstrous situations will be no less moral than what is seen in the theatre today.

Of course, even assuming that a certain segment of the public interested in serious artistic experiences will come to demand plays written in the style described above, such plays would still have to result from a *genuine creative necessity* felt by an author writing for the stage. If such a work were only a kind of *schematic nonsense*, devised in cold blood, artificially, without real need, it would probably arouse nothing but laughter, like those paintings with a bizarre form of subject matter which are created by those who do not suffer from a real 'insatiable pursuit of new forms,' but who manufacture them for commercial reasons or *pour épater les bourgeois.* Just as the birth of a new form, pure and abstract, without a direct religious basis, took place only through deforming our vision of the external world, so the birth of Pure Form in the theatre is also possible only through deforming human psychology and action.

We can imagine such a play as having complete freedom with respect to absolutely everything from the point of view of real life, and yet being extraordinarily closely knit and highly wrought in the way the action is tied together. The task would be to fill several hours on the stage with a performance possessing its own internal, formal logic, independent of anything in 'real life.' An invented, not *created*, example of such a work can only make our theory appear ridiculous, and from a certain point of view, even absurd (for some, even infuriating or, to put it bluntly, *idiotic*), but let us try.

Three characters dressed in red come on stage and bow to no one in particular. One of them recites a poem (it should create a feeling of urgent necessity at this very moment). A kindly old man enters leading a cat on a string. So far everything has taken place against a background of a black screen. The screen draws apart, and an Italian landscape becomes visible. Organ music is heard.

The old man talks with the other characters, and what they say should be in keeping with what has gone before. A glass falls off the table. All of them fall on their knees and weep. The old man changes from a kindly man into a ferocious 'butcher' and murders a little girl who has just crawled in from the left. At this very moment a handsome young man runs in and thanks the old man for murdering the girl, at which point the characters in red sing and dance. Then the young man weeps over the body of the little girl and says very amusing things, whereupon the old man becomes once again kindly and good-natured and laughs to himself in a corner, uttering sublime and limpid phrases. The choice of costumes is completely open: period or fantastic—there may be music during some parts of the performance. In other words, an insane asylum? Or rather a madman's brain on the stage? Perhaps so, but we maintain that, *if the play is seriously written and appropriately produced*, this method can *create works of previously unsuspected beauty*, whether it be drama, tragedy, farce, or the grotesque, all in a uniform style and unlike anything which previously existed.

On leaving the theatre, the spectator ought to have the feeling that he has just awakened from some strange dream, in which even the most ordinary things had a strange, unfathomable charm, characteristic of dream reveries, and unlike anything else in the world. Nowadays the spectator leaves the theatre with a bad taste in his mouth, or he is shaken by the purely biological horror and sublimity of life, or he is furious that he has been fooled by a whole series of tricks. For all its variety, the contemporary theatre almost never gives us the other world, other not in the sense of being fantastic, but truly that other world which brings to us an understanding of purely formal beauty. Occasionally something like this happens in the plays of writers of previous ages, plays which after all have their significance and greatness that we certainly do not want to deny them with any fanatical fury. This element which we are discussing can be found in some of the plays of Shakespeare and Słowacki,[2] for example, but never in its purest form, and therefore, despite their greatness, these plays do not create the desired effect.

The climax and the conclusion of the kind of play which we are proposing may be created in a complete abstraction from what might be called that debasing feeling of pure curiosity about real life, that tension in the pit of the stomach with which we watch a drama of real life, and which constitutes precisely the one and only appeal of plays today. Of course we would have to break this bad habit, so that *in a world with which, on the realistic level, we have no contact*, we could experience a metaphysical drama similar to the one which takes place among the notes of a symphony or sonata and only among them, so that the *dénouement* would not be an event of concern to us as part of real life, but only as something comprehensible *as the inevitable conclusion of the*

---

[2] The romantic poet and playwright Juliusz Słowacki (1809–1849), wrote over twenty verse dramas, many of them with mystical and grotesque elements.

*purely formal complications of sound patterns, decorative or psychological, free from the causality found in real life.*

The criticism of absolute freedom made against contemporary artists and their works by people who do not understand art can also be applied here. For example, why three characters, not five? Why dressed in red, not green? Of course, we cannot *prove* the necessity for that number and colour, but it should appear inevitable in so far as each element is a necessary part of the work of art once it has been created; while we are watching the play unfold, we ought not to be able to think of any other possible internal interrelationships. And we maintain that, if the work is to be created with complete artistic sincerity, it will have to compel the spectators to accept it as inevitable. It is certainly much more difficult with the theatre than with the other arts, because, as a certain expert on the theatre has asserted, the crowd as it watches and listens is an essential part of the performance itself, and moreover the play has to be a box-office success. But we believe that sooner or later the theatre must embark upon the 'insatiable pursuit of new forms,' which it has avoided until now, and it is to be hoped that extraordinary works, within the dimensions of Pure Form, still remain to be created, and that there will not simply be more 'renaisssance' and 'purification' or repetition ad nauseam of the old repertoire which really has nothing at all to say to anybody.

We must unleash the slumbering Beast and see what it can do. And if it runs mad, there will always be time enough to shoot it before it is too late.

# The Theatre of Cruelty: First Manifesto (1932)

## Antonin Artaud

The life's work of the French actor, author, designer, director, and—above all—theorist of the theatre Antonin Artaud (1896–1948) bristles with paradoxes. Though confined for many years to mental asylums, he had a committed following among the French intellectual elite. Though only fitfully successful as a stage and film actor, indeed a downright failure as a director—neither of his companies, the Théâtre Alfred Jarry (1926–9) and the Théâtre de la Cruauté (1935), managed to secure a lasting foothold in the theatrical life of Paris—his posthumous influence both inside and outside France has been immense. This is due in the main to the collection of his essays, *The Theatre and Its Double* (1938)—the very title of which suggested the mutually reflective relationship of theatre and life that was crucial to his thinking. His theories may have followed in the wake of those sketched out earlier by Jarry (see pp. 160–4) and Apollinaire (see pp. 165–70): he, too, denounced the rationalist, psychologically based theatre of the Western tradition; but he went further than they had done by totally rejecting the primacy of the text and demanding performances based on ritual, magic, terror, and ecstasy. Theatre according to Artaud should not *reflect* life but *change* it by involving and indeed overwhelming the audience in a powerful pre-rational and therapeutic experience. Influenced by what he had seen of Cambodian and Balinese dancers (in 1922 and 1931 respectively), he attached the highest importance to all the non-verbal aspects of performance.[1] But it was only the mistrust of language-as-adequate-communication and the disillusionment with rational structures of thought after the Second World War that was to give a currency to Artaud's views denied them during his own lifetime. Also, his demand that all the

Translated from the French by Helen Weaver, in Antonin Artaud, *Selected Writings* (New York: Farrar, Straus & Giroux, 1976), 242–51.

[1] For an assessment of Artaud's ideas, including his misunderstanding of oriental theatre, see Paul Goodman, 'Obsessed by Theatre', in Eric Bentley (ed.), *The Theory of the Modern Stage: An Introduction to Modern Theatre and Drama* (Harmondsworth: Penguin Books, 1968), 76–9. Martin Esslin's well-informed *Artaud* (London: John Calder, 1976) has fewer reservations in endorsing the Artaud myth. It is interesting to compare the above views with those of Jerzy Grotowski, whose work is often seen in a similar light to Artaud's—see 'He Wasn't Entirely Himself', in Grotowski, *Towards a Poor Theatre*, trans. Jörgen Andersen and Judy Barba (London: Methuen, 1969), 85–93.

complex elements of performance be rigorously co-ordinated met the growing trend of director's theatre: Peter Brook, Ariane Mnouchkine, Jean-Louis Barrault, Richard Schechner, Joseph Chaikin, Julian Beck, and Judith Malina as well as many other men and women of the theatre have all taken some ideas from Artaud. The two essays quoted below show related aspects of his philosophy. The (first) *Manifesto of the Theatre of Cruelty*, published in the October 1931 issue of the 'Nouvelle Revue Française', was intended (but failed) to raise sufficient funds for this proposed theatrical venture which in the event did not get under way until 1935. In it Artaud outlined his ideas on acting, lighting, sound, performance space, etc. *An End to Masterpieces* (1933), on the other hand, looked more closely at the intended effect of performances on spectators and gave a necessary gloss on what he meant by the word 'cruelty'.

We cannot go on prostituting the idea of the theatre, whose only value lies in its excruciating, magical connection with reality and danger.

Stated this way, the question of the theatre must arouse general attention, since theatre, because of its physical aspect and because it requires *expression in space* (the only real expression, in fact), allows the magical means of art and speech to be practiced organically and as a whole, like renewed exorcisms. From all this it follows that we shall not restore to the theatre its specific powers of action until we have restored its language.

That is to say: instead of relying on texts that are regarded as definitive and as sacred, we must first of all put an end to the subjugation of the theatre to the text and rediscover the notion of a kind of unique language halfway between gesture and thought. [...]

The question for the theatre, then, is to create a metaphysics of speech, gesture and expression in order to rescue it from its psychological and human stagnation. But all this can be of use only if there is behind such an effort a real metaphysical temptation, an appeal to certain unusual ideas which by their very nature cannot be limited or even formally defined. These ideas, which have to do with Creation, with Becoming, with Chaos, and are all of a cosmic order, provide an elementary notion of a realm from which the theatre has become totally estranged. These ideas can create a kind of passionate equation between Man, Society, Nature and Objects.

It is not a question, however, of putting metaphysical ideas directly on the stage but of creating various kinds of temptations, of indrafts of air around these ideas. And humour with its anarchy, poetry with its symbolism and its images provide a kind of elementary notion of how to channel the temptation of these ideas.

We must now consider the purely material aspect of this language. That is, of all the ways and means it has of acting on the sensibility.

It would be meaningless to say that this language relies on music, dance, pantomime, or mimicry. Obviously it utilizes movements, harmonies and rhythms but only insofar as they can converge in a kind of central expression, without favouring any particular art. [...]

It is with an altogether Oriental sense of expression that this objective and concrete language of the theatre serves to corner and surround the organs. It flows into the sensibility. Abandoning Western uses of speech, it turns words into incantations. It extends the voice. It utilizes vibrations and qualities of the voice. It wildly stamps in rhythms. It pile-drives sounds. It seeks to exalt, to benumb, to charm, to arrest the sensibility. It releases the sense of a new lyricism of gesture which, by its rapidity or its spatial amplitude, ultimately surpasses the lyricism of words. In short, it ends the intellectual subjugation to language by conveying the sense of a new and more profound intellectuality which hides itself under the gestures and signs, elevated to the dignity of particular exorcisms. [...]

## Technique

It is a question, therefore, of making the theatre, in the proper sense of the word, a function; something as localized and as precise as the circulation of the blood in the arteries, or the apparently chaotic development of dream images in the brain, and this by a powerful linkage, a true enslavement of the attention.

The theatre cannot become itself again—that is, it cannot constitute a means of true illusion—until it provides the spectator with the truthful precipitates of dreams in which his taste for crime, his erotic obsessions, his savagery, his fantasies, his utopian sense of life and of things, even his cannibalism, pour out on a level that is not counterfeit and illusory but internal.

In other words, the theatre must seek by every possible means to call into question not only the objective and descriptive external world, but the internal world, that is, man from a metaphysical point of view. It is only thus, we believe, that we may once again be able to speak about the rights of the imagination in connection with the theatre. Neither Humour nor Poetry nor Imagination mean anything unless, by an anarchic destruction generating a fantastic flight of forms which will constitute the whole spectacle, they succeed in organically calling into question man, his ideas about reality and his poetic place in reality.

But to regard theatre as a second-hand psychological or moral function, and to believe dreams themselves have only a replacement function, is to diminish the profound poetic bearing of both dreams and theatre. If the theatre, like dreams, is bloody and inhuman, it is in order to manifest and to root unforgettably in us the idea of a perpetual conflict and a spasm in which life is constantly being cut short, in which everything in creation rises up and struggles against our condition as already formed creatures, it is to perpetuate in a concrete and immediate way the metaphysical ideas of certain Fables whose very atrociousness and energy are enough to demonstrate their origin and their content of essential principles.

This being so, one sees that by its proximity to the principles that transfuse it poetically with their energy, this naked language of the theatre, a language that is not virtual but real, must make it possible, by utilizing the nervous magnetism of man, to transgress the ordinary limits of art and speech, in order to realize actively, that is to say magically, *in real terms*, a kind of total creation in which man can only resume his place between dreams and events.

## Themes

We have no intention of boring the audience to death with transcendent cosmic preoccupations. That there may be profound keys to thought and action with which to read the spectacle as a whole does not generally concern the spectator, who is not interested in such things. But they must be there all the same; and this concerns us.

THE SPECTACLE. Every spectacle will contain a physical and objective element perceptible to all. Cries, groans, apparitions, surprises, theatrical tricks of all kinds, the magical beauty of costumes taken from certain ritual models, dazzling lighting effects, the incantatory beauty of voices, the charm of harmony, rare notes of music, the colours of objects, the physical rhythm of movements whose crescendo and descrescendo will blend with the rhythm of movements familiar to everyone, concrete apparitions of new and surprising objects, masks, puppets larger than life, sudden changes of lighting, physical action of light which arouses sensations of heat and cold, etc.

MISE EN SCÈNE. It is in terms of *mise en scène*, regarded not merely as the degree of refraction of a text on the stage but as the point of departure of all theatrical creation, that the ideal language of the theatre will evolve. And it is in the utilization and handling of this language that the old duality beween author and director will disappear, to be replaced by a kind of unique Creator who will bear the double responsibility for the spectacle and the plot.

THE LANGUAGE OF THE STAGE. It is not a question of eliminating spoken language but of giving words something of the importance they have in dreams.

Also, one must find new methods of transcribing this language, which might be related to the methods of musical notation or might make use of some sort of code.

As for ordinary objects, or even the human body, elevated to the dignity of signs, it is obvious that one can derive inspiration from hieroglyphic characters, not only in order to transcribe these signs in a legible way that enables one to reproduce them at will, but also in order to compose on the stage symbols that are precise and immediately legible.

This code language and this musical notation will also be invaluable as a means of transcribing voices.

Since it is fundamental to this language to make a specialized use of intonations, these intonations must constitute a kind of harmonic balance, a kind of secondary distortion of speech that must be reproducible at will.

Similarly, the ten thousand and one facial expressions captured in the form of masks will be labelled and catalogued so that they can participate directly and symbolically in this concrete language of the stage; and this independently of their particular psychological utilization.

Furthermore, these symbolic gestures, these masks, these attitudes, these individual or group movements whose innumerable meanings constitute an important part of the concrete language of the theatre—evocative gestures, emotive or arbitrary attitudes, frenzied pounding out of rhythms and sounds—will be reinforced and multiplied by a kind of reflection of gestures and attitudes that consist of the mass of all the impulsive gestures, all the failed attitudes, all the slips of the mind and the tongue which reveal what might be called the impotences of speech, and in which there is a prodigious wealth of expressions, to which we shall not fail to have recourse on occasion.

There is, besides, a concrete idea of music in which sounds make entrances like characters, in which harmonies are cut in two and are lost in the precise entrances of words.

From one means of expression to another, correspondences and levels are created; and even the lighting can have a specific intellectual meaning.

MUSICAL INSTRUMENTS. They will be used for their qualities as objects and as part of the set.

Also, the need to act directly and profoundly upon the sensibility through the sense organs invites research, from the point of view of sound, into qualities and vibrations of sound to which we are absolutely unaccustomed, qualities which contemporary musical instruments do not possess and which compel us to revive ancient and forgotten instruments or to create new ones. They also compel research, beyond the domain of music, into instruments and devices which, because they are made from special combinations or new alloys of metals, can achieve a new diapason of the octave and produce intolerable or ear-shattering sounds or noises.

LIGHT.—LIGHTING. The lighting equipment currently in use in theatres is no longer adequate. In view of the peculiar action of light on the mind, the effects of luminous vibrations must be investigated, along with new ways of diffusing light in waves, or sheets, or in fusillades of fiery arrows. The colour range of the equipment currently in use must be completely revised. In order to produce particular tone qualities, one must reintroduce into lighting an element of thinness, density, opacity with a view to producing heat, cold, anger, fear, etc.

COSTUMES. As for costumes, and without suggesting that there can be any such thing as a standard theatrical costume that is the same for all plays, we shall as far as possible avoid modern dress—not because of any fetishistic and superstitious taste for the old, but because it seems perfectly obvious that certain age-old costumes intended for ritual use, although they were once of their time, retain a beauty and appearance that are revelatory by virtue of their closeness to the traditions that gave them birth.

THE STAGE.—THE AUDITORIUM. We are eliminating the stage and the auditorium and replacing them with a kind of single site, without partition or barrier of any kind, which will itself become the theatre of the action. A direct communication will be re-established between the spectator and the spectacle, between the actor and the spectator, because the spectator, by being placed in the middle of the action, is enveloped by it and caught in its cross-fire. This envelopment is the result of the very shape of the room.

For this reason we shall abandon existing theatre buildings and use some kind of hangar or barn, which we shall have reconstructed according to techniques that have resulted in the architecture of certain churches or certain sacred buildings, and certain Tibetan temples.

In the interior of this construction, special proportions of height and depth will prevail. The room will be enclosed by four walls without any kind of ornament, and the audience will be seated in the middle of the room, below, on movable chairs to allow them to follow the spectacle that will go on all around them. In effect, the absence of a stage in the ordinary sense of the word will allow the action to spread out to the four corners of the room. Special areas will be set aside, for the actors and the action, at the four cardinal points of the room. The scenes will be played in front of whitewashed walls designed to absorb the light. In addition, overhead galleries will run right around the periphery of the room as in certain Primitive paintings. These galleries will enable the actors to pursue each other from one part of the room to the other whenever the action requires, and will permit the action to spread out on all levels and in all perspectives of height and depth. A cry uttered at one end of the room can be transmitted from mouth to mouth, with successive amplifications and modulations, to the other end of the room. The action will unfold, will extend its trajectory from level to level, from point to point; paroxysms will suddenly break out, flaring up like fires in different places; and the quality of true illusion of the spectacle, like the direct and immediate hold of the action on the spectator, will not be an empty phrase. For this diffusion of the action over an immense space will mean that the lighting of a scene and the various lighting effects of a performance will seize the audience as well as the characters;—and several simultaneous actions, several phases of an identical action in which the characters, clinging together in swarms, will withstand all the assaults of the situations, and the external assaults of the elements and the storm, will have their counterpart in physical means of lighting, thunder or wind whose repercussions the spectator will undergo.

Nevertheless, a central area will be set aside which, without serving as a stage properly speaking, will enable the main part of the action to be concentrated and brought to a climax whenever necessary.

OBJECTS.—MASKS.—PROPS. Puppets, enormous masks, objects of unusual proportions will appear by the same right as verbal images, to emphasize the concrete aspect of every image and every expression—and the counterpart of this will be that all things which usually require their objective representation will be treated summarily or disguised.

SETS. There will be no sets. This function will be adequately served by hieroglyphic characters, ritual costumes, puppets thirty feet high representing the beard of King Lear in the storm, musical instruments as tall as men, objects of strange shape and unknown purpose.

IMMEDIACY. But, people will say, a theatre so removed from life, from facts, from current preoccupations ... From the present and events, yes! From profound preoccupations which are the prerogative of the few, no! In the *Zohar*,[2] the story of Rabbi Simeon who burns like fire is as immediate as fire.

WORKS. We shall not perform any written plays but shall attempt to create productions directly on stage around subjects, events or known works. The very nature and arrangement of the room require spectacle and there is no subject, however vast, that can be denied us.

SPECTACLE. There is an idea of total spectacle that must be revived. The problem is to make space speak, to enrich and furnish it; like mines laid into a wall of flat rocks which suddenly give birth to geysers and bouquets.

THE ACTOR. The actor is at once an element of prime importance, since it is on the effectiveness of his performance that the success of the spectacle depends, and a kind of passive and neutral element since all personal initiative is strictly denied him. It is an area in which there are no precise rules; and between the actor from whom one requires the mere quality of a sob and the actor who must deliver a speech with his own personal qualities of persuasion, there is the whole margin that separates a man from an instrument.

INTERPRETATION. The spectacle will be calculated from beginning to end, like a language. In this way there will be no wasted movement and all the movements will follow a rhythm; and since each character will be an extreme example of a type, his gesticulation, his physionomy, his costume will appear as so many rays of light.

THE CINEMA. To the crude visualization of what is, the theatre through poetry opposes images of what is not. From the point of view of action, moreover, one cannot compare a cinematic image which, however poetic, is limited by the properties of celluloid, to a theatrical image which obeys all the exigencies of life.

CRUELTY. Without an element of cruelty at the foundation of every spectacle, the theatre is not possible. In the state of degeneracy in which we live it is through the skin that metaphysics will be made to reenter our minds. [...]

---

[2] The Zohar, a commentary on the Pentateuch written in Aramaic, is the most important book of the Cabbala—the mystical line of Jewish thought which originated in the Middle Ages. Artaud studied this as well as other esoteric texts.

# An End to Masterpieces
## (1933)

## Antonin Artaud

One reason for the asphyxiating atmosphere in which we live without possible escape or recourse—and for which we are all responsible, even the most revolutionary among us—is this respect for what has already been written, formulated or painted, what has been given form, as if all expression were not finally exhausted and had not reached the point where things must fall apart if they are to begin again.

We must put an end to this idea of masterpieces reserved for a so-called elite, and which the mass of the people do not understand; we must realize that the mind has no restricted districts like those set apart for clandestine sexual encounters.

The masterpieces of the past are good for the past: they are not good for us. We have a right to say what has been said and even what has not been said in a way which pertains to us, which is immediate and direct, which corresponds to present modes of feeling and which everyone will understand.

It is idiotic to blame the masses for having no sense of the sublime, when we confuse the sublime with one of its formal manifestations, which are always dead manifestations. And if, for example, the modern mass audience no longer understands *Oedipus Rex*, I would go so far as to say that this is the fault of *Oedipus Rex* and not the fault of the audience.

In *Oedipus Rex* there is the theme of Incest and the idea that nature ridicules morality, and that there are forces at large somewhere which we would do well to beware of, whether we call these forces *destiny* or something else.

There is also the presence of an epidemic of the plague which is a physical embodiment of these forces. But all this is in costumes and in language which have lost all contact with the crude and epileptic rhythm of our time. Sophocles speaks grandly perhaps, but in a manner that is no longer relevant to the age. He speaks too subtly for this age, as if he were speaking beside the point.

Translated from the French by Helen Weaver, in Antonin Artaud, *Selected Writings* (New York: Farrar, Straus & Giroux, 1976), 252–9.

However, a mass audience that trembles at train wrecks, that is familiar with earthquakes, plague, revolution, war, that is sensitive to the disorderly throes of love, is capable of reaching all these high ideas and asks only to be made aware of them, provided one speaks to them in their own language and provided these ideas do not come to them by way of costumes and an overrefined language which belong to dead ages, ages that will never be brought to life again.

Today as in the past the masses are hungry for mystery: they ask only to become aware of the laws according to which destiny is revealed and perhaps to guess the secret of its manifestations.

Let us leave textual criticism to academic drudges and formal criticism to aesthetes, and recognize that what has been said need not be said again; that an expression does not work twice, does not live twice; that all words, once uttered, are dead and are effective only at the moment when they are uttered; that a form that has been used has no function but to urge us to look for another; and that the theatre is the only place in the world where a gesture, once made, can never be exactly duplicated.

If the masses do not come to literary masterpieces it is because these masterpieces are literary, that is, fixed; and fixed in forms that no longer respond to the needs of the time.

Far from blaming the masses and the public, we should blame the formal screen which we interpose between ourselves and the masses, and this new form of idolatry, this idolatry of fixed masterpieces which is one of the aspects of bourgeois conformity.

This conformity which causes us to confuse sublimity, ideas, things with the forms they have assumed down the ages and in ourselves—in our mentalities, the mentalities of snobs, fops and aesthetes whom the public no longer understands.

There is no point in accusing the bad taste of a public that slakes its thirst with nonsense, as long as one has not shown the public a valid spectacle [...].

The public which takes the false for the true has a feeling for the true and always responds to it when it does appear. However, it is not on the stage that one must look for truth today but in the street; and if one offers the crowds in the streets an opportunity to show its human dignity, it will always do so.

If the masses have lost the habit of going to the theatre; if we have all come to regard the theatre as an inferior art, a means of vulgar distraction, and to use it as an outlet for our bad instincts—this is because we have been told too often that it was theatre, that is, lies and illusion. It is because for four hundred years, that is, since the Renaissance, we have become accustomed to a purely descriptive and narrative theatre, a theatre that tells us about psychology.

It is because much ingenuity has been exerted to bring to life on the stage creatures that are plausible but detached, with the spectacle on one side and the audience on the other—and because the masses are no longer shown anything but the mirror image of what they are. [...]

Psychology, with its relentless effort to reduce the unknown to the known, that is, the daily and the ordinary, is the cause of this decline and this terrible loss of energy, which seems to me to have reached its lowest point. And it seems to me that both the theatre and we ourselves must have done with psychology. [...]

Stories about money, money anxieties, social climbing, throes of love untouched by altruism, sexuality sprinkled with an eroticism lacking in mystery, may be psychology, but they are not theatre. These anxieties, this lechery, these ruttings in the presence of which we are reduced to lip-smacking voyeurs, turn to revolution and to vinegar: we must become aware of this.

But this is not the most serious aspect.

If Shakespeare and his imitators have gradually instilled in us an idea of art for art's sake, with art on one side and life on the other, one could rely on this ineffectual and lazy idea as long as life outside held together. But it is now clear from too many signs that everything that once sustained our lives is coming apart, that we are all mad, desperate and sick. And I urge *us* to react.

This idea of a detached art, of poetry as something charming that exists only to beguile our leisure time, is a decadent idea, and it demonstrates loudly our capacity for castration. [...]

We must put an end to this superstition of text and of *written* poetry. [...] Beneath the poetry of texts there is poetry pure and simple, without form and without text. And just as the efficacity of those masks that are used in the magical rites of certain tribes is exhausted—and the masks are then good for nothing but to be put in museums—so the poetic efficacity of a text is exhausted; but the poetry and efficacity of the theatre are exhausted least quickly, since they include the action of what is expressed in gestures and in speech, and which never occurs twice in the same way. [...]

I am not one of those who believe that civilization must change so that the theatre can change; but I do believe that the theatre, utilized in the highest and most difficult sense, has the power to influence the aspect and formation of things; and the encounter on the stage of two passionate manifestations, two living centres, two nervous magnetisms is something as whole, as true and as decisive, even, as in life the encounter of two epidermises in a momentary lust.

That is why I propose a Theatre of Cruelty.—With that mania for depreciating everything that we all have today, as soon as I uttered the word 'cruelty' everyone immediately took it to mean 'blood'. But '*theatre of cruelty*' means a theatre that is difficult and cruel first of all for myself. And on the level of representation it is not a question of that cruelty which we can practice on each other by cutting up each other's bodies, by sawing away at our personal anatomies or, like Assyrian emperors, by sending each other packages of human ears, noses, or neatly severed nostrils through the mail, but of that much more terrible and necessary cruelty which things can practice on us. We are not free. And the sky can still fall on our heads. And the theatre has been created to teach us, first of all, that.

Either we shall be able to return by modern and present-day means to this superior idea of poetry and of poetry through the theatre which is behind the Myths told by the great ancient tragedians, either we shall be able once again to entertain a religious idea of the theatre, that is, without meditation, without useless contemplation, without vague dreams, to arrive at a consciousness and a mastery of certain dominant forces, certain notions that govern everything; and since notions when they are effective carry their own energy, to recover within ourselves those energies which ultimately create order and heighten the value of life, or we might just as well give up without a struggle at once and recognize that we are no longer good for anything but disorder, famine, blood, war and epidemics.

Either we shall bring all the arts back to one central attitude and necessity, finding an analogy between a gesture made in painting or the theatre and a gesture made by lava in a volcanic eruption, or we must stop painting, babbling, writing, and doing anything at all.

I propose to return to the theatre that elementary magical idea taken up by modern psychoanalysis, which consists of curing a patient by having him assume the external attitude of the state one would like to restore him to. [...]

I propose to return by way of the theatre to an idea of the physical understanding of images and of the means of inducing trances, as in Chinese medicine, which knows, over the whole extent of the human anatomy, what points must be punctured in order to regulate even the subtlest functions. [...]

The theatre is the only place in the world and the last collective means we still have of reaching the organism directly and, in periods of neurosis and base sensuality like the one in which we are immersed, of attacking this base sensuality by physical means which it cannot resist.

[...] I propose that we treat the spectators like snakes that are being charmed and that we lead them by way of the organism to the subtlest notions.

At first by crude means which are gradually refined. These crude immediate means hold their attention from the beginning.

That is why in the 'Theatre of Cruelty' the spectator is in the middle and the spectacle surrounds him.

In this spectacle, sound effects are constant; sounds, noises, cries are chosen first for their vibratory quality, then for what they represent.

Among these means, which are gradually refined, lighting also plays a part. Lighting which is not designed merely to colour or to illuminate, and which contributes its force, its influence, its suggestions. And the light of a green cavern does not have the same sensual effect on the organism as the light of a windy day.

After sound and light there is action and the dynamism of action: it is here that theatre, far from copying life, enters into communication, if it can, with pure forces. And whether one accepts or denies them, it is still permissible to speak of forces when referring to whatever it is that engenders energizing images in the unconscious, and gratuitous crime in the outside world.

A violent and concentrated action is a metaphor of lyricism: it evokes supernatural images, a bloodline of images, a bloody gush of images in the poet's mind as well as the spectator's.

Whatever conflicts may haunt the mind of an age, I defy the spectator to whom violent scenes have transferred their blood, who has felt a superior action passing through his own body, who has seen the extraordinary and essential movements of his thought suddenly illuminated in extraordinary events—violence and bloodshed having been placed at the service of the violence of thought—I defy this spectator to indulge outside the theatre in ideas of war, rioting or random murders.

Stated in this way, the idea seems pretentious and childish. And it will be argued that one example leads to another, that the attitude of healing leads to healing, and the attitude of murder leads to murder. Everything depends on the style and the purity with which things are done. There is a risk. But it should not be forgotten that although a theatrical gesture may be violent, it is disinterested; and that what the theatre teaches us is precisely the uselessness of the action which, once done, is no longer necessary, and the superior usefulness of that state which is not made use of by action but which, *restored*, produces sublimation.

Therefore, I propose a theatre in which violent physical images pound and hypnotize the sensibility of the spectator, who is caught in the theatre as if in a whirlwind of higher forces.

A theatre which, abandoning psychology, recounts the extraordinary, puts on the stage natural conflicts, natural and subtle forces, and which presents itself first of all as an exceptional force of redirection. A theatre which produces trances, as the dances of the Dervishes and the Isawas produce trances, and which addresses itself to the organism by precise means, and with the same means as the healing music of certain tribes which we admire on records but which we are incapable of originating among ourselves. […]

# The Theatre's New Testament (1964)

## Jerzy Grotowski

The Polish director Jerzy Grotowski (b. 1933) has brought a highly personal perspective to the trend in the second half of the twentieth century of assigning a secondary role to the dramatic text in the theatre. He has been compared to Artaud for drawing inspiration from oriental performing arts and rethinking the theatrical space so as to bring about a closer audience involvement; but he differs from his French predecessor in the technical precision of his work and in sacrificing stage technology in favour of a 'poor theatre'. Between 1959 and 1971, working first with the Theatre of Thirteen Rows (Opole) and then the Laboratory Theatre (Wrocław), he placed the performer firmly at the centre of the theatrical experience. Calling for a 'holy actor' prepared to give himself or herself unreservedly to the audience, he devised technical exercises to enable him or her to achieve this. Grotowski's influence has extended beyond Poland to Scandinavia, the United States, Italy, and Britain where he has lectured and taught; it was to spread yet further afield by the publication of *Towards a Poor Theatre* (1968). Edited by his Italian-born student Eugenio Barba (himself the conductor of distinguished experimental performance work in Scandinavia since 1964), this book consists of articles and interviews. The piece from which excerpts are given below was an interview with Barba in 1964, first published in the latter's *Alla Ricerca del Teatro Perduto* (In Search of the Lost Theatre, Padua, 1965). From the early 1970s onwards, Grotowski has turned away from theatre, living in California and Italy and devoting himself to 'paratheatrical experiences' and 'active culture'—intensive explorations which dispense with audiences altogether.

[...] What does the word theatre mean? This is a question we often come up against, and one to which there are many possible answers. To the academic,

Translated by Jörgen Andersen and Judy Barba, in Jerzy Grotowski, *Towards a Poor Theatre* (London: Methuen, 1969), 27–53.

the theatre is a place where an actor recites a written text, illustrating it with a series of movements in order to make it more easily understood. Thus interpreted the theatre is a useful accessory to dramatic literature. The intellectual theatre is merely a variation of this conception. Its advocates consider it a kind of polemical tribune. Here, too, the text is the most important element, and the theatre is there only to plug certain intellectual arguments, thus bringing about their reciprocal confrontation. It is a revival of the medieval art of the oratorical duel.

To the average theatre-goer, the theatre is first and foremost a place of entertainment. If he expects to encounter a frivolous Muse, the text does not interest him in the least. What attracts him are the so-called gags, the comic effects and perhaps the puns which lead back to the text. His attention will be directed mainly towards the actor as the centre of attraction. A young woman sufficiently briefly clad is in herself an attraction to certain theatre-goers who apply cultural criteria to her performance, though such a judgement is actually a compensation for personal frustration.

The theatre-goer who cherishes cultural aspirations likes from time to time to attend performances from the more serious repertoire, perhaps even a tragedy provided that it contains some melodramatic element. In this case his expectations will vary widely. On the one hand he must show that he belongs to the best society where 'Art' is a guarantee and, on the other, he wants to experience certain emotions which give him a sense of self-satisfaction. Even if he does feel pity for poor Antigone and aversion for the cruel Creon, he does not share the sacrifice and the fate of the heroine, but he nevertheless believes himself to be her equal morally. For him it is a question of being able to feel 'noble'. The didactic qualities of this kind of emotion are dubious. The audience—all Creons—may well side with Antigone throughout the performance, but this does not prevent any of them from behaving like Creon once out of the theatre. It is worth noticing the success of plays which depict an unhappy childhood. To see the sufferings of an innocent child on the stage makes it even easier for the spectator to sympathize with the unfortunate victim. Thus he is assured of his own high standard of moral values.

Theatre people themselves do not usually have an altogether clear conception of theatre. To the actor the theatre is first and foremost *himself*, and not what he is able to achieve by means of his artistic technique. He—his own private organism—*is* the theatre. Such an attitude breeds the impudence and self-satisfaction which enable him to present acts that demand no special knowledge, that are banal and commonplace, such as walking, getting up, sitting down, lighting a cigarette, putting his hands in his pockets, and so on. In the actor's opinion this is not meant to reveal anything but to be enough in itself for, as I said, he, the actor, Mr. X., *is* the theatre. And if the actor possesses a certain charm which can take in the audience, it strengthens him in his conviction.

To the stage-designer, the theatre is above all a plastic art and this can have positive consequences. Designers are often supporters of the literary theatre.

They claim that the décor as well as the actor should serve the drama. This creed reveals no wish to serve literature, but merely a complex towards the producer.[1] They prefer to be on the side of the playwright as he is further removed and consequently less able to restrict them. In practice, the most original stage-designers suggest a confrontation between the text and a plastic vision which surpasses and reveals the playwright's imagination. It is probably no mere coincidence that the Polish designers are often the pioneers in our country's theatre. They exploited the numerous possibilities offered by the revolutionary development of the plastic arts in the twentieth century which, to a lesser degree, inspired playwrights and producers.[2]

Does this not imply a certain danger? The critics who accuse the designers of dominating the stage, put forward more than one valid objective argument, only their premise is erroneous. It is as if they blame a car for travelling faster than a snail. This is what worries them and not whether the designer's vision dominates that of the actor and the producer. The vision of the designer is creative, not stereotyped, and even if it is, it loses its tautological character through an immense magnification process. Nevertheless, the theatre is transformed—whether the designer likes it or not—into a series of living tableaux. It becomes a kind of monumental 'camera obscura', a thrilling 'laterna magica'. But does it not then cease to be theatre?

Finally, what is the theatre to the producer? Producers come to the theatre after failing in other fields. He who once dreamed of becoming a playwright usually ends up as a producer.

The actor who is a failure, the actress who once played the young prima donna and is getting old, these turn to production.

The theatre critic who has long had an impotence complex towards an art which he can do no more than write about takes up producing.

The hypersensitive professor of literature who is weary of academic work considers himself competent to become a producer. He knows what drama is—and what else is theatre to him if not the realization of a text?

Because they are guided by such varied psychoanalytic motives, producers' ideas on theatre are about as varied as it is possible to be. Their work is a compensation for various phenomena. A man who has unfulfilled political tendencies, for instance, often becomes a producer and enjoys the feeling of power such a position gives him. This has led more than once to perverse interpretations, and producers possessing such an extreme need for power have staged plays which polemize against the authorities: hence numerous 'rebellious' performances.

---

[1] The word 'producer' is here used in the sense of 'director'.

[2] Examples of such a link in Poland between the visual arts and the theatre are the painter-playwright Stanisław Wyspiański (1869–1907) and Stanisław Witkiewicz (see pp. 182–7). Tadeusz Kantor (1915–1990), the director who was the first to prove the theatrical viability of Witkiewicz's plays was also a painter.

Of course a producer wants to be creative. He therefore—more or less consciously—advocates an autonomous theatre, independent of literature which he merely considers as a pretext. But, on the other hand, people capable of such creative work are rare. Many are officially content with a literary and intellectual theatre definition, or to maintain Wagner's theory that the theatre should be the synthesis of all the arts.[3] A very useful formula! It allows one to respect the text, that inviolable basic element, and furthermore it provokes no conflict with the literary and philological milieu. It must be stated, in parentheses, that every playwright—even the ones we can only qualify as such out of sheer politeness—feels himself obliged to defend the honour and rights of Mickiewicz,[4] Shakespeare, etc., because quite simply he considers himself their colleague. In this way Wagner's theory about 'the theatre as the total art' establishes *la paix des braves* in the literary field.

This theory justifies the exploitation of the plastic elements of scenography in the performance and ascribes the results to it. The same goes for the music, whether it be an original work or a montage. To this is added the accidental choice of one or more well known actors and from these elements, only casually co-ordinated, emerges a performance which satisfies the ambitions of the producer. He is enthroned on top of all the arts, although in reality he feeds off them all without himself being tied to the creative work which is carried out for him by others—if, indeed, anyone can be called creative in such circumstances.

Thus the number of definitions of theatre is practically unlimited. To escape from this vicious circle one must without doubt eliminate, not add. That is, one must ask oneself what is indispensable to theatre. Let's see.

Can the theatre exist without costumes and sets? Yes, it can.

Can it exist without music to accompany the plot? Yes.

Can it exist without lighting effects? Of course.

And without a text? Yes, the history of the theatre confirms this. In the evolution of the theatrical art the text was one of the last elements to be added. If we place some people on a stage with a scenario they themselves have put together and let them improvise their parts as in the Commedia dell'Arte, the performance will be equally good even if the words are not articulated but simply muttered.

But can the theatre exist without actors? I know of no example of this. One could mention the puppet-show. Even here, however, an actor is to be found behind the scenes, although of another kind.

Can the theatre exist without an audience? At least one spectator is needed to make it a performance. So we are left with the actor and the spectator. We

---

[3] See pp. 3–11.

[4] The sprawling 4-part play, *Forefathers' Eve* by Poland's leading poet, Adam Mickiewicz (1798–1855), was considered unstageable during the nineteenth century but has achieved full acceptance into the Polish repertoire since. Part III (1832) in particular is regarded as a great national dramatic poem. Grotowski directed this play in 1961 at Opole, in a production which intimately involved the spectators in the action.

can thus define the theatre as 'what takes place between spectator and actor'. All the other things are supplementary—perhaps necessary, but nevertheless supplementary. It is no mere coincidence that our own theatre laboratory has developed from a theatre rich in resources [...] into the ascetic theatre we have become in recent years: an ascetic theatre in which the actors and audience are all that is left. [...] This does not mean that we look down upon literature, but that we do not find in it the creative part of the theatre, even though great literary works can, no doubt, have a stimulating effect on this genesis. [...]

In order that the spectator may be stimulated into self-analysis when confronted with the actor, there must be some common ground already existing in both of them, something they can either dismiss in one gesture or jointly worship. Therefore the theatre must attack what might be called the collective complexes of society, the core of the collective subconscious or perhaps superconscious (it does not matter what we call it), the myths which are not an invention of the mind but are, so to speak, inherited through one's blood, religion, culture and climate.

I am thinking of things that are so elementary and so intimately associated that it would be difficult for us to submit them to a rational analysis. For instance, religious myths: the myth of Christ and Mary; biological myths: birth and death, love symbolism or, in a broader sense, Eros and Thanatos; national myths which it would be difficult to break down into formulas, yet whose very presence we feel in our blood when we read Part III of Mickiewicz's 'Forefathers' Eve', Słowacki's 'Kordian'[5] or the Ave Maria. [...]

[5] In his play, *Kordian* (1832), the Polish poet and dramatist Juliusz Słowacki (1809–49) took a more critical view of the destiny of Poland than that expressed by his friend and fellow exile Mickiewicz in *Forefathers' Eve* (see n. 4 above). In 1962 Grotowski produced this national romantic drama too, at Opole.

# The Holy Theatre: Happenings (1968)

## Peter Brook

In a long directorial career in theatre and opera, Peter Brook (b. 1925) has experimented with a wide variety of styles both in the classical and the modern repertoire. Beginning before the age of twenty, he has worked professionally with hardly a break—in Britain, where he was a director of the Royal Shakespeare Company from 1962 to 1970, in the United States as well as in Paris, where he established the International Centre of Theatre Research in 1970 and has headed an international company ever since. Leading this group of actors from different traditions, he has attempted to cross all but insurmountable cultural divides with productions in Iran and various parts of Africa. By keeping himself constantly open to fresh ideas, he has not allowed his approach to petrify; his justly famous production of Peter Weiss's *Marat/Sade* (1964; see p. 247) managed to combine the seemingly incompatible concepts of Brecht and Artaud. Essentially a practitioner, he made his most substantial contribution to theory with a series of Granada Northern Lectures at the Universities of Hull, Keele, Manchester, and Sheffield, published in 1968 under the title of *The Empty Space*. Distinguishing between what he called the Deadly, the Holy, the Rough and the Immediate Theatre, he drew on his own experiences to tease out what was and what was not vital and meaningful in contemporary theatre. Though a strong champion of improvisation and sympathetic to Artaudian ideas he showed himself to be aware of the pitfalls of unbridled irrationalism in performance—as exemplified by some of the wilder Happenings of the 1960s.

One look at the average audience gives us an irresistible urge to assault it—to shoot first and ask questions later. This is the road to the Happening.

A Happening is a powerful invention, it destroys at one blow many deadly forms, like the dreariness of theatre buildings, and the charmless trappings of

From Peter Brook, *The Empty Space* (London: McGibbon & Kee, 1968), 55–7.

curtain, usherette, cloakroom, programme, bar. A Happening can be anywhere, any time, of any duration: nothing is required, nothing is taboo. A Happening may be spontaneous, it may be formal, it may be anarchistic, it can generate intoxicating energy. Behind the Happening is the shout 'Wake up!' Van Gogh made generations of travellers see Provence with new eyes, and the theory of Happenings is that a spectator can be jolted eventually into new sight, so that he wakes to the life around him. This sounds like sense, and in Happenings, the influence of Zen and Pop Art combine to make a perfectly logical twentieth-century American combination. But the sadness of a bad Happening must be seen to be believed. Give a child a paintbox, and if he mixes all the colours together the result is always the same muddy browny grey. A Happening is always the brainchild of someone and unavoidably it reflects the level of its inventor: if it is the work of a group, it reflects the inner resources of the group. This free form is all too often imprisoned in the same obsessional symbols: flour, custard pies, rolls of paper, dressing, undressing, dressing-up, undressing again, changing clothes, making water, throwing water, blowing water, hugging, rolling, writhing—you feel that if a Happening became a way of life then by contrast the most humdrum life would seem a fantastic happening. Very easily a Happening can be no more than a series of mild shocks followed by let-downs which progressively combine to neutralize the further shocks before they arrive. Or else the frenzy of the shocker bludgeons the shockee into becoming still another form of the Deadly Audience—he starts willing and is assaulted into apathy.

The simple fact is that Happenings have brought into being not the easiest but the most exacting form of all. As shocks and surprises make a dent in a spectator's reflexes, so that he is suddenly more open, more alert, more awake, the possibility and the responsibility arise for onlooker and performer alike. The instant must be used, but how, what for? Here, we are back to the root question—what are we searching for anyway? Do-it-yourself Zen[1] hardly fits the bill. The Happening is a new broom of great efficacy: it is certainly sweeping away the rubbish, but as it clears the way the old dialogue is heard again, the debate of form against formlessness, freedom against discipline; a dialectic as old as Pythagoras, who first set in opposition the terms Limited and Unlimited. It is all very well to use crumbs of Zen to assert the principle that existence is existence, that every manifestation contains within it all of everything, and that a slap on the face, a tweak of the nose or a custard pie are all equally Buddha. All religions assert that the invisible is visible all the time. But here's the crunch. Religious teaching—including Zen—asserts that this visible-invisible cannot be seen automatically—it can only be seen given certain conditions. The conditions can relate to certain states or to a certain under-

[1] One definition of Zen Buddhism is that it is a 'direct assault upon the citadel of Truth, without reliance upon concepts of God or soul or salvation, or the use of scripture, ritual or vow' (Christmas Humphries).

standing. In any event, to comprehend the visibility of the invisible is a life's work. Holy art is an aid to this, and so we arrive at a definition of a holy theatre. A holy theatre not only presents the invisible but also offers conditions that make its perception possible. The Happening could be related to all of this, but the present inadequacy of the Happening is that it refuses to examine deeply the problems of perception. Naively it believes that the cry 'Wake up'! is enough: that the call 'Live!' brings life. Of course, more is needed. But what?

A Happening was originally intended to be a painter's creation—which instead of paint and canvas, or glue and sawdust, or solid objects, used people to make certain relationships and forms. Like a painting, a Happening is intended as a new object, a new construction brought into the world, to enrich the world, to add to nature, to sit alongside everyday life. To those who find Happenings dreary the supporter retorts that any one thing is as good as another. If some seem 'worse' than others, this, they say, is the result of the spectator's conditioning and his jaded eye. Those who take part in a Happening and get a kick out of doing so can afford to regard the outsider's boredom with indifference. The very fact that they participate heightens their perception. The man who puts on a dinner jacket for the opera, saying, 'I enjoy a sense of occasion', and the hippy who puts on a flowered suit for an all-night light-show are both reaching incoherently in the same direction. Occasion, Event, Happening—the words are interchangeable. The structures are different—the opera is constructed and repeated according to traditional principles, the light-show unfolds for the first and last time according to accident and environment; but both are deliberately constructed social gatherings that seek for an invisibility to interpenetrate and animate the ordinary.

# The London Controversy: Tynan v. Ionesco (1958)

It seems appropriate to end this section with some quotations from an unusual literary event: an eloquent head-on clash between the arguments *for* objective, realistic
drama and the counter-arguments *against* it. This controversy, fought out during the
months of June and July 1958 in the pages of the British Sunday newspaper, the
*Observer*, was triggered by a revival of Eugène Ionesco's one-act plays, *The Chairs*
and *The Lesson*, at the Royal Court Theatre, London. Kenneth Tynan (1927–80), at
the time the *Observer* drama reviewer who had carved out a solid reputation for himself as the champion of authors new to the British stage such as Brecht, Beckett, and
even Ionesco, now attacked Ionesco from a socially committed and realist point of
view. (Later, Tynan was to have a significant input into the newly formed National
Theatre's repertoire when he joined it as its literary adviser in 1963.) By way of reply,
in the following week's *Observer*, Ionesco made out a—perhaps paradoxically rational—case in defence of a drama of subjectivity unfettered by social concerns. Tynan
returned to the offensive in a second piece in the *Observer*. This critical jousting
brought in other commentators of the cultural scene on both sides of the fence—the
journalist Philip Toynbee, the art critic John Berger, the expert on German drama H. F.
Garten, the young playwright/director Keith Johnstone, the film and theatre director
Lindsay Anderson and George Devine, the director of the Royal Court Theatre, himself. When Orson Welles joined the fray as well, the controversy took on an even
wider resonance. Welles rejected Ionesco's claim that there was no room in drama for
any social questions. (However, this stand against subjectivist drama did not prevent
his directing Ionesco's *Rhinoceros*, admittedly a more socially 'relevant' play, two
years later at the very same Royal Court Theatre.) Ionesco penned yet another reply
to Tynan but the *Observer*, which had bought the English rights to it, failed to publish it; the article appeared later in the original French version in *Cahiers des saisons*,
no. 15 (Winter 1959).

Translated from the French by Donald Watson, in Eugène Ionesco, *Notes and Counter Notes* (London:
John Calder, 1964), 90–100.

# Kenneth Tynan in the *Observer*, 22 June 1958

## Ionesco: Man of Destiny?

[…] Ever since the Fry–Eliot 'poetic revival' caved in on them, the ostriches of our theatrical intelligentsia have been seeking another faith. Anything would do as long as it shook off what are known as 'the fetters of realism'. Now the broad definition of a realistic play is that its characters and events have traceable roots in life; Gorki and Chekhov, Arthur Miller and Tennessee Williams, Brecht and O'Casey, Osborne and Sartre have all written such plays. They express one man's view of the world in terms of people we can all recognize. Like all hard disciplines, realism can easily be corrupted. It can sink into sentimentality (N. C. Hunter),[1] half-truth (Rattigan),[2] or mere photographic reproduction of the trivia of human behaviour. Even so, those who have mastered it have created the lasting body of twentieth-century drama: and I have been careful not to except Brecht, who employed stylized production techniques to set off essentially realistic characters.

That, for ostriches, is what ruled him out of court. He was too real. Similarly, they preferred Beckett's '*Fin de Partie*', in which the human element was minimal, to 'Waiting for Godot,' which not only contained two tramps of mephitic reality but even managed to regard them, as human beings, with love. Veiling their disapproval, the ostriches seized on Beckett's more blatant verbal caprices and called them 'authentic images of a disintegrated society.' But it was only when M. Ionesco arrived that they hailed a messiah. Here at last was a self-proclaimed advocate of *anti-théâtre*: explicitly anti-realist, and by implication anti-reality as well. Here was a writer ready to declare that words were meaningless and that all communication between human beings was impossible. The aged (as in 'The Chairs') are wrapped in an impenetrable cocoon of hallucinatory memories; they can speak intelligibly neither to each other nor to the world. The teacher in 'The Lesson' can 'get through' to his pupil only by means of sexual assault, followed by murder. Words, that magic innovation of our species, are dismissed as useless and fraudulent.

Ionesco's is a world of isolated robots, conversing in cartoon-strip balloons of dialogue that are sometimes hilarious, sometimes evocative, and quite often neither, on which occasions they become profoundly tiresome. (As with shaggy-dog stories, few of M. Ionesco's plays survive a second hearing: I felt this particularly with 'The Chairs.') This world is not mine, but I recognize it to be a valid personal vision, presented with great imaginative aplomb and verbal audacity. The peril arises when it is held up for general emulation as the gateway to the theatre of the future, that bleak new world from which the humanist heresies of faith in logic and belief in man will forever be banished.

---

[1] Some of the plays of Norman Charles Hunter (1908–71), particularly his strongly cast *A Day by the Sea* (1953), were popular with London West End audiences and briefly gave the author the reputation of being the 'English Chekhov'.

[2] The critical reputation of Sir Terence Rattigan (1911–77) has undergone a number of reassessments.

M. Ionesco certainly offers an 'escape from realism': but an escape into what? A blind alley, perhaps, adorned with *tachiste* murals. Or a self-imposed vacuum, wherein the author ominously bids us observe the absence of air. Or, best of all, a funfair ride on a ghost train, all skulls and hooting waxworks, from which we emerge into the far more intimidating clamour of diurnal reality. M. Ionesco's theatre is pungent and exciting, but it remains a diversion. It is not on the main road: and we do him no good, nor the drama at large, to pretend that it is …

## Ionesco's reply in the *Observer*, 29 June 1958

### The Playwright's Role

I was of course honoured by the article Mr Tynan devoted to my two plays, 'The Chairs' and 'The Lesson', in spite of the strictures it contained, which a critic has a perfect right to make. However, since some of his objections seem to me to be based on premises that are not only false but, strictly speaking, outside the domain of the theatre, I think I have the right to make certain comments.

In effect, Mr Tynan says that it has been claimed, and that I myself have approved or supported this claim, that I was a sort of 'messiah' of the theatre. This is doubly untrue because I do not like messiahs and I certainly do not consider the vocation of the artist or the playwright to lie in that direction. I have a distinct impression that it is Mr Tynan who is in search of messiahs. But to deliver a message to the world, to wish to direct its course, to save it, is the business of the founders of religions, of the moralists or the politicians—who, incidentally, as we know only too well, make a pretty poor job of it. A playwright simply writes plays, in which he can offer only a testimony, not a didactic message—a personal, affective testimony of his anguish and the anguish of others or, which is rare, of his happiness—or he can express his feelings, comic or tragic, about life.

A work of art has nothing to do with doctrine. I have already written elsewhere that any work of art which was ideological and nothing else would be pointless, tautological, inferior to the doctrine it claimed to illustrate, which would already have been expressed in its proper language, that of discursive demonstration. An ideological play can be no more than the vulgarization of an ideology. In my view, a work of art has its own unique system of expression, its own means of directly apprehending the real.

Mr Tynan seems to accuse me of being deliberately, explicitly, anti-realist; of having declared that words have no meaning and that all language is incommunicable. That is only partly true, for the very act of writing and presenting plays is surely incompatible with such a view. I simply hold that it is difficult to make oneself understood, not absolutely impossible, and my play 'The Chairs' is a plea, pathetic perhaps, for mutual understanding. As for the idea of reality, Mr Tynan seems […] to acknowledge only one plane of reality: what is called the 'social' plane, which seems to me to be the most external, in other words the most superficial. That is why I think that writers like Sartre (Sartre the author of political melodramas), Osborne, Miller, Brecht, etc., are simply the new *auteurs du boulevard*, representatives of a left-wing conformism which is just as lamentable as the right-wing sort. These writers offer nothing that one does not know already, through books and political speeches.

But that is not all; it is not enough to be a social realist writer, one must also apparently be a militant believer in what is known as progress. The only worth-while authors, those who are on the 'main road' of the theatre, would be those who thought in a certain clearly defined way, obeying certain pre-established principles or directives. This would be to make the main road a very narrow one; it would considerably restrict the planes of reality (which are innumerable) and limit the field open to the investigations of artistic research and creation.

I believe that what separates us all from one another is simply society itself, or if you like politics. This is what raises barriers between men, this is what creates misunderstanding.

If I may be allowed to express myself paradoxically, I should say that the true society, the authentic human community, is extra-social—a wider, deeper society, that which is revealed by our common anxieties, our desires, our secret nostalgias. The whole history of the world has been governed by these nostalgias and anxieties, which political action does no more than reflect and interpret, very imperfectly. No society has been able to abolish human sadness, no political system can deliver us from the pain of living, from our fear of death, our thirst for the absolute; it is the human condition that directs the social condition, not vice versa.

This 'reality' seems to me much vaster and more complex than the one to which Mr Tynan and many others want to limit themselves. The problem is to get to the source of our malady, to find the non-conventional language of this anguish, perhaps by breaking down this 'social' language which is nothing but clichés, empty formulas, and slogans. The 'robot' characters which Mr Tynan disapproves of seem to me to be precisely those who belong *solely* to this or that *milieu* or social 'reality', who are prisoners of it, and who—being no more than social, seeking a solution to their problems by so-called social means—have become impoverished, alienated, empty. It is precisely the conformist, the *petit-bourgeois*, the ideologist of *every* society who is lost and dehumanized. If anything needs demystifying it is our ideologies, which offer ready-made solutions (which history quickly overtakes and refutes) and a language that congeals *as soon as it is formulated*. It is these ideologies which must be continually re-examined in the light of our anxieties and dreams, and their congealed language must be relentlessly split apart in order to find the living sap beneath.

To discover the fundamental problem common to all mankind, I must ask myself what *my* fundamental problem is, what *my* most ineradicable fear is. I am certain then to find the problems and fears of literally everyone. That is the true road into my own darkness, our darkness, which I try to bring to the light of day.

It would be amusing to try an experiment, which I have no room for here but which I hope to carry out some day. I could take almost any work of art, any play, and guarantee to give it in turn a Marxist, a Buddhist, a Christian, an Existentialist, a psychoanalytical interpretation and 'prove' that the work subjected to each interpretation is a perfect and exclusive illustration of each creed, that it confirms this or that ideology beyond all doubt. For me this proves another thing: that every work of art (unless it is a pseudo-intellectualist work, a work already comprised in some ideology that it merely illustrates, as with Brecht) is outside ideology, is not reducible to ideology. Ideology circumscribes without penetrating it. The absence of ideology in a work does not mean the absence of ideas: on the contrary it fertilizes them. In other words, it was not Sophocles who was inspired by Freud but obviously the other way round. Ideology is not the source of art. A work of art is the source and raw material of ideologies to come.

What then should the critic do? Where should he look for his criteria? Inside the work itself, its universe and its mythology. He must look at it, listen to it, and simply say whether it is true to its own nature. The best judgment is a careful exposition of the work itself. For that, the work must be allowed to speak, uncoloured by preconception or prejudice.

Whether or not it is on the 'main road'; whether or not it is what you would like it to be—to consider this is already to pass judgment, a judgment that is external, pointless and false. A work of art is the expression of an incommunicable reality that one tries to communicate—and which sometimes can be communicated. That is its paradox and its truth.

## Tynan's reply in the *Observer*, 6 July 1958

### Ionesco and the Phantom

M. Ionesco's article on 'The Playwright's Role' is discussed elsewhere in these pages by Mr Toynbee and several readers. I want to add what I hope will not be a postscript, for this is a debate that should continue.

As I read the piece I felt first bewilderment, next admiration, and finally regret. Bewilderment at his assumption that I wanted drama to be forced to echo a particular political creed, when all I want is for drama to realize that it is *part* of politics, in the sense that every human activity, even buying a packet of cigarettes, has social and political repercussions. Then, admiration: no one could help admiring the sincerity and skill with which, last Sunday, M. Ionesco marshalled prose for his purposes. And ultimately, regret: regret that a man capable of stating a positive attitude towards art should deny that there was any positive attitude worth taking towards life. Or even (which is crucial) that there was an umbilical connection between the two.

The position towards which M. Ionesco is moving is that which regards art as if it were something different from and independent of everything else in the world; as if it not only did not but *should* not correspond to anything outside the mind of the artist. This position, as it happens, was reached some years ago by a French painter who declared that, since nothing in nature exactly resembled anything else, he proposed to burn all of his paintings which in any way resembled anything that already existed. The end of that line, of course, is Action Painting.

M. Ionesco has not yet gone so far. He is stuck, to pursue the analogy, in an earlier groove, the groove of cubism, which has fascinated him so much that he has begun to confuse ends and means. The cubists employed distortion to make discoveries about the nature of objective reality. M. Ionesco, I fear, is on the brink of believing that his distortions are more valid than the external world it is their proper function to interpret. To adapt Johnson, I am not yet so lost in drama criticism as to forget that plays are the daughters of earth, and that things are the sons of heaven. But M. Ionesco is in danger of forgetting; of locking himself up in that hall of mirrors which in philosophy is known as solipsism.

Art is parasitic on life, just as criticism is parasitic on art. M. Ionesco and his followers are breaking the chain, applying the tourniquet, aspiring as writers to a condition of stasis. At their best, of course, they don't succeed: the alarming thing is that they try. As in physiology, note how quickly the brain, starved of blood, produces hallucinations and delusions of grandeur. 'A work of art,' says M. Ionesco, 'is the source and the raw material of ideologies to come.' O hubris! Art and ideology often interact on each other; but the plain fact is that they both spring from a common source. Both draw on human experience to explain mankind to itself; both attempt, in very different ways, to assemble coherence from seemingly unrelated phenomena; both stand guard for us against chaos. They are brothers, not child and parent. To say, as M. Ionesco does, that Freud was inspired by Sophocles is the direst nonsense. Freud merely found in Sophocles confirmation of a theory he had formed on the basis of empirical evidence. This does not make Sophocles a Freudian, or vice versa: it is merely a pleasing instance of fraternal corroboration.

You may wonder why M. Ionesco is so keen on this phantom notion of art as a world of its own, answerable to none but its own laws. Wonder no more: he is merely seeking to exempt himself from any kind of value-judgment. His aim is to blind us to the fact that we are all in some sense critics, who bring to the theatre not only those 'nostalgias and anxieties' by which, as he rightly says, world history has largely been governed, but also a whole series of new ideas— moral, social, psychological, political—through which we hope some day to free ourselves from the rusty hegemony of *Angst*. These fond ideas, M. Ionesco quickly assures us, do not belong in the theatre. Our job, as critics, is just to hear the play and 'simply say whether it is true to its own nature'. Not, you notice, whether it is true to ours; or even relevant; for we, as an audience, have forfeited our right to a hearing as conscious, sentient beings. 'Clear evidence of cancer here, sir.' 'Very well, leave it alone: it's being true to its own nature.'

Whether M. Ionesco admits it or not, every play worth serious consideration is a statement. It is a statement addressed in the first person singular to the first person plural; and the latter must retain the right of dissent. [...]

Cyril Connolly once said, once and wanly, that it was closing time in the gardens of the West; but I deny the rest of the suavely cadenced sequence, which asserts that 'from now on an artist will be judged only by the resonance of his solitude or the quality of his despair.'[3] Not by me, he won't. I shall, I hope, respond to the honesty of such testimonies: but I shall be looking for something more, something harder; for evidence of the artist who is not content with the passive role of a symptom, but concerns himself, from time to time, with such things as healing. M. Ionesco correctly says that no ideology has yet abolished fear, pain or sadness. Nor has any work of art. But both are in the business of trying. What other business is there?

---

[3] This statement by the editor of the magazine *Horizon*, which appeared in its final issue (Dec. 1949–Jan. 1950, p. 362), had become a cliché of intellectual discourse in Britain in the early 1950s.

# PART IV

**Political Theatre**

# Letter to a Creative Collaborator (1922)[1]

## Ernst Toller

The dramatist and poet Ernst Toller (1893–1939), generally classed as one of the leading German expressionist playwrights, was no ivory-tower writer: his prominent involvement with the uprising in Munich in 1918–19 caused him to be gaoled for four years after the defeat of the revolutionaries by government troops. He wrote the contemporary allegory *Masses and Man* (1920) as well as three further political plays in prison. The production of *Masses and Man* at the Berlin Volksbühne in 1921, while the author was still in gaol, represented a milestone in non-naturalistic staging technique, especially in its bold use of spotlights. The expressionistic devices employed by Toller (such as drastically pared-down settings, highly stylized language, characters reduced to posterlike two-dimensionality, the alternation of 'real' scenes with 'dream' scenes) reflected the playwright's sense of isolation from the life outside the prison walls; but as he himself was to recognize, they also manifested the unresolved contradictions in his own political attitude: on the one hand, the wish for revolutionary action, which implied the possible use of violence, and on the other hand a pacifist humanitarianism. In his later (rather less resonant) plays Toller, who throughout his life continued to be an anti-fascist activist, returned to a more conventional style of playwriting.

There are critics who object to the fact that, although the dream scenes had a dreamlike look, you gave the 'real scenes' a visionary appearance and thus blurred the boundaries between reality and dream.[2] I specially want to say to

Preface to the 2nd edition of Ernst Toller, *Masse-Mensch* (Masses and Man) (Potsdam: Gustav Kiepenheuer Verlag, 1922), 5–6. Translated from the German by George Brandt.

[1] The 'creative collaborator' in question was Jürgen Fehling, the highly innovative director of the play at the Volksbühne.

[2] *Masses and Man* consists of seven scenes—four 'realistic' ones alternating with three 'dream' scenes.

you that you have acted according to my intentions. These 'real scenes' are no naturalistic 'depictions of a *milieu*', the figures (except for the figure of Sonia) are not individualized.[3] *Whatever can be real in a drama like my 'Masses and Man'? Only the spiritual, the intellectual atmosphere.*

As a politician I act as if human beings as individuals, as groups, as functionaries, as wielders of power, as economic power brokers, as if any sort of actual conditions were real facts. As an artist I perceive the highly questionable nature of these 'real facts'. ('It is still an open question whether we personally exist.')

I see prisoners in a prison yard sawing wood in a monotonous rhythm. I am moved and think, Human beings. That one may be a worker, that one a peasant, that one perhaps a solicitor's clerk … I see the room in which the worker used to live, see his little peculiarities, the special gestures with which he would throw away a match, embrace a woman, walk through a factory gate in the evening. I see equally clearly the broad-backed peasant there, that little chicken-breasted solicitor's clerk. Then … suddenly … these are no longer the human beings X and Y and Z but ghastly puppets, fatefully driven by dimly perceived compulsions.

Two women once went past my cell window, to the iron bars of which I was clinging. Two old maids apparently. Both had close-cropped white hair, both wore dresses of the same shape, the same colour and the same cut, both were carrying a grey umbrella with white dots, both were waggling their heads.

Not for a split second did I see any 'real persons' who were going for a walk in the 'real Neuburg', in the narrow courthouse lane. A dance of death of two old maids, one old maid and her mirrored death, was staring me in the face.

The drama, *Masses and Man*, is a visionary image which virtually 'burst' out of me in a matter of two and a half days. The two nights which, confined to prison, I had to spend in my 'bed' in a dark cell were abysmally agonizing, I was as it were lashed by visions, by demonic visions, by visions somersaulting in grotesque leaps. In the morning I sat down at my table, shaken by a cold inward fever, and did not stop until my fingers, numbed and trembling, wouldn't serve me any longer. No one was allowed into my cell, I refused all cleaning up, I turned in uncontrolled rage on all my comrades who wanted to ask me questions, to help me in any way.

The blissfully onerous labour of reformulating and polishing took one year.

Today I take a critical view of the drama, *Masses and Man*, I have recognized the limitations of the form which derives from an inner inhibition—in spite of everything—of those days, a personal reticence which shyly avoided the artistic shaping of my personal experience, of a naked confession, and which

---

[3] The dramatis personae, in typical expressionist style, are depicted as types rather than individuals and remain nameless—except for the central figure of Soni Irene L. This character was based on Sonia Lerch, a middle-class fellow prisoner of Toller's who committed suicide in goal.

yet could not summon up the will to objectify in a purely artistic manner. The monstrous nature of the days of revolution had not turned into a spiritual *image* of the days of revolution, it was somehow still a painful, agonizing 'psychic *element*', a psychic '*chaos*'.

I am suprised at the incomprehension of critics. The reason may be (which is most probably the case) a formal inadequacy. But perhaps an additional reason is the fact that what for 'bourgeois' critics is a 'newspaper slogan', 'a phrase from a lead editorial' etc. means for those of us who live close to the proletarian people, who understand their inner world, *who create out of the psychological and intellectual world of the proletarian people*, the expression of the most shattering, the most convulsive ideological battles which take over the whole person.

So that's how it is: what seems to the 'bourgeois' a quarrel about dry-as-dust words in the social world and its artistic image, is for the proletarian a tragic division, a terrifying assault. What seems to the 'bourgeois' a 'deep' insight,' 'significant', the expression of the most moving intellectual struggles, leaves the proletarian totally unmoved.—

I need not emphasize that proletarian art, too, must lead on to humanity, that it must be comprehensive in the deepest sense—like life, like death. There is a proletarian art only to the extent that for the creative person the complexities of proletarian inner life are pathways to the shaping of the eternally human.

Fortress Niederschönenfeld, October 1921

# The Programme of the Proletarian Theatre (1920)

## Erwin Piscator

A comparison of Toller's explanation of the background of *Masses and Man* (see previous item) with the programme put forward by the director Erwin Piscator (1893–1966) as the policy for a newly established political theatre company clearly shows the wide differences between various forms of committed theatre, in Germany as elsewhere. The manifesto reproduced below was issued in 1920 on behalf of the Proletarian Theatre, a group recently founded under the auspices of several left-wing political parties as well as working-class and allied organizations; published in the special October 1920 issue of the magazine *Der Gegner*, this was later reproduced in Piscator's book, *Das Politische Theater* (1929), in which he argued the case for a socially progressive theatre on the basis of his own, by then substantial, production record. Though Piscator was to become the leading practitioner of agit-prop as well as more differentiated kinds of left-wing theatre in Germany, in his later work in the 1920s he did not actually follow the guidelines laid down in the manifesto over-literally: thus, he did not by any means eschew the employment of professional actors as suggested. What is hinted at in the programme, though not yet worked out in detail, is his groping his way towards an Epic Theatre. This apparently paradoxical concept (a literary work according to Aristotle was *either* epic *or* dramatic but could not be both) was pioneered by Piscator and taken up, with a significantly different inflection, by his friend Bertolt Brecht. Both men wished to see the social dimension in drama to be paramount, as against the older emphasis on the fate of the individual. But whereas for Brecht, 'epic' stood for the idea of 'narrative', i.e. detachment (see pp. 227–8), for Piscator it meant primarily 'large-scale', i.e. involving major social forces. This reading was to lead him to a highly technicized production style, including the use of film projections and complex stage machinery. He recognized the fact that at the time the Programme of the Proletarian Theatre was published there was as yet no suitable drama. This caused him either to reinterpret the classics in a Marxist sense (his controversial production of Schiller's *The Robbers* in 1926 being a case

Translated from the German by Hugh Rorrison, in Erwin Piscator, *The Political Theatre* (London: Eyre Methuen, 1980), 45–7.

in point) or to encourage new left-wing authors, often working in teams (including Brecht), in order to produce the kind of play required by the new age and—it was hoped—a new working-class audience. When Piscator became head of the West Berlin Freie Volksbühne in 1962, some four decades after the proletarian-revolutionary period, he did at last find and promote the work of congenial fact-based authors like Hochhuth, Kipphardt, and Weiss (see pp. 247–53).

The directors of the Proletarian Theatre (Proletarisches Theater) must aim for simplicity of expression, lucidity of structure, and a clear effect on the feelings of a working-class audience. Subordination of all artistic aims to the revolutionary goal: conscious emphasis on and cultivation of the idea of the class struggle.

The Proletarian Theatre wants to serve the revolutionary movement and therefore has a duty to the revolutionary workers. A committee chosen from among these workers will ensure that its cultural and propagandistic aims are realized.

It will not always be necessary to give priority to the message the author intended. On the contrary, as soon as the public and the theatre have worked together to achieve a common desire for revolutionary culture, almost any bourgeois play, no matter whether it demonstrates the decay of bourgeois society or whether it brings out the capitalist principle with special clarity, will serve to strengthen the notion of the class struggle and to add to our revolutionary understanding of its historical necessity. Such plays could well be preceded by an introductory lecture which would prevent misunderstanding or an undesirable effect. In certain circumstances the plays could also be altered (the conservative personality cult of the artist need not concern us) either by cutting the text or by building up certain scenes or, where necessary, even by adding a prologue or an epilogue to make the whole thing clear. In this way a large part of world literature can be pressed into the service of the revolutionary proletariat, just as the whole of world history can be used to propagate the idea of the class struggle.

The style used by the actor, the writer and the director must be wholly factual (similar in style to the Lenin or Chicherin[1] manifestos, whose easy, flowing rhythm and unmistakable simplicity produce a considerable emotional impact). Everything that is said must be unexperimental, unexpressionistic, relaxed, subordinated to the simple, unconcealed will and aims of the revolution. For this reason all neoromantic, expressionist and similar styles and problems, emerging as they do from the anarchistic, individualistic personal needs of bourgeois artists, must be eliminated at the outset.

---

[1] G. V. Chicherin (1872–1936), Russian revolutionary of aristocratic origin who was People's Commissar for Foreign Affairs in the Soviet Government from 1918 till 1928.

There must of course be no failure to exploit the new technical and stylistic possibilities of recent movements in the arts, so long as they serve the artistic aims we have described and do not serve some stylistic purpose of their own as part of some private artistic revolution or other. In all problems of style the guiding principle must be whether the vast circle of the proletarian audience will derive some benefit from it, or whether it will be bored or confused, or even infected by bourgeois notions. Revolutionary art can emerge only from the minds of the revolutionary workers. It will be the work of a character that was formed in common toil and in the common struggle by the selfless will of the masses. The workers' instinct for self-preservation will see to it that they achieve cultural and artistic freedom in the same measure as political and economic freedom. And this intellectual liberation must be Communist in character to correspond to the material liberation.

Two fundamental principles emerge for the Proletarian Theatre. The first relates to the fact that as an organization it must break with capitalist traditions and create a footing of equality, a common interest and a collective will to work, uniting directors, actors, designers and technical administrative personnel, and then uniting these people with the consumers (that is, the audience). It will gradually be able to do without 'professional actors' as it accumulates players from among its own audiences. These players will cease to be dabbling amateurs, for the first task facing the Proletarian Theatre is to spread and deepen the Communist idea, and this cannot be restricted to the activities of one professional group but must become the concern of a wider community in which the public has just as important a function as the stage. The first condition is that the actor must have a completely new attitude to the theme of the play in question. He can no longer set himself above each role or be indifferent to it any more than he can be totally absorbed in it, abandoning his own conscious will. Just as the Communist politician must deal with political or economic problems or any other social question, according to an immutable scale of common humanity in each case, and just as each individual in a political gathering must become a politician, so the actor in each of his roles must make every word, every gesture an expression of the proletarian, Communist idea, and in the same way each spectator, wherever he may be, whatever he may be saying or doing, must act in a fashion which stamps him unmistakably as a Communist. Skill and talent will not produce this result. The second task facing the Proletarian Theatre is to make an educative, propagandistic impact on those members of the masses who are as yet politically undecided or indifferent, or who have not yet understood that a proletarian state cannot adopt bourgeois art and the bourgeois mode of 'enjoying' art. The method of utilizing traditional literature which I mentioned at the outset should become the accepted method of doing this. In these old plays we still find the old world with which even the most sheltered among us are familiar, and here too we shall see that all propaganda starts off by using the existing state of affairs to point to the desirable state of affairs.

This brings the writer face to face with an important task. He, too, must cease to be the autocrat he has always been in the past, and must learn to put his own ideas and original touches to the back of his mind and concentrate on bringing out the ideas which are alive in the pysche of the masses. He must cultivate trivial forms which have the merit of being clear and easily under-stood by all, and he must learn from political leaders. Just as they have to sense and interpret in advance the forces and tendencies which are developing within the masses, and not to sugar-coat for the masses a policy which is historically and psychologically alien to them or is only familiar to them because of evil practices in times past, so the writer must become the point at which the proletarian will to culture crystallizes, the flint on which the workers' desire for truth will ignite.

# The Modern Theatre is the Epic Theatre: Notes to the opera *Aufstieg und Fall der Stadt Mahagonny* (1930)

## Bertolt Brecht

The figure of Eugen Berthold Friedrich ('Bert') Brecht (1898–1965) is bound to loom large in any consideration of dramatic theory in the twentieth century. Poet, director, and playwright, he let his theorizing arise out of and feed back into theatrical practice —whenever, that is, he was able to get near a theatre; for the greater part of his exile from Germany, between 1933 and 1946, this was rarely the case. Brecht's thinking about drama and performance has influenced men and women of the theatre— writers, directors, designers, actors—all over the world, partly because of the strength of the plays that embody his theoretical position, partly because of the incisiveness of the theory in its own right, and partly because of the prestige of the Berliner Ensemble which he founded in 1949 and which he led until the time of his death. This impact can be traced even when those touched by it do not share the philosophical stance, viz. Marxism, which underlay his writings from the mid-1920s onwards. Indeed, quite a few of his devices have been taken over somewhat mechanically, particularly the famous 'alienation' or 'estrangement' effect; this may become little more than a stylistic flourish when simply used as an aesthetic, rather than as a consciousness-raising, device. Brecht's theories, which over time came to embrace all aspects of play structure as well as theatrical performance, represented a creative engagement with the aesthetic implications of Marxism; to the dismay of some, they turned out very different from the unventuresome Socialist Realism obligatory in the Soviet theatre under Stalin. In common with other Marxists, and indeed theorists of many different schools, he raised the fundamental question of what theatre was *for*; but his desire to use it for helping to bring about social change caused him to go beyond, indeed generally to avoid, the purveying of straightforward, ready-made progressive messages. Even in his *Lehrstücke* (didactic plays) for amateur use, he set up dialectics designed to produce more than unthinking assent: he wished to re-educate the spectators (and indeed the actors) by appealing to their rational, i.e. critical, faculties. This essentially cool idea of drama, Epic Theatre, which he enlarged on in a good many of

Translated from the German by John Willett, in *Brecht on Theatre* (London: Methuen, 1964), 33–42.

his theoretical writings, was formulated most explicitly in the following Notes to the opera, *Rise and Fall of the City of Mahagonny*. The centre-piece of these Notes, the much quoted table listing the different characteristics of Dramatic and Epic Theatre, must be taken with a pinch of salt: as note 2 indicates (see p. 227), these seeming polar opposites are not in fact absolute antitheses. The epic style represents a *shift* towards greater rationality, not a total exclusion of all emotion. But Brecht's polemical intentions tempted him to state his case in provocative terms; it is therefore necessary to be alive to the undertone of irony in many of his formulations—and to think things out for oneself.

## Opera—with Innovations!

For some time past there has been a move to renovate the opera. Opera is to have its form modernized and its content brought up to date, but without its culinary character being changed. Since it is precisely for its backwardness that the opera-going public adores opera, an influx of new types of listener with new appetites has to be reckoned with; and so it is. The intention is to democratize but not to alter democracy's character, which consists in giving the people new rights, but no chance to appreciate them. Ultimately it is all the same to the waiter whom he serves, so long as he serves the food. Thus the *avant-garde* are demanding or supporting innovations which are supposedly going to lead to a renovation of opera; but nobody demands a fundamental discussion of opera (i.e. of its function), and probably such a discussion would not find much support.

The modesty of the *avant-garde*'s demands has economic grounds of whose existence they themselves are only partly aware. Great apparati like the opera, the stage, the press etc., impose their views as it were incognito. For a long time now they have taken the handiwork (music, writing, criticism, etc.) of intellectuals who share in their profits—that is, of men who are economically committed to the prevailing system but socially near-proletarian—and processed it to make fodder for their public entertainment machine, judging it by their own standards and guiding it into their own channels; meanwhile the intellectuals themselves have gone on supposing that the whole business is concerned only with the presentation of their work, is a secondary process which has no influence over their work but merely wins influence for it. This muddled thinking which overtakes musicians, writers and critics as soon as they consider their own situation has tremendous consequences to which far too little attention is paid. For by imagining that they have got hold of an apparatus which in fact has got hold of them they are supporting an apparatus which is out of their control, which is no longer (as they believe) a means of furthering output but has become an obstacle to output, and specifically to their own output as soon as it follows a new original course which the apparatus finds awkward or opposed to its own aims. Their output then becomes a matter of delivering the goods. Values evolve which are based on the fodder principle. And this leads to a general habit of judging works of art by their suitability for the apparatus without ever judging the apparatus by its suitability for the work. People say, this or that is a good work; and they mean (but do not say) good for the apparatus. Yet this apparatus is conditioned by the society of the day and only accepts what can keep it going in that society. We are free to discuss any innovation which doesn't threaten its social function—that of providing an evening's entertainment. We are not free to discuss those which threaten to change its function, possibly by fusing it with the educational system or with the organs of mass communication. Society absorbs via the apparatus whatever it needs in order to reproduce itself. This means that an innovation will pass if it is calculated to rejuvenate existing society, but not if it is going to change it—irrespective of whether the form of the society in question is good or bad.

The *avant-garde* don't think of changing the apparatus, because they fancy that they have at their disposal an apparatus which will serve up whatever they freely invent, transforming itself spontaneously to match their ideas. But they are not in fact free inventors: the apparatus goes on fulfilling its function with or without them; the theatres play every night; the papers come out so many times a day; and they absorb what they need; and all they need is a given amount of stuff.[1]

You might think that to show up this situation (the creative artist's utter dependence on the apparatus) would be to condemn it. Its concealment is such a disgrace.

And yet to restrict the individual's freedom of invention is itself a progressive act. The individual is increasingly drawn into enormous events that are going to change the world. No longer can he simply 'express himself'. He is brought up short and put into a position where he can fulfil more general tasks. The trouble, however, is that at present the apparati do not work for the general good; the means of production do not belong to the producer; and as a result his work amounts to so much merchandise, and is governed by the normal laws of mercantile trade. Art is merchandise, only to be manufactured by the means of production (apparati). An opera can only be written for the opera. [...]

## Opera—

[...] Our existing opera is a *culinary opera*. It was a means of pleasure long before it turned into merchandise. It furthers pleasure even where it requires,

---

[1] The intellectuals, however, are completely dependent on the apparatus, both socially and economically; it is the only channel for the realization of their work. The output of writers, composers, and critics comes more and more to resemble raw material. The finished article is produced by the apparatus. [Brecht's note.]

or promotes, a certain degree of education, for the education in question is an education of taste. To every object it adopts a hedonistic approach. It 'experiences' and it ranks as an 'experience'.

Why is *Mahagonny* an opera? Because its basic attitude is that of an opera: that is to say, culinary. Does *Mahagonny* adopt a hedonistic approach? It does. Is *Mahagonny* an experience? It is an experience. For … *Mahagonny* is a piece of fun. [...]

*Mahagonny* is nothing more or less than an opera.

## —with Innovations!

Opera had to be brought up to the technical level of the modern theatre. The modern theatre is the epic theatre. The following table shows certain changes of emphasis as between the dramatic and the epic theatre.[2]

| DRAMATIC THEATRE | EPIC THEATRE |
| --- | --- |
| plot | narrative |
| implicates the spectator in a stage situation | turns the spectator into an observer, but |
| wears down his capacity for action | arouses his capacity for action |
| provides him with sensations | forces him to take decisions |
| experience | picture of the world |
| the spectator is involved in something | he is made to face something |
| suggestion | argument |
| instinctive feelings are preserved | brought to the point of recognition |
| the spectator is in the thick of it, shares the experience | the spectator stands outside, studies |
| the human being is taken for granted | the human being is the object of the inquiry |
| he is unalterable | he is alterable and able to alter |
| eyes on the finish | eyes on the course |
| one scene makes another | each scene for itself |
| growth | montage |
| linear development | in curves |
| evolutionary determinism | jumps |
| man as a fixed point | man as a process |
| thought determines being | social being determines thought |
| feeling | reason |

---

[2] This table does not show absolute antitheses but mere shifts of accent. In a communication of fact, for instance, we may choose whether to stress the element of emotional suggestion or that of plain rational argument. [Brecht's note.]

When the epic theatre's methods begin to penetrate the opera the first result is a radical *separation of the elements*. The great struggle for supremacy between words, music and production—which always brings up the question 'which is the pretext for what?': is the music the pretext for the events on the stage, or are these the pretext for the music? etc.—can simply be by-passed by radically separating the elements. So long as the expression 'Gesamtkunst-werk' (or 'integrated work of art')³ means that the integration is a muddle, so long as the arts are supposed to be 'fused' together, the various elements will all be equally degraded, and each will act as a mere 'feed' to the rest. The process of fusion extends to the spectator, who gets thrown into the melting pot too and becomes a passive (suffering) part of the total work of art. Witchcraft of this sort must of course be fought against. Whatever is intended to produce hypnosis, is likely to induce sordid intoxication, or creates fog, has got to be given up.

## Words, music and setting must become more independent of one another

### (a) Music
For the music the change of emphasis proved to be as follows:

| DRAMATIC OPERA | EPIC OPERA |
|---|---|
| The music dishes up | the music communicates |
| music which heightens the text | music which sets forth the text |
| music which proclaims the text | music which takes the text for granted |
| music which illustrates | which takes up a position |
| music which paints the psycho-logical situation | which gives the attitude |

Music plays the chief part in our thesis.⁴

### (b) Text
We had to make something instructive and straightforward of our fun, if it was not to be irrational and nothing more. The form employed was that of the moral tableau. The tableau is performed by the characters in the play. The text had to be neither moralizing nor sentimental, but to put morals and senti-mentality on view. Equally important was the spoken word and the written

---

³ This is a clear reference to the Wagnerian concept of music-drama as the 'total' or 'integrated' work of art which was meant to supersede the older type of opera. For Wagner's theories, see pp. 3–11.

⁴ The large number of craftsmen in the average opera orchestra allows of nothing but associative music (one barrage of sound breeding another); and so the orchestral apparatus needs to be cut down to thirty specialists or less. The singer becomes a reporter, whose private feelings must remain a private affair. [Brecht's note.]

word (of the titles). Reading seems to encourage the audience to adopt the most natural attitude towards the work.[5]

### (c) Setting

Showing independent works of art as part of a theatrical performance is a new departure. Neher's projections adopt an attitude towards the events on the stage; as when the real glutton sits in front of the glutton whom Neher has drawn.[6] In the same way the stage unreels the events that are fixed on the screen. These projections of Neher's are quite as much an independent component of the opera as are Weill's music and the text. They provide its visual aids.

Of course such innovations also demand a new attitude on the part of the audiences who frequent opera houses.

## Effect of the Innovations: A Threat to the Opera?

It is true that audience had certain desires which were easily satisfied by the old opera but are no longer taken into account by the new. What is the audience's attitude during an opera; and is there any chance that it will change?

Bursting out of underground stations, eager to become as wax in the magicians' hands, grown-up men, their resolution proved in the struggle for existence, rush to the box office. They hand in their hat at the cloakroom, and with it they hand their normal behaviour: the attitudes of 'everyday life'. Once out of the cloakroom they take their seats with the bearing of kings. How can we blame them? You may think a grocer's bearing better than a king's and still find this ridiculous. For the attitude that these people adopt in the opera is unworthy of them. Is there any possibility that they may change it? Can we persuade them to get out their cigars?

Once the content becomes, technically speaking, an independent component, to which text, music and setting 'adopt attitudes'; once illusion is sacrificed to free discussion, and once the spectator, instead of being enabled to have an experience, is forced as it were to cast his vote; then a change has been launched which goes far beyond formal matters and begins for the first time to affect the theatre's social function.

In the old operas all discussion of the content is rigidly excluded. If a member of the audience had happened to see a particular set of circumstances portrayed and had taken up a position *vis-à-vis* them, then the old opera would have lost its battle: the 'spell would have been broken'. Of course there were elements in the old opera which were not purely culinary; one has to

---

[5] For the significance of titles, see Brecht's 'Notes to the Threepenny Opera', quoted in Willet, *Brecht on Theatre*, 43.

[6] The stage designer Caspar Neher (1897–1962), a lifelong friend of Brecht's who collaborated with him both before the latter's emigration from Germany in 1933 and after his return to Europe from the United States in 1948, had been responsible for the scenery of the first production of *The Rise and Fall of the Town of the City of Mahagonny* (Leipzig, 1930); this included a striking use of projections.

distinguish between the period of its development and that of its decline. *The Magic Flute, Fidelio, Figaro* all included elements that were philosophical, dynamic.[7] And yet the element of philosophy, almost of daring, in these operas was so subordinated to the culinary principle that their *sense* was in effect tottering and was soon absorbed in sensual satisfaction. Once its original 'sense' had died away the opera was by no means left bereft of sense, but had simply acquired another one—a sense *qua* opera. The content had been smothered in the opera. Our Wagnerites are now pleased to remember that the original Wagnerites posited a sense of which they were presumably aware. Those composers who stem from Wagner still insist on posing as philosophers. A philosophy which is of no use to man or beast, and can only be disposed of as a means of sensual satisfaction. [...]

What is the point, we wonder, of chasing one's own tail like this? Why this obstinate clinging to the pleasure element? This addiction to drugs? Why so little concern with one's own interests as soon as one steps outside one's own home? Why this refusal to discuss? Answer: nothing can come of discussion. To discuss the present form of our society, or even of one of its least important parts, would lead inevitably and at once to an outright threat to our society's form as such.

We have seen that opera is sold as an evening entertainment, and that this puts definite bounds to all attempts to transform it. We see that this entertainment has to be devoted to illusion, and must be of a ceremonial kind. Why?

In our present society, the old opera cannot be just 'wished away'. Its illusions have an important social function. The drug is irreplaceable; it cannot be done without.[8]

Only in the opera does the human being have a chance to be human. His entire mental capacities have long since been ground down to a timid mistrustfulness, an envy of others, a selfish calculation. The old opera survives not just because it is old, but chiefly because the situation which it is able to meet is still the old one. This is not wholly so. And here lies the hope for the new opera. Today we can begin to ask whether opera hasn't come to such a pass that further innovations, instead of leading to the renovation of this whole form, will bring about its destruction.[9]

---

[7] These products of the early phase of rising bourgeois ideology had *some* progressive, liberal, and even socially critical elements.

[8] The life imposed on us is too hard; it brings us too many agonies, disappointments, impossible tasks. In order to stand it we have to have some kind of palliative. There seem to be three classes of these: overpowering distractions, which allow us to find our sufferings unimportant, pseudo-satisfactions which reduce them and drugs which make us insensitive to them. Something of the kind is indispensable. The pseudo-satisfactions offered by art are illusions if compared with reality but are none the less psychologically effective for that, thanks to the part played by the imagination in our inner life. (Freud, *Das Unbehagen in der Kultur* ['Civilization and its Discontents', Vienna: Internationaler Psychoanalytischer Verlag, 1930]), p. 22. Such drugs are sometimes responsible for the wastage of great stores of energy which might have been applied to bettering the human lot. (*Ibid.*, p. 28) [Brecht's note.]

[9] Such, in the opera *Mahagonny*, are those innovations which allow the theatre to present moral tableaux (showing up the commercial character both of the entertainment and of the persons entertained) and which put the spectator in a moralizing frame of mind. [Brecht's note.]

Perhaps *Mahagonny* is as culinary as ever—just as culinary as an opera ought to be—but one of its functions is to change society; it brings the culinary principle under discussion, it attacks the society that needs operas of such a sort; it still perches happily on the old bough, perhaps, but at least it has started (out of absent-mindedness or bad conscience) to saw it through …
[…]

Real innovations attack the roots.

## For Innovations—against Renovation!

The opera *Mahagonny* was written two years ago, in 1927. In subsequent works attempts were made to emphasize the didactic more and more at the expense of the culinary element. And so to develop the means of pleasure into an object of instruction, and to convert certain institutions from places of entertainment into organs of mass communication.[10]

---

[10]  Brecht was to quote this sentence in *A Short Organum for the Theatre* (1948)—see p. 233.

# A Short Organum for the Theatre (1948)

## Bertolt Brecht

This, the fullest exposition of Brecht's theory of drama and theatre, was written in Switzerland in 1948, on his return to Europe from American exile. It represents a partial revision of his earlier doctrine (see the previous item, pp. 224–31) which had emphasized the social function of drama to the near-exclusion of aesthetic considerations. In the *Short Organum for the Theatre* Brecht allowed more ample room to aesthetics but did not repudiate the notion of theatre as a socially responsive and responsible instrument—which to him meant interpreting life from a socialist point of view. Drama *qua* text is linked here with all the aspects of stage production, and this includes the much discussed A-effect, particularly in relation to acting technique. Brecht had dealt with the question of alienation in acting before in a number of articles, e.g. *A Dialogue about Acting* (see Willett, *Brecht on Theatre*, 26–9), the notes to the *Threepenny Opera: The Literarization of the Theatre* (ibid. 43–7), notes to *Man is Man: The Question of Criteria for Judging Acting* (ibid. 53–7), notes to *The Mother: Indirect Impact of the Epic Theatre* (ibid. 57–62), *Alienation Effects in Chinese Acting* (ibid. 91–9), *The Street Scene* (ibid. 121–9), *A Short Description of a New Technique of Acting which Produces an Alienation Effect* (ibid. 136–47), as well as *The Messingkauf Dialogues* (London: Methuen, 1965). But the essay, substantial sections from which are quoted below, shows alienation to cover a wider ground: it is all part of the general 'consciousness-raising' which every aspect of theatre is supposed to bring about. The title of the essay is a tribute to Francis Bacon's Latin treatise, *Novum Organum* (1620), in which the Jacobean statesman and philosopher, whom Brecht greatly admired, had argued in favour of an experimental rather than a dogmatic approach to the study of nature.

Translated from the German by John Willett, in *Brecht on Theatre* (London: Methuen, 1964), 179–205.

# Prologue

The following sets out to examine an aesthetic drawn from a particular kind of theatrical performance which has been worked out in practice over the past few decades. In the theoretical statements, excursions, technical indications occasionally published in the form of notes to the writer's plays, aesthetics have only been touched on casually and with comparative lack of interest. There you saw a particular species of theatre extending or contracting its social functions, perfecting or sifting its artistic methods and establishing or maintaining its aesthetics—if the question arose—by rejecting or converting to its own use the dominant conventions of morality or taste according to tactical needs. This theatre justified its inclination to social commitment by pointing to the social commitment in universally accepted works of art, which only fail to strike the eye because it was the accepted commitment. As for the products of our own time, it held that their lack of any worthwhile content was a sign of decadence: it accused these entertainment emporiums of having degenerated into branches of the bourgeois narcotics business. [...] The battle was for a theatre fit for the scientific age, and where its planners found it too hard to borrow or steal from the armoury of aesthetic concepts enough weapons to defend themselves against the aesthetics of the Press they simply threatened 'to transform the means of enjoyment into an instrument of instruction, and to convert certain amusement establishments into organs of mass communication':[1] i.e. to emigrate from the realm of the merely enjoyable. [...] And yet what we achieved in the way of theatre for a scientific age was not science but theatre, and the accumulated innovations worked out during the Nazi period and the war—when practical demonstration was impossible—compel some attempt to set this species of theatre in its aesthetic background, or anyhow to sketch for it the outlines of a conceivable aesthetic. To explain the theory of theatrical alienation except within an aesthetic framework would be impossibly awkward. [...]

Let us therefore cause general dismay by revoking our decision to emigrate from the realm of the merely enjoyable, and even more general dismay by announcing our decision to take up lodging there.[2] Let us treat the theatre as a place of entertainment, as is proper in an aesthetic discussion, and try to discover which type of entertainment suits us best. [...]

# 3

From the first it has been the theatre's business to entertain people, as it also has of all the other arts. It is this business which always gives it its particular dignity; it needs no other passport than fun, but this it has got to have. We should not by any means be giving it a higher status if we were to turn it, for

---

[1] See pp. 231 for Brecht's own *Notes to the Opera Mahagonny*.
[2] A humorous reference to Brecht's own exile and his return to Europe from America.

example, into a purveyor of morality; it would on the contrary run the risk of being debased, and this would occur at once if it failed to make its moral lesson enjoyable, and enjoyable to the senses at that: a principle, admittedly, by which morality can only gain. Not even instruction can be demanded of it: at any rate, no more utilitarian lesson than how to move pleasurably, whether in the physical or in the spiritual sphere. The theatre must in fact remain something entirely superfluous, though this indeed means that it is the superfluous for which we live. Nothing needs less justification than pleasure.

## 4

Thus what the ancients, following Aristotle, demanded of tragedy is nothing higher or lower than that it should entertain people. Theatre may be said to be derived from ritual, but that is only to say that it becomes theatre once the two have separated; what it brought over from the mysteries was not its ritual function, but purely and simply the pleasure which accompanied this. And the catharsis of which Aristotle writes—cleansing by fear and pity, or from fear and pity—is a purification which is performed not only in a pleasurable way, but precisely for the purpose of pleasure. To ask or to accept more of the theatre is to set one's own mark too low. [...]

## 7

And different periods' pleasures varied naturally according to the system under which people lived in society at the time. The Greek demos [literally the demos of the Greek circus³] ruled by tyrants had to be entertained differently from the feudal court of Louis XIV. The theatre was required to deliver different representations of men's life together: not just representations of a different life, but also representations of a different sort. [...]

## 9

And we must always remember that the pleasure given by representations of such different sorts hardly ever depended on the representation's likeness to the thing portrayed. Incorrectness, or considerable improbability even, was hardly or not at all disturbing, so long as the incorrectness had a certain consistency and the improbability remained of a constant kind. All that mattered was the illusion of compelling momentum in the story told, and this was created by all sorts of poetic and theatrical means. Even today we are happy to overlook such inaccuracies if we can get something out of the spiritual purifications of Sophocles or the sacrificial acts of Racine or the unbridled frenzies of Shakespeare, by trying to grasp the immense or splendid feelings of the principal characters in these stories.

---

³ Actually the circus was a Roman, not a Greek, institution.

## 10

For of all the many sorts of representation of happenings between humans which the theatre has made since ancient times, and which have given entertainment despite their incorrectness and improbability, there are even today an astonishing number that also give entertainment to us.

## 11

In establishing the extent to which we can be satisfied by representations from so many different periods—something that can hardly have been possible to the children of those vigorous periods themselves—are we not at the same time creating the suspicion that we have failed to discover the special pleasures, the proper entertainment of our own time?

## 12

And our enjoyment of the theatre must have become weaker than that of the ancients, even if our way of living together is still sufficiently like theirs for it to be felt at all. We grasp the old works by a comparatively new method—empathy—on which they rely little. Thus the greater part of our enjoyment is drawn from other sources than those which our predecessors were able to exploit so fully. We are left safely dependent on beauty of language, on the elegance of narration, on passages which stimulate our private imaginations: in short, on the incidentals of the old works. These are precisely the poetical and theatrical means which hide the imprecisions of the story. [...] And according to Aristotle—and we agree there—narrative is the soul of drama. We are more and more disturbed to see how crudely and carelessly men's life together is represented, and that not only in old works but also in contemporary ones constructed according to the old recipes. Our whole way of appreciation is starting to get out of date.

## 13

It is the inaccurate way in which happenings between human beings are represented that restricts our pleasure in the theatre. The reason: we and our forbears have a different relationship to what is being shown.

## 14

For when we look about us for an entertainment whose impact is immediate, for a comprehensive and penetrating pleasure such as our theatre could give us by representations of men's life together, we have to think of ourselves as children of a scientific age. Our life as human beings in society—i.e. our life—is determined by the sciences to a quite new extent. [...]

## 19

The same attitude as men once showed in face of unpredictable natural cata-strophes they now adopt towards their own undertakings. The bourgeois class, which owes to science an advancement that it was able, by ensuring that it alone enjoyed the fruits, to convert into domination, knows very well that its rule would come to an end if the scientific eye were turned on its own under-takings. And so that new science which was founded about a hundred years ago and deals with the character of human society was born in the struggle between rulers and ruled. Since then a certain scientific spirit has developed at the bottom, among the new class of workers whose natural element is large-scale production: from down there the great catastrophes are spotted as undertakings by the rulers.

## 20

But science and art meet on this ground, that both are there to make men's life easier, the one setting out to maintain, the other to entertain us. In the age to come art will create entertainment from the new productivity which can so greatly improve our maintenance, and in itself, if only it is left unshackled, may prove to be the greatest pleasure of them all.

## 21

If we want now to surrender ourselves to this great passion for producing, what ought our representations of men's life together look like? What is that productive attitude in face of nature and society which we children of a scientific age would like to take up pleasurably in the theatre?

## 22

That attitude is a critical one. [...]

## 23

The theatre can only adopt such a free attitude if it lets itself be carried along by the strongest currents in its society and associates itself with those who are necessarily most impatient to make great alterations there. The bare wish, if nothing else, to evolve an art fit for the times must drive our theatre of the scientific age straight out into the [industrial] suburbs, where it can stand as it were wide open, at the disposal of those who live hard and produce much, so that they can be fruitfully entertained there with their great problems. They may find it hard to pay for our art, and immediately to grasp the new method of entertainment, and we shall have to learn in many respects what they need and how they need it; but we can be sure of their interest. [...] The theatre has to become geared into reality if it is to be in a position to turn out effective representations of reality, and to be allowed to do so.

## 24

But this makes it simpler for the theatre to edge as close as possible to the apparatus of education and mass communication. For although we cannot bother it with the raw material of knowledge in all its variety, which would stop it from being enjoyable, it is still free to find enjoyment in teaching and inquiring. It constructs its workable representations of society, which are then in a position to influence society, wholly and entirely as a game: for those who are constructing society it sets out society's experiences, past and present alike, in such a manner that the audience can 'appreciate' the feelings, insights and impulses which are distilled by the wisest, most active and most passionate among us from the events of the day or the century. They must be entertained with the wisdom that comes from the solution of problems, with the anger that is a practical expression of sympathy with the underdog, with the respect due to those who respect humanity, or rather whatever is kind to humanity; in short, with whatever delights those who are producing something.

## 25

And this also means that the theatre can let its spectators enjoy the particular ethic of their age, which springs from productivity. A theatre which converts the critical approach—i.e. our great productive method—into pleasure finds nothing in the ethical field which it must do and a great deal that it can. Even the wholly anti-social can be a source of enjoyment to society so long as it is presented forcefully and on the grand scale. [...]

## 26

For such an operation as this we can hardly accept the theatre as we see it before us. Let us go into one of these houses and observe the effect which it has on the spectators. Looking about us, we see somewhat motionless figures in a peculiar condition: they seem strenuously to be tensing all their muscles, except where these are flabby and exhausted. They scarcely communicate with each other; their relations are those of a lot of sleepers, though of such as dream restlessly [...] Seeing and hearing are activities, and can be pleasant ones, but these people seem relieved of activity and like men to whom something is being done. This detached state, where they seem to be given over to vague but profound sensations, grows deeper the better the work of the actors, and so we, as we do not approve of this situation, should like them to be as bad as possible. [...]

## 29

That is the sort of theatre which we face in our operations, and so far it has been fully able to transmute our optimistic friends, whom we have called the children of the scientific era, into a cowed, credulous, hypnotized mass. [...]

## 33

The theatre as we know it shows the structure of society (represented on the stage) as incapable of being influenced by society (in the auditorium). Oedipus, who offended against certain principles underlying the society of his time, is executed: the gods see to that; they are beyond criticism.[4] Shakespeare's great solitary figures, bearing on their breast the star of their fate, carry through with irresistible force their futile and deadly outbursts; they prepare their own downfall; life, not death, becomes obscene as they collapse; the catastrophe is beyond criticism. Human sacrifices all round! Barbaric delights! We know that the barbarians have their art. Let us create another. [...]

## 35

We need a type of theatre which not only releases the feelings, insights and impulses possible within the particular historical field of human relations in which the action takes place, but employs and encourages those thoughts and feelings which help transform the field itself.

## 36

The field has to be defined in historically relative terms. In other words we must drop our habit of taking the different social structures of past periods, then stripping them of everything that makes them different; so that they all look more or less like our own, which then acquires from this process a certain air of having been there all along, in other words of permanence pure and simple. Instead we must leave them their distinguishing marks and keep their impermanence always before our eyes, so that our own period can be seen as impermanent too. [...]

## 37

If we ensure that our characters on the stage are moved by social impulses and that these differ according to the period, then we make it harder for our spectator to identify himself with them. He cannot simply feel: that's how I would

---

[4] An inaccurate outline of *King Oedipus*, at the end of which the eponymous hero, blinded by his own hand, is shown ready to continue his life; or of its sequel, *Oedipus at Colonus*, in which he is revealed to be rising to mythical stature at the time of his death.

act, but at most can say: if I had lived under those circumstances. And if we play works dealing with our own time as though they were historical, then perhaps the circumstances under which he himself acts will strike him as equally odd; and this is where the critical attitude begins. [...]

# 39

If a character responds in a manner historically in keeping with his period, and would respond otherwise in other periods, does that mean that he is not simply 'Everyman'? It is true that a man will respond differently according to his circumstances and his class; if he were living at another time, or in his youth, or on the darker side of life, he would infallibly give a different response, though one still determined by the same factors and like anyone else's response in that situation at that time. So should we not ask if there are not any further differences of response? Where is the man himself, the living, unmistakable man, who is not quite identical with those identified with him? It is clear that his stage image must bring him to light, and this will come about if this particular contradiction is recreated in the image. The image that gives historical definition will retain something of the rough sketching which indicates traces of other movements and features all around the fully-worked-out figure. [...]

# 40

Such images certainly demand a way of acting which will leave the spectator's intellect free and highly mobile. He has again and again to make what one might call hypothetical adjustments to our structure, by mentally switching off the motive forces of our society or by substituting others for them: a process which leads real conduct to acquire an element of 'unnaturalness', thus allowing the real motive forces to be shorn of their naturalness and become capable of manipulation.

# 41

It is the same as when an irrigation expert looks at a river together with its former bed and various hypothetical courses which it might have followed if there had been a different tilt to the plateau or a different volume of water. And while he in his mind is looking at a new river, the socialist in his is hearing new kinds of talk from the labourers who work by it. And similarly in the theatre our spectator should find that the incidents set among such labourers are also accompanied by echoes and by traces of sketching.

## 42

The kind of acting which was tried out at the Schiffbauerdamm Theater in Berlin between the First and Second World Wars, with the object of producing such images, is based on the 'alienation effect' (A-effect). A representation which alienates is one which allows us to recognize its subject, but at the same time makes it seem unfamiliar. The classical and mediaeval theatre alienated its characters by making them wear human or animal masks; the Asiatic theatre even today uses musical and pantomimic A-effects. Such devices were certainly a barrier to empathy, and yet this technique owed more, not less, to hypnotic suggestion than do those by which empathy is achieved. The social aims of these old devices were entirely different from our own.

## 43

The old A-effects quite remove the object represented from the spectator's grasp, turning it into something that cannot be altered; the new are not odd in themselves, though the unscientific eye stamps anything strange as odd. The new alienations are only designed to free socially conditioned phenomena from that stamp of familiarity which protects them against our grasp today.

## 44

For it seems impossible to alter what has long not been altered. We are always coming on things which are too obvious for us to bother to understand them. What men experience among themselves they think of as 'the' human experience. A child, living in a world of old men, learns how things work there. He knows the run of things before he can walk. If anyone is bold enough to want something further, he only wants it as an exception. Even if he realizes that the arrangements made for him by 'Providence' are only what has been provided by society he is bound to see society, that vast collection of beings like himself, as a whole that is greater than the sum of its parts and therefore not in any way to be influenced. [ … ] To transform himself from general passive acceptance to a corresponding state of suspicious inquiry he would need to develop that detached eye with which the great Galileo observed a swinging chandelier. He was amazed by this pendulum motion, as if he had not expected it and could not understand its occurring, and this enabled him to come on the rules by which it was governed. Here is the outlook, disconcerting but fruitful, which the theatre must provoke with its representations of human social life. It must amaze its public, and this can be achieved by a technique of alienating the familar.

## 45

This technique allows the theatre to make use in its representations of the new social scientific method known as dialectical materialism. In order to unearth society's laws of motion this method treats social situations as processes, and traces out all their inconsistencies. It regards nothing as existing except in so far as it changes, in other words is in disharmony with itself. This also goes for those human feelings, opinions and attitudes through which at any time the form of men's life together finds its expression. [...]

## 47

In order to produce A-effects the actor has to discard whatever means he has learnt of getting the audience to identify itself with the characters which he plays. Aiming not to put his audience into a trance, he must not go into a trance himself. His muscles must remain loose, for a turn of the head, e.g. with tautened neck muscles, will 'magically' lead the spectators' eyes and even their heads to turn with it, and this can only detract from any speculation or reaction which the gesture may bring about. His way of speaking has to be free from parsonical sing-song and from all those cadences which lull the spectator so that the sense gets lost. Even if he plays a man possessed he must not seem to be possessed himself, for how is the spectator to discover what possessed him if he does?

## 48

At no moment must he go so far as to be wholly transformed into the character played. The verdict: 'He didn't act Lear, he was Lear' would be an annihilating blow to him. He has just to show the character, or rather he has to do more than just get into it; this does not mean that if he is playing passionate parts he must himself remain cold. It is only that his feelings must not at bottom be those of the character, so that the audience's may not at bottom be those of the character either. The audience must have complete freedom here. [...]

## 50

There needs to be yet a further change in the actor's communication of these images, and it too makes the process more 'matter-of-fact'. Just as the actor no longer has to persuade the audience that it is the author's character and not himself that is standing on the stage, so also he need not pretend that the events taking place on the stage have never been rehearsed, and are now happening for the first and only time. [...] He narrates the story of his character by vivid portrayal, always knowing more than it does and treating its 'now' and 'here' not as a pretence made possible by the rules of the game but as something to be distinguished from yesterday and some other place, so as to make visible the knotting-together of events.

## 51

This matters particularly in the portrayal of large-scale events or ones where the outside world is abruptly changed, as in wars and revolutions. The spectator can then have the whole situation and the whole course of events set before him. He can for instance hear a woman speaking and imagine her speaking differently, let us say in a few weeks' time, or other women speaking differently at that moment but in another place.[5] This would be possible if the actress were to play as though the woman had lived through the entire period and were now, out of her memory and her knowledge of what happened next, recalling those utterances of hers which were important at the time; for what is important here is what became important. To alienate an individual in this way, as being 'this particular individual' and 'this particular individual at this particular moment', is only possible if there are no illusions that the player is identical with the character and the performance with the actual event.

## 52

We shall find that this has meant scrapping yet another illusion: that everyone behaves like the character concerned. 'I am doing this' has become 'I did this', and now 'he did this' has got to become 'he did this, when he might have done something else.' It is too great a simplification if we make the actions fit the character and the character fit the actions: the inconsistencies which are to be found in the actions and characters of real people cannot be shown like this. The laws of motion of a society are not to be demonstrated by 'perfect examples', for 'imperfection' (inconsistency) is an essential part of motion and of the thing moved. It is only necessary—but absolutely necessary—that there should be something approaching experimental conditions, i.e. a counter-experiment should now and then be conceivable. Altogether this is a way of treating society as if all its actions were performed as experiments.

## 53

Even if empathy, or self-identification with the character, can be usefully indulged in at rehearsals (something to be avoided in a performance) it has to be treated just as one of a number of methods of observation. [...] But it is the crudest form of empathy when the actor simply asks: what should I be like if this or that were to happen to me? what would it look like if I were to say this and do that?—instead of asking: have I ever heard somebody saying this or seen somebody doing that? in order to piece together all sorts of elements with

[5] There is a clear recollection here of Helene Weigel's performance, playing the lead—Pelagea Vlassova—in Brecht's dramatization of Gorki's *The Mother*, first staged in Berlin in January 1932. See also Willett, *Brecht on Theatre*, 57–62 and 81–4 respectively for Brecht's Notes to *The Mother* ('Indirect Impact of the Epic Theatre', 1933) and his Criticism of the New York production of *The Mother* (1935).

which to construct a new character such as would allow the story to have taken place—and a good deal else. The coherence of the character is in fact shown by the way in which its individual qualities contradict one another.

## 54

Observation is a major part of acting. The actor observes his fellow-men with all his nerves and muscles in an act of imitation which is at the same time a process of the mind. For pure imitation would only bring out what had been observed; and this is not enough, because the original says what it has to say in too subdued a voice. To achieve a character rather than a caricature, the actor looks at people as if they were playing him their actions, in other words as if they were advising him to give their actions careful consideration.

## 55

Without opinions and objectives one can represent nothing at all. Without knowledge one can show nothing; how could one know what would be worth knowing? Unless the actor is satisfied to be a parrot or a monkey he must master our period's knowledge of human social life by himself joining in the war of the classes. [...] Nobody can stand above the warring classes, for nobody can stand above the human race. Society cannot share a common communication system so long as it is split into warring classes. Thus for art to be 'unpolitical' means only to ally itself with the 'ruling' group.

## 56

So the choice of viewpoint is also a major element of the actor's art, and it has to be decided outside the theatre. Like the transformation of nature, that of society is a liberating act; and it is the joys of liberation which the theatre of a scientific age has got to convey. [...]

## 61

The realm of attitudes adopted by the characters towards one another is what we call the realm of gest. Physical attitude, tone of voice and facial expression are all determined by a social gest: the characters are cursing, flattering, instructing one another, and so on. The attitudes which people adopt towards one another include even those attitudes which would appear to be quite private, such as the utterances of physical pain in an illness, or of religious faith. These expressions of a gest are usually highly complicated and contradictory, so that they cannot be rendered by any single word and the actor must take care that in giving his image the necessary emphasis he does not lose anything, but emphasizes the entire complex. [...]

## 64

Splitting such material into one gest after another, the actor masters his character by first mastering the 'story'. It is only after walking all round the entire episode that he can, as it were by a single leap, seize and fix his character, complete with all its individual features. Once he has done his best to let himself be amazed by the inconsistencies in its various attitudes, knowing that he will in turn have to make them amaze his audience, then the story as a whole gives him a chance to pull the inconsistencies together; for the story, being a limited episode, has a specific sense, i.e. only gratifies a specific fraction of all the interests that could arise.

## 65

Everything hangs on the 'story'; it is the heart of the theatrical performance. For it is what happens *between* people that provides them with all the material that they can discuss, criticize, alter. Even if the particular person represented by the actor has ultimately to fit into more than just the one episode, it is mainly because the episode will be all the more striking if it reaches fulfilment in a particular person. The 'story' is the theatre's great operation, the complete fitting together of all the gestic incidents, embracing the communications and impulses that must now go to make up the audience's entertainment.

## 66

Each single incident has its basic gest: Richard Gloster courts his victim's widow. The child's true mother is found by means of a chalk circle. God has a bet with the Devil for Dr Faustus's soul. Woyzeck buys a cheap knife in order to do his wife in, etc.[6] The grouping of the characters on the stage and the movements of the groups must be such that the necessary beauty is attained above all by the elegance with which the material conveying that gest is set out and laid bare to the understanding of the audience.

## 67

As we cannot invite the audience to fling itself into the story as if it were a river and let itself be carried vaguely hither and thither, the individual episodes have to be knotted together in such a way that the knots are easily noticed. The episodes must not succeed one another indistinguishably but must give us a chance to interpose our judgment. (If it were above all the obscurity of the original interrelations that interested us, then just this circumstance would

---

[6] This refers to the following plays: Shakespeare's *Richard III*, I. ii; Brecht's own *Caucasian Chalk Circle*, Sc. vi; Goethe's *Faust*, 'Prologue in Heaven'; and Büchner's *Woyzeck*, Sc. xviii.

have to be sufficiently alienated.) The parts of the story have to be carefully set off one against another by giving each its own structure as a play within the play. To this end it is best to agree to use titles like those in the preceding paragraph. The titles must include the social point, saying at the same time something about the kind of portrayal wanted, i.e. should copy the tone of a chronicle or a ballad or a newspaper or a morality. [...] In short: there are many conceivable ways of telling a story, some of them known and some still to be discovered. [...]

## 70

The exposition of the story and its communication by suitable means of alienation constitute the main business of the theatre. Not everything depends on the actor, even though nothing may be done without taking him into account. The 'story' is set out, brought forward and shown by the theatre as a whole, by actors, stage designers, mask-makers, costumiers, composers and choreographers. They unite their various arts for the joint operation, without of course sacrificing their independence in the process.

## 71

It emphasizes the general gest of showing, which always underlies that which is being shown, when the audience is musically addressed by means of songs. Because of this the actors ought not to 'drop into' song, but should clearly mark it off from the rest of the text; and this is best reinforced by a few theatrical methods such as changing the lighting or inserting a title. For its part, the music must strongly resist the smooth incorporation which is generally expected of it and turns it into an unthinking slavey. Music does not 'accompany' except in the form of comment. It cannot simply 'express itself' by discharging the emotions with which the incidents of the play have filled it. [...] Thus music can make its point in a number of ways and with full independence, and can react in its own manner to the subjects dealt with; at the same time it can also quite simply help to lend variety to the entertainment.

## 72

Just as the composer wins back his freedom by no longer having to create atmosphere so that the audience may be helped to lose itself unreservedly in the events on the stage, so also the stage designer gets considerable freedom as soon as he has no longer to create the illusion of a room or a locality when he is building his sets. It is enough for him to give hints, though these must make statements of greater historical or social interest than does the real setting. [...]

## 73

For choreography too there are once again tasks of a realistic kind. It is a relatively recent error to suppose that it has nothing to do with the representation of 'people as they really are'. If art reflects life it does so with special mirrors. Art does not become unrealistic by changing the proportions but by changing them in such a way that if the audience took its representations as a practical guide to insights and impulses it would go astray in real life. It is of course essential that stylization should not remove the natural element but should heighten it. Anyhow, a theatre where everything depends on the gest cannot do without choreography. Elegant movement and graceful grouping, for a start, can alienate, and inventive miming greatly helps the story.

## 74

So let us invite all the sister arts of the drama, not in order to create an 'integrated work of art'[7] in which they all offer themselves up and are lost, but so that together with the art of acting they may further the common task in their different ways; and their relations with one another consist in this: that they lead to mutual alienation. [...]

## 77

That is to say, our representations must take second place to what is represented, men's life together in society; and the pleasure felt in their perfection must be converted into the higher pleasure felt when the rules emerging from this life in society are treated as imperfect and provisional. In this way the theatre leaves the spectator productively disposed even after the spectacle is over. [...]

---

[7] Brecht's stress on the relative independence of the various arts that together make up a theatrical performance is in deliberate contradiction to Wagner's championing of the 'total' or 'integrated work of art'. For Wagner's theory of the *Gesamtkunstwerk*, see pp. 3–11.

# The Material and the Models: Notes Towards a Definition of Documentary Theatre (1968)

## Peter Weiss

The striking change of tack in the dramatic work of novelist/essayist/poet/painter/film-maker Peter Weiss (1916–82) was due to no mere personal whim: it reflected changes in world politics during the 1960s and 1970s. German-born, living in Sweden where he wrote sometimes in Swedish but mostly in German, the author had come to worldwide notice with the play generally known by its abbreviated title: *Marat/Sade* (1964). In this dramatized clash of revolutionary commitment (Marat) versus aristocratic individualism (the Marquis de Sade) Weiss combined Artaudian with Brechtian devices and gave a platform to both sides of the argument. Exchanging this neutrality for a socialist stance shortly after, Weiss wrote several documentary plays, the most rigorous of which was *The Investigation* (1965): this was based verbatim on the Frankfurt trials of Auschwitz camp personnel (1963–5). Interestingly enough, it was Erwin Piscator who first produced this documentary masterpiece at the Freie Volksbühne in Berlin—over forty years after issuing his own call for a fact-based theatre (see Piscator, pp. 221–3). The essay quoted below, which expresses Weiss's later point of view, was delivered as a paper to the Brecht Dialogue held at the Berliner Ensemble (12–16 February 1968); it was subsequently published in the West German magazine, *Theater heute* (1968).

The realistic theatre of actuality has taken numerous forms since the days of the 'Proletcult' movement, of agitprop, of the experiments of Piscator and the didactic plays of Brecht.[1] Today its diverse forms are lumped together under various names such as political theatre, documentary theatre, theatre of

Translated from the German by Heinz Bernard, in *Theatre Quarterly*, 1/1 (Jan.–Mar. 1971), 41–3.

[1] The 'Proletcult Theatre' was a Russian agit-prop group formed shortly after the Revolution for which S. M. Eisenstein (better known as a film-maker of worldwide reputation) worked for a while.—Brecht's specifically didactic plays were written between 1929 and 1934.

protest, anti-theatre.[2] Accepting the difficulty of classifying all the different forms of a basic dramatic kind, the attempt will be made here to discuss one of its variants, that which is exclusively concerned with documenting an event and which can therefore be called Documentary Theatre.

# I

Documentary Theatre is a theatre of reportage. Records, documents, letters, statistics, stock-exchange bulletins, annual reports of banks and companies, government declarations, speeches, interviews, statements by well-known personalities, newspaper and broadcast reports, photos, newsreels and other contemporary documents are the basis of the performance. Documentary Theatre refrains from all invention; it gathers authentic material and re-produces it on the stage, unaltered in content, edited in form. In contrast to the haphazard nature of the news with which we are bombarded daily on all sides, a selection based on a definite theme, generally of a social or political character, is shown on the stage. This critical selection and the principles by which the montage of snippets of reality is effected determine the quality of the documentary drama.

# II

Documentary Theatre is a reflection of life as it is brought to us by the mass media. The work of Documentary Theatre is determined by critical questions of different kinds:

a) Critique of concealment. Are reports in the press, on radio and TV slanted towards the point of view of dominant interests? What are we not told? Who benefits by the omissions? To whose advantage is it when certain social phenomena are hushed up, modified, idealized?

b) Critique of falsification of reality. Why are an historical figure, a period or an epoch eliminated from consciousness? Whose position is strengthened by the suppression of historical facts? Who gains from the deliberate distortion of decisive and significant events? Which social strata are anxious to conceal the past? How do the deliberate distortions manifest themselves? How are they received?

c) Critique of lies. What are the consequences of an historical deception? What does a contemporary situation built on lies look like? What difficulties do we have to take into account in seeking out the truth? Which influential organs, what powerful groupings will do anything to prevent the truth from becoming known?

---

[2] 'Antitheatre' was the name of the group run in Munich in the 1960s by the German actor, play-wright, and film-maker Rainer Werner Fassbinder (1946–82); this was not, however, a politically committed company.

## III

Although the means of communication have now reached maximum extension and bring us news from all over the world, the causes and relationships of the decisive events which shape our present and our future remain hidden from us. We are denied access to the personal papers of the people responsible for actions of which we only see the end results. A Documentary Theatre which wants to deal, for instance, with the murders of Lumumba, of Kennedy, of Che Guevara, with the massacre in Indonesia, with what went on behind the scenes during the Indo-China negotiations in Geneva, with the latest Middle East conflict, or with the preparations of the United States government for war in Vietnam is first of all up against the artificial fog behind which the world's rulers hide their manipulations.

## IV

A Documentary Theatre aimed against those groups who are interested in a policy of obscurantism and opacity, aimed against the tendency of the mass media to keep the population in a state of stupefaction and bewilderment, is in the same starting position as any citizen wishing to make his own enquiries; his hands are tied, and eventually he takes the only road still open to him: that of public protest. Documentary Theatre, like the spontaneous open-air demonstration with its placards, slogans and choric chants, represents a reaction against the state of things as they are and a demand for an explanation.

## V

Street demonstrations, giving out leaflets, marching in ranks, mingling with large crowds: these are concrete actions showing direct results. Improvised as they are, they have a strong dramatic quality; their development is unpredictable; at any moment they can explode into a confrontation with the forces of law and order, thus pointing out the contradictions within society. Documentary Theatre which presents and sums up the latent seeds of rebellion tries to retain the quality of topicality in its expression. But even at the point of composing the text for a closed performance—to be given at a certain time and in a confined space, with actors and spectators—Documentary Theatre works in conditions different from those which apply to direct political action. The stage of the Documentary Theatre no longer represents immediate actuality but an image of a segment of that actuality torn out of its living context.

## VI

Documentary Theatre, so long as it does not take the form of a street spectacle, cannot compare with the reality content of an authentic political event. It can never measure up to the dynamic expressions of opinion which are generated in a public forum. It cannot issue a challenge to the state and the administration from a theatre with the same force as a march on government buildings or on military centres. Even when it attempts to free itself from the framework which defines it as an artistic medium, when it renounces any aesthetic considerations and does not try to be a finished product but a mere declaration of militancy, giving the impression of bursting into spontaneous existence and of acting without preparation[3]—the result is nevertheless a form of artistic expression, and it has to become a form of artistic expression if it is to have any validity.

## VII

The fact is that a Documentary Theatre, which aims to be a political forum first of all and which renounces all aesthetic considerations, calls into question its right to exist. In that case, practical political activity outside the theatre would be more effective. Only when it has transmuted into an artistic form the reality it has laid bare by its probing, checking and critical activity can it achieve any true validity in dealing with that reality. On such a stage the drama can become an instrument for forming political opinion. But we have to discuss how the specific forms of expression of Documentary Theatre are to be understood, in contrast to traditional artistic concepts.

## VIII

The strength of Documentary Theatre lies in its ability to shape a useful pattern from fragments of reality, to build a model of current events. It does not stand at the centre of events, it adopts the position of the spectator and analyst. By means of its montage technique, it emphasizes significant details in the chaotic material of external reality. Through the confrontation of contradictory details it shows up an existing conflict to which, on the basis of the assembled documentation, it then brings a suggested solution, an appeal, or a point of principle. All that which in open improvisation, in politically coloured 'happenings'[4] leads to diffuse tension, to emotional sympathy, to an illusion of participation in current events, is in Documentary Theatre dealt with attentively, consciously and reflectively.

## IX

Documentary Theatre submits facts for examination. It shows the differing responses to events and statements. It shows the origins of these responses.

---

[3] Compare Boal's Theatre of the Oppressed—see pp. 254–60.
[4] For Happenings, see pp. 205–7.

One side gains by an event. Another side loses. The parties confront each other. Their interdependence is revealed. The bribery and blackmail are illustrated by which this interdependence is to be sustained. The losses appear alongside the gains. The winners defend themselves. They present themselves as the guardians of order. They show how they administer their property. In contrast to them, the losers. The traitors in the ranks of the losers, hoping for advancement for themselves. The others, striving not to lose even more. A constant clash of unequal parties. Insight into inequality made so concrete it becomes unbearable. Injustices so evident they demand immediate intervention. Situations so rooted in fraud they can only be altered by force. Opposing ideas on the same subject are articulated. Assertions are compared with actual conditions. Protestations, promises are followed by actions which contradict them. The results of decisions made in secret conclaves are analyzed. Whose position has been strengthened, who was undermined by them? The silence, the evasions of the participants are documented. Evidence is submitted. Conclusions are drawn, based on recognizable models. Real persons are characterized as the representatives of certain social interests. Actions motivated by social and economic factors are shown, not individual conflicts. Documentary Theatre which is concerned with what is typical, as opposed to quickly exhausted external appearances, deals not with stage characters and naturalistic descriptions but with groups, with fields of force, with tendencies.

# X

Documentary Theatre takes sides. Many of its themes inevitably demand judgement. In such a theatre, objectivity is apt to be a concept used by a ruling group to excuse its actions. The call for restraint and understanding is shown to come from those who do not wish to lose their privileges. The attacks by the Portuguese colonizers against Angola and Mozambique, the measures taken by the South African Republic against the African population, the aggression by the United States against Cuba, the Dominican Republic and Vietnam can only be presented as one-sided crimes. In the description of rapine and genocide, the technique of painting in black and white is justified, with no conciliatory traits for the aggressor, with every kind of solidarity for the underdog.

# XI

Documentary Theatre can take on the form of a tribunal. Here, too, it cannot claim the authenticity of the Court at Nuremberg, the Auschwitz trial in Frankfurt, a hearing of the American Senate or the Russell Tribunal;[5] but the questions, the point of attack articulated in the real court-room can be stated

---

[5] The Bertrand Russell Peace Foundation, established in 1963, set up an International War Crimes Tribunal to investigate such 'police actions' as the Vietnam War.

in a fresh way. It can, by virtue of the distance gained, pursue arguments from points of view not considered at the original trial. The participants are placed in an historical context. At the same time as their actions are presented, the development is traced of which these actions are the result, and attention is drawn to further possible consequences. Through their actions, the machinery which continues to shape reality is demonstrated. All non-essentials, all digressions can be eliminated so as to lay bare the basic problem. What is lost are the elements of surprise, local colour, sensation; what is gained are universal truths. Moreover, Documentary Theatre can draw the audience into the action, which is not possible in a real court-room; it can put the audience in the position of the accused or the accuser; it can make them members of a committee of enquiry; it can contribute to the understanding of a complex situation or stir up to the uttermost an attitude of resistance.

## XII

A few more examples of the formal handling of documentary material.

a) Reports, and parts of reports, divided rhythmically into carefully timed sections. Brief moments, consisting of just one fact, one exclamation, are relieved by longer, more complicated units. A quotation is followed by the enactment of a situation. By quick cutting, a situation is switched to another, contrasting one. Single speakers confront a number of speakers. The scenario consists of antithetical pieces, of sequences of similar examples, of contrasting forms, of changing orders of magnitude. Variations on a theme. Raising the pitch of events. Insertion of disturbances, dissonances.

b) The factual material is shaped by means of language. In quotations, typicality is emphasized. Personalities are caricatured, situations drastically simplified. Reports, comments, résumés are turned into songs. Choirs and mime are introduced. Gestural portrayals of the action, parody, use of masks and scenic effects. Musical accompaniment, sound effects.

c) Interruptions of the reportage. Cutting away to a reflection, to a monologue, to a dream, to contradictory conduct. These breaks in the course of the action, causing uncertainty which may create a shock effect, show how an individual or a group are affected by the events portrayed. Laying bare the inner reality as a reply to external events. These violent switches should not, however, lead to confusion but must draw attention to the many facets of the event; the means used should be a verifiable experience rather than an end in themselves.

d) Dissolving the structure. Not a calculated rhythm but raw material, compact or in a loose stream, when showing social struggles, portraying a revolutionary situation, reporting from the theatre of war. Presentation of the violence in the clash of forces. But here, too, the tumult on stage, the experience of alarm and indignation must not remain vague and unresolved. The more distressing the material, the more necessary it is to reach a conspectus, a synthesis.

# XIII

Hand in hand with the attempts of Documentary Theatre to develop a convincing form goes the search for a suitable venue. If the performance takes place in a commercial theatre, with high prices of admission, the Documentary Theatre is caught up in the very system it wants to attack. If it moves outside the Establishment, it is forced into places frequented by a small coterie of the likeminded. Instead of having an effective influence on conditions, it often merely demonstrates its impotence in opposition to those who preserve those conditions. Documentary Theatre must gain access to factories, schools, sports grounds, meeting-halls. As it breaks away from the aesthetic assumptions of traditional theatre, it constantly needs to question its own means and to develop new techniques suited to new conditions.

# XIV

Documentary Theatre is only possible when it consists of a regular working group, schooled politically and sociologically, and is capable of scientific investigation, supported by a comprehensive archive. Documentary drama is valueless if it is afraid of definitions, if it shows only the conditions and not the causes underlying them, if it does not reveal the need and the possibility of eliminating these conditions, if it remains fixed in a posture of a frantic attack without actually hitting the opponent. Documentary Theatre is therefore opposed to the kind of drama whose main theme is its own fury and despair and which clings to the concept of a hopeless and absurd world. Documentary Theatre asserts the alternative: that reality, however opaquely it may present itself, can be explained in every detail.

# Poetics of the Oppressed
## (1974)

### Augusto Boal

Much of the work of the Brazilian theoretician, director and playwright Augusto Boal (b. 1931) represents political theatre at its most direct and committed—an attempt to abolish the gap between performers and spectators to the greatest extent possible. Imprisoned and tortured for his radical views in Brazil in 1971, he spent many years as an exile in Argentina, Peru, and France. His Forum Theatre in Paris (1978–86) developed improvisational techniques involving the audience, problem-solving games intended potentially to change real-life situations. Boal has also worked professionally in different European countries and in the USA. Returning to Brazil in 1986, he founded the Theatre of the Oppressed Centre in Rio de Janeiro. His book, *Theatre of the Oppressed*, which combines a series of scholarly essays on the European tradition of dramatic theory with a description of his practical work in Brazil, Argentina, and Peru, has been translated into twenty-five languages.

[…] The bourgeoisie already knows what the world is like, *their* world, and is able to present images of this complete, finished world. The bourgeoisie presents the spectacle. On the other hand, the proletariat and the oppressed classes do not know yet what their world will be like; consequently their theatre will be the rehearsal, not the finished spectacle. […]

I have been able to observe the truth of this view during all my activities in the people's theatre of so many and such different countries of Latin America. Popular audiences are interested in experimenting, in rehearsing, and they abhor the 'closed' spectacles. In those cases they try to enter into a dialogue with the actors, to interrupt the action, to ask for explanations without waiting politely for the end of the play. Contrary to the bourgeois code of manners,

Translated from the Spanish by Charles A. and Maria-Odilia Leal McBride, in Augusto Boal, *Theater of the Oppressed* (New York: Urizen Books, 1979), 142–55.

the people's code allows and encourages the spectator to ask questions, to dialogue, to participate.

All the methods I have discussed[1] are forms of rehearsal-theatre, and not a spectacle-theatre. One knows how these experiments will begin but not how they will end, because the spectator is freed from his chains, finally acts, and becomes a protagonist. Because they respond to the real needs of a popular audience they are practised with success and joy.

But nothing in this prohibits a popular audience from also practising a more 'finished' form of theatre. [...] Some of these forms were:

1) *Newspaper theatre:* [...] It consists of several simple techniques for transforming daily news items or any other non-dramatic material into theatrical performances.

a) Simple reading: the news item is read detaching it from the context of the newspaper, from the format which makes it false or tendentious.

b) Crossed reading: two news items are read in crossed (alternating) form, one throwing light on the other, explaining it, giving it a new dimension.

c) Complementary reading: data and information generally omitted by the newspapers of the ruling classes are added to the news.

d) Rhythmical reading: as a musical commentary, the news is read to the rhythm of the samba, tango, Gregorian chant, etc., so that the rhythm functions as a critical 'filter' of the news, revealing its true content, which is obscured in the newspaper.

e) Parallel action: the actors mime parallel actions while the news is read, showing the context in which the reported event really occurred; one hears the news and sees something else that complements it visually.

f) Improvisation: the news is improvised on stage to exploit all its variants and possibilities.

g) Historical: data or scenes showing the same event at other historical moments, in other countries, or in other social systems, are added to the news.

h) Reinforcement: the news is read or sung with the aid or accompaniment of slides, jingles, songs, or publicity materials.

i) Concretion of the abstract: that which the news often hides in its purely abstract information is made concrete on the stage: torture, hunger, unemployment, etc., are shown concretely, using graphic images, real or symbolic.

j) Text out of context: the news is presented out of the context in which it was published; for example, an actor gives the speech about austerity previously delivered by the Minister of Economics while he devours an enormous dinner [...]

---

[1] Earlier on in this essay Boal lists some of the techniques he employed when working with the People's Theatre in Peru in August 1973; this was part of a programme of fighting illiteracy among workers, slum dwellers, and peasants, many of whom spoke languages other than Spanish. The techniques he developed for preparing the actor-spectators involved in this project were (*a*) physical awareness training; (*b*) making the body more expressive; and (*c*) different playmaking methods based on the experiences drawn from people's actual lives and the problems confronting them.

2) *Invisible theatre*: It consists of the presentation of a scene in an environment other than the theatre, before people who are not spectators. The place can be a restaurant, a sidewalk, a market, a train, a line of people, etc. The people who witness the scene are those who are there by chance. During the spectacle, these people must not have the slightest idea that it is a 'spectacle', for this would make them 'spectators'.

The invisible theatre calls for the detailed preparation of a skit with a complete text or a simple script; but it is necessary to rehearse the scene sufficiently so that the actors are able to incorporate into their acting and their actions the intervention of the spectators. During the rehearsal it is also necessary to include every conceivable intervention from the spectators; these possibilities will form a kind of optional text.

The invisible theatre erupts in a location chosen as a place where the public congregates. All the people who are near become involved in the eruption and the effects of it last long after the skit is ended. [...]

It is necessary to emphasize that the invisible theatre is not the same thing as a 'happening' or the so-called 'guerilla theatre'.[2] In the latter we are clearly talking about 'theatre', and therefore the wall that separates actors from spectators immediately arises, reducing the spectator to impotence: a spectator is always less than a man! In the invisible theatre the theatrical rituals are abolished; only the theatre exists, without its old worn-out patterns. The theatrical energy is completely liberated, and the impact produced by this free theatre is much more powerful and lasting. [...]

3) *Photo-romance*: In many Latin American countries there is a genuine epidemic of photo-romances, subliterature on the lowest imaginable level, which furthermore always serves as a vehicle of the ruling classes' ideology. The technique here consists of reading to the participants the general lines in a plot of a photo-romance without telling them the source of this plot. The participants are asked to act out the story. Finally, the acted-out story is compared to the story as it is told in the photo-romance, and the differences are discussed.

For example: a rather stupid story taken from Corín Tellado, the worst author of this brutalizing genre, started like this:

A woman is waiting for her husband in the company of another woman who is helping her with the housework ...

The participants acted according to their customs: a woman at home expecting her husband will naturally be preparing the meal; the one helping her is a neighbour who comes to chat about various things; the husband comes

---

[2] 'Happenings', such as the ones set up by the American painter Allan Kaprow in the 1960s, were one-off events set up by non-professional performers in non-theatrical venues. These tended to abolish the boundary between 'actors' and spectators; they combined logically disconnected activities in a manner reminiscent of dada and surrealism but had no direct political or social aim. (See Brook, pp. 205–7.) 'Guerilla theatre'—as practised for instance by the (professional) American Living Theatre, also during the 1960s—similarly avoided theatrical venues and made a direct appeal to spectators: but in contrast to Happenings sought to intervene directly in politics.

home tired after a long day's work, the house is a one-room shack, etc. etc. In Corín Tellado, on the contrary, the woman is dressed in a long evening gown, with pearl necklaces, etc.; the woman who is helping her is a black maid [...] The house is a marble palace; the husband comes home after a day's work in his factory, where he had an argument with the workers [...]

This particular story was sheer trash, but at the same time it served as a magnificent example of ideological insight. The well dressed woman received a letter from an unknown woman, went to visit her and discovered her to be a former mistress of her husband; the mistress stated that the husband had left her because he wanted to marry the factory owner's daughter, that is, the well dressed woman. To top it all, the mistress exclaimed:

'Yes, he betrayed me, deceived me. But I forgive him because, after all, he has always been very ambitious, and he knew very well that with me he could not climb very high. On the other hand, with you he can go very far indeed!' [...]

And the young wife, not to be outdone, pretends to be ill so that he will have to remain at her side and so that, as a result of this trick, he will finally fall in love with her. What an ideology! This love story is crowned with a happy ending rotten to the core. Of course the story, when told without the dialogues and acted out by peasants, takes on an entirely different meaning. When at the end of the performance the participants are told of the origin of the plot they have just acted out, they experience a shock. And this must be understood: when they read Corín Tellado they immediately assume the passive attitude of 'spectators'; but if they first of all have to act out a story themselves, afterwards, when they do read Corín Tellado's version, they will no longer assume a passive, expectant attitude but instead a critical, comparative one. [...] And they will be prepared to detect the poison infiltrating the pages of those photo-stories, or the comics and other forms of cultural and ideological domination. [...]

4) *Breaking the repression:* The dominant classes crush the dominated ones through repression; the old crush the young through repression; certain races subjugate certain others through repression. [...]

The capitalist does not ask the working man if he agrees that the capital should belong to one and the labour to another; he simply places an armed policeman at the factory door and that is that—private property is decreed.

The dominated class, race, sex, or age group suffers the most constant, daily, and omnipresent repression. The ideology becomes concrete in the figure of the dominated person. [...] There is not an oppression by the masculine sex in general of the feminine sex in general: what exists is the concrete oppression that men (individuals) direct against women (individuals).

The technique of breaking repression consists in asking a participant to remember a particular moment when he felt especially repressed, accepted that repression, and began to act in a manner contrary to his own desires. That moment must have a deep personal meaning: I, a proletarian, am oppressed; we proletarians are oppressed; therefore the proletariat is oppressed. It is necessary to pass from the particular to the general, not vice versa, and to deal with something that has happened to someone in particular, but which at the same time is typical of what happens to others.

The person who tells the story also chooses from among the rest of the participants all the other characters who will participate in the reconstruction of the incident. Then, after receiving the information and directions provided by the protagonist, the participants and the protagonist act out the incident just as it happened in reality—recreating the same scene, the same circumstances and the same original feelings.

Once the 'reproduction' of the actual event is over, the protagonist is asked to repeat the scene but this time without accepting the repression, fighting to impose his will, his ideas, his wishes. The other participants are urged to maintain the repression as in the first performance. The clash that results helps to measure the possibility one often has to resist and yet fails to do so; it helps to measure the true strength of the enemy. It also gives the protagonist the opportunity of trying once more and carrying out, in fiction, what he had not been able to do in reality. But […] the fact of having rehearsed a resistance to oppression will prepare him to resist effectively in a future reality, when the occasion presents itself once more.

On the other hand, it is necessary to take care that the generic nature of the particular case under study be understood. In this type of theatrical experiment the particular instance must serve as the point of departure, but it is indispensable to reach the general. […]

5) *Myth theatre*: It is simply a question of discovering the obvious behind the myth: to tell a story logically, revealing its evident truths.

In a place called Motupe there was a hill, almost a mountain, with a narrow road that led through the trees to the top; halfway to the top stood a cross. One could go as far as the cross: to go beyond it was dangerous; it inspired fear, and the few who had tried had never returned. It was believed that some sanguinary ghosts inhabited the top of the mountain. But the story is also told of a brave young man who armed himself and climbed to the top, where he found the 'ghosts'. They were in reality some Americans who owned a gold mine located precisely on the top of that mountain. […]

The myths told by the people should be studied and analysed and their hidden truths revealed. In this task the theatre can be extraordinarily useful.

6) *Analytical theatre*: A story is told by one of the participants and immediately the actors improvise it. Afterwards each character is broken down into all his social roles and the participants are asked to choose a physical object to symbolize each role. For example, a policeman killed a chicken thief. The policeman is analysed:

a) He is a worker because he rents his labour power; symbol: a pair of overalls;

b) He is a bourgeois because he protects private property and values it more than human life; symbol: a necktie or a top hat, etc.;

c) he is a repressive agent because he is a policeman; symbol: a revolver.

This is continued until the participants have analysed all his roles: head of a family (symbol: the wallet, for example), member of a fraternal order, etc., etc. It is important that the symbols be chosen by the participants present and that they be not imposed 'from above'. For a particular community the symbol for the head of a family might be a wallet, because he is the person who controls the household finances and in this way controls the family. For another community this symbol may not communicate anything, that is, it may not be a symbol; then an armchair may be chosen ...

Having analysed the character or characters [...], a fresh attempt to tell the story is made, but taking away some of the symbols from each character, and consequently some social roles as well. Would the story be exactly the same if:

a) the policeman did not have the top hat or the necktie?

b) the robber had a top hat or necktie?

c) the robber had a revolver?

d) the policeman and the robber both had the same symbol for the fraternal order?

The participants are asked to make varying combinations and the proposed combinations must be performed by the actors and criticized by all those present. In this way they will realize that human actions are not the exclusive and primordial result of individual psychology: almost always, through the individual speaks his class!

7) *Rituals and masks*: The relations of production (infrastructure) determine the culture of a society (superstructure).

Sometimes the infrastructure changes but the superstructure for a while remains the same. [...]

This particular technique of a people's theatre [...] consists precisely in revealing the superstructure, the rituals which reify all human relationships, and the masks of behaviour that these rituals impose on each person according to the role he plays in society and the rituals he must perform.

A very simple example: a man goes to a priest to confess his sins. How will he do it? Of course, he will kneel, confess his sins, hear the penitence, cross himself and leave. But do all men confess always in the same way before all priests? Who is the man and who is the priest?

In this case we need two versatile actors to stage the same confession four times:

First scene: the priest and the parishioner are landlords;

Second scene: the priest is a landlord and the parishioner is a peasant;

Third scene: the priest is a peasant and the parishioner is a landlord;

Fourth scene: the priest and the parishioner are peasants.

The ritual is the same in each instance, but the different social masks will cause the four scenes to be different also.

This is an extraordinarily rich technique which has countless variants: the same ritual changing masks; the same ritual performed by people of one social class and later by people of another class; exchange of masks within the same ritual; etc. etc.

## Conclusion: 'Spectator', a Bad Word!

[...] The spectator is less than a man and it is necessary to humanize him, to restore him to his capacity for action in all its fulness. He too must be a subject, an actor on an equal plane with those generally accepted as actors, who must also be spectators. All these experiments of a people's theatre have the same objective—the liberation of the spectator, on whom the theatre has imposed finished visions of the world. And since those responsible for theatrical performances are in general people who belong directly or indirectly to the ruling classes, obviously their finished images will be reflections of themselves. The spectators in the people's theatree (i.e., the people themselves) cannot go on being the passive victims of those images.

[...] (The) poetics of Aristotle is the *poetics of oppression*: the world is known, perfect or about to be perfected, and all its values are imposed on the spectators, who passively delegate power to the characters to act and think in their place. In so doing the spectators purge themselves of their tragic flaw—that is, of something capable of changing society. A catharsis of the revolutionary impetus is produced! Dramatic action substitutes for real action.

Brecht's poetics is that of the enlightened vanguard: the world is revealed as subject to change, and the change starts in the theatre itself, for the spectator does not delegate power to the characters to think in his place, although he continues to delegate power to them to act in his place. The experience is revealing on the level of consciousness, but not globally on the level of action. Dramatic action throws light upon real action. The spectacle is a preparation for action.

The *poetics of the oppressed* is essentially the poetics of liberation: the spectator no longer delegates power to the characters either to think or to act in his place. The spectator frees himself; he thinks and acts for himself! Theatre is action!

Perhaps the theatre is not revolutionary in itself; but have no doubts, it is a rehearsal of revolution!

# Political Dynamics: The Feminisms (1986)

## Michelene Wandor

The poet, critic, and playwright Michelene Wandor (b. 1940), who has written extensively for the stage, for television and radio (including serial dramatizations of literary classics), is a leading British feminist author. The following excerpt from her book on sexual politics and the theatre, *Carry on, Understudies*, represents an informed and committed insider's viewpoint. In *Look Back in Gender* (London: Methuen, 1987) Ms Wandor dealt with questions of sexuality and the family in post-war British drama. She has also run playwriting workshops, given poetry readings, and edited plays by women.

Because of the scarcity value of women playwrights and of plays which take either a female-gendered perspective, or which are largely or entirely about women, it is all too easy sometimes for them to be casually labelled with one of the many new clichés which have sprung up during the 1970s: 'feminist theatre', 'women's theatre', 'plays for women'—all these convey some important clue as to the bias or content of a play, but they are not analytical. They are useful sign-posts; but they can be used by misogynists in order to sneer at and ghettoise new work by and about women. Or they can be used in a blanket sort of way to imply support and approval (nothing wrong with that) and to forestall any criticism or comment. It seems to me both exciting and important to try to understand precisely the way in which the ideas generated through political feminism have affected (or not) the work of women and men playwrights. We are, after all, talking about the complex ways in which imaginative work is both a product of its own time and a response to it, and writing a work of fiction (in this case, a play), even if it has documentary sources, is an engagement with the relationship between the conscious knowledge and ideas of the writer, and the

From Michelene Wandor, *Carry on, Understudies* (London: Routledge & Kegan Paul, 1986), 130–9.

way s/he then digests that knowledge and creates a fictional, imaginative world. This imaginative world cannot simply be 'checked off' against 'reality'. It is an act of illusion, since it creates its own internal rules, it is part of a tradition—or traditions—whether the writer is aware or not, and it constantly alludes to empirically verifiable bits of the real world, and to the imaginations and emotions of its audiences. There is no simple way in which neat correlations between politics and art (feminism and theatre) can be made; but it is essential that some attempt is made, in order to understand the plays better. It is not a game to pass abstract value judgments [...]

First of all, some clarification on the nature of feminism. Or rather, of the feminisms. Feminism is not a crude or a homogeneous thing. It has a history (a number of histories, indeed) and has taken different forms at different times. Having said that, it is important to stress that just because a play is by a woman, or includes women characters, or has an all-female cast, it does not necessarily mean that the play will be sympathetic to feminism, even though it may be about emotions and actions which are not commonly seen on the stage. Because a play is about women does not necessarily mean that it is about feminism; and if it is, it is important to try to understand how it refracts its feminist influences. For the purposes of this discussion, I have limited the description of feminism to its three major tendencies—as they have emerged during the 1970s. There are of course other gradations, and there are overlaps between the three tendencies, but they each stem from a different theoretical explanation of why women are where they are in society, and they each have a different set of political and tactical priorities for responding to the analysis, and bringing about social change. The three tendencies share three important features: (1) All three tendencies seek to bring about some sort of change in the position of women. (2) All three tendencies challenge both the idea and the fact of male dominance. (3) All three tendencies assert the importance of self-determination for women. However, each tendency interprets this principle, at both the personal/individual and the social/collective levels, in different ways. But they do all challenge the crudeness of a biological determinism that says that women are biologically weaker than, and inferior to, men, and that women's social and cultural inferiority therefore follows on. All three feminisms, then, challenge the oppressiveness of different aspects of the social/sexual division of labour. [...]

The three kinds of feminism, then:

# 1 Radical feminism

Radical feminism springs from the direct, gut response of all women to the day-to-day irritations which women feel and experience. Radical feminism articulates these responses, analyses and politicizes the details of oppression. It challenges very directly the notion that men are biologically superior to women, and it does so by claiming that what women do and think and feel is socially valuable and important. Radical feminist theory argues that the oppression of women predates capitalism, and that therefore all subsequent forms of social injustice stem from the basic sexual antagonism between men and women. Thus for radical feminism 'men' (i.e. biological and social male-ness) are seen as the primary enemy, and everything that is 'bad' in the world (i.e. war, aggression) is seen as 'male', and everything 'good' (caring, nurturing) is seen as 'female'. It will be seen that radical feminism simply inverts the model of sexist values and produces a reverse moral system, in which—instead of men on top and women below—women are on top and the men below. [...]

Radical feminism offers a dualist analysis of social structure divided simply along gender lines, and this position leads to the very crude view that there is such a thing as a 'women's culture' and a 'women's language' which is entirely separate from that of men. The seductive but inaccurate notion that our language has been 'made' by men with no meanings for women would, if taken to its logical conclusion, mean that men and women would never understand one another. It is more accurate to say that men have more power over some aspects of the language, and it is that power which women challenge.

It is of course true that in a common-sense, everyday way, one often feels that men and women talk a different 'language'; but when such idiomatic expression is used instead of real cultural analysis, a very dangerous thing happens. In theatre, for example, such a view can be used to justify the idea that plays about women have no interest or relevance for men; that they are, in fact, 'for' women alone. In effect, this means that men are let off the hook, both as theatre workers and as members of the audience. They can shrug off what women are saying and the forms their imaginations take, instead of being challenged on the grounds of their own ignorance and prejudice. It may be true (it often is) that women in the audience of a play about women are more likely to understand or respond to what they are seeing, but that does not mean that men can't. [...]

Because of its dualist gender philosophy and its hostility to anything that it defines as essentially 'male', radical feminism has little or no interest in any class analysis, and no desire or interest in any political relationship with social-ism or the labour movement, or any of the left-wing groups and parties.

## 2 Bourgeois feminism or emancipationism

[...] Basically bourgeois feminism simply seeks a larger share of social power for a small number of women—the 'women at the top' syndrome. It often takes the apparently liberal line of 'men and women are different, but can be equal', but in practice this usually means that the real basis of power relations between the sexes (personal and political) is concealed. Bourgeois feminism accepts the world as it is and sees the main challenge for women as simply a matter of 'equalling up' with men; in other words, what men already do is seen as the norm. Bourgeois feminism also has a little touch of radical feminism in there with this approach: unlike radical feminism, it does not challenge many of the aspects of feminity with which women are lumbered. The reverse. It asserts that women, if they really want to and try hard enough, can make it to the top, and they have added strength because they can use their feminine wiles to twist men round their little fingers on the way there; thus they reveal a curious combination of total acceptance of men as the norm, together with an element of contempt for the sexual weakness of men who can be subject to the lures and power of flirtation and women's sexual power. This produces an odd hybrid: bourgeois radical feminism, in which women simultaneously depend on men and despise them [...]

In other respects, however, bourgeois feminism is very different indeed from radical feminism: it places total stress on individual effort, which produces the token woman surrounded by men and served by other women; this means that bourgeois feminism has no interest in any idea of solidarity or sisterhood—the reverse, since such an idea is bound to conflict with the notion of individual self-advancement. And because bourgeois feminism accepts the status quo (with a bit more power for women) it also—like radical feminism—has no interest in a class analysis, and certainly no interest whatsoever in socialism or the labour movement.

However, like radical feminism it has important strengths: it is absolutely straightforward about the importance of women taking responsibility for power. It stresses the need for women to take charge of territories normally seen as the 'male' preserve, and in its emphasis on the individual it provides a model (or an image) for woman [...] as a responsible agent determining her own life and development. [...]

One recent development shows how bourgeois feminism is becoming more and more influential in the theatre in the 1980s, and that is the way that many women use the term 'actor' as if it were the generic term which includes 'actress' as part of its meaning. This is actually a retrograde step, since there is a very real gender distinction necessary in describing male and female performers, and to allow the word 'actor' to be the 'norm' is to help perpetuate the unconscious assumption that the actress is some kind of secondary or divergent category. In fact there is a perfectly good generic term [...], and that is 'performer', which after all is the best general description of the job. [...]

## 3 Socialist feminism

Socialist feminism draws together elements from the kind of class analysis developed by Karl Marx and others since, and the radical feminism which developed in the early 1970s. In terms of its theory, it aims to analyse and understand the way in which power relations based on class interact with power relations based on gender—again, at both the individual and social level. Socialist feminism recognizes that there are times and issues over which solidarity between women can cut across class or cultural barriers, but it also recognizes the importance of struggles based on class, which necessarily involve men, and that women can have important differences among themselves, based on class difference.

Theoretically and strategically, socialist feminism is more far-reaching than either bourgeois or radical feminism; where radical feminism proposes a real surge of energy and solidarity between women, it does so by devaluing and ignoring men; bourgeois feminism values social power for women, but has no concern for class issues and is still absolutely defined by men as the norm. Socialist feminism, on the other hand, proposes changes both in the position of women as women, and in the power relations of the very basis of society itself—its industrial production and its political relations. [...]

I would imagine that the reader will have gathered by the way I have approached these three feminist tendencies that my own political choice lies with the socialist-feminist. This does not mean that I am claiming that it is morally 'better'—indeed [...], there are aspects of feminism which the other two tendencies are more able to confront clearly and head-on. [...] It is also important to remember that the accounts of feminism which I have given are analytical and do not correspond simply with the real life experience of every woman at every moment. In practice the political consciousness of any feminist is made up of all the various elements, with different aspects dominant in different women, and at different times. A feminist working in a very traditional theatre situation, where attitudes are very reactionary, is likely to find herself experiencing strong, gut, radical-feminist angers; a woman in a position of power in the theatre (as artistic director, say) has to face and deal with both her desires for power and her actual objective power at work. And a feminist who is in a position to work democratically with others (say in a 'fringe' group) is more likely to be exploring ways of sharing power and control over work with others, with taking responsibility for herself and her work as a woman.

Since the feminist ideas are complex, and since it is also impossible to make crude correlations between ideology, the individual and their objective situation, one must also approach the evaluation of plays from a political point of view with caution. [...] The relationship between the conscious idea in social circulation and what happens in the imagination of the writer is both too exciting and too important to be reduced to a political label. And yet the political analysis is absolutely essential, if we are to understand what it is that writers have been doing in the 1970s and 1980s. [...]

# PART V

---

## Semiotics

# Dynamics of the Sign in the Theatre (1940)

## Jindřich Honzl

Jindřich Honzl (1894–1953) differed from other members of the Prague Linguistic Circle to which he belonged, the group of scholars who from 1926 onwards applied the new science of semiotics to a wide range of subjects including theatre, in that he combined an intimate knowledge of stage practice with theoretical scholarship. A writer, teacher, and editor, he was also a stage director who made his mark in Czech theatrical life, his work ranging from proletarian mass spectacles to surrealist productions; as a theorist, he attempted to reconcile surrealism with structuralism. In 1926 he co-founded the Liberated Theatre, which specialized in avant-garde drama. In addition to those productions of his mentioned in the essay below, he also directed such plays as Jarry's *Ubu Roi* and Cocteau's *Orphée*. Honzl was a film-maker too, and he was deeply involved in film education. From 1939 till 1941 he ran the 99 Seats Theatre; in 1948 he became the head of the National Theatre in Prague. *Dynamics of the Sign in the Theatre* first appeared in the journal of the Prague Linguistic Circle, *Slovo a slovesnost* (Word and Poetics), no. 6 (1940), 177–88.

Everything that makes up reality on the stage—the playwright's text, the actor's acting, the stage lighting—all these things in every case stand for other things. In other words, dramatic performance is a set of signs.

Otakar Zich expressed such a view in his *Aesthetics of Dramatic Art* when he advanced the notion that 'dramatic art is an art of images and is so, moreover, in absolutely every respect.'[1] Thus the actor represents a dramatic character [...], the scenery represents the locale where the story unfolds [...], bright

Translated from the Czech by Irwin R. Titunik, in Ladislav Matejka and I. R. Titunik (eds.), *Semiotics of Art* (Cambridge, Mass.: MIT Press, 1976), 74–93.

[1] Otakar Zich, *Estetika dramatického uměni* (Aesthetics of Dramatic Art (Prague, 1931), 45. [Honzl's note.] Zich (1879–1934), not himself a member of the Prague Linguistic Circle, attempted to grasp the complexity of dramatic art in terms of a single system of systems.

lighting represents daytime, dim lighting denotes night-time, music represents some happening (the noise of battle), and so forth. Zich explains that though the stage certainly involves architectural constructions, still it cannot in his view be consigned to the domain of architecture because architecture does not want to stand for anything and, hence, does not have any image function. The stage has no other function than to stand for something else, and it ceases to be the stage if it does not represent something. [...]

Moreover, from this instance of the semiotic character of the stage we can draw an analogy to other aspects of the theatrical performance. [...] Although the stage is usually a construction, it is not its constructional nature that makes it a stage but the fact the it *represents* dramatic place. The same can be said about the actors: the actor is usually a person who speaks and moves about the stage. However, the fundamental nature of an actor does not consist in the fact that he is a person speaking and moving about the stage but that he *represents someone, that he signifies a role in a play*. Hence it does not matter whether he is a human being; an actor could be a piece of wood as well. If the wood moves about and its movements are accompanied by words, then such a piece of wood can represent a character in a play, and the wood becomes an actor. [...]

And if a mere voice, heard from the wings of a stage or over the radio, properly signifies a dramatic character, then such a voice is an actor. Precisely such an acoustic actor appears in Goethe's *Faust*: in the usual performances of this play we perceive the role of God in the prologue merely as a voice. Finally, in radio plays, voice and sound represent not only dramatic characters but also all the other facts that make up the reality of the theatre: the stage, scenery, props and lighting. [...]

And much to our amazement, we are discovering that stage 'space' need not be spatial but that sound can be a stage and music can be a dramatic event and scenery can be a text.

First of all, let us deal with the stage and those signs that denote it. We may say that the stage can be represented by any real space or, in other words, a stage can equally well be a structure or a town square surrounded by spectators or a meadow or a hall in an inn. But even when a stage is such a space, it need not be denoted solely by its spatial nature. We have already used the example of a radio stage [...] However, even the conventional theatre can provide us with examples of a nonspatial denotation of a stage, for example, sound representing a stage. In the last act of Chekhov's *The Cherry Orchard* it is precisely the orchard that plays the main role. The cherry orchard is on the stage but in such a way that we cannot see it. It is not represented spatially but acoustically, as the blows of axes cutting down the orchard are heard in the last act. [...]

Zich's notion has the stage always still in a theatre, in the architecturally denoted place 'where plays and operas are performed.' It was precisely concrete artistic work that dared to move into the areas where the theory of theatre had not yet entered, even though it had already pointed in that direction. Modern theatre has had the effect precisely of freeing the stage from its previously permanent architectural constants.

Cubo-futuristic theatrical experiments[2] turned our attention to stages and theatres other than those built for the tsarist ballet, the box displays of high society, or for the cultural activity of small-town amateurs. Through these experiments we discovered the theatre of the street, we became fascinated by the theatricality of a sports field and admired the theatrical effects created by the movements of harbour cranes, and so on. Simultaneously we discovered the stage of the primitive theatre, the performances of a barker, children's games, circus pantomimes, the tavern theatre of strolling players, the theatres of masked celebrating villagers. The stage could arise anywhere—any place could lend itself to theatrical fantasy.

With the freeing of the stage, other aspects of theatrical performance were released from their confinements. Scenery of wooden frames and painted canvas awoke from its spell. Stylized theatre from as early as the time of the Théâtre d'Art in France, or G. Fuchs and A. Appia in Germany, the Society of New Drama in Russia, and of Kvapil in Bohemia[3] adhered to scenic signs that might be called scenic metonymies.[4] [...] A part represented the whole. But a part could indicate several different wholes: a Venetian column and a flight of stairs sufficed for almost all the scenes in *The Merchant of Venice*, excepting scenes in Portia's or Shylock's rooms or in the garden.[5] The column and the flight of steps were used not only as scenery for the street but also for the harbour, the square, and the court of justice. The attributive scenery of the stylized stage always sought to use devices of one single meaning whenever possible. True, a Venetian column could be placed in a square or in a street or made part of a house. But in each and every case it meant a Venetian building

---

[2] This portmanteau word links futurist theatrical practice (for Marinetti's *The Futurist Synthetic Theatre*, see pp. 176–81) with cubism, the movement in painting which converted three-dimensional objects to the two-dimensional picture surface and often combined views from different angles into one image, thus breaking decisively with the perspective vision that had dominated Western art since the Renaissance. The linkage of these two ideas underlines the non-representational aspect of avant-garde theatre in the 1920s and 1930s.

[3] The short-lived Paris Théâtre d'Art (1890–2), run by the young poet Paul Fort (1872–1960), initiated a reaction against naturalism; the early work of Maeterlinck was championed there.—Georg Fuchs (1868–1940) helped to found the Munich Artists' Theatre in 1908, with a 'relief stage' that drastically simplified scenic staging and brought the actor closer to the audience; his book, *Die Revolution des Theaters* (Revolution in the Theatre) was widely influential.—The Swiss designer Adolphe Appia (1862–1928) fundamentally altered scenic thinking by his writings about non-naturalistic settings in which he stressed the space-creating potential of electric lighting. (See pp. 145–6.)—The Society of New Drama was the name given in 1904 by Vsevolod Emilievich Meyerhold (1874–1940) to his company which was dedicated to symbolist drama.—Jaroslav Kvapil (1868–1950), librettist and playwright, had a distinguished career at the National Theatre in Prague, first as dramaturge from 1900 until 1911 and then as the artistic director until 1920; he produced many symbolist (as well as naturalistic) plays there.

[4] Derived from classical rhetoric, the concept of 'metonymy' (a *pars pro toto* figure, e.g. crown = royal authority) was one of the cornerstones of early semiological thought, forming a contrast to 'metaphor', a figure that applies the name of one object to another.

[5] This production by Kvapil was part of the Shakespearian cycle he staged at the National Theatre

and nothing but a Venetian building, of which it could be a part. With the advent of cubo-futuristic theatre new materials appeared on the stage, and formerly undreamt-of things acquired various representative functions. The theatre of Russian constructivism[6] used a construction made of planks to represent a factory yard, a garden pavilion, a wheat field or a flour mill. [...] Meyerhold's construction for *Tarelkin's Death*[7] was simply a crate combined with a cylindrical object of the same material whose circular end faced the audience and could have suggested any number of things, but none of them without ambiguity. Perhaps the most definite idea it conjured up, in this case, was that of a meat grinder. But it could equally well have indicated a circular window or a round cage or a huge mirror, circularity being its most striking feature. [...]

It is only when we see the actor pacing back and forth in the cylindrical structure like a prisoner and clutching its slats like bars that we realize the function of this stage prop: it is a cell. Simultaneously, however, there remain in our minds all the associations of form that originated during our first glance at the said prop. The idea of a 'meat grinder' in combination with the idea of a 'prison cell' acquires a mutual polarization of new meanings.

If we examine other stage sets used by Meyerhold in his stagings of that period, we frequently see a system of suspended planes, staircases and props whose meaning as a sign is completely indeterminate. The critics of these performances and sets often spoke of 'abstract scenery'. Neither Meyerhold nor any other stage artist was concerned with abstract scenery. His stage sets had very concrete tasks and functions. Indeterminate in shape and colour, they became signs only when used for the actor's actions. It can be said that *a representative function was not expressed by means of form or colour, but by the actor's actions* on the stage construction. [...]

The desire for freedom of expression and technique is a tendency that has constantly had a determining effect on art. The theatre brought about by the cubo-futuristic revolt 'for fresh air' introduced new theatrical devices and dispensed with many others. Russian constructivism rid the stage of scenery, wings, borders and backdrops. As a result the stage lost the possibility of localizing an action through the use of painted signs indicating an interior or exterior. That was not all, however. Not only did directors reject scenery, stage front and rear, borders and wings, but they also departed from the bare stage that remained after their revolt. [...] The directors who succeeded them (Okhlopkov, Gropius's theatre design)[8] did away with a stage completely or,

---

[6] *Constructivism*: a Russian artistic movement (by no means limited to, but particularly important in, the theatre) which used non-traditional materials in abstract designs inspired by industrial processes and engineering.

[7] The production in 1922 of this play, written by Alexander Vasilievich Sukhovo-Kobylin in 1869 but not staged at the time for censorship reasons, was aggressively non-naturalistic, employing circus-like effects and sight gags.

[8] The Soviet director Nikolai Pavlovich Okhlopkov (1900–67) experimented extensively with different actor-audience relationships by varying the seating and the acting areas, especially at the Realistic

more precisely, placed the stage among the spectators so that any free place in front of, above, next to, or behind the audience could be a stage. Thus they consigned to oblivion all those rare and precious stage mechanisms that, in obedience to a single demand by the director, lowered a section of stage or piece of scenery or a prop or even an actor from the height of the fly gallery, rotated the rear part of a stage set to the front, shifted prepared scenery from the wings, raised up whole stage areas with scenery intact through trapdoors, and so on.[9] [...] To represent or signify the spatial location of a play became problematical with the abandonment of many of the conventions established between stage and auditorium by long-standing tradition. [...]

When the foundations of theatrical structure are shaken in this way, measures must immediately be taken to adapt to new modes of operation. [...] One theatrical function is to locate a play spatially: to signify a lawn or bar-room, to represent a cemetery or a banqueting hall. This is an essential function of the stage which must be implemented just as much by a stage using constructions as by a stage using scenery, and just as much by a stage located in the midst of the spectators as by one that is traditionally located. Signs whose function it is to promote the spectators' understanding always involved the designation of a space. [...] The fact that the signs are supposed to designate the space in which an action takes place does not mean that they must be spatial signs. [...] On the centralized stage possibilities are extremely limited for the placing of objects, large pieces of furniture, or scenery signs. While the constructivist stage concentrated on the actor's actions, the centralized stage is often solely dependent on the actor per se. Okhlopkov's theatre has acquainted us with a number of superb instances of the actor becoming a sign for spatial location. Here one found not only actor-scenery and actor-set, but even actor-furniture, actor-props.

Okhlopkov created an *actor-sea* by having a young man dressed in a neutral manner (in blue, that is 'invisible', overalls with a blue mask on his face) shake a blue-green sheet attached to the floor in such a way that the rippling of the blue-green sheet expressively replaced the waves of a sea canal. He created *actor-furniture* by having two 'invisibly' attired actors kneel opposite each other and stretch between them a tablecloth into the quadrilateral shape of a table. An *actor-prop* originated by placing next to the actor playing the role of the captain, another actor dressed in blue overalls who held up the handle of the ship's horn the moment when the captain, pulling the handle, blasts a signal to the sailors. [...]

---

Theatre in Moscow (1930–7).—The design by Walter Gropius of a 'total theatre', drawn up in 1926 for Erwin Piscator (see pp. 220–1), was never realized. It included a revolving arena stage, a stage surrounding the auditorium, a ceiling and screens onto which films could be projected, etc.

[9] It is a fact, however, that the increasingly sophisticated stage machinery developed from the Renaissance onwards until the present day continues to be part of the vocabulary of modern theatre architecture, in spite of the development of the non-illusionistic stage during the twentieth century.

Every student of the theatre immediately saw analogies between Okhlopkov's staging procedures and the methods employed by ancient Chinese and Japanese theatres. [...]

It would be wrong, however, to think that this changeable method of dramatic expression is a specialty of the Chinese and Japanese theatre or of a Russian innovator from the year 1935. Similar methods of dramatic expression can be found in many Czech dramatic performances. I should like to mention my own production of *The Teacher and the Pupil* (by V. Vančura) in cooperation with the painter Jindřich Stýrský at the Municipal Theatre in Brno in 1930.

The fourth act of the play is situated at the edge of town. In order to indicate this fact we made use of a *dramatic mask*. But we took this dramatic mask from the face of the actor, relocated it, and applied it as a spatial *sign on the stage*. Projected across a wide area of the cyclorama was a face whose lower part was covered with a scarf in the manner of highwaymen. This face, with evil eyes below a forehead covered by a hat, arched above the stage and shaded that area in which the spectator usually sees a sky with floating clouds.

*Through relocation,* the dramatic mask acquired a new meaning. [...]

In my production of Apollinaire's *The Breasts of Tiresias* in 1927,[10] the poet's words were changed into painter's images. We transformed the actors into letters which then moved like figures about the stage. The different combinations of letters created different verses.

In the production of Goll's *Methusalem* (1927) *stage props* (bread, a bottle, and so on) appeared in the play as characters who rebel against Methusalem.[11] [...]

It is in the changeability of the theatrical sign that the main difficulty of defining theatrical art lies. Definitions of this concept either narrow down theatricality to the manner of expression of our conventional drama and opera theatres or expand it to such an extent that it becomes meaningless.

It is on the basis of changes of the theatrical sign that we explain yet another theoretical confusion that hinders research of the problem of who or what is the central creative element of dramatic expression. If we say that it is the playwright, then we are certainly correct as regards numerous cases and examples. However, we still would not grasp the essence of many historical examples of theatre and could not prove that in all cases it is the word of the playwright that represents the axis of theatrical art. The entirely free theme or wholly unthematic characters of improvised Italian comedies and similar forms show that even the playwright and his text are susceptible of the changes we have discussed earlier. Similarly, we cannot regard as completely true the statement that the main bearer of theatrical art is the actor. As a proof of this I have in mind the static positioning of actors on the stage (characteristic of many

---

[10] For Apollinaire's preface to *The Breasts of Tiresias*, see pp. 165–70.

[11] For Goll's preface to *Methusalem*, see pp. 174–5. The stage props suggested here do not figure in Goll's text, but a number of stuffed animals (e.g. a bear, a parrot, a cuckoo, and a stag's head) do have speaking parts in it.

dramatic styles of both past and present) which converts theatre into a dialogue recital carried out by stationary figures [...] or anaesthetizes the actor into a puppet with prearranged stilted movements, thus changing the traditional acting function into a function of a stage prop or structure. And should a modern director say that he himself is the centre of dramatic creation, we can agree with his statement only in the instances where he demonstrates this to us. Should he speak of the theatrical art of past times when there was no director, then we cannot but disagree with him.

We do not mean by this to prove that the text, actor, and director are auxiliary or dispensable factors that merely affect the balance of theatrical structure. We wish to show only that every historical period actualizes a different component of dramatic expression and that the creative forces of one factor can replace or suppress others without decreasing the strength of the dramatic effect. We could also prove that certain periods directly demand such shifts in the balance of the dramatic structure. [...] However, if we go into the matter more deeply, we find that the actor's function is always present even though it may change into, or appear in the guise of, another function. Similarly, we must allow that what we call the organizational force of the director was present in every historical period of the theatre, even when there was no director as such. [...]

A number of theories of theatre built around changeability have been advanced in the effort to organize or unify the multiplicity of dramatic material, devices and procedures. The best known of these is undoubtedly Wagner's concept of theatre as 'collective art' (*das Gesamtkunstwerk*).[12]

Multiplicity of devices is organized by the 'collective art' (*Gesamtkunstwerk*) in such a way that individual components unite in a result, provide a 'collective effect'. Thus the dramatic character is present not only on the stage but also in the orchestra; we experience its inner state, development and fate not only from words and actions we see on the stage but also from the sounds we hear. Here it is a matter of the parallelism of the musical stream, the dramatic action, the words, scenery, props, lighting and all other factors. [...]

This principle of 'collective art' [...] assumes that the intensity of dramatic effect, that is, the strength of the spectator's impression, is directly proportional to the *number of perceptions* that synchronically flood the senses and mind of the spectator at any given moment. The task of the dramatic artist (in the Wagnerian sense) is to equalize the effects of various dramatic devices in order to produce impressions of the same impact.

Thus, this theory does not recognize changes of the theatrical sign which can use different materials for its implementation. On the contrary, Wagner's *Gesamtkunstwerk* theory indirectly claims that there is no specific, unitary dramatic material but that there are diverse materials which must be kept apart and treated side by side. Accordingly, there is no dramatic art as such, but

---

[12] For some of Wagner's ideas on the collaboration of the arts, see pp. 3–11.

there are music, text, actor, scenery, stage props, and lighting, which collectively make up dramatic art. Thus dramatic art cannot exist by itself but only as a collective manifestation of music, poetry, architecture, histrionics, and so on. Dramatic art results as the sum of the other arts.

With regard to the spectator and to the psychology of perception, I am of the opinion that this theory is incorrect. Uppermost is the problem of whether the spectator perceives acoustic and visual signs simultaneously and with the same intensity or whether he concentrates on one aspect only in the course of perception. When trying to solve this question, we must also bear in mind the fact that it is a matter of the perception of *artistic signs* and that this is a special case of perception. If the spectator's mind has to concentrate in order to understand the semiotic value of certain facts, it can certainly be presumed that it also concentrates on perception of a particular kind, visual or acoustic. However, should the concentrated attention of the spectator perceive both visually and acoustically, we cannot speak even in this instance of a *sum* of impressions but only of a special relation of one kind of perception to the other, of the *polarization of these perceptions.*

After all, we encounter among spectators people who visit a theatre to listen to music or to a poet or to see the performance of a certain actor, and so on. However, even persons without special interests find themselves, when attending a theatre, listening only to the music at one moment and captivated by the actor or enchanted by the poetic text at another moment. I would say that nearly all theatregoers fall into this category. At the same time, however, the interest of the spectator does not pass from one device to another merely by chance; it does so deliberately. If we observe the audience at a theatre we see that its members turn their eyes to the same spot on the stage, that they all have the same interest in a single actor at one moment or interest in the observation of the scenery at another moment. The psychology of the spectators' perception thus prevents us from accepting the assumptions of the Wagnerian theory of 'collective art'. [...]

If it were true that dramatic art is the sum of various arts [...], there would, for example, be no theatre of artistic expression whose sole means would be the actor himself, that is, an actor without stage, words, music, scenery, and so on. And indeed recognition as a theatrical performance must be accorded even to a pantomime[13] that is conducted in an empty circus ring solely by the actions of a player. [...]

Apart from the dispute over the *Gesamtkunstwerk,* one could also mention other theories of theatrical art which are similarly confused because their authors, unable or unwilling to understand the special character of dramatic material, too incautiously transferred the relations of poetry, painting, music and other arts to dramatic art.

---

[13] The word is used here in the sense of a mime performance rather than the traditional English pantomime.

I commenced my study with a quotation from Zich and I should like to conclude by returning to Zich's views. [...] According to Zich the specific character of the theatrical unit is the *combination* of 'two simultaneous, inseparable but *heterogeneous* components, that is, visual components (optical) and audible components (acoustic).'

However, even this 'combination' does not prevent us from seeking and finding a unity in dramatic art, from declaring that it is a single integral art. The binary character of the materials, that is, the visual and acoustic character of dramatic devices does not negate the unity of the essence of theatre art.

Since the acoustic and the visual can change places on the stage, it may happen that one of the components submerges below the surface of the spectator's conscious attention. [...]

Let us note, furthermore, that the silent film was also once called visual *theatre* and that the radio play could be called acoustic *theatre*. Thus the specific character of theatre art does not lie in the division of its devices into acoustic and visual ones. It is necessary to seek the essence of theatre art elsewhere.

It is my belief that with our analysis of the changeability of the theatrical sign we have undertaken a task that can test the trustworthiness of many definitions of theatrical art and decide whether those definitions make provision for the old and the new types of theatre that have originated in different social structures, in different historical periods, under the influence of different poetic or dramatic personalities, as the result of many technical inventions, and so on. I am also of the opinion that we should restore respect for the old theory of theatrical art which sees its essence in *acting*, in *action*.

In this light, the theatricality of dramatic character and that of place and of plot will not appear to us as things permanently separated from one another. [...]

Action, taken as the essence of dramatic art, unifies word, actor, costume, scenery and music in the sense that we could then recognize them as different conductors of a single current that either passes from one to another or flows through several at one time. Now that we have used this comparison, let us add that this current, that is, dramatic action, is not carried by the conductor that exerts the least resistance (dramatic action is not always concentrated only in the performing actor) but rather theatricality is frequently generated in the overcoming of obstacles caused by certain dramatic devices (special theatrical effects when, for instance, action is concentrated solely in the words or in the actor's motions or in offstage sounds, and so on), in the same way that a filament fibre glows just because it has resistance to an electric current. [...]

Modern theatre begins the very moment scenery is evaluated according to the function it fulfils in the actual dramatic action. The fact that the Théâtre d'Art in the nineties restricted its scenery to 'a backdrop and a number of movable curtains' has to be explained, from our viewpoint, as a recognition of the real function of stage scenery in plays whose theatricality and action are created verbally (Maeterlinck). If the German Shakespearean stage was limited to a Gothic arch or a column against a blue backdrop, it was a result of the aware-ness that a stage set participates in a Shakespearean play solely as a simple scenic sign informing the spectator of the change of scene.[14]

The new limitations in stage art resulting from Russian constructivism spring from the idea of dramatic performance which is manifested by *the player's movements* and everything that serves these movements; acrobatic props or contraptions, a movable wall or floor, and so on. [...]

The examples I have employed show clearly that there are no permanent laws or invariable rules for the unification of dramatic devices via the flow of dramatic action. In its autonomous development, which is an integral feature of the development of every art, the theatre actualizes different aspects of theatricality at different times. E.g., Maeterlinck's symbolism actualizes the verbal text as the bearer of dramatic action (Maeterlinck's play *Les Aveugles* (The Blind) *is acted out* through the dialogue of immobile actors conversing on stage).[15] Russian constructivism, on the other hand, *acts* by means of the dance or the 'biomechanical movements of the actor'.[16]

The changeability of the hierarchical scale of components of dramatic art corresponds to the changeability of the theatrical sign. I have attempted to throw light on both. I wanted to demonstrate the changeability that makes stage art so varied and all-attractive but at the same time so elusive of definition. Its protean metamorphoses have sometimes even caused the very existence of a theatrical art to be doubted. [...] It was only a combination of separate arts. Theatre had not located either its core or its unity. I have shown that it has both, that it is one and many like the Triune God of Saint Augustine.

[14] Jocza Savits (1847–1915) pioneered a 'Shakespearian stage' at the Munich Court Theatre between 1888 and 1906, anticipating William Poel's re-creation of Elizabethan staging methods in England.

[15] For some of Maeterlinck's ideas on theatre, see pp. 115–21.

[16] 'Biomechanics' was the name given by Meyerhold to his system of actor training which stressed physiology rather than psychology.

# Semiotics of Theatrical Performance (1977)

## Umberto Eco

The career of Umberto Eco (b. 1932) has shown—at least—two distinct faces. He has achieved international fame as a writer of fiction: one of his novels, *The Name of the Rose* (1980), a medieval mystery story, has been translated into twenty languages and was made into a film in 1986. But he is also Italy's leading semiotician who enjoys a worldwide reputation. At the University of Bologna, where he has been Director of the Institute of Communications and the Performing Arts since 1959, his Chair of Semiotics was the first appointment explicitly so designated at any university. Professor Eco has served as Secretary-General of the International Association of Semiotic Studies. As well as at Bologna, he has taught at Florence, at Yale, at Columbia, the University of New York, Northwestern University (Chicago), and the University of São Paolo. His wide reading in *belles-lettres* has always informed his more strictly scholarly writings. In addition to a number of books in Italian (some on medieval subjects), he published *A Theory of Semiotics* (Indiana University Press, 1976), in English. This general study of the subject does not refer to drama as such. However, in a collection of essays, *The Limits of Interpretation*, he has specifically considered drama from the point of view of performance. Actually, drama is only lightly touched on in this book which, in a wide-ranging survey of related topics, takes in such diverse matters as literary serials, fakes and forgeries, Pirandello (as a theorist of humour) and other aesthetic questions seen in a semiotic light. Initially inclined towards an 'open methodology' that would give the interpreter a major role in determining the meaning of any given text, Professor Eco later came around to the view that there was an inherent hard core of meaning and that interpretation had been given too much theoretical scope.

*Drama Review*, 21/1 (T73) (Mar. 1977), 107–17; repr. in a shortened version in Umberto Eco, *The Limits of Interpretation* (Bloomington: Indiana University Press, 1994), 101–10.

[...] Semiotics can be conceived of either as a unified theoretical approach to the great variety of systems of signification and communication, and in this sense it constitutes a metalinguistic discourse dealing with any of its objects by means of homogeneous categories, or it can be conceived as a description of those various systems insisting on their mutual differences, their specific structural properties, their idiosyncracies—from verbal language to gestures, from visual images to body positions, from musical sounds to fashions. It shows a wide range of 'languages' ruled by different conventions and laws. It can investigate those various domains either at the elementary level of their consecutive units (such as words, colour spots, physical formants of sounds, geometrical or topological shapes) or at the more complex level of texts and discourses—that is, narrative structures, figures of speech, and so on.

What, then, are the specific object and the starting level of a semiotics of theatre, since theatre is, among the various arts, the one in which the whole of human experience is co-involved, the very place in which complete 'son et lumière' events take place, in which human bodies, artifacts, music, literary expressions[...] are in play at the same moment? [...] I could [...] list many researchers and different approaches, but you might get the impression that the semiotics of theatre is nothing but an arithmetic sum of the semiotic analyses of other forms of communication.

However, the first duty of a new (or old) theory is not only to isolate its own object but also to do it in a more essential way than before. What we ask a theory for, is to give us back an old subject illuminated by a new light in order to realize that only from that point of view the object can be really understood. Is semiotics able to do that? I am not sure of it. Semiotics is a very young discipline, only two thousand years old, and it has a terrific task to perform, since nearly everything seems to fall under its headings.

One of its main temptations is to start straight away from the most complex phenomena, instead of rediscovering the most basic features of a given 'language'. Among the various semiotic disciplines, only their older sister (or mother?), linguistics, has demonstrated enough wisdom and prudence to avoid, at its first steps, the analysis of texts. [...]

The same is true with a semiotics of theatrical performance. In order to try to formulate it, we should begin with a positively naive attitude, assuming that we do not know what Molière did, who Samuel Beckett was, how Stanislavsky made somebody feel himself to be an apple or how Bertolt Brecht made an apple appear to be a piece of criticism of capitalist society.

Let me start with an example proposed (without thinking of theatre) by the founding father of American semiotics, C. S. Peirce. He once wondered what kind of sign could have been defined by a drunkard exposed in a public place by the Salvation Army in order to advertise the advantages of temperance. He did not answer this question. I shall do it now. Tentatively. [...] Even though trying to keep a naive attitude, we cannot eliminate some background knowledge. [...] Therefore we immediately suspect that in that sudden epiphany of intoxication lies the basic mystery of (theatrical) performance.

As soon as he has been put on the platform and shown to the audience, the drunken man has lost his original nature of 'real' body among real bodies. He is no more a world object among world objects—he has become a semiotic device, he is now a *sign*. A sign, according to Peirce, is something that stands to somebody for something else in some respect or capacity—a physical presence referring back to something absent. What is our drunken man referring back to? To a drunken man. But not to *the* drunk who he is, but to *a* drunk. The present drunk—insofar as he is a member of a class—is referring us back to the class of which he is a member. He *stands* for the category he belongs to. There is no difference, in principle, between our intoxicated character and the word 'drunk'.

Apparently this drunk stands for the equivalent expression, 'There is a drunken man,' but things are not that simple. The physical presence of the human body along with its characteristics could stand either for the phrase, 'There is a drunken man in this precise place and in this precise moment,' or for the one, 'Once upon a time there was a drunken man'; it could also mean, 'There are many drunken men in the world.' As a matter of fact, in the example I am giving, and according to Peirce's suggestion, the third alternative is the case. To interpret this physical presence in one or in another sense is a matter of convention, and a more sophisticated theatrical performance would establish this convention by means of other semiotic media—for instance, words. But at the point we are, our tipsy-sign is open to any interpretation. He stands for all the existing drunken men in our real world and in every possible world. He is an open expression (or sign-vehicle) referring back to an open range of possible contents.

Nevertheless, there is a way in which this presence is different from the presence of a word or of a picture. It has not been actively produced (as one produces a word or draws an image)—it has been *picked up* among the existing physical bodies and it has been shown or *ostended*. [...] Ostention is one of the various ways of signifying, consisting in de-realizing a given object in order to make it stand for an entire class. But ostension is, at the same time, the most basic instance of performing.

You ask me, 'How should I be dressed for the party this evening?' If I answer by showing you my tie framed by my jacket and say, 'Like this, more or less,' I am signifying by ostension. My tie does not mean my actual tie but your possible tie (which can be of a different stuff and colour) and I am 'performing' by representing to you the you of this evening. [...] My performance, which was eminently visual and behavioural, has been accompanied by a verbal metalinguistic message establishing some criteria of pertinence. 'More or less' signified 'making an abstraction from the particular stuff, colour and size of *my* tie.' [...]

The same happens with our intoxicated man. It is not necessary that he have a specific face, a specific eye colour, a moustache or a beard, a jacket or a sweater. It is, however, necessary (or at least I think so) that his nose be red or violet; his eyes dimmed by liquid obtuseness; his hair, his moustache and his beard ruffled and dirty; his clothes splashed with mud, sagging and worn-out. [...] The list of these characteristics is established by a social code, a sort of iconographic convention. The very moment our sergeant of the Salvation Army has chosen the *right* drunk, he has made recourse to a socialized knowledge. His choice has been semantically oriented. He has been looking for the right man just as one looks for the right word.

Nevertheless, there is something that distinguishes our drunkard from a word. A word is a sign, but it does not conceal its sign-quality. We conventionally accept that through words someone speaks about reality, but we do not confuse words with things (except in cases of mental illness). [...] In the case of our elementary model of mise-en-scène, the drunk is a sign, but he is a sign that pretends not to be accepted as a sign, he has to be recognized as a 'real' spatio-temporal event, a real human body. In theatre, there is a 'square semiosis.' With words, a phonic object stands for other objects made with different stuff. In the mise-en-scène an object, first recognized as a real object, is then assumed as a sign in order to refer back to another object (or to a class of objects) whose constitutive stuff is the same as that of the representing object.

I stress this point because it makes evident a crucial semiotic question: that is, the difference between so-called *natural* and artificial signs. Everybody agrees on the fact that words and pictures are signs insofar as they are intentionally produced by human beings in order to communicate. But many semioticians wonder whether medical symptoms, animal imprints or unintentional body movements are to be considered as signs. [...] Is there a difference between signification by means of intentional and artificial devices ruled by a convention (such as words or road signals) and signification as inferred from natural and unintentional events such as symptoms and imprints? [...]

Our drunk is representing drunkenness. His red nose has been selected as a natural unintentional event able to intentionally (the intention belongs to the Salvation Army, not to him) represent the devastating effects of intemperance. But what about his teeth? There is no specific convention establishing that an average drunken man lacks his incisors or has a set of black teeth. But if our intoxicated man possesses those characteristics, this would work very well. Insofar as the man becomes a sign, those of his characteristics that are not pertinent to the purposes of representation also acquire a sort of vicarious representative importance. The very moment the audience accepts the convention of the mise-en-scène, every element of that portion of the world that has been framed (put upon the platform) becomes significant. [...]

I should, however, stress that, until now, I have incorrectly put together natural and unintentional signs. I have done it on purpose because it is a kind of confusion frequently made by many semioticians. But we should disambiguate it.

On the one hand, I can produce a false natural event, as when I purposely produce a false imprint in order to fool somebody. I can produce a false symptom by painting red spots on my face to pretend I have measles.

On the other hand, I can produce unintentionally what is usually conceived to be intentional (the most typical examples are psychoanalytic slips of the tongue or those common errors that everybody makes when speaking a foreign language), but I also can produce intentionally what is usually believed to be unintentional. For instance, his pronunciation shows that a man is, let me say, a Frenchman speaking English. The choice of English words is an intentional act, the way of pronouncing them, even though semiotically important (it means: 'I am a Frenchman') is unintentional. But what about a fictional character purposefully emitting French-like phonemes in order to mean 'I am French', while he is perfectly all-American—maybe a CIA agent trying to get political information by talking with a French Communist [...]? Is there a difference between an actor who, to pretend having been whipped, draws red lines on his shoulders and another one (a more professional actor more religiously following the principles of realism) who really wounds himself in order to get really bleeding traces?

I have no clear and definite responses for these questions. I only wanted to make clear to what an extent the elementary problems of dramatic fiction are strictly linked with the basic problems of general semiotics.

[...] It is not theatre that is able to imitate life; it is social life that is designed as a continuous performance and, because of this, there is a link between theatre and life.

Let me outline an elementary matrix considering eight possible types of interaction in emitting and receiving unintentional behaviour as signs. Let me list under 'E' the intention of the emitter ('+' meaning the behaviour is intentional and '−' that it is not), under 'A' the intentionality or the unintentionality of the reaction of the addressee and under 'I' the intention that the addressee attributes (or does not attribute) to the emitter.

|   | E | A | I |
|---|---|---|---|
| 1 | + | + | + |
| 2 | + | + | − |
| 3 | + | − | (+) |
| 4 | + | − | (−) |
| 5 | − | + | + |
| 6 | − | + | − |
| 7 | − | − | (+) |
| 8 | − | − | (−) |

Case number 1: An actor hobbles along, pretending to be a lame person. The addressee understands that he is doing it voluntarily.

Case 2: I simulate a limp in order to make the addressee believe that I am lame, and the addressee consciously receives this piece of information, believing that my behaviour is unintentional. This represents the typical case of successful simulation.

Cases 3 and 4: In order to get rid of a boring visitor, I drum on the desk with my fingers to express nervous tension. The addressee receives this as a subliminal stimulus that irritates him; he is unable to attribute to me either intentionality or unintentionality, although later he might (or might not) realize what happened and attribute plus or minus intentionality to my act.

Cases 5 and 6: Being bored by the same visitor, I unintentionally drum with my fingers. The visitor realizes the situation and attributes plus or minus intention to me.

Case 6 is also the one of the patient emitting an involuntary slip of the tongue during a conversation with his psychoanalyst, who understands the sign and recognizes that it was not intentionally emitted.

Cases 7 and 8 are variations of cases 3 and 5, with a different misunderstanding strategy.

In fact one can get from this matrix all the basic plots of Western comedy and tragedy, from Menander to Pirandello, or from Chaplin to Antonioni. But the matrix might be further complicated by adding to it a fourth item; that is, the intention that the emitter wishes the addressee to attribute to him. 'I tell you $p$ so that you believe that I am lying and that, in fact, I meant $q$ while $p$ is really the case.' [...] An Italian scholar, Paola Pugliatti (1976) has applied this matrix to the well-known 'nothing' uttered by Cordelia, examining the different interplay of interpretations and misunderstandings taking place between Cordelia and King Lear, Cordelia and France, King Lear and Kent and so on. But [...] Paolo Valesio (1980) has further complicated this analysis by interpreting the 'nothing' of Cordelia as a witty rhetorical device aimed not to convince Lear but rather to inform France about her mental disposition and rhetorical ability.

Coming back to our poor tipsy guinea pig [...], his presence could be reconsidered in the light of the above matrix. [...] In the very presence of that drunken man, we are witnessing the crucial antinomy that has haunted the history of western thought for two thousand years. It is known as the 'liar paradox'—someone asserts that all he is telling is false.

In the same way, should the drunken man open his devastated mouth and utter something like 'I love liquor' or 'Don't trust alcohol'... Well, we ought to face at that precise moment the linguistic and logical set of problems concerning the difference between the *sujet de l'énonciation* and the *sujet de l'énoncé*. Who is speaking, *qui parle*? That intoxicated individual? The class he is representing? The Salvation Army? [...]

In a certain sense every dramatic performance (be it on the stage or on the screen) is composed by two speech acts. The first one is performed by the actor who is making a performative statement—'I am acting.' By this implicit statement the actor tells the truth since he announces that *from that moment on* he will lie.

The second one is represented by a pseudo-statement where the subject of the statement is already the character, not the actor. Logically speaking, those statements are referentially opaque. When I say, 'Paul has said that Mary will come,' I am responsible for the truth of *p*. The same happens in a dramatic performance. Because of the first performative act, everything following it becomes referentially opaque. Through the decision of the performer ('I am another man') we enter the possible world of performance, a world of lies in which we are entitled to celebrate the suspension of disbelief.

There is a difference between a narrative text and a theatrical performance. In a narrative, the author is supposed to tell the truth when he is speaking as subject of the act of utterance, and his discourse is recognized as referentially opaque only when he speaks about what Julien Sorel and David Copperfield have said.[1] But what about a literary text in which Thomas Mann says 'I' and the 'I' is not Thomas Mann but Serenus Zeitblom telling what Adrian Leverkühn has said?[2] At this moment, narrative becomes very similar to theatre. [...]

Once this is said—once the methodological standpoint that both fiction and reportage are instances of mise-en-scène—it remains to ask, 'How does a character speak who acts as an element of mise-en-scène?' Do his words have a univocal meaning? Do they mean one thing only and nothing else?

In 1938, the Soviet folklorist Bogatyrev,[3] in a fundamental paper on signs in theatre, pointed out that signs in theatre are not signs of an object but signs of a sign of an object. He meant that, beyond their immediate denotation, all the objects, behaviours and words used in theatre have an additional *connotative* power. For instance, Bogatyrev suggested that an actor playing a starving man can eat some bread as bread—the actor connoting the idea of starvation, but the bread eaten by him being denotatively bread. But under other circumstances, the fact of eating bread could mean that this starving man eats only a poor food, and therefore the piece of bread not only denotes the class of all possible pieces of bread, but also connotes the idea of poverty.

However, our drunken man does something more than connote drunkenness. In doing so, he is certainly realizing a figure of speech, a metonymy, since he stands for the cause of his physical devastation; he is also an antonomasia,[4] since he, individually taken, stands for his whole category—he is the drunken man par excellence. But (according to the example of Peirce) he is also realizing an irony by antonymy.[5] He, the drunk, the victim of alcoholism, stands

---

[1] Julien Sorel and David Copperfield are the heroes of Stendhal's *Le Rouge et le noir* (1830) and Dicken's *David Copperfield* (1850) respectively.

[2] In Thomas Mann's novel, *Doktor Faustus* (1949), Serenus Zeitblom is the first-person narrator of the life and death of the composer Adrian Leverkühn.

[3] Pyotr Grigor'evich Bogatyrev (1893–1971), Russian folklorist, a formalist who participated in the Prague School while living in Czechoslovakia between the wars.

[4] *Metonymy*: the substitution of an attribute or adjunct of an object for the object itself. *Antonomasia*: the substitution of a person's attribute for that person's proper noun.

[5] *Antonymy*: naming something (ironically) for its opposite.

ironically for his contrary; he celebrates the advantages of temperance. He implicitly says, 'I am so, but I should not be like this, and you should not become like me.' Or, at another level, 'Do you see how beautiful I am? Do you realize what a glorious sample of humanity I am representing here?' But in order to get the irony, we need the right framing: in this case, the standards of the Salvation Army surrounding him.

Since we have approached the rhetorical level, we are obliged to face the ideological one. Our drunken man is no longer a bare presence. He is not even a mere figure of speech. He has become an ideological abstraction: temperance vs. intemperance, virtue vs. vice. Who has said that to drink is bad? Who has said that the spectacle of intoxication has to be interpreted as an ironical warning and not as an invitation to the most orgiastic freedom? Obviously, the social context. The fact that the drunk has been exposed under the standards of the Salvation Army obliges the audience to associate his presence with a whole system of values.

What would have happened if the drunk had been exposed under the standard of a revolutionary movement? Would he have still signified 'vice' or rather 'the responsibility of the system,' 'the results of bad administration,' 'the whole starving world'? Once we have accepted that the drunk is also a figure of speech, we must begin to look at him also as an ideological statement. A semiotics of the mise-en-scène is constitutively a semiotics of the production of ideologies.

All these things, this complex rhetorical machinery, are moreover made possible by the fact that we are not only looking at a human body endowed with some characteristics—we are looking at a human body standing and moving within a physical space. The body could not stagger if there were not an environing space to give it orientation—up and down, right and left, to stand up, to lie down. Were the bodies two or more, space would establish the possibility of associating a given meaning to their mutual distances. In this way we see how the problems of the mise-en-scène refer back to the problems of many other semiotic phenomena, such as proxemics (the semiotics of spatial distances) or kinesics (the semiotics of gestures and body movements). And we realize that the same semiotic parameters can be applied to the semiotics of theatre, of cinema, of architecture, of painting, of sculpture.

From the idiosyncratic character of the theatrical phenomenon we have arrived at the general problems of semiotics. Nevertheless, theatre has additional features distinguishing it from other forms of art and strictly linking it with everyday conversational interaction—for instance, the audience looking at the drunk can laugh, can insult him and he can react to people's reaction. Theatrical messages are shaped also by the feedback produced from their destination point.

So the semiotics of theatrical performance has shown, during our short and introductory analysis, its own *proprium*, its distinguishing and peculiar features. A human body, along with its conventionally recognizable properties, surrounded by or supplied with a set of objects, inserted within a physical space, stands for something else to a reacting audience. In order to do so, it has been framed within a sort of performative situation that establishes that it has to be taken as a sign. [...]

# Psychic Polyphony (1986)

## Marvin Carlson

The American scholar Marvin Albert Carlson (b. 1935), who has taught theatre and drama at Cornell and Indiana University, is perhaps best known for his authoritative contributions to the history of the French, German, and Italian theatre from the eighteenth century onwards. Professor Carlson's interests have extended from theatre history into the field of theatre theory in general and theatre semiotics in particular. The following essay from his book on the latter subject highlights a hitherto insufficiently theorized aspect of performance.

Until relatively modern times, Western theatrical theory has been largely dominated by an orientation toward the dramatic script, and the techniques and procedures developed for the analysis of dramatic structures and phenomena were often essentially the same as those already successfully employed in the analysis of nondramatic literary texts. Unquestionably such strategies have provided a rich variety of insights, but at the same time, they have obscured important aspects of theatre, especially when these were not readily accessible to the sort of analysis developed for material created for reading rather than for enactment.

In recognition of this, much modern theatrical theory has followed the direction exemplified by Marco de Marinis, who has argued that the performed play cannot be built upon or projected from the 'virtual mise en scène of the printed text, which has its own semiotic.' Instead it must be viewed as a new phenomenon, a 'spectacle text' which employs the written text only as one element in a multicoded, multidimensional, and pluralistic new textual system.[1]

From Marvin Carlson, *Theatre Semiotics: Signs of Life* (Bloomington: Indiana University Press, 1990), 95–108. The notes are by Marvin Carlson, unless otherwise stated, as are all the translations.

[1] Marco de Marinis, 'Lo spettacolo come testo 1', *Versus* 21 (Sept.–Dec. 1978), p. 57.

Early in this century Stark Young suggested that the stage performance should be viewed as 'translation' of a text into another artistic 'language',[2] but this metaphor can be misleading unless one acknowledges that the process is not really akin to changing from one linguistic system to another but rather from one expressive system into another which is phenomenologically different. Many semioticians have suggested that the performed play 'speaks' not one language but many, emitting what Barthes called a 'thickness of signs'.[3] Bert States, however, has called attention to an extremely important commonality among the various sign-systems employed by the theatre, suggesting that most of these produce 'a language whose words consist to an unusual degree of things that *are* what they seem to be.'[4]

Nothing is more basic to the theatrical experience than this physical reality. 'A play,' says Thornton Wilder, 'visibly represents pure existing, while a novel is a past reported in the present, what one mind, claiming to omniscience, asserts to have existed.'[5] The written text of the play occupies a somewhat uneasy position between these two. The omniscient narrator typical of the novel is not fully manifested here, but even so the drama does not reach us directly, but filtered through a quasi-authorial presence most obviously manifested in the stage directions. With an author like Shaw, the stage directions take us almost into the generic realm of the short story or novel, but even a dramatist as sparing in such indications as Shakespeare provides occasional suggestions for setting or movement, and of course must attribute all lines to the proper speaker. Clearly, reading the printed 'Bernardo: Who's there?' is an experience much closer to reading the novelistic ' "Who's there?" cried Bernardo' than to seeing and hearing an actor speak the line. The roots of the word 'theatre' (from *theatron*, a place for seeing), 'spectator' (from *spectare*, to watch) and 'auditorium' (from *audire*, to hear) all reflect the necessary physicality and presence of the theatre experience.

Theatrical performance thus occupies a strange, even uncanny position midway between arts of absence, such as the novel or the cinema, and the experience of presence we have in everyday life. Indeed, David Cole sees the essence of the theatre's power as resting precisely in this doubleness, where all elements—actors, scenery, lighting, etc.—exist both in themselves and as part of the mythical *illud tempus*, both as realities and as ideograms.[6]

This element of presence gives to all theatrical signs what States calls an affective corporeality, a certain irreducible 'thingness', which may in fact

[2] Stark Young, 'Translations,' *Immortal Shadows* (New York: C. Scribner's Sons, n.d.), p. 3.
[3] Roland Barthes, *Critical Essays*, trans. Richard Howard (Evanston, 1972), 262. Tadeusz Kowzan analyses thirteen different theatrical sign systems in 'The Sign in the Theatre', *Diogenes* 61 (1968), pp. 52–80.
[4] Bert O. States, *Great Reckonings in Little Rooms* (Berkeley, 1985), p. 20.
[5] Thornton Wilder, 'Some Thoughts on Playwriting,' *The Intent of the Artist*, ed. Augusto Centeno (Princeton, 1941), p. 89.
[6] David Cole, *The Theatrical Event: A 'Mythos,' A Vocabulary, a Perspective* (Middletown, Conn., 1975), pp. 155–6.

interfere at times with their most efficient use as aesthetic devices. It was precisely this corporeality of theatrical signs which led Charles Lamb to consider all performances of Shakespeare inevitably inferior to reading. The reading of a tragedy he called 'a fine abstraction. It presents to the fancy just so much of external appearances as to make us feel that we are among flesh and blood, while by far the greater and better part of our imagination is employed upon the thoughts and internal machinery of the character.' In reading, 'some dim images of royalty—a crown and sceptre, may float before our eyes' without durability or clear definition, while staging requires 'full and cumbersome' coronation robes and the 'shiftings and re-shiftings of a Romish priest at a mass.'[7]

It is easy to see why Lamb prefers the flexibility and artistic control of 'externals' offered by the written text. Here precisely as much detail and duration can be given to an object like a crown as the situation requires, from a fleeting image to a richly described artifact, and such an image can be instantly evoked or dismissed. The theatre, however, normally requires a real object with physical substance and permanence which demands the attention of both actors and audience. Unquestionably Lamb has isolated a critical difference between theatre and the written text, but while stressing the advantages gained by the written text through the absence of permanent corporeal objects, he has ignored the compensatory effects available to performance through an artistic utilization of such objects.

It is true that a physical crown provides no 'dim image of royalty,' but it may be a powerful visual metaphor, the strength of which has been recognised by dramatists in all ages. The triumphant rebel holding at last the physical symbol of power in his hands or the dying despot whose fallen crown has rolled just beyond the reach of his grasping fingers are the sort of powerful images that fix an entire dramatic situation in our imagination and our memory. Indeed, Goethe defines the theatrical in terms of just this sort of physical embodiment, 'immediately symbolic to the eye,' citing as an example the moment when Prince Hal removes the crown from his sleeping father, places it upon his own head, and struts proudly about.[8] Similarly the robing of the new pope in Brecht's *Galileo* takes advantage of precisely the ponderous presence which so troubled Lamb to create a powerful and memorable theatrical sequence.

Duration is often combined with presence to create striking effects on the stage completely unrealizable in print. Barthes in *Image, Music, Text* suggests that a text should no longer be regarded as a line of words releasing a single 'theological' meaning (the 'message of an author-God'), but as a multidimensional space 'in which a variety of meanings, none of them original, blend and

[7] Charles Lamb, 'On the Tragedies of Shakespeare, Considered with Reference to Their Fitness for Stage Representation', *The Works of Charles and Mary Lamb*, ed. E. V. Lucas, 5 vols. (New York, 1903), 1: pp. 110–11.

[8] Johann Wolfgang von Goethe, *Sämtliche Werke*, 40 vols. (Stuttgart, 1902–7), 26: p. 52.

clash.'[9] This spatial conception of a text as a field in which many voices compete for attention has a distinctly theatrical flavour, since the author-God is much more clearly a *Dieu caché* on the stage than in the written text. Certain voices are given corporeal reality, and the multidimensional space is not figurative but real. This Barthean view of a multivocal text has proven enormously fruitful in modern critical analysis, but the form of the written text will always guarantee that such a multiplicity cannot be directly realized there, as it can in the theatre. Many voices may indeed be present in a written text, but all must be channelled by the nature of the medium into the single expressive device of the written line. Jindřich Honzl spoke of words, actors, costumes, scenery, and music in the theatre as working in sharp contrast to this single 'conductor,' as being 'different conductors of a single current that either passes from one to another or flows through several at one time.'[10]

The single conductive line of the written text presents a serious obstacle to the author who wishes to keep an idea or an image steadily in the reader's mind while speaking of other things. In fact there is no literary device which can guarantee the permanence in the reader's consciousness of anything the words themselves are not at that moment considering. Lamb's 'dim images' of crown and sceptre may well drift away as the text focuses on other matters even when the author *wants* them to remain present. The multiple channels of theatrical reception, however, allow simultaneous statements to be made by a variety of presences, often with powerful emotional effect. In Ingmar Bergman's *King Lear*, the crown, taken off by Lear in the first scene, remains downstage near the footlights throughout the play (even during the intermission, when it is picked out by a soft spotlight) as a constant and moving reminder of the initial disruptive act and of the subsequent leaderless condition of the realm.

Costumes and scenery almost inevitably make some kind of continuous commentary in the theatre. Thus an audience remains constantly aware, whatever else may be happening, of the steady rain and gloom outside the Alving house in *Ghosts*, of the formidable array of ancestral portraits surrounding poor Johannes Rosmer in *Rosmersholm*, of the heavy presence of the two great overarching elm trees in *Desire under the Elms* which, if O'Neill's stage directions are followed, 'brood oppressively over the house... like exhausted women resting their sagging breasts and hands and hair on its roof.'[11] When these texts are merely read, it is most difficult, once the opening stage directions are passed, to keep such images visually present in the mind as other matters clamour for attention.

The multiple perception of presences is unquestionably a central feature in the particular power of the theatre. Mukařovský, summarizing the

---

[9] Roland Barthes, *Image, Music, Text*, trans. Stephen Heath (New York, 1977), p. 146.

[10] See Honzl, pp. 277. [GB's note.]—Jindřich Honzl, 'Dynamics of the Sign in the Theatre,' trans. Irwin Titunik, *Semiotics of Art: Prague School Contributions*, ed. Ladislau Matejka and Irwin Titunik (Cambridge, Mass., 1976), p. 91. [Carlson's note.]

[11] Eugene O'Neill, *The Plays of Eugene O'Neill*, 3 vols. (New York, 1941), 1: p. 202.

contributions of the Prague Linguistic Circle in his 1941 article 'On the Current State of the Theory of the Theatre,' observed that the theatre is essentially 'an interplay of forces moving through time and space and pulling the spectator into the interplay which we call a stage production, a performance.'[12] Only recently has theatre theory again begun to address this insight and to recognize that a production must in theory and in practice be conceived in time, must be considered from multiple and simultaneous perspectives, and must recognize all the while that every viewing will put together these different perspectives in different combinations.

Even more central to the power of theatre than the various 'presences' of properties, scenery, and other visual and auditory elements are the living presences of the actors, whose various psychic drives also 'blend and clash' in a particularly striking and powerful manner. To this specifically theatrical phenomenon I have assigned the term 'psychic polyphony'. Some of the workings and implications of this phenomenon will be the central concern of the present essay.

In performance, characters, like crowns, utilize duration and presence to create a complex perceptual web which, thanks to the simultaneous accessibility of different 'conductors' in performance, allows the spectator a freedom of response quite different from and more inclusive than that offered by the printed text. Modern reader-response theory has stressed the creative role of the reader in engaging a text, but whatever the freedom open to the interpretative process, the arrangement of stimuli upon which this interpretation is based is controlled to a far greater extent on the printed page. It is true that directors, designers, and actors do not *normally* encourage a free play of audience focus about the stage (although certain modern experimental performances have stood out as exceptions to the norm). An important part of theatre art traditionally has been that of guiding the spectators' attention to the proper element of the spectacle. Cultural norms also help to discourage a 'free play' of attention across a perceptual field. Nevertheless, all theatre practitioners realize that focus on stage, as opposed to focus in print, is loosely controlled and while the average audience may devote the major part of its attention to the central focus of the scene, this will almost invariably be supplemented with selective and personally chosen attention to secondary areas of focus, and even to characters and scenic elements not currently stressed at all. The very fact that the stage makes the elms or the portraits of Rosmer's ancestors accessible whether they are being spoken of or not means that the spectator may at any time give them primary focus, according to the free play of his or her desire or predisposition.

This relative freedom of the theatrical spectator to select the object of focus and to create a unique and individual synchronic 'reading' as the play moves

[12] Jan Mukařovský, 'On the Current State of the Theory of the Theatre,' *Structure, Sign and Function*, trans. John Burbank and Peter Steiner (New Haven, 1978), p. 203.

forward diachronically has particular implications for the way characters are created, sustained, and perceived on the stage. A long-standing rule for actors is to remember that no matter how small their part, whenever they are on stage someone is likely always to be giving them central, if monetary, attention. The theatre has sought, with differing success in different periods, to accommodate this wandering focus by training its minor actors to present a clear contribution to the main action. The inanimate object on stage, so long as it can be initially assimilated into the world of the play, presents no further problem. But the actor, who shares the audience's double awareness of reality and pretence, must continually demonstrate to the spectator that he is 'in character', since the fact that he is physically present serves always as a reminder of this 'real' existence, an existence that may be foregrounded at any moment by choice, by inattention, or by some mishap.

The indifference of some producers to this matter aroused much protest in the nineteenth century while directors such as Saxe-Meiningen, Antoine and Stanislavski were lauded for their efforts to ensure that every character on stage, no matter how insignificant, was at all times a fit subject for audience contemplation. In a memorable passage in Stanislavski's *Creating a Role*, the Stanislaski-like director Tortsov demonstrates something of the attention that went into such an effect by interrogating an extra who is playing a gondolier in *Othello*. Although this extra only appears as part of the crowd aroused by Iago and Roderigo at Brabantio's house at the opening of the play, Tortsov expects him to know his position in the household, his duties, his relation to his fellows and master, so that when he appears on stage it will be as a fully developed individual pursuing an action thought out and motivated in impressive detail.[13] A spectator focusing upon this gondolier should discover an element contributing distinctly to the total flow of the action just as Iago is.

Among the recent strategies for the analysis of the creation and interpretation of dramatic characters have been several showing a clear debt to the narratological structural analyses of Propp and Greimas. Although neither of these was primarily interested in the drama, their work has in turn reawakened interest in two hitherto rather neglected theorists with similar structural concerns, Georges Polti and Étienne Souriau, both of whom proposed dramatic taxonomies based upon 'dramatic situations'. For Polti these were a somewhat whimsical collection of nouns such as 'madness,' 'adultery,' and 'disaster,' and of phrases such as 'all sacrificed for a passion,' 'falling prey to misfortune,' or 'necessity of sacrificing loved ones.'[14] Souriau developed a more complex analysis based on six 'functions'—the 'thematic force' which seeks a goal, the goal sought, the receiver of profit from this goal, an opposing force, a helper, and an arbitrator.[15] Greimas's six actantial roles—subject, object, sender,

---

[13] Constantin Stanislavski, *Creating a Role*, trans. E. R. Hapgood (New York, 1961), p. 8.

[14] See Polti, pp. 12–18. [GB's note.] Georges Polti, 'Les 36 situations dramatiques,' *Mercure de France* 12 (1894). [Carlson's note.]

[15] Étienne Souriau, *Les deux cent mille situations dramatiques* (Paris, 1950), p. 144.

receiver, opponent, and helper—are closely related to Souriau's functions and have been similarly employed for the analysis of dramatic structure.

Critics of this approach have complained of its taxonomic rigidity and its focus upon distribution of roles and relationships in an ultimately reductive manner. Actantial roles may shift rapidly about during a narrative, and a character may be simultaneously playing several roles in several different actions —subject in one; opponent, receiver, or helper in yet others. The physical plurality of theatrical performance makes this multiplicity particularly evident. Tortsov's conversation with the actor playing the gondolier reminds us that even the most minor character on the stage may be seen, and according to Stanislavski should be played, as the protagonist in his own life drama, responsible for the action, successful or not, which he attempts to carry out within the dramatic situation. In Stanislavskian terms he must seek the 'creative objective at the heart of every motivational unit, an objective which carries in itself the germ of the action.'[16] The actions thus developed are united in what Stanislavski calls the through-line of action leading toward the ultimate goal of the character, the super-objective.

Obviously, not all of the proposed actions of the various characters on stage can be fulfilled. [...]

No matter who is speaking or taking the centre focus, we have the option as spectators to place our own focus on any other psychic presence on stage, and thus to interpret the pattern of actions and counter-actions in a great variety of ways at the same theatrical moment. Figure and ground may be thought of as simultaneous to one another.

An important part of the unique power of the theatre has always been derived from this psychic polyphony—the simultaneous expression of a number of different psychic lines of action, allowing the spectator a choice of focus and a variety in the process of combination. The potential power of mere physical and psychic presence, even (and sometimes especially) when a character speaks little or not at all, was clearly recognized from the beginning of Western drama. The silence of Cassandra for almost three hundred lines after her entrance with Agamemnon in the *Oresteia* is a device of enormous power on stage, though in the printed text her presence during the emotion-packed scene between Agamemnon and Clytemnestra may be almost totally forgotten. In the theatre however, like the crown in Bergman's *Lear*, simply by her presence she brings to our mind, as Kitto observes, 'a whole train of associated ideas, like a remembered scent or tune.'[17] At the same time, through our continual realization of the steadily growing emotional investment she has in the scene being enacted, she builds up during this extended period an overwhelming psychic expectation, discharged at last in her unearthly cry to Apollo, one of the most chilling moments in the Greek theatre.

[16] Constantin Stanislavski, *An Actor Prepares*, trans. E. R. Hapgood (New York, 1936), p. 110.
[17] H. D. F. Kitto, *Greek Tragedy* (London, 1950), p. 76.

In more normal stage interaction we see a constantly shifting pattern of actions and reactions, contributed to by everyone present and offering a multiple psychic perspective to the observer. The plays of Chekhov, with which, of course, Stanislavski is particularly associated, provide especially clear examples of psychic polyphony, and it is this, I would suggest, which makes Chekhov notoriously less effective in print than on the stage. It is extremely difficult, if not impossible, to read a play like *Three Sisters* or *The Cherry Orchard* while keeping a continuously clear idea of the physical and psychic plenitude of all of the characters on stage, especially of those with very little to say. It is harder still to focus freely among those to observe their reactions, gestures, and expressions no matter who is speaking, as one may so easily do in the theatre. Yet it is precisely this continuous interplay which lies at the very heart of the Chekhovian theatre.

Certain theatrical scenes seem created as if to call attention to this multiple perspective and certainly to capitalize upon it. One of the most famous is the play within a play in *Hamlet*. Here we have the players themselves as one (already multiple) focus of attention. We have the grouping Claudius, Gertrude, and Polonius, each watching the play, as we know, with quite different concerns. We have another grouping elsewhere on stage of Ophelia and Hamlet, watching the play, the king, and each other, and finally we have Horatio, stationed by Hamlet in yet another location to provide another perspective on the king's reactions. Horatio, of course, has also his own concerns, and we can be fairly certain that he will also be keeping a watchful eye on his beloved, if somewhat erratic, friend. To be complete, we should also include other members of the court—guards, ladies and gentlemen, and so on, whose reactions also distinctly contribute to the overall effect of the scene as presented, though they may well be forgotten when it is only read. The spectator has phenomenological access at every instant to every one of these perspectives. [...]

The theatrical tableau has often been used as a striking device for calling attention to psychic polyphony by holding it, as it were, on a sustained chord. A well-known example is the screen scene in Sheridan's *The School for Scandal*. Robert Scholes has called the moment of revelation in this scene 'one of the great moments of pure stagecraft in the history of the theatre,' at which 'all the layers of ironic perception are allowed to discharge into laughter and applause.' The silent exchange of looks in the tableau, Scholes continues, 'can be sustained as long as the actors can mime and the audience interpret additional nuances of meaning.'[18]

The ironies of this classic scene and the audience's enjoyment of them depend precisely upon the psychic plurality which is a distinctive feature of theatre art. Each of the participants in this tableau—Joseph and Charles Surface, Lady Teazle and Sir Peter—brings to the scene his or her own fully

[18] Robert Scholes, *Semiotics and Interpretation* (New Haven, 1982), p. 79.

developed character and line of action, and in this moment of comic crisis the audience's perception is free to wander freely, relishing the variety of reactions and interrelations simultaneously available. Wherever one looks there is a new source of delight, and each spectator may choose the order in which he or she reads the scene—focusing upon Joseph's discomfiture, Charles' delight, Lady Teazle's embarrassment, or Sir Peter's astonishment—in whatever order or whatever combination proves most attractive. This freedom might be contrasted with a filming of the same scene, where the camera would inevitably make these choices for us, devoting a set number of frames in a set order to close-ups of each of the participants for a totally different phenomenological effect.

Many memorable moments in the theatre are built upon this same device. The discovery of Natasha and Belyev by Rakitin and Arkady in the fourth act of Turgenev's *A Month in the Country* has a dynamic closely analogous to Sheridan's scene and generates a similar prolonged delight in the audience. In each of these examples the psychic interchange continues during the period of physical paralysis, since the characters are reacting not only to the new situation but also to each other's reactions.

A somewhat different effect is obtained when everyone on stage reacts simultaneously to a single stimulus, but without particular attention to one another. A notable example of such a tableau concludes Gogol's *Inspector General* [...].

The Gogol tableau stands somewhere between the tableau emphasizing a moment of intense psychic interplay, like those in *The School for Scandal* and *A Month in the Country*, and another sort of tableau where the primary interest is not psychic, but pictorial or emblematic. The psychic tableau attempts to justify itself to some extent realistically—its participants remain frozen in shock or surprise as they might in a similar crisis in real life. Emblematic tableaux are not, of course, devoid of psychological content, but the justification for the 'freezing' of the scene is usually not psychological but pictorial, as in the nineteenth-century melodramas where all the actors at a moment of high excitement struck simultaneous 'attitudes' to form an applause-attracting 'picture,' or when stage action is developed so as to lead to a visual 'quotation' of a famous painting or sculptural group, and the action freezes not for internal reasons, but simply so that the reproduction can be appreciated. Cross-fertilization of narrative paintings and theatre was particularly popular during the nineteenth century, when certain plays were created primarily to provide scenes reproducing famous paintings and when painters often selected as subjects scenes in plays (Shakespeare being particularly favoured).[19] [...]

The outstanding recent example of the common nineteenth-century practice of developing an entire play around the stage re-creation of a well-known

---

[19] This interplay, with related phenomena in literature, has been studied in Martin Meisel, *Realizations* (Princeton, 1983).

portrait is surely Sondheim's *Sunday in the Park with George*, the first act of which concludes with the stage re-creation of Seurat's *A Sunday Afternoon on the Island of La Grande Jatte*. The second act [...] begins with the same tableau, but now that it is continued, our reaction shifts from the visual delight of the re-creation to the tension engendered by the forced immobility of what we now focus on as living presences. The opening song of this act, 'It's Hot Up Here,' sung as the tableau is maintained, expresses the continuing discomfort of those beings trapped in Seurat's 'Painting.' Even frozen in position, however, their psychic interplay continues ('The soldiers have forgotten us'). [...]

The mutability of dramatic sign may, as Bogatyrev and Honzl have observed, result in an actor's being treated according to a particular theatrical convention as an abstract quality or even an inanimate object,[20] but it is almost impossible to prevent the psychic presence of the actor from 'bleeding through' the convention and thus continuing to affect the reception of the piece. *Sunday in the Park with George* plays amusingly upon the difference between the live actor who becomes an element in a tableau and the tableau representation of an actor without life in the two soldiers in the painting. [...] Shakespeare explores the comic potential of life 'bleeding through' in his depiction of the labourers of Athens appearing as 'Wall' and 'Moonshine' in the interlude of Pyramus and Thisbe in *A Midsummer Night's Dream*.

The insistence on psychic presence adds piquancy to the emblematic tableau on stage, but it also adds a certain instability which is not always in the best interests of the desired frozen 'effect'. The statue of the Commendatore in *Don Giovanni*, for example, is always a bit distracting, since the audience generally (correctly) assumes that the statue is being counterfeited by a real actor and is thus highly sensitive not only to any inadvertent movement before the statue 'comes to life,' but also to the psychic presence emanating even from a very rigid figure which they seek to 'read into' the psychic polyphony of the scene.

Even dramatists sometimes seem to feel that their lesser characters function like lesser characters in a novel, existing only to the degree that they are created by the author and thus condemned, like Lamb's images of royalty, to only that portion of existence required by the machinery of the action. Thus Strindberg in his preface to *Miss Julie* says that he deliberately portrayed the supporting character of Christine in a 'somewhat abstract' manner because 'ordinary people are, to a certain degree, abstract in the performance of their daily work—conventional, and showing only one side of themselves—and as long as the spectator feels no need to see their other sides, my abstract portrayal of them will serve well enough.'[21] It is true that we learn less about the character

---

[20] Peter Bogatyrev, 'Forms and Functions of Folk Theatre,' trans. Bruce Kochis, and Honzl, 'Dynamics of the Sign', *Semiotics of Art*, ed. Matejka and Titunik, pp. 51–56; pp. 74–93.

[21] See Strindberg, p. 95. [GB's note.]—August Strindberg, *Plays* (New York, 1964), p. 107. [Carlson's note.]

Christine during this play than about Jean and Miss Julie, but when portrayed by a real, living actress, she is in no way more abstract than they, and while she is on stage makes just as legitimate a claim upon audience attention.

Dramatically speaking, a character may be 'unrealized,' as the Son claims to be in Pirandello's *Six Characters in Search of an Author*, but he can no more project a 'dim image' of a person than the stage crown can present Lamb's 'dim image of royalty.' When such a character appears on the stage, the physical and psychic presence of the actor who embodies him will necessarily provide an unavoidable measure of realization. A character on stage may be unclear or inconsistent, but he will always necessarily participate fully in the diverse structure of presence, and thus in the changeable tensions of the drama's reception. Whether an actor has developed a particular contextual world, like Stanislavski's gondolier, or not, as a living being he possesses always the potential of being viewed as the protagonist of his own drama, entangled with and yet separate from the drama of every other character. Thus the web of competing through-lines of action, which Stanislavski considered the basis of the dramatic situation, is always potentially involved in the theatre. Analysis like his encourages us to recognize at least some of the ways in which the multiplicity of actantial patterns, which I have called psychic polyphony, make a central contribution to the almost endless variety of readings constantly offered by theatrical performance, and beyond that, to the specifically theatrical pleasure offered by this freedom of reading and the simultaneity of multiple perception.

# The Signs of Stage and Screen (1987)

## Martin Esslin

Martin Esslin (b. 1918 in Vienna) has throughout his life combined a practical involvement in drama with a critical and theoretical interest in different aspects of the subject. He read English and Philosophy at the University of Vienna and trained as a director at the Reinhardt Seminar of Dramatic Art. Having fled to England from Nazism, he joined the BBC in 1940 as a producer and scriptwriter; from 1963 to 1977 he served as Head of Radio Drama. He was awarded the OBE in 1972. Changing to a teaching career, he was the Professor of Drama at Stanford University, California, from 1977 till 1988. Professor Esslin has written extensively on various aspects of modern drama, notably on Brecht, Pinter, Beckett, and Artaud. His *Theatre of the Absurd* (1962) was a pioneering study of what was then a new dramatic phenomenon; it gave general currency to the (admittedly controversial) term, 'absurdism'.

[...]

## 2

As regards the 'live' theatre its only truly distinctive feature, and one that constitutes an immense advantage vis-à-vis the mechanically reproduced forms of drama, is its ability to establish an immediate inter-action between performers and audience, a continuous feed-back of reactions.

That the performance unrolls itself in the presence of the audience, that it allows spontaneous modifications of its pre-set and rehearsed elements in the light of the actual circumstances prevailing during the performance, that unforeseen inspiration as well as mistakes can occur, all these factors enhance the excitement of the event for performers as well as spectators. Even more important is the fact that the reaction of the spectators can be made instantly manifest to the performers, by their laughter, their silence with bated breath, their spontaneous applause, or in certain forms of oriental drama by loud exhortation or verbal encouragement. In the light of such reactions the actors can immediately modify and adapt their performance.

From Martin Esslin, *The Field of Drama* (London: Methuen, 1987), 91–105.

Audiences vary from performance to performance, owing to a multitude of factors: a full house produces a more receptive mood than an empty one; bad weather outside, the political situation, or simply the presence of large cohesive groups of spectators (coach parties from the suburbs, foreign tourists) modify the collective individuality of the audience, its reactions as a crowd subject to the specific characteristics of a mass-psychological entity. Actors touring with a play from city to city are, moreover, convinced that the quickness of reaction, the readiness to respond of audiences varies from place to place. [...] Experienced performers have learned to gauge the crowd response to the point where, as the saying goes, 'they can hold the audience in the palm of their hands'. Experienced and skilled actors can subdue the audience as the matador subdues the bull.

This phenomenon amounts to a continuous process of feed-back between the performers and the audience: by reacting to the audience, the actors modify the audience's reaction and that modified reaction, in turn, is felt by the actors—and so on.

Equally important is the fact that this is not merely a two-way traffic. Each member of the audience also reacts to the reaction of the other members of the audience: if the person next to me laughs loudly, I shall probably, because laughter is contagious, laugh more loudly or intensely myself. [...]

That the multiple feed-back effect of live performance is of inestimable value in enhancing the experience of the event, both for the actors and the spectators, is beyond doubt. Yet although, of course, the heightened intensity of the experience, the greater degree of concentration it produces in the individual spectator, may contribute to the spectator's ability to derive meaning from the performance, it hardly constitutes a distinct system of signs in the sense in which semiotics uses the term. This leaves us with the additional meaning-generating abilities of the two cinematic dramatic media—the cinema and television.

## 3

The mechanically reproduced and photographic forms of drama—the feature film and the television play—differ from live dramatic performance in that the spectator in the mechanically transmitted media has no direct contact with the performers, that their work has to be brought to him through the mediation of the camera.

Insofar as drama of this type tends to be recorded on film or videotape—live television drama has become exceedingly rare—the dramatic action, moreover, has already happened outside the spectator's own time-frame. It thus lacks a certain element of the unexpected, the spontaneous event—or, indeed, potential mishap—which enhances the excitement of live performance.

In the theatre the spectator is presented with a predetermined, given space, the stage. This space may be fixed, rigidly circumscribed and static, surrounded by a proscenium arch and thus resembling a picture within a frame; or it may be an open arena; or, indeed, in 'environmental' productions, it may surround both spectators and actors;[1] it may be used to represent and accommodate different locations, environments, 'sets', made palpably visible or merely imagined (as in the Elizabethan theatre). But that space itself, whatever shape it takes, will always be a 'given'. It is static, it remains constantly and unmoving in front of, or around, the spectator.

Within this space, which constantly remains within the range of his focused and peripheral vision, he can look wherever he feels the focus of the action resides at any given moment. As the spectator in the theatre focuses his attention, he has to make choices as to where he will look at any stage of the performance:[2] at the hero's action, or the villain's reaction, up at Juliet, or down at Romeo in the balcony scene, and so on. In that respect the spectator in a live performance does what the camera does for him in the cinematic forms of drama: he creates a sequence of close-ups and long-shots, a freely chosen 'montage' of focused images. At times when it was the fashion for members of the audience to use 'opera glasses', they quite consciously created 'close-ups' of the leading players or singers for themselves. The same process goes on, even with the naked eye. [...]

In this respect the difference between the cinematic and the live dramatic media merely derives from the fact that the spectator is freer to compose his own 'editing' of the action. [...]

A much more decisive difference between live and cinematic drama lies in the fundamental distinction between the theatrical and the cinematic space. Whereas the stage (whether of the 'peep-show' type, an open arena or 'in the round') confronts the spectator throughout the performance and is its basic 'given', the cinema or television screens are doors through which the spectator freely enters a space which is infinitely variable and constantly changing. The spectator in the theatre 'confronts' a space, the spectator in the cinema and television 'is sucked into' and propelled through a sequence of different spaces. Because the camera acts as the spectator's eye, the spectator enters any space into which the camera takes him: he speeds along in a car, runs in and out of houses, approaches and recedes from objects. This increases the spectator's 'mobility' in space'. He can be propelled to any point the director wants him to be.

On the other hand his total control over the spectator's eye through his control of the camera also allows the director to *restrict* the spectator's vision at will: he can show him the hand of the murderer without revealing the face which would give away the murderer's identity, he can concentrate on the feet of a milling crowd without showing us in what street, or in what room those people are moving. [...]

---

[1] Compare Artaud's ideas on staging methods—see p. 193.
[2] See pp. 294–8 for Marvin Carlson's similar description of the spectator's selective focusing of attention during a theatrical performance.

Not only does the camera guide the spectator's eye from point to point, making him look more closely at a detail or step back and take a wider view—providing, in other words, a number of different 'shots'—but the creator of the cinematic drama also determines the dynamic of the way in which each partial image is fused into a continuous, meaningfully linked sequence, with its own rhythm and narrative line.

So, what in the theatre remained the spectator's freely (albeit semi-subconsciously) selected assemblage of a sequence of visual impressions through his shifting focus of attention, becomes, in the cinematic forms of drama, a carefully judged and pre-determined artistic process, a principle of narration. In this process the selection of viewpoints ('shots') and their rhythmic fusion (through the 'panning' or 'travelling' of the camera), followed by their assemblage on film or videotape into a continuous, carefully regulated and judged sequence—in other words, 'editing' or 'montage' of pre-recorded images—becomes an additional, immensely powerful generator of meaning. Hence most of the thinking about the aesthetics of the cinematic media revolves around the techniques arising out of this *deictic* function[3] of the camera and the rhythmics and dynamics of fusing its images into a carefully controlled stream of visual statements.

Film theoreticians tend to distinguish between, on the one hand, the 'mise-en-scène'—which comprises all the sign systems that create meaning on the stage and is the *given* that is being photographed—and, on the other hand, the 'art of the director', which involves the selection and composition of 'shots'. As a result the 'mise-en-scène' (being essentially identical with the methods of staging in the theatre) tends to get short shrift in contemporary film criticism, with the acting, design, and above all the script being treated as secondary elements.

It is true that the director's and editor's influence on the acting, for example, is considerable. Weak moments can be eliminated, and 'montage' can achieve powerful effects merely through suggestive juxtaposition of shots. [...]

Nevertheless the concentration of various schools of film aesthetics on the specifically 'filmic' aspects of cinematic drama has had the consequence of devaluing the contribution of the other sign systems. The 'auteur' theory of cinema, for example, which postulates the director as the sole creator of the film and tends to regard the contribution of writer, designer, cameraman and editor and all the other creative artists involved as secondary, not only patently falsifies an existing state of affairs, as most films are the product of a multitude of more or less fortuitously assembled contributors, but has led to the comparative neglect of the contribution of all other artists—writers, designers and above all actors—in the more intellectually ambitious forms of film criticism. [...]

---

[3] *Deictic*: a semiological term for the function of *pointing* or *indicating*.

It is significant that in the television medium, where, for economic reasons, much less time and effort can be expended on re-taking the same scene over and over again, and where there is even less time to edit the material, considerable writers like Harold Pinter, Tom Stoppard, David Mercer, Samuel Beckett, have been able to create drama of a high order of literary and artistic integrity, presented in a cinematic form. Indeed, in the case of Beckett, the 'auteur' concept works more convincingly than in the cinema: here the 'auteur' is the writer, who is enabled to give concrete form to his imagination by being allowed to direct his own text. Even in the cinema itself some major masterpieces have resulted from the work of directors who wrote their own scripts or of writers who have had the good fortune of being able to direct—or otherwise control—the realization of their dramatic ideas— Keaton, Chaplin, Orson Welles, Jean Cocteau and Woody Allen are cases in point here.

## 4

[...] Techniques like the flashback, the dynamic montage of long and short scenes, frequent change of the place of action, the use of recorded voice-overs, or narrators who are present on stage and weave in and out of the action, have become commonplace in contemporary stage drama. While these developments may appear revolutionary after a long period dominated by classical and naturalistic conventions which insisted on a strict three- or five-act structure or the convention of the missing fourth wall, the cinema here merely renewed links with the much freer medieval and Elizabethan conventions of drama, which also used a montage of short scenes, as well as narration (as Shakespeare did in *Pericles* or in *Henry V* and *The Winter's Tale* to cite but the most obvious examples).

Yet it is undoubtedly under the influence of the cinema—and radio which uses narrators with even greater frequency—that the techniques of stage drama have been opened up and freed from the constraints of the 'well-made play'. Audiences used to the cinema will now readily accept epic drama relying on complex levels of narration like Brecht's *The Caucasian Chalk Circle*, or reversals of the chronological time sequence as in Pinter's *Betrayal* or Caryl Churchill's *Top Girls*.

What the theatre retains as its own peculiar strength is its ability to suggest real objects through symbolic action: an actor can mime drinking from a non-existent glass or using a non-existent gun on the stage, while the cinema owing to its photographic nature and hence its need for greater realism is compelled to use real objects. On the other hand the deictic nature of the camera, its ability to point to a small object by moving it into close-up has greatly increased the cinema's ability to use real objects in the role of symbols. The cinema can use the visual equivalent of the Wagnerian 'Leitmotiv' by associating objects, or even whole landscapes, with particular ideas or emotions.

**5**

Some of the most important distinctions between the three visual dramatic media—the stage, cinema and television—derive from the differing conditions under which they are viewed by their audiences.

Here the cinema and the live theatre share—as against television—the important characteristic that their products are watched by crowds assembled in darkened rooms: thus the reactions of their audiences are governed by the phenomena of collective 'mass' rather than individual psychology. Moreover, in both cases, the performance is perceived as an event in itself, an occasion for the sake of which one has made an effort (leaving home, buying a ticket etc.), whereas television is casually entered into, and equally casually opted out of.

In the theatre the audience is in the presence of the purveyors of the communication—the actors. This sets off the complex process of feed-back between the audience and the actors and among members of the audience mentioned earlier.

In the cinema the feed-back between audience and performers is eliminated, but the perception by the audience of its own reaction remains extremely powerful. Here the ability of the medium to direct the attention of all audience members to the same details by the manipulation of their viewpoint actually strengthens the uniformity of the audience's response. Hence, for example, the hysterical bursts of laughter that can be aroused by the best of film farce.

In television drama this mass-psychological response is totally absent. Not only does the television audience lack the surrounding crowd, they are also free from the constraints upon people sitting in a darkened, crowded room and therefore more or less compelled to sit through the whole performance. The television audience can leave the performance at the flick of a switch. Hence the much lower intensity of response to television drama, hence also the frantic concentration of television drama upon supense-enhancing effects, the insistence on packing suspense-provoking incidents into the first minutes of a play—and, in comedy, the use of studio audience or canned laughter, in order to exploit the contagious nature of laughter in the hope that it will make even solitary viewers join in. [...]

Television, being constantly available on tap in the home, is perceived by the audience as a continuous stream of entertainment. Thus each individual item or programme will inevitably receive some additional or unintended meaning by being juxtaposed with other items that precede or follow it. The perception of a news report about a space flight will affect and be affected by a science fiction film before or after it, a political play by the news that follows or precedes it.

The paradox here is that, in the case of commercial television, moreover, this continuum is itself constantly fragmented and interrupted by extraneous material in the form of advertisements. Hence the production of 'meaning', the purveying of subtler types of dramatic information, is more difficult on television, and frequently leads to more insistent pointing, more heavy underlining of semiotic information in television film and drama. [...]

The advent of the distribution of videotaped films constitutes a new aspect of the gradual merging of cinematic and televisual drama. Taped cinema films are seen as small screens by small numbers of people in non-theatrical conditions. Hence an important aspect of the creation of meaning in the cinema is being lost. On the other hand the film will unfold without commercial interruption on the home screen, and the viewing of the film will—if it has been bought or rented—have more of a sense of occasion than a casually turned-on television play.

# 6

If we now try to systematize the different elements that create the first—denotational—level of the 'meaning' of a dramatic performance, we might arrive at the following tabulation:

**Sign systems common to all dramatic media**
1. Framing systems outside the drama proper
   a. Architectural framework and ambiance surrounding the performance
   b. Title, generic description, pre-publicity
   c. Prologue, title sequence, epilogue etc.
2. Sign systems at the actor's disposal
   a. Personality, balance of 'casting'
   b. Delivery of the text
   c. Facial expression
   d. Gesture, body language
   e. Movement in space
   f. Make-up, hairstyle
   g. Costume
3. Visual sign systems
   a. Basic spatial configuration
   b. Visual representation of locale
   c. Colour scheme
   d. Properties
   e. Lighting
4. The text
   a. Basic lexical, syntactic, referential meaning of the words
   b. Style—high/low, prose/verse etc.
   c. Individualization of characters
   d. Overall structure—rhythm—timing
   e. Text as action—subtext

    5. Aural sign systems
      a. Music.
      b. Non-musical sounds

### Sign systems confined to Cinema and Television
    1. Sign systems derived from camera work
      a. Static shots: long-shot, medium and full close-up
      b. Panning shots
      c. Travelling shots[4]
      d. Slow motion, and accelerated motion shots
    2. Sign systems derived from the linking of shots
      a. Dissolve
      b. Crossfade[5]
      c. Split screen[6]
      d. Sharp cut
    3. The sign system of editing
      a. Montage
      b. Use of the rhythmic flow of images

[...] All such tables, as all attempts at a systematization of such complex phenomena, must be highly tentative, especially in this field, where the overlap between, and the mutual merging of, the distinct systems constantly complicates matters. [...]

These, then, are the means, the tools by which the originators of a dramatic performance can establish their characters, paint their background and environment, tell their story.

Yet there is always more to a story than merely its basic outline. Once the actual, factual, *denotational* level has been established, other levels of meaning intervene. The originators of the performance (writer, director, designer, composer) may ultimately aim at those higher levels—the moral, political, philosophical message they want to convey—but those levels must be firmly based on the denotational meaning of the signs they have presented to their audience. [...]

---

   [4] *Panning shots*: up-and-down or sideways camera movements from a fixed (tripod) position, comparable to the viewpoint of a person standing but looking around. *Travelling* (or more normally, tracking) *shots*: camera movements in space (including car or crane shots).

   [5] Presumably this expression, more common in radio parlance, covers shots fading in from, or out of, black—and occasionally white or another colour.

   [6] Actually, there are a great many other (optical or video) ways of manipulating shots, not to mention the endless possibilities of computer-generated images.

# Avant-Garde Theatre and Semiology: A Few Practices and the Theory Behind Them (1982)

## Patrice Pavis

Patrice Pavis (b. 1947) is a leading French theorist of drama and performance who has taught at the Theatre Institute of the University of Paris 3 and at the University of Paris 8. He has written extensively about theatrical semiology, including reception theory, and about Marivaux on the stage. His *Dictionnaire du théâtre* gives a full explanation of the basic terms and concepts of theatrical analysis.

Avant-garde theatre and semiology perform a curious ballet: they avoid each other at first, for want of being acquainted, as if they were going through an identity crisis, not quite knowing how to define themselves and, *a fortiori*, how to behave *vis-à-vis* each other. It is certain that the artistic avant-garde in no way resembles a domain precisely marked out in time, space, style or method; as for semiology, even if its place in theatre studies is no longer in dispute, it still hesitates between a theoretical model, abstract and often difficult to put into practice, and a concrete, but too descriptive, application.

Let us therefore not ask semiology if it can be applied to the avant-garde and what it enables us to discover about it; this would be a naive question rendered false from the outset: one can always apply a method to one's subject, even if it is with a very mixed success, and there is no reason why the semiologist should not tackle contemporary theatre events and describe certain signifying systems of the performance. It is much more productive to turn the question and the perspective about and to examine how the avant-garde uses or disqualifies certain semiotic practices in its creative work.

In this we can better understand the characteristic union of avant-garde and theory, at a time when the artistic subject is very often called upon to

Translated from the French by Jill Daugherty (1981), in Patrice Pavis, *Languages of the Stage: Essays in the Semiology of the Theatre* (New York: Performing Arts Journal Publications, 1982), 181–91.

formulate its own theory and to integrate this metalanguage into its very content, and when establishing a theory very much resembles an artistic operation, since it takes a lot of imagination to create explanatory models more or less adapted to their subject. Nothing, however, has been decided as regards the type of semiology which would be best suited to the avant-garde, and it is by examining the use or the rejection of semiotic tools in avant-garde theatrical art that we can appreciate the integration of the avant-garde and semiology.

It is obviously not the first time that an artistic movement and a theory have met and enriched each other. One only has to think of futurism and formalism in Russia, Czech structuralism and the art of the thirties,[1] the *nouveau roman* and the theory of narration, structuralism and the rereading of the classics, etc. What seems to be new, in the relationship between theatrical practice and theory, is a willingness not to separate and oppose approaches and to check the validity of the one against the other. [...] Now—is this the sign of over-exaggerated abstraction and theorising?—it is certain that the notion of *mise en scène*, which for a century, ever since the birth of the official avant-garde in 1887,[2] has been the end result of a centralizing and controlled conception of meaning in the theatre, is today in a state of crisis. Perhaps because the spectator's role has become too rigid (the *mise en scène* being considered the source of and the key to the meaning furnished by the author of the performance), he is wrongly expected to find a continuity and a centring in what is, on the stage, but a multitude of performance practices and texts. To replace the structural notion of *mise en scène* by that of an author of the performance or director is thus to fall back into a problematic situation that the avant-garde had indeed resolved to transcend: that of an autonomous subject who is the source of meaning and who controls the totality of the signs, as the playwright or actor did formerly. Thus meaning is not assumed in advance, it emerges from the bringing into view (*la mise en regard*), by the stage practices, of the different signifying systems always out of step in relation to one another, and which necessitate, in order to be recentred, the intervention of the perception of a 'spectator-director' [...].

In order to understand this outcome, [...] we should consider how the notions of *sign* and *theatrical language*, used both by the avant-garde and semiology, are necessary but at the same time insufficient to describe the theatre of today and its critical analysis. These are notions that were useful for the first theorization and a first semiology, but that today, by being identified with space and visuality, could easily hamper both theoretical advance and contemporary practice.

---

[1] See Honzl, pp. 269–78.
[2] 1887 is the year in which Antoine's *Théâtre Libre* and Paul Fort's *Théâtre d'Art* were founded. [Pavis's note.]

# The Death of the Sign?

The avant-garde distrusts and tries to free itself from the sign but always succumbs to it in the end: such is the attraction-repulsion movement that was best personified by Artaud in his criticism of the theatre founded on the text and psychology.[3] Artaud wanted to create 'a new physical language based on signs and no longer on words'.[4] But the signs, 'stage images' or animated hieroglyphs, were unable to form a veritable language, since that would have frozen the theatre by reducing it to a desiccated and codified language, as limited, in the long run, as the alphabet and the sounds of articulate language. Faced with this contradiction inherent in any 'artistic language' seeking to form a semiological system having its own units and its own specific way of functioning, the avant-garde had to choose between two solutions and two diametrically opposed aesthetics: (1) entirely give up the idea of the sign and the codification of the *mise en scène* or (2) multiply signs and units until the signifying structure degenerates into an infinite series of identical patterns.

(1) In the first case, a whole trend of research into improvisation tries to escape from the constraint of re-petition or re-presentation; it refuses the idea of a separation between sign and thing, stage and life. The perfect example is that of The Living Theatre and their search for an expression freed from all prior codification, for an original and spontaneous language.[5] This trend is a direct descendant of Artaud's research. Analysing contemporary theatre (that of the thirties, which is still so close to the present-day output), Artaud was quick to diagnose its 'desiccation', its inability to take hold of life in the theatrical and gestural event; he proposed to replace it by a 'directly communicative language,' composed of gestures, incantation, gesticulation and scenic rhythm, a 'new physical language based on signs and no longer on words'. But this new language, even if it goes beyond dialogue and the discursive, could not come into being outside of a system of signs, i.e. a codification that, sooner or later, is likely to become solidified in a system as rigid as that of speech.

This was a phenomenon, moreover, of which Artaud was wholly aware [...]. This double movement of Artaud—the search for and rejection of a specifically theatrical language—is characteristic of the avant-garde: driven by the desire to create its own units without lapsing for that very reason into the codification of language, it hesitates between the indefinable *expressiveness* of the artistic language and the desiccating *codification* of a too mechanical semiology.

(2) On the other hand, the 'serial' trend has reacted in a manner apparently opposed to this fossilization of the sign: by multiplying the sign *ad infinitum*,

---

[3] See pp. 195–9.

[4] Antonin Artaud, *Le Théâtre et son double* (Paris: Gallimard, 1964), p. 81. [Pavis's note.]

[5] The Living Theatre, founded in 1948 by Julian Beck (1925–85) and Judith Malina (b. 1926), at first staged existing playtexts but from an Artaudian perspective; however, during the company's stay in Europe (1964–8) and its subsequent visit to Brazil (1970–1), it moved more and more into the field of collective creation, each member of the company making an original contribution to the performance.

by repeating it to satiety or by varying it very slightly. The series has become the privileged avatar of structure and even of myth. We know, ever since Walter Benjamin,[6] that in the era of mechanical reproduction the work of art acquires a completely new meaning and that it ceases to be founded on the ritual to enter straight away the domain of the political [...] For a serial work of art, this new context, in which everything is multipliable and repetitive, becomes one of the constituent principles of its creation. Thus, in the fifties, the theatre of the absurd turned the repetition of a situation or *leitmotiv* into the symptom of its blind submission to the series principle, admitting its inability to recount a unique and original story in which the meaning—moral, lesson, argument—could no longer refer to a stable and exemplary analysis of reality.[7] In the same formal manner, the 'theatre of everyday life' (... of Franz Xaver Kroetz, Michel Deutsch, Jean-Paul Wenzel, etc.)[8] chooses to retell a 'story without a story' or a banal news item, stereotyped formulas that ideology and its sounding-boards drum into our ears all day long. [...] An author such as Michel Vinaver[9] delights in hunting down the typical and banal phrases of a conversation between office workers (*Les Travaux et les jours/Work and Days*) or business executives (*À la Renverse/Bending Over Backwards*). In all these examples, the repetitions are the scarcely emphasized parody of the classical tragic play whose hero performs in the myth a liberating and meaningful action. These plays and this dramaturgy indicate that the basic *myth* or more simply the tale to be told are relayed by the *series* and thematic variation. [...]

Whatever the trends of the present-day theatre of research, whether these be the negation of the sign or its parodic affirmation, the relationship between the sign and the thing appear profoundly disturbed. The sign seems to have lost its stable relationship between signifier and signified and to have lapsed into two extreme avatars: (1) the *hieroglyph* (a motivated 'sign' that refers to the thing by pointing to it rather than signifying it: this is the case of spontaneous or improvised theatre); (2) the *serial* form in which the sign has no more than a syntactical value for 'serial theatre'. Avant-garde theatre has brought about a crisis in the semiotic and referential relationship of the sign with the world. It has lost all confidence in a mimetic reproduction of reality by the theatre,

---

[6] The essay by the progressive German-Jewish thinker, Walter Benjamin (1892–1940), *The Work of Art in the Age of its Technical Reproducibility*, of which there were three different drafts, first appeared in a (not entirely faithful) French translation in 1936. Its wide influence only came about when it was published in German in 1955, and in an English translation in 1969. The essay's concern with dramatic representation centred on the cinema rather than the theatre.

[7] The repetition of situations and the piling up of objects were prominent features of the absurdist plays of Eugène Ionesco. See pp. 208–14.

[8] The German playwright Franz Xaver Kroetz (b. 1946) has frequently dramatized the lives of the inarticulate. Michel Deutsch and Jean-Paul Wenzel worked at the Théâtre National de Strasbourg in the 1970s, influenced to some extent by the work of German contemporary playwrights.

[9] The work of Michel Vinaver (b. 1927), French novelist and dramatist, is frequently described as being part of the 'théâtre du quotidien' (the theatre of everyday life), a description that does not actually cover all the aspects of his plays.

without having invented a semiological system and an autonomous theatrical language capable of taking its place. Semiology doubtless owes its rapid development to this calling into question of the mimetic nature of art and the refusal of the stage to presume to imitate a pre-existent exterior world.

It is amusing to note that this crisis in mimetism and representation dates back to the end of the nineteenth century, when naturalism and symbolism combined forces under the aegis of the director. Theatre, and in a similar manner literary theory, decided to depend no longer, in order to define themselves, on the exterior world, but to elaborate their own semiotic units and to concentrate on their different possibilities of combination rather than on their meaning. However, if they have not succeeded up to the present day in defining a semiological system and an autonomous theatrical language, it is because they have proved to be too ambitious and dogmatic, hoping to find (like Artaud) a universal language and a specificity that practice and continual invention of new forms do not cease to refute. What one could term 'avant-gardes of specificity' are all those experiments that try to define theatre by a criterion judged necessary and self-sufficient: the actor, space, *mise en scène*, spectator participation, etc. However, none of these criteria is tenable in the long run, with the result that it is becoming impossible to found a semiology based on such specific criteria.

Curiously enough, this has had repercussions on theatrical practice, since a reversal in the relationship between theatrical expression and exterior reality has taken place. Formerly, when the sign was innocent, art was conceived of as the imitation of an objective exterior fact, and the success of the artistic act was measured according to the affinity between sign and thing. Today art no longer seeks to be mimetic, it tries to take the scope of the work of art as its starting point, as its first reality, and is only interested in the referent as a trace in the sign. This is the case of the verbal frescoes of Vinaver [...]: the referent is a stock of stereotypes and stylistic devices that the plays use as raw material, without bothering about the global and realistic reconstitution of the business enterprise or capitalist society. If it so happens that these fragments of ideology and jargon reconstitute a fictional universe closely resembling our own world, this could only be by 'pure coincidence' ... or as the result of the productive work of the spectator.

If the concept of language, sign or specificity is thus in a state of crisis, crystallizing but also blocking avant-garde thought, this is probably because it has linked its fate too closely to the notions of *mise en scène* and spatiality. Indeed everything indicates that it is the encounter between *mise en scène* and artistic language, conceived of as the bringing into view and into space (*mise en vue et en espace*) of meaning, that dominates avant-garde research today, a domination that *another* avant-garde, that of time, rhythm and voice, is seeking to break. Perhaps one should see in this mutation the failure or at least the limits of a semiology based solely on a Cartesian examination, measurable, geometric and, in a word, *spatial*, of the theatrical performance.

It has so often been repeated that theatre has nothing to do with literature, [...] that spatiality and the geometric and visual measurement of signs have been made, a trifle hastily, the only specific criterion of theatre. [...]

Jean-François Lyotard[10] has come in time to remind us of the limited and paralysing nature of such an artistic and semiotic vision by locating the semiological block in the undertaking of the man of space that Artaud was. [...]

Artaud's failure was his wanting to counter the fossilization of the theatre by putting in its place a vision of the theatre that was too spatial and not sufficiently inner and pulsational, his searching for an impossible scenic and gestural language, his forming an idea likewise too specific, in this case too spatial and visual, of the theatrical event.

If today the avant-garde transcends the exclusively spatial, geometric and content-orientated vision of the theatre, it is obviously not through a return to the text, to psychology or linear narrativity. It is a transcendence toward other repressed components of the stage: voice, rhythm, inner duration, the absence of hierarchy between sign systems, the semiological creativity of the spectator, the part played by chance [...] in any theatrical performance.

## Two Semiologies for One Theatre?

We therefore have to ask ourselves if the two ways, that of space and that of temporal event, are necessarily opposed and exclusive, and whether they condemn any semiological theory to be split up into two discourses foreign to each other. According to this schema we would have, on the one hand, a *semiology of space*: starting from an 'empty space' (Peter Brook) to be filled with a predetermined framework[11] (... fundamentally stable and limited, hence reassuring), and on the other hand, a *semiology of time*, which no longer starts off from units that are foreseeable [...], which neither measures nor divides space but creates it as needed, using as its starting point the play event. The latter semiology organizes an experience of the actor and the spectator in a non-structured series of discourses, rhythms, verbal exchanges, relays between image and word—all elements of stage enunciation.

The semiology of space and the theatrical practice it describes are well known because ever since the recognition of *mise en scène* they have reigned supreme over theory and the stage. From the time of naturalism and symbolism up to Brechtian critical realism, space has been considered the frame of reference within which lie *mise en scène* and meaning. For naturalism, space is the only environment in which man moves and where he finds his place according to social determinisms. With Brecht we reach another peak of spatialization, since *mise en scène* is entrusted with making visual the social

---

[10] See Jean-François Lyotard, 'La dent, la paume', in *Des Dispositifs pulsionnels* (Paris: Christian Bourgeois Editeur, 1980), pp. 89–98. [Pavis's note.]

[11] See Peter Brook's *The Empty Space* (London: McGibbon & Kee, 1968).

relations of the characters by emphasizing their *Gestus* or the basic arrangement of the scenic figures. The alienation-effect theory is proof of the takeover by space of the production of meaning in the theatre, for it makes visible the character behind the apparent character [...][12]

Even if space lost all sense of direction and unity, meaning continues to be more or less readable in it. Thus in Brook's film version of Peter Weiss's *Marat/Sade*,[13] the camera relativizes space by multiplying the viewpoints of the prison-bath of the Asylum of Charenton. However, a movement backwards of the camera shows, on several occasions, the director of the institution outside the place of action, separated from the public by a row of bars. This ironic zoom movement re-establishes immediately the boundary between inside and outside, and situates the discourse on liberty in a visual counter-discourse on imprisonment. Even fragmented and disorganized, this type of space [...] still has meaning; it puts the pieces together again and reassures the spectator who can project himself into it. This kind of avant-garde and semiology are based on the clear perception of the borderline between signs, spaces, the dramatic work and the outside world. [...]

On the contrary, the semiology and practice founded on time no longer have an expanse to fill, but a duration and rhythm to maintain. Space no longer exists except in reference to the whereabouts of the actor; it is often not pertinent to the production of meaning.[14] [...] Of this theatre we can catch a few 'glimpses' or rather 'sounds', through a rhythm (as in the *Sprechstücke* of Peter Handke,[15] a voice (those of the 'immaterial' characters of Marguerite Duras), a hackneyed repetition of ideological speech (that of Vinaver's garrulous heroes), or a narrative presence of a 'performer'.

The present success of *performance* can be explained by the rediscovery of the temporal 'event' aspect unique to the theatre. After all, the theatre is always the presence of a living being in front of me, the actor who lives in a time and space that are also mine. Instead of re-presenting and playing an exterior situation and a stable referent, the *performer* admits to being a fugitive and elusive being, willing to go 'a little way' with the spectator. In all these examples, there is no longer a referential space doubling and illustrating the text, no longer a visible and foreseeable functioning of the spectacle/theatre event that the spectator has to encompass with his gaze and mind. It is a question of the

---

[12] See *A Short Organum for the Theatre*, pp. 240–6.

[13] Peter Brook made a film of his stage production for the Royal Shakespeare Company in 1965 of Peter Weiss's *The Persecution and Assassination of Marat as Performed by the Inmates of the Asylum of Charenton under the Direction of the Marquis de Sade*, usually abbreviated as *Marat/Sade*.

[14] See 'Espace' in Pavis' *Dictionnaire du théâtre* (Paris, Éditions sociales, 1980), pp. 151–9. [Pavis's note.]

[15] 'Speech plays' by the Austrian playwright Peter Handke (b. 1942), such as *Offending the Audience* and *Self-Accusation* (1966) as well as *Kaspar* (1968), do away altogether with the traditional dramatic categories of time, place, plot, and character in order to concentrate entirely on the enunciation of words.

listener letting himself be borne by the rhythm of the enunciation and concentrating on his task as structurer of materials delivered pell-mell, hence the insistence on the process of the elaboration of meaning, more than on meaning itself. [...] In these theatrical practices, the boundary line between sense and nonsense, work of art and life, is ceaselessly being moved back, so that any limit seems conventional and capable of being repressed.

Numerous texts thus play on the experience of limits. [...] But this is only to remind us all the better in the end that any psychological, social or artistic excess is in fact controlled by the frontiers of the institution or the work of art. Scenic space and the screen protect us from this overflowing of life, the boundary is not wiped out, but its very mobility indicates the impossibility of counting on fixed units and a stable semiological system. [...]

Other more radical theatrical experiments play still more systematically on the frontier between gesture and word, total improvisation and fixed repetition. [...] The interest of these experiments is to make one feel the moment of drift or of capsizing between gesture and word, to show how the text [...] can be the result of a gestural 'trying out'. There is nothing surprising in the fact that it is the voice that serves as mediation between these two heterogeneous elements: the body (supposedly improvisable and therefore liberated) and the text (supposedly repeatable and fixed). [...] By insisting on the vocal signifier [...], artistic and theoretical practice is less interested in the utterances (visible, comprehensible and made concrete in scenic space) than in the enunciation (place of the enunciating subjects, noises and failures of their production). [...]

## What avant-gardes?

It is easy to propose a typology of the avant-garde in the theatre according to this space/time dichotomy. [...] Such a typology would, however, have only a limited interest, since it would help deepen the gulf that divides the two avant-gardes by assimilating space to exuberant theatricality and scenic writing, and time to an aural theatre [...] and a theatricality inherent in dramatic language. [...]

Today one could take these two tendencies as the standard-bearers of two kinds of theatre. Though they describe it theoretically, they are not, however, distinct and necessarily contradictory categories. There would, moreover, be a certain danger (from which semiology might even fail to recover) in dividing theatrical production and analysed spectacle into space and time; it would be the same danger (and the same theoretical and practical impossibility) that exists in separating utterance and enunciation, content and form, fable and recounting discourse [...]

In all these examples, the avant-garde plays with semiology and its theoretical position is far from certain; it questions and contests the fact that the sign can be considered the minimal unit, even the spatial and representative base of the scenic unit; it postpones, however, the death of the sign [...] Like philosophy, the avant-garde and semiology are still in the age of the sign and the performance/representation [...] We have not yet reached the post-avant-garde, but are still in the period of avant-postmodernism. Theatre finds in these labels and borderline cases, not its end, but its very substance.

# Select Bibliography

## Books

### (a) Anthologies and Handbooks

ALTERNBERD, LYNN, and LEWIS, LESLIE L., *A Handbook for the Study of Drama* (New York: Macmillan, 1966).

BARBA, EUGENIO, *The Secret Art of the Performer: A Dictionary of Theater Anthropology*, trans. Richard Fowler (London: Routledge, 1991).

BENEDIKT, MICHAEL, and WELLWARTH, GEORGE E. (eds.), *Modern French Plays: An Anthology from Jarry to Ionesco* (London: Faber & Faber, 1964).

BENTLEY, ERIC (ed.), *The Theory of the Modern Stage: An Introduction to Modern Theatre and Drama* (Harmondsworth: Penguin, 1968).

BETSKO, KATHLEEN, and KOENIG, RACHEL (eds.), *Interviews with Contemporary Women Playwrights* (New York: Beech Tree Books, 1987).

BOYER, ROBERT D., *Realism in European Theater and Drama: A Bibliography* (Westport, Conn.: Greenwood Press, 1979).

BROWNSTEIN, OSCAR LEE, and DAUBERT, DARLENE M., *Analytical Sourcebook of Concepts in Dramatic Theory* (Westport, Conn.: Greenwood Press, 1981).

CALDERWOOD, JAMES LEE, and TOLIVER, HAROLD EARL, *Perspectives on Drama* (New York: Oxford University Press, 1968).

CAMERON, KENNETH M., and HOFFMAN, THEODORE J. C., *A Guide to Theatre Study* (New York: Macmillan, 2nd edn., 1974).

CLARK, BARRATT HARPER (ed.), *European Theories of the Drama: An Anthology of Dramatic Theory and Criticism*, rev. Henry Popkin (New York: Crown Publications, 1947).

COLE, TOBY (ed.), *Playwrights on Playwriting*, with an introduction by John Gassner (New York: Hill & Wang, 1961).

CORRIGAN, ROBERT W. (ed.), *Theater in the 20th Century* (New York: Grove Press, 1963).

DUKORE, BERNARD F. (ed.), *Dramatic Theory and Criticism: Greek to Grotowski* (New York: Holt, Rinehart and Winston, 1974).

HESS-LÜTTICH, ERNEST W. B. (ed.), *Multimedial Communication, ii: Theatre Semiotics* (Tübingen: Gunter Narr Verlag, 1982).

LAUTER, PAUL, *Theories of Comedy* (Garden City: Doubleday, 1964).

MATTHEWS, BRANDER (ed.), *Papers on Playmaking* (New York: Hill and Wang, 1957).

[R. R. Bowker Company], *Performing Arts 1876–1981 Books: Including an International Index of Current Serial Publications* (New York: R. R. Bowker Co., 1981).

SCHUTZMAN, MADY, and COHEN-CRUZ, JAN (eds.), *Playing Boal: Theatre, Therapy, Activism* (London: Routledge, 1994).

STEADMAN, SUSAN M., *Dramatic Re-visions: An Annotated Bibliography of Feminism and Theatre 1972–1988* (Chicago: American Library Association, 1991).

WAGER, WALTER (ed.), *The Playwrights Speak*, with an introduction by John Russell Taylor (London: Longmans, 1969).

WHALON, MARION K., *Performing Arts Research: A Guide to Information Sources* (Detroit: Gale Research Co., 1976).

### (b) Other

ABEL, LIONEL, *Metatheatre: A New View of Dramatic Form* (New York: Hill & Wang, 1963).

ALTER, JEAN, *A Socio-Semiotic Theory of Theater* (Philadelphia: Pennsylvania University Press, 1991).

ANDERSON, MAXWELL, *The Essence of Tragedy and Other Footnotes and Papers* (Washington, DC: Anderson House, 1939).

APOLLONIO, UMBRO (ed.), *Futurist Manifestos* (London: Thames and Hudson, 1973).

APPIA, ADOLPHE, *Staging Wagnerian Drama*, trans. P. Loeffler (Basle: Birkhäuser, 1982).

—— *Music and the Art of the Theatre*, trans. Robert W. Corrigan and Mary Douglas Dirks, ed. Barnard Hewitt (Coral Gables, Fla.: University of Miama Press, 1962).

—— *The Work of Living Art: A Theory of the Theatre*, trans. H. D. Albright (Coral Gables, Fla.: University of Miama Press, 1960).

—— *Essays, Scenarios and Designs*, trans. Walther B. Vollbach (Ann Arbor: UMI Research Press, 1989).

ARCHER, FRANK, *How to Write a Good Play* (London: Sampson Low, Marston & Co., 1892).

ARCHER, WILLIAM, *Play-Making: A Manual of Craftsmanship* (London: Chapman & Hall, 1912).

ARTAUD, ANTONIN, *Selected Writings*, trans. Helen Weaver (New York: Farrar, Straus & Giroux, 1976).

—— *The Theatre and Its Double*, trans. by Caroline Richards (New York: Grove Press, 1958).

—— *The Theatre and Its Double*, trans. by Victor Corti (London: Calder & Boyars, 1970).

ASTON, ELAINE, *An Introduction to Feminism and Theatre* (London: Routledge, 1995).

—— and SAVONA, GEORGE, *Theatre as Sign-system: A Semiotics of Text and Performance* (London: Routledge, 1991).

AUSTIN, GAYLE, *Feminist Theories for Dramatic Criticism* (Ann Arbor: University of Michigan Press, 1990).

BAKER, GEORGE PIERCE, *Dramatic Technique* (London: Jonathan Cape, 1919).

BAKHTIN, MIKHAIL, *The Dialogic Imagination*, trans. by Michael Holquist (Austin: Texas University Press, 1982).

BALMFORTH, RAMSDEN, *Ethical and Religious Values of Drama* (London: Allen & Unwin, 1925).

—— *The Problem-play and Its Influence on Modern Thought and Life* (London: Allen & Unwin, 1928).

BAMBER, LINDA, *Comic Women: Tragic Men: A Study of Gender and Genres* (Stanford, Calif.: Stanford University Press, 1982).

BARBA, EUGENIO, *Beyond the Floating Islands*, ed. Ferdinando Taviani (New York: Performing Arts Journal Press, 1986).

BARKER, HOWARD, *Arguments for a Theatre* (Manchester: Manchester University Press, 2nd ed., 1993).

BARRY, JACKSON G., *Dramatic Structure: The Shaping of Experience* (Berkeley and Los Angeles: University of California Press, 1970).

BARTHES, ROLAND, *Critical Essays*, trans. Richard Howard (Evanston, Ill.: Northwestern University Press, 1972).

—— *Image—Music—Text*, trans. Stephen Heath (London: Fontana, 1977).

BECKERMAN, BERNARD, *Dynamics of Drama: Theory and Method of Analysis* (New York: Alfred Knopf, 1970).

—— *Theatrical Presentation: Performer, Audience, Act* (New York: Routledge, 1990).

BEN CHAIM, DAPHNA, *Distance in the Theatre: The Aesthetics of Audience Response* (Ann Arbor: UMI Research Press, 1981, 1984).

BENNETT, SUSAN, *Theatre Audiences: A Theory of Production and Reception* (London: Routledge, 1990).

BENTLEY, ERIC, *The Playwright as Thinker* (New York: Meridian, 1955).

—— *The Life of the Drama* (London: Methuen, 1966).

—— *The Theatre of Commitment: And Other Essays on Drama in Our Society* (London: Methuen, 1968).

BERGSON, HENRI, *Laughter: An Essay on the Meaning of the Comic*, trans. Cloudesley Brereton and Fred Rothwell (London: Macmillan, 1911).

BERMEL, ALBERT, *Artaud's Theatre of Cruelty* (New York: Taplinger, 1977).

BLAU, HERBERT, *The Impossible Theater: A Manifesto* (New York: Macmillan, 1964).

—— *The Audience* (Baltimore: Johns Hopkins University Press, 1991).

—— *To All Appearances: Ideology of Performance* (London: Routledge, 1992).

BOAL, AUGUSTO, *Theater of the Oppressed*, trans. Charles A. and Maria-Odilia Leal McBride (New York: Urizen Books, 1979).

BONNER, FRANCES et al., *Imagining Women: Cultural Representations and Gender* (Cambridge: Polity Press, 1992).

BORCHMEYER, DIETER, *Richard Wagner: Theory and Theatre*, trans. Stewart Spencer (Oxford: Clarendon Press, 1991).

BOULTON, MARJORIE, *The Anatomy of Drama* (London: Routledge and Kegan Paul, 1960).

BRANDT, GEORGE W., *British Television Drama* (Cambridge: Cambridge University Press, 1981).

BRECHT, BERTOLT, *The Messingkauf Dialogues*, trans. John Willett (London: Methuen, 1965).

—— *Brecht on Theatre*, ed. John Willett (London: Eyre Methuen, 1964).

BROOK, PETER, *The Empty Space* (London: McGibbon & Kee, 1968).

BROWN, JANET, *Feminist Drama: Definition and Critical Analysis* (London: Scarecrow Press, 1979).

BRUNETIÈRE, FERDINAND, *The Law of the Drama*, trans. Philip M. Hayden, with an Introduction by Henry Arthur Jones, Dramatic Museum Publications, ser. 1, no. 3 (New York: Columbia College, 1914).

BRUSTEIN, ROBERT, *The Theatre of Revolt* (Boston: Little, Brown, 1964).

BRYER, JACKSON, *The Playwright's Art: Conversations with Contemporary American Dramatists* (New Brunswick, NJ: Rutgers University Press, 1995).

BURNS, ELIZABETH, *Theatricality: A Study of Convention in the Theatre and in Social Life* (London: Longman, 1972).

—— and BURNS, TOM (eds.), *Sociology of Drama and Literature: Selected Readings* (Harmondsworth: Penguin Education, 1973).

CARLSON, MARVIN, *Theories of the Theatre: A Historical and Critical Survey, from the Greeks to the Present* (Ithaca: Cornell University Press, 1984).

—— *Theatre Semiotics: Signs of Life* (Bloomington: Indiana University Press, 1990).

CARTER, LAWSON A., *Zola and the Theater* (New Haven: Yale University Press, 1963).

CASE, SUE-ELLEN, *Feminism and Theatre* (London: Macmillan, 1988).

—— (ed.), *Performing Feminisms: Feminist Critical Theory and Theatre* (Baltimore: Johns Hopkins University Press, 1990).

CAUTE, DAVID, *The Illusion: An Essay on Politics, Theatre and the Novel* (London: André Deutsch, 1971).

CHAIKIN, JOSEPH, *The Presence of the Actor* (New York: Atheneum, 1977).

COLE, DAVID, *The Theatrical Event: A 'Mythos,' a Vocabulary, a Perspective* (Middletown, Conn.: Wesleyan University Press, 1975).

CONSTANTINIDES, STRATOS E., *Theatre under Deconstruction? A Question of Approach* (New York: Garland Publishing Co., 1993).

CORRIGAN, ROBERT W., *Comedy: Meaning and Form* (San Francisco: Chandler, 1965).

—— *Tragedy: Vision and Form* (San Francisco: Chandler, 1965).

COURTNEY, RICHARD, *Drama and Intelligence: A Cognitive Theory* (Montreal and Kingston: McGill-Queen's University Press, 1990).

—— *Drama and Feeling: An Aesthetic Theory* (Montreal and Kingston: McGill-Queen's UP, 1995).

CRAIG, EDWARD GORDON, *On the Art of the Theatre* (London: Heinemann, 1911).

—— *Craig on Theatre*, ed. Michael Walton (London: Methuen, 1983).

DAWSON, S. W., *Drama and the Dramatic* (London: Methuen, 1970).

DIXON, W. M., *Tragedy* (London: Edward Arnold, 1924).

DOLAN, JILL, *The Feminist Spectator as Critic* (Ann Arbor: UMI Research Press, 1988).

DÜRRENMATT, FRIEDRICH, *Writings on Theatre and Drama*, trans. H. M. Waidson (London: Jonathan Cape, 1976).

EAGLETON, MARY, *Feminist Literary Theory: A Reader* (Oxford: Blackwell, 1986).

ECO, UMBERTO, *The Limits of Interpretation* (Bloomington: Indiana University Press, 1994).

ELAM, KEIR, *The Semiotics of Theatre and Drama* (London: Methuen, 1980).

ELIOT, T. S., *Poetry and Drama* (London: Faber & Faber, 1951).

ELLIS FERMOR, UNA, *The Frontiers of Drama* (London: Methuen, 2nd edn., 1964).

ERVINE, ST. JOHN GREER, *How to Write a Play* (London: Allen and Unwin, 1928).

ESSLIN, MARTIN, *The Anatomy of Drama* (London: Temple Smith, 1976).

—— *The Field of Drama: How the Signs of Drama Create Meaning on Stage and Screen* (London: Methuen, 1987).

FERGUSSON, FRANCIS, *The Idea of a Theater: The Art of Drama in a Changing Perspective* (Princeton: Princeton University Press, 1949).

FISCHER-LICHTE, ERIKA, *The Semiotics of Theatre*, trans. Jeremy Gaines and Doris L. Jones (Bloomington: Indiana University Press, 1992).

FOREMAN, RICHARD, *Plays and Manifestos*, ed. Kate Davy (New York: New York University Press, 1976).

FREYTAG, GUSTAV, *Freytag's Technique of the Drama*, trans. Elias J. MacEwan (Chicago: S. C. Griggs, 1896).

FUCHS, GEORG, *Revolution in the Theatre*, condensed and adapted by Constance Connor Kuhn (Ithaca, NY: Cornell University Press, 1959).

FURST, LILIAN R., and SKRINE, PETER, *Naturalism*, The Critical Idiom, 18 (London: Methuen, 1971).

GASSNER, JOHN (ed.), *Ideas in the Drama* (New York: Columbia University Press, 1964).

GEROULD, DANIEL (ed. & trans.), *Twentieth-Century Polish Avant-Garde Drama: Plays, Scenarios, Critical Documents* (Ithaca: Cornell University Press, 1977).

GOLDMAN, ALBERT, and SPRINCHORN, EVERT (eds.), *Wagner on Music and Drama* (New York: E. P. Dutton, 1964).

GOLDMAN, EMMA, *The Social Significance of Modern Drama* (Boston: R. G. Badger, 1914).

GOODLAD, J. S. R., *A Sociology of Popular Drama* (London: Heinemann, 1971).

GRANT, DAMION, *Realism*, The Critical Idiom, 9 (London: Methuen, 1970).

GRANVILLE-BARKER, HARLEY, *On Poetry in Drama* (London: Sidgwick, 1937).

—— *On Dramatic Method* (New York: Dramabook, Hill & Wang, 1956).

GRAVER, DAVID, *The Aesthetics of Disturbance: Anti-Art in Avant-Garde Drama* (Ann Arbor: University of Michigan Press, 1995).

GRIFFITHS, STUART, *How Plays are Made: A Guide to the Technique of Play Construction and the Basic Principles of Drama* (London: Heinemann Educational Books, 1982).

GROSS, ROBERT, *Words Heard and Overheard: The Main Text in Contemporary Drama* (New York: Garland Publishing Co., 1990).

GROSS, ROGER, *Understanding Playscripts: Theory and Method* (Bowling Green, Oh.: Bowling Green University Press, 1974).

GROTOWSKI, JERZY, *Towards a Poor Theatre*, trans. by Jörgen Andersen and Judy Barba (London: Methuen, 1969).

GUTHKE, KARL, *Modern Tragicomedy* (New York: Random House, 1966).

HAMILTON, CLAYTON, *The Theory of the Theatre, and Other Principles of Dramatic Criticism* (New York: Henry Holt & Co., rev. edn., 1939).

HANNA, GILLIAN, *Feminism and Theatre*, Theatre Papers, 2nd ser., no. 8 (Totnes: Dartington College of Arts, 1978).

HARRIS, MARK, *The Case for Tragedy* (New York: G. P. Putnam's Sons, 1932).

HART, LINDA, *Making a Spectacle: Feminist Essays on Contemporary Women's Theatre* (Ann Arbor: University of Michigan Press, 1989).

HAUGEN, EINAR, *Ibsen's Drama: Author to Audience* (Minneapolis: Minnesota University Press, 1979).

HEBBEL, FRIEDRICH, *Maria Magdalena* (1844), trans. Paula Green (Boston: R. G. Badger, 1914).

HELBO, ANDRÉ, *The Theory of Performing Arts* (Amsterdam: John Benjamin, 1987).

—— (ed.), *Approaching Theater* (Baltimore: Johns Hopkins University Press, 1990).

HENNEQUIN, ALFRED, *The Art of Playwriting* (Boston: Houghton and Co., 1890).

HINCHLIFFE, ARNOLD, *The Absurd*, The Critical Idiom, 5 (London: Methuen, 1969).

HOLDERNESS, GRAHAM, *The Politics of Theatre and Drama* (London: Macmillan, 1992).

HOLUB, ROBERT C., *Reception Theory: A Critical Introduction* (London: Methuen, 1984).

HORNBY, RICHARD, *Script into Performance: A Structuralist View of Play Production* (Austin: University of Texas Press, 1977).

—— *Drama, Metadrama and Perception* (Lewisburg: Bucknell University Press, 1986).

HOY, CYRUS, *The Hyacinth Room: An Investigation into the Nature of Comedy, Tragedy, and Tragicomedy* (London: Chatto & Windus, 1964).

IONESCO, EUGÈNE, *Notes and Counter-Notes*, trans. Donald Watson (London: John Calder, 1964).

ISSACHAROFF, MICHAEL, and JONES, ROBIN F. (eds.), *Performing Texts* (Philadelphia: University of Pennsylvania Press, 1988).

JARRY, ALFRED, *Ubu Roi*, trans. Barbara Wright (London: Gaberbocchus Press, 1951).

JASPERS, KARL, *Tragedy Is Not Enough*, trans. Harald A. T. Reiche et al. (London: Gollancz, 1953).

JAUSS, HANS ROBERT, *Toward an Aesthetic of Reception*, trans. Timothy Bahti (London: Harvester Press, 1982).

JONES, ROBERT EDMOND, *The Dramatic Imagination: Reflections and Speculations on the Art of Theatre* (New York: Theatre Arts Books, 1941).

JOURDAIN, ELEANOR F., *The Drama in Europe in Theory and Practice* (London: Methuen, 1924).

KAPROW, ALLAN, *Assemblages, Environments and Happenings* (New York: Abrams, 1966).

KATRAK, KETU H., *Wole Soyinka and Modern Tragedy: A Study of Dramatic Theory and Practice* (Westport, Conn.: Greenwood Press, 1986).

KAUFMANN, WALTER, *Tragedy and Philosophy* (Garden City, NY: Anchor Books, Doubleday & Co., 1969).

KAYSSAR, HELEN, *Feminist Theatre* (Houndmills: Macmillan, 1984).

—— *Feminist Theatre and Theory* (Basingstoke: Macmillan, 1996).

KENNEDY, ANDREW K., *Dramatic Dialogue:*

*The Duologue of Personal Encounter* (Cambridge: Cambridge University Press, 1983).

KERR, WALTER, *How Not to Write a Play* (New York: Simon & Schuster, 1955).

KIRBY, MICHAEL STANLEY, *Happenings: An Illustrated Anthology* (New York: E. P. Dutton, 1965).

—— *Futurist Performance* (New York: E. P. Dutton, 1971).

—— *A Formalist Theater* (Philadelphia: Pennsylvania University Press, 1987).

KLAF, FRANKLIN S., *Strindberg: The Origin of Psychology in Modern Drama* (New York: Citadel Press, 1963).

KOMESU, OKIFUMI, *The Double Perspective of Yeats's Aesthetic* (Gerrard's Cross: Colin Smythe, 1984).

KONRAD, LINN BRATTETEIG, *Modern Drama as Crisis: The Case of Maurice Maeterlinck*, American University Studies, ser. 2, vol. 25 (New York: Peter Lang, 1986).

KOSTELANETZ, RICHARD, *The Theatre of Mixed Means* (New York: Dial Press, 1968).

KRIEGER, MURRAY, *The Tragic Vision* (Chicago: University of Chicago Press, 1960).

KUMIEGA, JENNIFER, *The Theatre of Grotowski* (London: Methuen, 1985).

LABELLE, MAURICE MARC, *Alfred Jarry: Nihilism and the Theatre of the Absurd* (New York: New York University Press, 1980).

LANGER, SUSANNE K., *Feeling and Form* (New York: Scribner's, 1953).

LAWSON, JOHN HOWARD, *Theory and Technique of Playwriting* (New York: Hill & Wang, rev. edn., 1970).

LEVINE, IRA A., *Leftwing Dramatic Theory in the American Theatre* (Ann Arbor: UMI Research Press, 1985).

LEVITT, PAUL M., *A Structural Approach to the Analysis of Drama* (The Hague: Mouton, 1971).

LEWISOHN, LUDWIG, *The Modern Drama: An Essay in Interpretation* (New York: B. W. Huebsch, 1915).

—— *The Drama and the Stage* (New York: Harcourt, Brace & Co., 1922).

LUCAS, F. L., *Tragedy* (London: Hogarth Press, rev. edn., 1957).

MACDONALD, ERIK, *Theater at the Margins: Text and the Post-Structural Stage* (Ann Arbor: University of Michigan Press, 1993).

MACGOWAN, KENNETH, *A Primer of Playwriting* (New York: Doubleday, 1962).

MCGRATH, JOHN, *A Good Night Out: Popular Theatre: Audience, Class and Form* (London: Eyre Methuen, 1981).

MAETERLINCK, MAURICE, *The Treasure of the Humble*, trans. Alfred Sutro (London: George Allen, 1897).

MARINETTI, FILIPPO TOMMASO, *Selected Writings*, trans. R. W. Flint (London: Secker & Warburg, 1972).

MARTIN, MARIANNE W., *Futurist Art and Theory, 1909–1915* (Oxford: Clarendon Press, 1968).

MATEJKA, LADISLAV & TITUNIK, I. R. (eds.), *Semiotics of Art* (Cambridge, Mass.: MIT Press, 1976).

MATTHEWS, BRANDER, *A Study of the Drama* (Boston: Houghton Mifflin, 1910).

MEIER, ERIKA, *Realism and Reality: The Function of Stage Directions in the New Drama from Thomas William Robertson to Bernard Shaw*, Cooper Monograph on English and American Literature, no. 12 (Bern: A. Francke Verlag, 1967).

MELCHER, EDITH, *Stage Realism in France between Diderot and Antoine* (Bryn Mawr, Penn.: n.p., 1928).

MELROSE, SUSAN, *A Semiotics of the Dramatic Art* (London: Macmillan, 1994).

MELZER, ANNABELLE HENKIN, *Latest Rage the Big Drum: Dada and Surrealist Performance* (Baltimore: Johns Hopkins Press, 1994).

MEYERHOLD, VSEVOLOD EMILIEVICH, *Meyerhold on Theatre*, ed. and trans. Edward Braun (London: Methuen, rev. edn., 1991).

MILLER, ARTHUR, *The Theatre Essays of Arthur Miller*, ed. and introd. Robert A. Martin (London: Methuen, 2nd edn., 1994).

NATALLE, ELIZABETH J., *Feminist Theatre: A Study in Persuasion* (Metuchen, NJ: Scarecrow Press, 1985).

NATHAN, GEORGE JEAN, *The Critic and the Drama* (New York: Knopf, 1922).

NICOLL, ALLARDYCE, *Film and Theatre* (London: Harrap, 1936).

—— *The Theatre and Dramatic Theory* (London: Harrap, 1962).

NIETZSCHE, FRIEDRICH, *The Birth of Tragedy, and The Case of Wagner*, trans. Walter Kaufmann (New York: Vintage Books, 1967).

NORTHAM, JOHN R., *Ibsen's Dramatic Method: A Study of the Prose Dramas* (London: Faber, 1953).

O'DRISCOLL, ROBERT and REYNOLDS, LORNA (eds.), *Yeats and the Theatre* (London: Macmillan, 1975).

OSWALD, LAURA, *Jean Genet and the Semiotics of Performance* (Bloomington: Indiana University Press, 1989).

O'TOOLE, JOHN, *The Process of Drama* (London: Routledge, 1992).

OWEN, HARRISON, *The Playwright's Craft* (London: Thomas Nelson, 1947).

PAGE, ADRIAN, *The Death of the Playwright? Modern British Drama and Literary Theory* (London: Macmillan, 1992).

PALMER, D. J. (ed.), *Comedy: Developments in Criticism. A Casebook* (London: Macmillan, 1984).

PAVIS, PATRICE, *Languages of the Stage: Essays in the Semiology of the Theatre*, trans. Jill Daugherty (New York: Performing Arts Journal Publications, 1982).

—— *Theater at the Crossroads of Culture*, trans. Loren Kruger (London: Routledge, 1992).

PEACOCK, RONALD, *The Art of Drama* (London: Routledge & Kegan Paul, 1957).

PFISTER, MANFRED, *The Theory and Analysis of the Drama*, trans. J. Halliday (Cambridge: Cambridge University Press, 1988).

PISCATOR, ERWIN, *The Political Theatre*, trans. Hugh Rorrison (London: Eyre Methuen, 1980).

PLUNKA, GENE A. (ed.), *Antonin Artaud and the Modern Theater* (London: Associated University Press, 1994).

POLTI, GEORGES, *The Thirty-Six Dramatic Situations*, trans. Lucille Ray (Cincinatti: Writer's Digest, 1931).

PRIESTLEY, JOHN BOYNTON, *The Art of the Dramatist* (London: Heinemann, 1957).

QUINN, MICHAEL L., *The Semiotic Stage: Prague School Theatre Theory* (New York: Peter Lang, 1995).

RAPHAEL, DAVID DAICHES, *The Paradox of Tragedy* (Bloomington: Indiana University Press, 1960).

REES, G. BRYCHAN, *Hebbel as a Dramatic Artist: A Study of His Dramatic Theory and of Its Relationship to His Dramas* (London: G. Bell & Sons, 1930).

REYNOLDS, P., *Drama: Text into Performance* (Harmondsworth: Penguin, 1986).

ROBERTS, PATRICK, *The Psychology of Tragic Drama* (London: Routledge & Kegan Paul, 1975).

ROSE, MARGARET, *The Symbolist Theatre Tradition from Maeterlinck and Yeats to Beckett and Pinter* (Milan: Edizioni Unicopli, 1989).

ROZIK, ELI, *The Language of the Theatre* (Glasgow: University of Glasgow Press, 1992).

SARTRE, JEAN-PAUL, *Sartre on Theater*, ed. Michel Contat and Michel Rybalka, trans. Frank Jellinek (London: Quartet Books, 1976).

SCHECHNER, RICHARD, *Environmental Theater* (Indianapolis: Bobbs Merril, 1972).

—— *The End of Humanism* (New York: Performing Arts Journal Press, 1982).

—— *Between Theatre and Anthropology* (Philadelphia: University of Pennsylvania Press, 1985).

—— *Performance Theory* (London: Routledge, rev. edn., 1988).

—— and APPEL, WILLA (eds.), *By Means of Performance* (Cambridge: Cambridge University Press, 1990).

—— and SCHUMAN, MANDY, *Ritual, Play and Performance/Readings in the Social Sciences* (New York: Seabury Press, 1976).

SCHEVILL, JAMES, *Breakout! In Search of New Theatrical Environments* (Chicago: Swallow Press, 1973).

SCHLUETER, JUNE, *Metafictional Characters in Modern Drama* (New York: Columbia University Press, 1979).

SCHMID, HERTA, and VAN KESTEREN, ALOYSIUS, *Semiotics of Drama and Theatre: New Perspectives in the Theory of Drama & Theatre*, Linguistic and Literary Studies in Eastern Europe, 10 (Amsterdam: John Benjamin, 1984).

SCHWARZ, ALFRED, *From Büchner to Beckett: Dramatic Theory and the Modes of Tragic Drama* (Athens, Oh.: Ohio University Press, 1978).

SELLIN, ERIC, *The Dramatic Concepts of Artaud* (Chicago: University of Chicago Press, 1968).

SENELIK, LAURENCE, *Russian Dramatic Theory from Pushkin to the Symbolists* (Austin: University of Texas Press, 1981).

SHAW, GEORGE BERNARD, *Our Theatre in the Nineties*, 3 vols. (London: Constable, 1932).

—— *Major Critical Essays: The Quintessence of Ibsenism. The Perfect Wagnerite. The Sanity of Art* (London: Constable, 1932).

—— *Pen Portraits and Reviews* (London: Constable, 1932).

—— *Prefaces* (London: Odhams Press, 1938).

—— *Plays and Players: Essays on the Theatre*, sel. A. C. Ward (London: Oxford University Press, 1952).

—— *Shaw on Theatre*, ed. E. J. West (London: McGibbon & Kee, 1960).

SHAW, LEROY, *The Playwright and Historical Change: Dramatic Strategies in Brecht, Hauptmann, Kaiser, Wedekind* (Madison: University of Wisconsin Press, 1970).

SILK, MICHAEL STEPHEN, and STERN, J. P., *Nietzsche on Tragedy* (Cambridge: Cambridge University Press, 1981).

SOYINKA, WOLE, *Myth, Literature and the*

*African World* (Cambridge: Cambridge University Press, 1976).

STANISLAVSKY (Stanislavski), CONSTANTIN (Konstantin), *An Actor Prepares*, trans. Elizabeth Reynolds Hapgood (London: Geoffrey Bles, 1936).

—— *Building a Character*, trans. Elizabeth Reynolds Hapgood (London: Max Reinhardt, 1950).

—— *Stanislavsky on the Art of the Stage*, trans. with an Introductory Essay on Stanislavsky's 'System' by David Magarshack (London: Faber & Faber, 1950).

—— *Creating a Role*, trans. by Elizabeth Reynolds Hapgood (New York: Theatre Arts Books, 1961).

—— *Selected Works*, compiled by Oksana Korneva (Moscow: Raduga Publishers, 1984).

STATES, BERT O., *Irony and Drama: A Poetics* (Ithaca: Cornell University Press, 1971).

—— *'Great Reckonings in Little Rooms': On the Phenomenology of the Theater* (Berkeley: University of California Press, 1986).

STEINER, GEORGE, *The Death of Tragedy* (London: Faber & Faber, 1961).

—— *Language and Silence* (New York: Atheneum, 1967).

STRINDBERG, AUGUST, Preface to *Miss Julie*, in *The Plays*, i, trans. Michael Meyer (London: Secker & Warburg, 1964).

STYAN, J. L., *The Elements of Drama* (Cambridge: Cambridge University Press, 1960).

—— *The Dark Comedy: The Development of Modern Comic Tragedy* (Cambridge: Cambridge University Press, 1968).

—— *Drama, Stage and Audience* (Cambridge: Cambridge University Press, 1975).

SYMONS, ARTHUR, *Plays, Acting and Music: A Book of Theory* (London: Constable, 1909).

SZONDI, PETER, *Theory of Modern Drama*, trans. Michael Hays, 'Theory and History of Literature' series, vol. 29 (Minneapolis: University of Minnesota Press, 1983).

TAYLOR, JOHN RUSSELL, *The Rise and Fall of the Well-Made Play* (New York: Hill & Wang, 1967).

TENNANT, PETER F., *Ibsen's Dramatic Technique* (Cambridge: Cambridge University Press, 1948).

THOMPSON, ALAN REYNOLDS, *The Anatomy of Drama* (Berkeley and Los Angeles: University of California Press, 1946).

TURNER, VICTOR, *Process, Performance and Pilgrimage* (New Delhi: Concept Publishing Co., 1979).

—— *From Ritual to Theatre: The Human*

*Seriousness of Play* (New York: Performing Arts Journal Publications, 1982).

—— *The Anthropology of Performance* (New York: Performing Arts Journal Publications, 1986).

VAN DRUTEN, JOHN, *The Playwright at Work* (New York: Harper, 1953).

VAN LAAN, THOMAS F., *The Idiom of Drama* (Ithaca: Cornell University Press, 1970).

VELTRUSKÝ, JIŘÍ, *Drama as Literature* (Lisse: Peter de Ridder Press, 1977).

WAGNER, RICHARD, *Prose Works*, 8 vols., trans. William Ashton Ellis (London: K. Paul, Trench, Trübner & Co., 1892–9).

WANDOR, MICHELENE, *Carry on, Understudies* (London: Routledge & Kegan Paul, 1986).

—— *Look Back in Gender* (London: Methuen, 1987).

WELLWARTH, GEORGE, *The Theatre of Protest and Paradox* (London: McGibbon & Kee, 1965).

—— *Modern Drama and the Death of God* (Madison: University of Wisconsin Press, 1986).

WHITAKER, THOMAS R., *Fields of Play in Modern Drama* (Princeton University Press, 1977).

WILLETT, JOHN, *The Theatre of Bertolt Brecht: A Study from Eight Aspects* (London: Eyre Methuen, 1977).

WILLIAMS, RAYMOND, *Modern Tragedy* (London: Chatto & Windus, 1966).

—— *Drama in a Dramatised Society: An Inaugural Lecture* (Cambridge: Cambridge University Press, 1975).

WITKIEWICZ, STANISŁAW IGNACY, *The Mother and Other Unsavoury Plays*, ed. & trans. Daniel Gerould and C. S. Durer (New York: Applause Books, 1966).

—— *Beelzebub Sonata: Plays, Essays and Documents*, trans. Daniel Gerould and Jadwiga Kosicka (New York: Performing Arts Journal Publications, 1980).

WORTHEN, WILLIAM, *Modern Drama and the Rhetoric of Theater* (Berkeley and Los Angeles: University of California Press, 1992).

WRIGHT, ELIZABETH, *Psychoanalytic Criticism: Theory in Practice* (London: Methuen, 1984).

YEATS, WILLIAM BUTLER, *Essays and Introductions* (London: Macmillan, 1961).

YOUNG, STARK, *The Theatre* (New York: Hill & Wang Dramabook, 1958).

ZOLA, EMILE, *The Experimental Novel and Other Essays*, trans. Belle M. Sherman (New York: Cassell Publishing Co., 1893).

## Articles and Essays

ADDINGTON, DAVID, 'Art and Silence in the Theatre', *Indiana Speech Journal*, 10 (1976), 1–8.

—— 'Ego Involvement: Another Approach to Empathy', *Empirical Research in Theatre* (Center for Communication Research, Bowling Green University, Summer 1981), 22–31.

ALTER, JEAN, 'From Text to Performance', *Poetics Today*, 2/3 (Spring 1981), 131–9.

ARESTAD, SVERRE, 'Ibsen's Concept of Tragedy', *Publications of the Modern Language Association of America*, 74 (June 1959), 285–97.

AUSLANDER, PHILIP, 'Holy Theatre and Catharsis', *Theatre Research International*, 9/1 (1984), 16–29.

AUSTIN, GAYLE, 'Women/Text/Theatre', *Performing Arts Journal*, 9/2–3 (1985), 185–90.

BARAKA, IMAMU AMIRI (LeRoi Jones), 'The Revolutionary Theatre (1966)', in Baraka, *Selected Plays and Prose* (New York: Morrow, 1979), 131 *et seq.*

BARBA, EUGENIO, 'Theatre Anthropology', trans. Richard Fowler, *Drama Review*, 26/2 (Summer 1982), 5–32.

—— 'The Nature of Dramaturgy: Describing Actions at Work', *New Theatre Quarterly*, 1/1 (Feb. 1985), 75–8.

BARKER, DONALD, 'A Structural Theory of Theatre', *Yale/Theatre*, 8/1, 55–61

BARTHES, ROLAND, 'Barthes on Theatre', trans. Richard Howard, *Theatre Quarterly*, 9/33 (Spring 1979), 25–30.

BASSNETT, SUSAN, 'An Introduction to Theatre Semiotics', *Theatre Quarterly*, 10/38 (Summer 1980), 47–53.

—— 'Towards a Theory of Women's Theatre', in Herta Schmid and Aloysius Van Kesteren (eds.), *Semiotics of Drama and Theatre*, Linguistic and Literary Studies in Eastern Europe, 10 (Amsterdam: John Benjamin, 1984), 445–66.

—— 'Structuralism and After: Trends and Tendencies in Theatre Analysis, Part 1', *New Theatre Quarterly*, 1/1 (Feb. 1985), 79–82; 'Part 2', *NTQ*, 1/2 (May 1985), 205–7.

—— 'Struggling with the Past: Women's Theatre in Search of a History', *New Theatre Quarterly*, 5/18 (May 1989), 107–12.

BENSTON, A. N., 'From Naturalism to the Dream Play: A Study of the Evolution of Strindberg's Unique Theatrical Form', *Modern Drama*, 7 (Feb. 1965), 382–98.

BLAU, HERBERT, 'Ideology and Performance', *Theatre Journal*, 35/4 (Dec. 1983), 441–60.

BOGATYREV, PETR, 'The Interconnection of Two Similar Semiotic Systems: The Puppet Theatre and the Theatre of Living Actors', *Semiotica*, 47 (1983), 44–7.

BOND, EDWARD, 'The Writer's Theatre', in *Edward Bond: A Companion to the Plays*, ed. Malcolm Hay and Philip Roberts (London: TQ Publications, 1978), 70 *et seq.*

BRADBROOK, MURIEL, 'Yeats and the Noh Drama of Japan', in *Aspects of Dramatic Form in the English and Irish Renaissance: The Collected Papers of Muriel Bradbrook*, iii (Brighton: Harvester Press, 1983).

BRAINERD, BARRON, and NEUFELDT, VICTORIA, 'On Marcus Methods for the Analysis of the Strategy of a Play', *Poetics*, 10 (1974), 31–74.

BRANDT, GEORGE WILLIAM, 'Twentieth-Century Comedy', in W. D. Howarth (ed.), *Comic Drama: The European Heritage* (London: Methuen, 1978), 165–86.

BURNS, ELIZABETH, 'Conventions of Performance' (1972), in Elizabeth and Tom Burns (eds.), *Sociology of Literature and Drama* (Harmondsworth: Penguin Education, 1973), 348–58.

BYERS-PEVITTS, BEVERLEY, 'Imagining Women in Theatre: Departures from Dramatic Tradition', *Theatre Annual*, 40 (1985), 1–6.

CAINE, CINDY S. A. M., 'Structure in the One-Act Play', *Modern Drama*, 12, 390–8.

CANNING, CHARLOTTE, 'Constructing Experience: Theorising a Feminist Theatre History', *Theatre Journal*, 45 (1993), 529–40.

CARLSON, MARVIN, 'Modern Drama: A Selective Bibliography of Bibliographies', *Modern Drama*, 8 (1965), 112–18.

CASE, SUE-ELLEN, and FORTE, JEANIE K., 'From Formalism to Feminism', *Theatre*, 16/2 (1985), 62–5.

CHAIKIN, JOSEPH, 'The Open Theatre (Questions by Richard Schechner)', *Tulane Drama Review*, 9/2 (1964), 191–7.

CHIARAMONTE, NICOLA, 'Antonin Artaud', *Encounter*, 39/2 (Feb. 1968), 532–8.

CLEVENGER, THEODORE, 'Behavioral Research in Theatre', *Educational Theatre Journal*, 17 (May 1965), 118–21.

CONSTANTINIDES, STRATOS, 'Is Theatre under Deconstruction?', *Journal of Dramatic Theory and Criticism*, 4/1 (1989), 31–52.

COURTNEY, WILLIAM LEONARD, 'Modern Social Drama as Influenced by the Novel', *Fortnightly Review*, 77 (1902), 666–74.

—— 'Realistic Drama', *Fortune*, 98 (May 1913), 945–62.

D'ANGELO, N., 'George Bernard Shaw's Theory of Stage Representation', *Quarterly Journal of Speech* (June 1929), 330–49.

DAVY, KATE, 'Constructing the Spectator: Reception, Context and Address in Lesbian Performance', *Performing Arts Journal*, 10/2 (1986), 43–52.

DEÁK, FRANTIŠEK, 'Structuralism in Theatre: The Prague School Contribution', *Drama Review*, 20/4 (Dec. 1976), 83–94.

DE MARINIS, MARCO, 'The Dramaturgy of the Spectator', *Drama Review*, 31/2 (Summer 1987), 100–14.

—— 'Toward a Cognitive Semiotic of Theatrical Emotions', *Versus*, 41, 5–20.

DERRIDA, JACQUES, 'The Theatre of Cruelty and the Closure of Representation', in *Writing and Difference*, trans. Alan Bass (Chicago: University of Chicago Press, 1978), 232–50.

DIAMOND, ELIN, 'Brechtian Theory/Feminist Theory: Toward a Gestic Feminist Criticism', *Drama Review*, 32/1 (Spring 1988), 82–94.

DICKERSON, GLENDA, 'The Cult of True Womanhood: Toward a Womanist Attitude in Africa-American Theatre', *Theatre Journal*, 40 (1989), 178–87.

DICKINSON, THOMAS H., 'Drama of Intellectualism', *Drama*, 7 (Aug. 1912), 148–62.

—— 'Dramatic Art as an Expression of Society', *Forum*, 53 (Jan. 1915), 121–32.

DOLAN, JILL, 'In Defense of the Discourse: Materialist Feminism, Postmodernism, Poststructuralism . . . and Theory', *Drama Review*, 33/3 (Fall 1989), 58–71.

DUVIGNAUD, JEAN, 'The Theatre in Society: Society in the Theatre', trans. Tom Burns, in Elizabeth and Tom Burns (eds.), *Sociology of Drama and Literature* (Harmondsworth: Penguin Education, 1973), 82–100.

ECO, UMBERTO, 'Semiotics of Theatrical Performance', *Drama Review*, 21/1 (Mar. 1977), 107–17.

EISENSTEIN, SERGEI MIKHAILOVICH, 'Montage of Attractions', trans. D. and E. Gerould, *Drama and Theatre*, 9 (Fall 1970), 10 *et seq.*

ERVINE, ST. JOHN, 'On Learning to Write Plays', *Living Age*, 308 (1 Jan. 1921), 36–9.

ESSLIN, MARTIN, 'Violence in Drama', *Encore*, 49 (May–June 1964), 6–16.

—— 'The Theatre of Cruelty', *New York Times Magazine* (4 Mar. 1966), 22–3, 71–4.

—— 'The Stage: Reality, Symbol, Metaphor', in *Themes in Drama 4: Drama & Symbolism*, ed. James Redmond (Cambridge: Cambridge University Press, 1982), 1–12.

FÉRAL, JOSETTE, 'Performance and Theatricality: The Subject Demystified', *Modern Drama*, 25/1 (Mar. 1982), 170–81.

FLETCHER, JOHN, 'Symbolic Functions in Dramatic Performance', in James Redmond (ed.), *Themes in Drama 4: Drama & Symbolism* (Cambridge: Cambridge University Press, 1982), 13–28.

FREUD, SIGMUND, 'Psychopathic Characters on the Stage (1905 or 1906)', trans. James Strachey with Anna Freud, in *The Standard Edition of the Complete Psychological Works*, vii (London: Hogarth Press, 1953), 305–10.

FRIEDMAN, SHARON, 'Feminism as Theme in Twentieth-Century American Women's Drama', *American Studies*, 25 (Spring 1984), 69–89.

FRY, CHRISTOPHER, 'Poetry in the Theatre', *Saturday Review* (21 Mar. 1953), 18–19, 33.

GAUTHIER, E. P., 'Zola on Naturalism in Art and History', *Modern Language Notes*, 70 (Nov. 1955), 514–17.

GELDERMAN, CAROL W., 'The Male Nature of Tragedy', *Prairie Schooner*, 49/3 (1975), 220–36.

GILLESPIE, PATTI, 'Feminist Theatre: Rhetorical Phenomenon', *Quarterly Journal of Speech*, 64 (1978), 284–94.

GOODALL, JANE, 'The Plague and Its Powers in Artaudian Theatre', *Modern Drama*, 33/4 (1990), 529–42.

GOSSMAN, LIONEL, 'Signs in the Theatre', *Theatre Research International* (1977), 1–15.

GROTOWSKI, JERZY, 'For a Total Interpretation', *World Theatre*, 15/1 (1966), 18–22.

—— 'Jerzy Grotowski on the Theatre of Sources (interviewed by T. Burzyński)', *The Theatre in Poland*, 11 (1979), 24.

GRUBBS, HENRY ALEXANDER, 'Alfred Jarry's Theories of Dramatic Technique', *Romanic Review* (Oct. 1936).

GURVITCH, GEORGES, 'The Sociology of the Theatre' (1955), trans. Petra Morrison, in Elizabeth and Tom Burns (eds.), *Sociology of Drama and Literature* (Harmondsworth: Penguin Education, 1973), 71–81.

HAMMOND, B., 'Theatre Semiotics: An Academic Job Creation Scheme?', in 'Semiotics and the Theatre: 1983 Alsager Seminar', *Interface*, 2 (1984), 78–89.

HELBO, ANDRÉ, 'The Semiology of Theatre or: Communication Swamped', *Poetics Today*, 2/3 (Spring 1981), 105–11.

HENDERSON, ARCHIBALD, 'Henrik Ibsen and Social Progress', *Arena*, 33 (Jan. 1905), 23–30.

HITE, ROGER, CZEREPINSKI, JACKIE, and ANDERSON, DEAN, 'Transactional Analysis: A New Perspective for the Theatre', *Empirical Research in Theatre* (Center for Communication Research, Bowling Green University, Summer 1973), 1–17.

INGARDEN, ROMAN, 'The Functions of Language in the Theatre', in *The Literary Work of Art*, trans. George Grabowicz (Evanston, Ill.: Northwestern University Press, 1973), 377–96.

IRIBARNE, LOUIS, 'Revolution in the Theatre of Witkacy and Gombrowicz', *Polish Review*, 18/1–2 (1973), 58–76.

IRVING, L., 'The Drama as a Factor in Social Progress', *Fortune*, 101 (Aug. 1914), 268–74.

JENKINS, LINDA WALSH, 'Locating the Language of Gender Experience', *Women and Performance: A Journal of Feminist Theory*, 2/1 (1984), 5–20.

KAPLAN, D. M., 'Character and Theatre: Psychoanalytic Notes on Modern Realism', *Tulane Drama Review*, 10/4 (Summer 1966), 93–108.

KAUFMANN, R. W., 'Drama and Morality', *Forum*, 51 (May 1914), 664–72.

KERR, S. P., 'What are Immoral Plays?', *Westminster Review*, 155 (Apr. 1901), 444–50.

KIRBY, MICHAEL, 'Structural Analysis/Structural Theory', *Drama Review*, 20/4 (Dec. 1976), 51–68.

—— 'Nonsemiotic Performance', *Modern Drama* 21 (Mar. 1982), 110 *et seq.*

KITCHIN, LAURENCE, 'The Theatre of Cruelty', *Listener*, 70/1799 (19 Sept. 1963), 87–9.

KOHTES, MARTIN MARIA, 'Invisible Theatre: Reflections on an Overlooked Form', *New Theatre Quarterly*, 9/33 (Feb. 1993), 85–9.

KOTT, JAN, 'The Icon and the Absurd', *Drama Review*, 14/1 (Fall 1969), 17–24.

—— 'Witkiewicz and Artaud: Where the Analogy Ends', *Theatre Quarterly*, 5/18 (June–Aug. 1975), 69–73.

KOWZAN, TADEUSZ, 'The Sign in the Theatre', *Diogenes*, 61 (1968), 52–80.

KRISTEVA, JULIA, 'Modern Theater Does Not Take (A) Place', *Substance*, 18–19 (1977), 131–4.

LEVINE, CARL, 'Social Criticism in Shaw and Nietzsche', *Shaw Review*, 10 (1967), 9–17.

LEVY, DEBORAH, 'Questions of Survival: Towards a Postmodernist Feminist Theatre', *New Theatre Quarterly*, 9/35 (Aug. 1993), 255–65.

LOOMIS, R. S., 'Defense of Naturalism', *International Journal of Ethics*, 29 (Jan. 1919), 188–201.

MCDOWELL, FREDERICK P. W., 'Another Look at Bernard Shaw: A Reassessment of His Dramatic Theory, His Practice, and His Achievement', *Drama Survey*, 1/1 (1961), 34–53.

MCNAMARA, BROOKS, 'Performance Space: The Environmental Tradition', *Architectural Association Quarterly* (Apr.–June 1975), 3–10.

MAETERLINCK, MAURICE, 'The Modern Drama', in *The Double Garden*, trans. by Alfred Sutro (New York: Dodd, Mead & Co., 1904).

MAROWITZ, CHARLES, 'Notes on the Theatre of Cruelty', *Tulane Drama Review*, 11/2 (1966), 152–72.

MARTIN, CAROL, 'Feminist Analysis across Cultures: Performing Gender in India', *Women and Performance: A Journal of Feminist Theory*, 3/2 (1987–8), 33–40.

MILLER, ARTHUR, 'Tragedy and the Common Man', *New York Times* (27 Feb. 1949).

—— 'On Social Plays', in *A View from the Bridge* (London: Cresset Press, 1957), 1–17.

—— Introduction to *The Collected Plays*, i (London: Cresset Press, 1958), 3–55.

MILLER, JONATHAN, 'Plays and Players', in R. A. Hinde (ed.), *Non-Verbal Communication* (Cambridge: Cambridge University Press), 359–72.

MILNE, TOM, 'Cruelly, cruelly (The Theatre of Cruelty)', *Encore*, 48 (Mar.–Apr. 1964), 299–311.

MOHOLY-NAGY, LÁSZLÓ, 'Theater, Circus, Variety', in Walter Gropius, Oskar Schlemmer, et al., *The Theater of the Bauhaus*, trans. Arthur S. Wensinger (Middletown, Conn.: Wesleyan University Press, 1961), 49–70.

MOORE, C. L., 'The Modern Drama: Should Plays Preach?', *Dial*, 58 (Apr. 1915), 287–9.

MORGAN, MARGERY M., 'Shaw, Yeats, Nietzsche and the Religion of Art', *Komos*, 1 (1967), 24–34.

MOSS, JANE, 'Women's Theatre in Quebec: Choruses, Monologues and Dialogues', *Quebec Studies*, 1/1 (1983), 276–85.

—— 'The Body as Spectacle: Women's Theatre in Quebec', *Women and Performance: A Journal of Feminist Theory*, 3/1 (1986), 5–16.

Navarro de Zuvillaga, Javier, 'The Disintegration of Theatrical Space', *Architectural Association Quarterly*, 8/4 (1976), 24–31.

O'Neill, Eugene, 'Memoranda on Masks', repr. in Oscar Cargill, N. Bryllion Fagin, and William J. Fisher (eds.), *O'Neill and His Plays* (New York: New York University Press, 1961).

Orr, Robert H., 'The Surprise Ending: One Aspect of the Dramatic Technique of J. M. Synge', *English Literature in Translation*, 15 (1972), 105–15.

Osborne, John, 'Zola, Ibsen and the Development of the Naturalist Movement in Germany', *Arcadia*, 2 (1967), 196–203.

—— 'Naturalism and the Dramaturgy of the Open Drama', *German Life and Letters*, 23 (1970), 119–28.

Parsons, Mabel H., 'Strindberg, Reality and the Dream Play', *Poet Lore*, 26 (Nov.–Dec. 1916), 763–73.

Passow, Wilfried, 'The Analysis of Theatrical Performance', *Poetics Today*, 2/3 (Spring 1981), 237–54.

Pavis, Patrice, 'Semiology and the Vocabulary of Theatre', trans. Susan Bassnett, *Theatre Quarterly*, 10/40 (1981), 74–8.

—— 'Problems of the Semiology of Theatrical Gesture', *Poetics Today*, 2/3 (1981), 65–93.

—— 'Notes toward a Semiotic Analysis (concerning *Disparitions*)', *Drama Review*, 23/4 (Dec. 1979), 93–104.

—— 'The Classical Heritage of Modern Drama', *Modern Drama*, 29/1 (1986).

Pirandello, Luigi, 'On Humor', trans. Teresa Novel, *Tulane Drama Review*, 10/3 (Spring 1966), 46–59.

Rajan, Balachandra, 'Yeats, Synge and the Tragic Understanding', *Yeats Studies*, 2 (1972), 66–79.

Reinelt, Jeanelle, 'Feminist Theory and the Problem of Performance', *Modern Drama*, 32 (1989), 48–57.

Revzina, O. G., and Revzin, I. I., 'A Semiotic Experiment on Stage: The Violation of the Postulate of Normal Communication as a Dramatic Device', *Semiotica*, 14/3 (1975), 245–68.

Ruffini, Franco, 'Horizontal and Vertical Montage in the Theatre', trans. Susan Bassnett, *New Theatre Quarterly*, 2/5 (Feb. 1986), 29–37.

Sacksteder, William, 'Elements of the Dramatic Model', *Diogenes*, 52 (1975), 26–54.

Sartre, Jean-Paul, 'Forgers of Myths', trans. by Rosamund Gilder, in Rosamund Gilder, Hermine Rich Isaacs, et al. (eds.), *Theatre Arts Anthology* (New York: Theatre Arts Books, 1951), 135–42.

Savona, Jeannette Laillou, 'French Feminism and Theatre: An Introduction', *Modern Drama*, 27 (1984), 504–5.

Schechner, Richard, 'Approaches to Theory/Criticism', *Tulane Drama Review*, 10/4 (Summer 1966), 20–53.

—— '6 Axioms for Environmental Theatre', *Drama Review*, 12/3 (Spring 1968), 41–64.

—— 'Drama, Script, Theatre, Performance', *Drama Review*, 17/3 (Sept. 1973), 5–36.

Scheler, Max, 'On the Tragic', trans. Bernard Stambler, *Cross Currents*, 4/2 (Winter 1954), 180 *et seq.*

Serpieri, Alessandro, et al., 'Toward a Segmentation of the Dramatic Text', *Poetics Today* (1981), 163–200.

Seymour, Alan, 'Artaud's Cruelty', *London Magazine*, 3/12 (Mar. 1964), 59–64.

Shanks, E., 'Realism in the Theatre', *Outlook* (London), 51 (9 June 1923), 470.

Shevtsova, Maria, 'The Sociology of Theatre. Part One: Problems and Perspectives', *New Theatre Quarterly*, 5/17 (Feb. 1989), 23–35; 'Part Two: Theoretical Achievements', *NTQ* 5/18 (May 1989), 180–94; 'Part Three: Performance', *NTQ* 5/19 (Aug. 1989), 282–300.

Simmel, Georg, 'On the Theory of Theatrical Performance', (1923), trans. Tom Burns, in Elizabeth and Tom Burns (eds.), *Sociology of Drama and Literature* (Harmondsworth: Penguin Education, 1973), 304–10.

Sklar, Roberta, 'Towards Creating a Women's Theatre', *Drama Review*, 24/2 (June 1980), 23–40.

Sologub, Fyodor, 'The Theatre of One Will', *Drama Review*, 21/4 (Dec. 1977), 85–99.

Sontag, Susan, 'Film and Theatre', *Tulane Drama Review*, 11/1 (1966), 24–37.

—— 'The Death of Tragedy', and 'Happenings: An Art of Radical Juxtaposition', in *Against Interpretation* (London: Eyre & Spottiswoode, 1967), 132–9, 263–74.

Sprinchorn, Evert, 'Strindberg and the Greater Naturalism', *Drama Review*, 13 (Winter 1968), 119–20.

—— 'The Zola of the Occult: Strindberg's Experimental Method', *Modern Drama*, 17 (1974), 351–66.

States, Bert O., 'Chekhov's Dramatic Strategy', *Yale Review*, 56 (1967), 212–24.

STEPHENS, JUDITH, 'The Compatibility of Traditional Dramatic Forms and Feminist Expressions', *Theatre Annual*, 40 (1985), 7–23.

SUVIN, DARKO, 'Reflections on Happenings', *Drama Review*, 14/3 (1970), 125–44.

SYNGE, JOHN MILLINGTON, Preface to *The Playboy of the Western World* (Dublin: Maunsell & Co., 1911), v–vii.

TAN, ED, 'Cognitive Processes in Reception', in Ernest Hess-Lüttich (ed.), *Multimedial Communication*, ii: *Theatre Semiotics* (Tübingen: Gunter Narr Verlag, 1982), 156–203.

TURCO, ALFRED JR., 'Ibsen, Wagner and Shaw's Changing View of "Idealism"', *Shaw Review*, 17 (1974), 78–85.

UBERSFELD, ANNE, 'The Pleasure of the Spectator', trans. Pierre Bouillaget and Charles Jose, *Modern Drama*, 25/1 (Mar. 1982), 127–39.

VANDEN HEUVEL, MICHAEL, 'Complementary Spaces: Realism, Performance and a New Dialogics of Theatre', *Theatre Journal*, 44/1 (1992), 47–58.

VELTRUSKÝ, JIŘÍ, 'The Prague School Theory of Theatre', *Poetics Today*, 2/3 (1981), 225–35.

—— 'Man and Object in the Theater' (1940), in Paul L. Garvin (ed.), *A Prague School Reader on Esthetics, Literary Structure and Style* (Washington: Georgetown University Press, 1964), 83–91.

WANDOR, MICHELENE, 'The Fifth Column: Feminism and Theatre', *Drama*, 152 (1984), 5–9.

—— 'Culture, Politics and Values in Plays by Women in the 1980s', *Englisch-amerikanische Studien*, 3/4 ('Englisches Drama seit 1980', Dec. 1986), 441–8.

WEIGHTMAN, JOHN, 'Ibsen and the Absurd', *Encounter*, 45/4 (Oct. 1975), 48–52.

WEISS, AURÉLIU, 'The Interpretation of Dramatic Works', trans. Emerson Marks, *Journal of Aesthetics and Art Criticism*, 23 (1964–5), 317 *et seq.*

—— 'G. B. Shaw and Stage Directions', *British Journal of Aesthetics*, 8 (1968), 49–53.

WEISS, PETER, 'The Material and the Models: Notes towards a Definition of Documentary Theatre', trans. Heinz Bernard, *Theatre Quarterly*, 1/1 (Jan.–Mar. 1971), 41–3.

WILDER, THORNTON, 'Some Thoughts on Playwriting' (1941), in Augusto Centeno (ed.), *The Intent of the Artist* (New York: Russell and Russell, 1970).

WITKIEWICZ, STANISŁAW IGNACY, 'A Few Words about the Role of the Actor in the Theatre of Pure Form', trans. Daniel Gerould, *Theatre Quarterly*, 5/18 (June–Aug. 1975), 66–8.

WITTIG, SUSAN, 'Towards a Semiotic Theory of the Drama', *Educational Theatre Journal*, 26 (1974), 441–51.

# Index

Note: **Bold face** figures indicate page references to key passages.

absurdism, *see* Theatre of the Absurd
Académie Française xi, 19, 26, 102
acting ix, x, xvii, 80, 139, 140, 141, 142, 144;
  Artaud on 191–4, 198–9; Brechtian
  239–45; in different media 302, 303–5;
  feminist 264; futurist 179, 180, 181;
  Grotoswski on 200–4; interaction with
  audience 299–300, 308–9; as magic 58,
  59–60; naturalistic 97–8; noh 130; non-
  realistic 156–7, 162–4, 167–9, 183, 185–7;
  as part of Gesamtkunstwerk 5–6, 8–9,
  10; performance art 145, 148–52, 313–15;
  as 'presence' 289–90, 292–3; a
  respectable profession 48–9; as a sign
  system 269, 270, 272, 273, 274–8, 280,
  283–7; should be text-based 75–6; skills
  132–7; spectators as actors 254–60;
  symbolist 116, 122–5, 126; *see also* masks
Aeschylus: *Agamemnon* 294; *The
  Eumenides* 118; *The Libation Bearers*
  118; *Prometheus* 42, 111, 118; *The
  Suppliants* 118
agitprop xvi, 220, 247
Albee, Edward: *Who's Afraid of Virginia
  Woolf?* xii
alienation (A) effect 232, **240–6**, 313; *see
  also* acting, Brecht
Allen, Woody 303
Anderson, Lindsay 208
Andreyev, Leonid Nikolayevich 177
Anouilh, Jean xii, 39
Antoine, André 80, 89, 293, 308 n. 2
Antonioni, Michelangelo 284
Appia, Adolphe 132, **145–52**, 271
Apollinaire, Guillaume xvi, 160, 171, 188;
  *The Breasts of Tiresias* **165–70**, 173 n. 1,
  274

Archer, William 41
Aristophanes 52, 167, 174
Aristotle ix, xii, xiii, 16, 50, 115, 220, 227,
  234, 235; catharsis 36–7, 196, 234, 260;
  The Three Unities 21, 46–7, 81, 82 n. 1;
  *Poetics* xi, 36, 108; *Rhetoric* 37
Artaud, Antonin xvi, 66, 169 n. 4, 171, 182,
  200, 205, 247, 299, 301 n. 1; against the
  classics 195–9; errors 309, 311, 312; The
  Theatre of Cruelty xiii, xv, **188–94**
Aubignac, François Hédelin d' ix
audience, the x, xv; activating the 225,
  227, 229, 236–8, 246, 252, 254–60; in a
  black box 55, 56–8, 59, 60–1; as a community 3, 5–7, 44, 145, 150, 151; decoding
  the performance 282, 290, 291, 293,
  294–6, 308, 312; feminist audiences 263;
  middle-class audiences 77, 78–9; naïve
  audiences 90, 91, 123–4, 160–2, 177, 179,
  181, 201; need to be dominated 188, 191,
  193, 195–6, 198–9, 203–4; need for
  sensation 132, 136–7, 206–7; for naturalism 84; for non-naturalism 154, 157,
  166, 172–3, 183–7; psychology 276–7;
  response to stimuli 32, 37; responses in
  different media 299–302, 304–5;
  involvement in ritual 66–7;
  revolutionary audiences 221, 222–3;
  audiences seen historically 48, 50–4
Augier, Guillaume Victor Émile 84
auteur theory 302–3

Bacon, Francis 232
ballet, *see* dance
Balzac, Honoré de 84, 86–7
Barker, Howard **55–61**; *The Bite of the
  Night* 57

Barrault, Jean-Louis 189

Barthes, Roland 289, 290–1

Basch, Victor 166, 167

Beaumarchais, Pierre-Augustin Caron de:
*The Barber of Seville* 20; *The Marriage of Figaro* 21–2, 23

Beck, Julian 66, 189, 309 n. 5

Beckett, Samuel xi, xv, 208, 280, 299, 303;
*End Game* 209; *Krapp's Last Tape* 115;
*Waiting for Godot* 209

Beethoven, Ludwig van 3, 9; *Fidelio* 230

Benjamin, Walter 310

Bentley, Eric **35–41**, 106

Bergman, Ingmar 291, 294

Binyon, Laurence 123

Blake, William 36, 64, 124, 129

Blok, Alexander Alexandrovich: *The Fairground Booth* 132; *The Triumph of Death* 136; *The Unknown Woman* 136, 137

Boal, Augusto xiii, xvi, **254–60**

Bogatyrev, Pyotr Grigoryevich xvii, 285, 297

Brecht, Bertold Eugen Friedrich ('Bert') xv, xvi, 35, 45, 162 n. 6, 205, 208, 209, 220, 221, 247, 260, 280, 299, 312; Epic Theatre xii, 39, **224–31**, 303; ideology 47–8, 57, 60, 211, 212; *The Caucasian Chalk Circle* 303; *Galileo* 290; *The Mother* 242; *Mother Courage and Her Children* 48 n. 1; *A Short Organum for the Theatre* xii, 39, **232–46**

Breton, André 165

Brieux, Eugène 99, 101, 105

Brook, Peter 66, 189, **205–7**, 312, 313

Büchner, Karl Georg: *Woyzeck* 50–1, 244

Buddhism 130, 206, 212


Calderón de la Barca, Pedro 24, 76, 124

catharsis, *see* Aristotle

Cervantes Saavedra, Miguel de 24; *Don Quixote* 94

Chaikin, Joseph 66, 189

Chaplin, Charles 174, 284, 303

Chekhov, Anton Pavlovich xi, 209; *The Cherry Orchard* xii, 270, 295; *Three Sisters* 295

Churchill, Caryl: *Top Girls* 303

cinema xii, xv, 48, 89, 136 n. 11, 147, 165, 174, 176, 178, 179, 277, 286, 289, 296; inherently realistic 167; limitations of 133–4, 194; nature of **300–6**

Clair, René 136

Claudel, Paul 49, 177

Cocteau, Jean xii, 153, 303; *Oedipus Rex* 155; *Orpheus* 39, 269

Coleridge, Samuel Taylor x

comedy/the comic xiv, 35–6, 45, 60, 77, 166, 167, 201, 284; to be abolished 181; based on the will 21, 23, 24; mechanics of **25–34**, 104; misunderstood 161; naturalistic 88; the only genre for 20th century 50–4; *see also commedia dell'arte*, farce, (the) grotesque

*commedia dell'arte* xvi, 132, 133, 134, 203, 274

Corneille, Pierre 14, 42, 87, 102; *Le Cid* 20, 21

costume(s) xvi, 80, 128, 133, 141, 142, 144, 185, 186, 187, 195–6, 203, 245; Artaudian 192–3, 194; drama 82, 83, 85, 86; ritual 65; as sign 277, 291; simple costumes for verse drama 125

Craig, Edward Henry Gordon 122, 132, **138–44**, 145, 153

Crébillon, Prosper Jolyot de 43


dance 60, 91, 141, 142, 144, 169, 190, 271; as part of the *Gesamtkunstkwerk* 8, 9; ritual 65, 66; as stage choreography 96, 245, 246; in the Theatre of Pure Form 186; in theatricalism 137; in verse drama 126–8, 130

D'Annunzio, Gabriele: *The Daughter of Jorio* 180; *More than Love* 180

décor, *see* setting

De Marinis, Marco 288

Devine, George 208

dialectical materialism 240–1; *see also* Marx/Marxism

dialogue 79, 90, 95, 119–21, 257, 309

Diderot, Denis ix

director, the 145, 168–70, 189, 265, 292, 293; as all-round artist 138–44, 148–9, 150, 191; the dominant 49, 272–5; a failed artist 202–3; in film and TV 302–3

Donnay, Maurice 161

*drame* ix, xii, 85, 181, 186; *see also* romanticism

Dryden, John 102, 128

Dulac, Edmond 126

Dumas, Alexandre, *fils* 14, 84; *Le Demi-Monde* (The Outer Edge of Society) 20, 23

Duras, Marguerite 313
Dürrenmatt, Friedrich xii, **45–54**

Eco, Umberto xvii, **279–87**
Elam, Keir xvii
Eliot, Thomas Stearns 49, 209
Epic Theatre, *see* Brecht
Esslin XV, **209–306**
Euripides 21, 43, 173
expressionism xv, 89, 153–7, 171; dream
    plays 158–9, 217–18; as melodrama 39;
    revolutionary art and 221
Evreinov, Nikolai Nikolayevich 132

farce 23, 24, 38, 91, 160, 181, 186; Atellan
    134; medieval French 32
Fehling, Jürgen 217
Fellini, Federico 136
feminism 256–7, **261–6**
Fenollosa, Ernest 126
film, *see* cinema
French Academy, *see* Académie Française
Freud, Sigmund 107, 212, 213, 230 n. 8
Freytag, Gustav xiii
Frisch, Max 49
Fry, Christopher 209
Fuchs, Georg 132, 271
futurism xv, **176–81**, 182, 271, 272, 308

Garten H. F. 208
*Gesamtkunstwerk* ('total' or 'integrated
    work of art'), *see* acting, dance, music,
    Wagner
Giraudoux, Jean 39
Goethe, Johann Wolfgang von 3, 13, 14 n.
    5, 17, 24, 48, 72–3, 141, 290; *The Elective
    Affinities* 72; *Faust* 13, 50 n. 1, 72, 244,
    270; *Götz von Berlichingen* 73
Gogol, Nikolai Vasilievich: *The Inspector
    General* 296
Goll, Yvan **171–5**; *Methusalem, the Eternal
    Bourgeois* 171, 174–5, 274
Gorki, Maxim 209; *The Mother* 242 n. 5
Gozzi, Carlo 13, 14, 15
Greimas, A. J. 293–4
grotesque, the 21, 53, 82 n. 1, 132, 134–7,
    173, 186
Grotowski, Jerzy 66, 188 n. 1, **200–4**

Handke, Peter 58 n. 4, 313
happenings xv, 146, **205–7**, 250, 256
Hebbel, Friedrich: *Genevieve* 74; *Mary
    Magdalene* 71–80

Hellman, Lillian 39
hero/ine, the 22–3, 50–1, 61, 91, 108–11, 155,
    301; classical and romantic 82, 86–7;
    comic 27–8, 133, 134, 135; false heroics
    101, 103; the modern type of 93–4; tragic
    36, 37, 42, 43, 116–19, 201; types of 14, 16
Hochhuth, Rolf 221; *Soldiers: An
    Obiturary for Geneva*, 59
Hochwälder, Fritz 49
Hoffmann, Ernst Theodor Amadeus 135,
    137
Honzl, Jindřich **269–78**, 291, 297
Horace ix, x
Hugo, Victor xi, 21, 36, 85, 87, 166; *Hernani*
    82 n. 2; Preface to *Cromwell*, 82 n. 1.
Hunter, Norman Charles 209

Ibsen, Henrik Johan xi, 112, 123, 177; *A
    Doll's House* 100; *Ghosts* 91 n. 1, 291;
    *Hedda Gabler* xii, 100; *John Gabriel
    Borkman* 100–1; *The Master Builder*
    120–1; *Rosmersholm* 100, 291, 292; *When
    We Dead Awaken* 100–1; *The Wild Duck*
    100–1
improvisation 96, 146, 203, 205–6; false
    75, 104; futuristic 179; as a political tool
    249, 250, 254, 255, 258; radical 305, 314;
    see also *commedia dell'arte*, happenings
Ionesco, Eugene xv, xvi, 160, **208–14**; *The
    Bald Prima Donna* 171; *The Chairs* 181
    n. 8, 208–10; *The Lesson* 40, 208–10;
    *Rhinoceros*, 208

Jacques-Dalcroze, Émile 145
Jarry, Alfred xvi, **160–4**; *King Ubu* 160,
    165, 169 n. 5, 188, 269
Johnstone, Keith 208
Jones, Robert Edmond 155
Julien, Jean 170

kabuki 132, 137
Kant, Immanuel 13, 73
Kantor, Tadeusz 202
Keaton, Buster 303
Kipphardt, Heinar 221
Kowzan, Tadeusz xvii
Kroetz, Franz Xaver 310
Kvapil, Jaroslav 271

Labiche, Eugène Marin 33–4; *Célimare the
    Beloved* 20, 21; *An Italian Straw Hat* 23,
    29–30, 33; *Monsieur Perrichon's Journey*
    32

La Chaussée, Pierre-Claude Nivelle de 166

Lamb, Charles 290, 291, 297

Lesage, Alain René: *Gil Blas* 21–1

Lessing, Gotthold Ephraim viii, 24, 50

Living Theatre 256 n. 2, 309; *see also* Beck, Malina

Lugné-Poe, Aurélien-François 160

Lukács, György xvi

Lyotard, Jean-François 312

Maeterlinck, Maurice Polydore Marie Bernard **115–21**, 177, 271 n.3, 277; *The Blind* 278

Malina, Judith 66, 189, 309 n. 5

Marinetti, Filippo Tommaso xv, 160, **176–81**, 271

make-up 90, 97–8, 162–3

Marx, Karl/Marxism xvi, 45, 47, 212, 224, 236–9, 247–53, 264–5; Proletarian Theatre 220–3

mask, the xvi, 8, 160, 163–4, 240, 252, 274; Artaud on 191, 192, 194, 197; classical and modern masks 172–3, 174; Italian masks 133; Japanese-type masks 126, 128–9, 130; O'Neill on 153–7; ritual masks 65, 259–60, 271; see also *commedia dell'arte*, ritual

Meiningen, Duke George II of (Saxe-) 148, 293

melodrama **35–41**, 153, 201, 296

Menander 284

Mercer, David 303

Meyerhold, Vsevolod Emilievich **132–7**, 271 n. 3, 272, 278 n. 16

Mickiewicz, Adam Bernard 203, 204

Miller, xii, 39, 209, 211; *Death of a Salesman* **106–12**

Mnouchkine, Ariane 189

Molière (Poquelin, Jean-Baptiste) 25, 32, 49, 88, 93, 101, 103, 161, 174, 280; *Amphitryon* 31; *The Blunderer* 31; *The Cheats of Scapin* 27, 28; *The Forced Marriage* 26; *George Dandin* 31; *The Imaginary Invalid* 26–7; *The Misanthrope* 27–8; *The Miser* 161; *The School for Husbands* 31; *The School for Wives* 21, 23, 31; *Tartuffe* 20, 27

Morris, William 124

Mounet-Sully, Jean 163

Mounin, Georges xvii

Mozart, Wolfgang Amadeus: *Don Giovanni* 297; *The Magic Flute* 230; *The Marriage of Figaro* 230

Mukařovský, Jan 291–2

music ix, 53, 102, 117, 149, 169, 184, 186, 203, 240, 280, 306; Artaud on 190, 191, 192; Brecht on 225, 228, 245; as part of the *Gesamtkunstwerk* 3–4, 8, 9, 275, 276; as a political tool 252, 255; in ritual 65, 66; as a sign 270, 291; in verse drama 126, 127; *see also* Beethoven, Mozart, opera, Wagner

naturalism xv, 80, 122, 145, 161, 165, 176, 271 n. 3, 311, 312; conventions of 303; needed in 19th century **83–8**, 90–8; shortcomings of 22, 38, 40, 41, 60, 134, 166, 170

Neher, Caspar 229

neoclassicism xi, xii, xiii, 81–3, 86–8, 134, 150; *see also* tragedy

Nerval, Gérard de 13

Nietzsche, Friedrich Wilhelm: *The Birth of Tragedy* xiii

noh drama xvi, 122, 124–31, 155

Odets, Clifford 39

Okhlopkov, Nikolai Pavlovich 272–4

one-act play 47, 95–6

O'Neill, Eugene Gladstone xvii, 39, 106, **153–7**; *Desire under the Elms* 291; *The Great God Brown* 154, 156; *Lazarus Laughed* 156; *Strange Interlude* xv

opera 3, 4, 10, 87, 155, 207, **224–31**, 270, 274

Osborne, John 209, 211

ostention 281

parody 39, 53, 160, 310

performance, *see* acting

Pierce, Charles Sanders xvii, 280–1, 285

Pinter, Harold xv, 299; *Betrayal* 303; *Landscape and Silence* 115

Pirandello, Luigi 35, 279, 284; *Six Characters in Search of an Author* 298

Plautus 174

Plutarch 53

Poe, Edgar Allen 137

Polti, Georges: *The Thirty-Six Dramatic Situations* xiii, **12–18**, 293

Pound, Ezra Loomis 122, 126

Prague Linguistic Circle xvii, 269, 292

Propp, Vladimir 293

psychology  xvi, 89–90, 132, 176, 182, 312;
audience  300–2, 304–5; character
analysis essential  81, 86–7; complex
92–5, 98; dramatically trivial  42, 43, 116,
118, 137, 172, 177, 183, 184, 185, 190, 197,
199, 309; Freudian symbolism  106–7; of
perception  276; character portrayed by
masks  154
public, the, *see* audience, the
puppets  203, 218; acting modelled on  128,
164, 275; puppeteers  73; as signs  270; a
source of comedy  26, 28–9; theatrical
use of  191, 194

Racine, Jean  14, 87, 102, 149, 161, 234;
*Bajazet*  23; *Berenice*  118; *The Litigants*
29; *Phaedra*  20, 23
radio drama  270, 277, 303
Rattigan, Terence Mervin  209
reader-response theory  xiv, 292
realism  xiv–xv, 59, 150, 157, 167, 172, 186,
209, 303; *see also* naturalism
Regnard, Jean: *The Universal Legatee*  20,
23
Reinhardt, Max  138

Savits, Jocza  278
scene painting  6–7, 141, 146–7, 149; *see also*
settings
Schechner, Richard  xvi, 62, 66, 189
Schiller, Johann Christoph Friedrich  xiii,
3, 9 n. 4, 13, 24, 50, 51, 136; *The Robbers*
220; *Wallenstein* trilogy  51
Scribe, Augustin Eugène  43, 102, 104, 166;
*Favoritism, or the Climb up*  20
Semper, Gottfried  4
settings  xvi, 80, 90, 160, 289; design
overrated  201–2, 203; for different
genres  82, 83; grotesque  137;
illusionism condemned  128;
importance of design  141, 142, 145–50;
an independent work of art  229, 245;
naturalistic  96–7; non-illusionistic
124–5, 161–2, 184; painting as part of
*Gesamtkunstwerk*  6, 7, 9; as signs  269,
273–7, 289, 291, 292; unnecessary  194
Shakespeare, William  3, 41, 75, 76, 82 n. 1,
103, 128, 129, 172, 186, 203, 238, 296; his
audience  124; better read than
performed  290; his greatness  161, 234;
ignored the 'rules'  21; outdated  197;
pastiche  85; staging  48, 277–8; his

tragic heroes  50, 51; *Hamlet*  xiv, 23, 72,
116, 117, 155, 163, 289, 295; *Henry V*  303;
*Julius Caesar*  53, 156; *King Lear*  116, 194,
241, 284, 291, 294; *Macbeth*  116, 125, 160;
*The Merchant of Venice*  271–2; *A
Midsummer Night's Dream*  297; *Othello*
23, 117, 293; *Pericles*  303; *Richard III*  37,
244; *Romeo and Juliet*  100, 301; *The
Winter's Tale*  303
Shaw, George Bernard  xiii, 35, 36, **99–105**,
112, 177, 289; *The Devil's Disciple*  39;
*Man and Superman*  39; *Saint Joan*  39
Sheridan, Richard Brinsley  295–6
Słowacki, Juliusz  186, 204
Socialism, *see* Marx/Marxism
Sologub, Fyodor: *Vanka the Steward and
Johan the Page*  136
Sondheim, Stephen: *Sunday in the Park
with George*  297
Sophocles  17, 21, 124, 212, 213, 234; *Ajax*
118; *Antigone*  xiii, 42, 43, 52, 58, 118, 201;
*Electra*  118; *Oedipus Rex*  42, 72, 111, 118,
125, 195, 238; *Oedipus at Colonus*  118,
238; *Philoctetes*  118–19
Souriau, Étienne *The 200,000 Dramatic
Situations*  xiii, 293
spectators, *see* (the) audience
Spinoza, Baruch  73
stage design, *see* settings
stage lighting  xvi, 90, 145, 184, 189, 203,
217, 271 n. 3, 275, 276, 289, 305; Brechtian
57, 245; importance of  141, 142, 144, 156,
191, 192, 193, 198; opposition to
footlights  97, 98, 163; simple, for verse
drama  127
Stanislavky, Konstantin Sergeyevich  132,
138, 280, 293, 294, 295, 298
States, Bert O.  289
Stoppard, Tom  303
Stravinsky, Igor  155
street theatre  x, xvii, 57, 249–50, 256, 270,
271
Strindberg, Johan August  38, 115; *To
Damascus*  158; *A Dream Play*  **158–9**;
*The Father*  91, 95; *Miss Julie*  xv, 77 n. 6,
**89–98**, 158, 297–8
stylization  135, 137, 209, 246, 271
Sukhovo-Kobylin, Alexander Vasilievich:
*Tarelkin's Death*  272
surrealism  xv, 171–2, 174, 269, 274; first
mention of  165, 166
Suzuki, Tadashi  66

symbolism  xv, 122, 125, 128, 165, 176, 204,
271 n. 3; denied  167, 185; a director's
medium  311; political  258–9; surface
154; as theatricalism  189, 191, 192; *see
also* Maeterlinck, O'Neill, Yeats

television drama  xv, 67, 300–1, 303–6
Tellado, Corín  256–7
theatre architecture  x, 4, 137, 152, 189, 273,
300–1, 305; call for drastic reform  169,
193, 198; constants in  270, 271; part of
the *Gesamtkunstwerk*  5–6, 9, 11;
inadequate reform  142; intimate  98;
out-of-date  48
Théâtre d'Art  271, 277, 308 n. 2
Theatre of the Absurd  xv, 136 n. 13, 171,
182, **208–14**, 253, 299, 310
Tirso de Molina (Téllez, Gabriel): *The
Trickster of Seville and the Stone Guest*
135
Toller, Ernst: *Masses and Man*  **217–19**, 220
Toynbee, Philip  208, 212
tragedy/the tragic  ix, xii, 3, 7, 60–1, 76, 93,
96, 137, 161, 186, 290, 310; to be abolished
181; ambivalence in  91; appropriateness
of tragedy to the age  50–3, 81–3, 85–7,
100–1, 167, 234; basic situations  13–14,
284; and class  71, 78–9, 108–11;
coincidence in  38; choice in  43; in
daily life  **115–21**, 175; and melodrama
40–1, 201; and the 'rules'  20–1, 46–7;
simple and complex  16; status of  22–5;
the 'tragic victory'  109–10
Turgenev, Ivan Sergeyevich: *A Month in
the Country*  296

vaudeville  26, 29, 30, 31, 32, 91, 166, 181
Vega Carpio, Lope Félix de  24, 49

verse drama  102, 122, 124–5, 126–31, 168,
186 n. 2
villain, the  15, 155, 301; the cheater cheated
32; as 'hero' of melodrama  36, 37, 39,
102, 103
Vinaver, Michel  311, 313; *Bending Over
Backwards*  310; *Work and Days*  310
Voltaire (Arouet, François-Marie)  43

Wagner, Richard  xii, xiv, **3–11**, 99, 138, 141,
145, 149, 230; *Gesamtkunstwerk*  4, 9–11,
203, 228, 246, 275–6; *Leitmotiv*  4, 303
Walkley, Alfred Bingham  101
Wandor, Michelene  261–5
Wedekind, Frank  136
Weiss, Peter  xvi, 221, **247–53**; *The
Investigation*  247; *Marat/Sade*  205, 247,
313
Welles, Orson  208, 303
well-made play  43, 99, **102–5**, 178, 303
Wilder, Thornton Niven  289
Williams, Thomas Lanier ('Tennessee')
39, 209
Witkiewicz, Stanisław Ignacy  **182–7**, 202
Wolzogen, Ernst von  134
Wyspiański, Stanisław Mateusz Ignacy
202

Yeats, William Butler  xvi, 115, **122–31**, 153;
*On Baile's Strand*  127 n. 3; *The
Dreaming of the Bones*  131 n. 11; *The
Green Helmet*  127 n. 3; *At the Hawk's
Well*,  126–9
Young, Stark  289

Zen, *see* Buddhism
Zich, Otakar  269–70, 277
Zola, Émile Édouard Charles Antoine  xv,
**80–8**, 89, 101